A SILENT REVOLUTION?

A Silent Revolution?

Gender and Wealth in English Canada, 1860–1930

PETER BASKERVILLE

McGill-Queen's University Press
Montreal & Kingston • London • Ithaca

© McGill-Queen's University Press 2008

ISBN 978-0-7735-3411-7 (cloth)
ISBN 978-0-7735-3470-4 (pbk)

Legal deposit third quarter 2008
Bibliothèque nationale du Québec

Printed in Canada on acid-free paper that is 100% ancient forest free
(100% post-consumer recycled), processed chlorine free

This book has been published with the help of a grant from the Canadian
Federation for the Humanities and Social Sciences, through the Aid to
Scholarly Publications Programme, using funds provided by the Social
Sciences and Humanities Research Council of Canada.

McGill-Queen's University Press acknowledges the support of the Canada
Council for the Arts for our publishing program. We also acknowledge the
financial support of the Government of Canada through the Book Publishing
Industry Development Program (BPIDP) for our publishing activities.

Library and Archives Canada Cataloguing in Publication

Baskerville, Peter A. (Peter Allan), 1943–
    A silent revolution? : gender and wealth in English Canada,
1860–1930 / Peter Baskerville.

Includes bibliographical references and index.
ISBN 978-0-7735-3411-7 (bnd)
ISBN 978-0-7735-3470-4 (pbk)

1. Women – Canada – Economic conditions – 19th century. 2. Women –
Canada – Economic conditions – 20th century. 3. Women – Employment
– Canada – History – 19th century. 4. Women – Employment – Canada –
History – 20th century. 5. Marital property – Canada – History. 6. Women
– British Columbia – Victoria – Economic conditions – 19th century –
Case studies. 7. Women – British Columbia – Victoria – Economic
conditions – 20th century – Case studies. 8. Women – Ontario –
Hamilton – Economic conditions – 19th century – Case studies. 9.
Women – Ontario – Hamilton – Economic conditions – 20th century –
Case studies. I. Title.

HQ1453.B375 2008   331.40971'09034   C2008-900928-2

Typeset by Jay Tee Graphics Ltd. in 10.5/13 New Baskerville

Contents

APPENDICES

Acknowledgments

While I did not realize it at the time, I first undertook research for this book in 1991. Engaged in another project, I uncovered evidence of considerable borrowing by women from loan companies in late nineteenth-century Victoria and Vancouver, British Columbia. The extent of that behaviour intrigued me, and over the next decade and more, sometimes in conjunction with different projects and at other times as a focus in its own right, I sought to determine the extent of women's financial and economic activity in an era when women were not thought to be very active in such matters and to offer explanations for what I have come to argue was a very significant involvement by women, married and otherwise, in matters of capital. This book is the result of that protracted inquiry.

Given the volume of evidence that underlies the arguments presented in this book, research has been a wonderfully (for me at any rate) collaborative process. The hard work of entering data from such routinely generated sources as censuses, assessment rolls, real and chattel mortgage records, loan company financial ledgers, bank and insurance shareholding records, wills, and probates, to list a few of the larger databases created, could not have been done by one individual. I am indebted in more ways than they can know to the following for both their assistance in assembling the evidence necessary for the writing of this book and for the many valuable conversations concerning the data that I had with them: Jill Ainsley, Martin Ainsley, Danielle Baskerville, Ian Baskerville, Mina Baskerville, Melanie Buddle, Raymond Frogner, Robin Grazley, Darryl Green, John Gow, Lisa Helps, Takaia Larsen, Theresa McFarland, Brandy Patterson, Monica Perry, Chris Roberts, Chris Unruh, and Tamara Vrooman. For technical assistance I thank

Patrick Frisby, computer assistant with the Canadian Century Research Infrastructure Project (CCRI) at the University of Victoria. Also for his technical assistance, and for much more than that, I extend my gratitude to Doug Thompson, project coordinator of the CCRI at the University of Victoria.

I am indebted to the Social Sciences and Humanities Research Council of Canada for a research grant that facilitated much work on this project and to the Aid to Scholarly Publications Programme of Canada for a grant to publish this book. A small part of chapter 4 appeared in a different form in "Women and Investment in Late Nineteenth Century Urban Canada: Victoria and Hamilton, 1880–1901," *Canadian Historical Review* 80 (1999): 191–219. I thank the publisher for the right to use that material. For comments on one or more of the many papers that were presented at sundry conferences preceding the book's completion, I thank Annalee Lepp, Larry McCann, Lynne Marks, and Eric Sager of the University of Victoria; Bettina Bradbury and Gordon Darroch of York University; Livio Di Matteo of Lakehead University; Lisa Dillon of the University of Montreal; Chad Gaffield, president of the Social Sciences and Humanities Research Council of Canada; Robin Grazely of Queen's University; Lisa Helps of the University of Toronto; and Kris Inwood of Guelph University. Special thanks go to the two anonymous persons chosen by McGill-Queen's University Press to review this book. Their sympathetic and constructively supportive comments are much appreciated. I thank Don Akenson for his encouragement, Roger Martin for his astute management of the manuscript, Joan McGilvray for her editorial advice, and Elizabeth Hulse for her meticulous and professional job of copy-editing. My final thanks are, as always, to Fran. She knows why.

A SILENT REVOLUTION?

Introduction

A traditional literature has argued that from the early nineteenth century to at least the end of the Victorian era, urban middle- and even working-class married women were best understood as operating in spheres separate from those of men.[1] A married woman's place was in the home as a helpmate to her husband. It is not hard to find nineteenth-century commentaries in support of such an interpretation. Indeed, the "separate spheres" ideology underlay much gender discourse in late nineteenth-century Canada. "Scripture does map out woman's sphere of life," the editor of the Toronto *Mail* proclaimed in May 1893; "it confers upon her a sacred place in which, through her exclusion from the hurly-burly of contention, she can easily exercise a gentle sway over the sterner sex, and an ennobling influence on the race." Women could work before marriage, the *Canada Christian Monthly* allowed in 1875. "But after marriage all is changed; they must ask for what they require rather than have it paid to them quarterly." George Gage, a boot and shoe merchant in Hamilton, agreed: when, in 1886, his bride of two weeks took $10 "out of the till to buy something ... he told her the next time she wanted to buy anything to let him buy it and not to take money out of the till." Even widows, British Columbia's attorney general, grumbled in January 1873, "knew, as a rule, nothing of business." In 1900 the *Canadian Grocer* saw fit to copy an article from the *Ladies' Home Journal* which argued that businesswomen were a declining breed, "having proven themselves incapable of meeting the demands of modern business ... for which they were never intended [, business affairs being] distasteful to the sensitive feminine mind and fine womanly temperament." That sensitivity and fine temperament was, in the minds of many in the late nineteenth century, best suited for running a home and a family.[2]

Closer reading of the business press and other literary sources suggests a contested reality. It was wrong, a Victoria newspaper editor argued in 1873, to deny women "participation in worldly matters beyond the precinct of the drawing room or nursery ... beyond the sphere of their domestic duties." In January 1894 the *Canadian Grocer* reprinted an article which argued that "women are destined to take a prominent place in the retail stores of the country." The result would be, the writer warned, "that the male grocers will have to take up some other line." Three years earlier a Mrs McKeown became probably the first woman elected to the Hamilton Retail Grocer's Association. The "wife in business" made the chances of success for "the average married merchant ... better than those of the average bachelor dealer," a writer in the *Canadian Grocer* proclaimed in 1893.[3] Throughout the 1890s the current business affairs section of the *Canadian Grocer* was peppered with notes on women: registering businesses in their own names, selling their affairs, filing for bankruptcy, and, on occasion, challenging their husbands. Carson Dieckman sued his wife for repossession of his grocery business, which he claimed he had signed over to her while under the influence of alcohol. His wife contested the claim, replying that he "was perfectly sober and that she took the business, paid all the debts, and saved it from ruin."[4]

These mixed messages suggest that traditional conceptions of women's role in society were being challenged. As has been well documented by historians of women and gender, gender ideology is not fixed; rather, it is always under construction. During the last quarter of the nineteenth century, feminists toured many Canadian cities arguing for extended political and social rights for women no matter what their marital status.[5] Against the backdrop of often uncertain economic growth, provincial politicians began to pass legislation designed to mould families to better facilitate provincial and national economic expansion. Politicians debated and passed a series of measures concerning inheritance and property ownership that offered the possibility of some degree of shared power between husbands and wives and even (albeit to a lesser extent) children within families. Unevenly implemented across provinces and always contested, these measures were poised on the razor's edge of protecting families from speculative capitalism while maintaining for the male head his traditional patriarchal rights.

"An Act to Protect the Property of a Wife Deserted by her Husband," passed in the colony of Vancouver Island in 1862, along with similar acts passed in New Brunswick in 1851, Prince Edward Island in 1860, and Nova Scotia in 1866, and legislation concerning inheritance practices are cases in point. The "Deserted Wives" acts provided protection for abandoned wives from the seizure by their husbands of earnings and property. At the same time they allowed husbands to petition for the revocation of such protection. Moreover, the acts were to apply only to already broken homes, not to homes where inequities did not include desertion.[6] Laws relating to inheritance and dower were normative, not mandatory. Thus for intestate holdings primogeniture was amended in most jurisdictions in the last quarter of the nineteenth century, and equal division among children put in place. That stipulation, and the long-standing notion of dower – the wife's life entitlement to one-third of the husband's real property – was not, however, always binding on the right of the husband or father to write a will bequeathing his goods in any way he wished.[7] Legislators hoped that the law's example would be instructive, while allowing individual freedom.

Without doubt the most contentious and far-reaching legislation concerning family and capitalist relations passed in this period were a series of Married Women's Property Laws (MWPLs).[8] Before the passage of these laws, wives were unable to own or sell property, keep wages earned by their own labour, and sue or be sued. Common law held that "husband and wife are one person, and the husband is that person." As the *Upper Canada Law Journal* affirmed in 1856, women "entering the married state ... in the eye of the law ... may be said to cease to exist."[9] On the eve of the passage of the first MWPL in British Columbia, the editor of the Victoria *Standard* summed up the legal situation facing married women by comparing it to that of "the coloureds in the United States." "They have no rights which their husbands are bound to respect."[10] Marriage settlements, whereby the intended wife could put her assets into trust, thus protecting them from her husband's use, were possible but rarely employed, and even when they were adopted, the wife had to accede to the will of the trustees of her estate, trustees who at times could include her husband.[11] MWPLs were passed throughout English-speaking North America and England in the years leading up to and beyond the second half of the nineteenth century.[12] New Brunswick passed the first such act in the British North American colonies in 1851, followed by a second in 1877. Upper Canada passed its first act in 1859. Ontario adopted more significant legislation, patterned after British law, in 1872, 1873, and 1884; British Columbia followed suit in 1873 and 1886, and Nova Scotia in 1884 and 1898. It is appropriate to note here that this book focuses mainly on practice in English-speaking urban Canada, that is, that part of Canada outside Quebec. It does so because the prime intent is to test the effect of the MWPLs and several other laws on women's lived experience. Given the different civil legal regime in effect in Quebec compared to the rest of Canada, it seemed wise to focus on the English Canadian civil law jurisdiction and to mention Quebec law and practice only in the context of the wider argument.

As discussed above, the first set of property laws focused only on abandoned women. The second phase, generally following legislation in England, gave to a married woman greater control of property: in most jurisdictions she was allowed to hold real and personal property and earnings in her own name. She could dispose of personal property but not real estate.

These laws were significant advances. By the end of the 1870s, married women could legally make money and purchase but not dispose of real estate. By the end of the 1880s (in Nova Scotia the 1890s) they were able to dispose of real as well as personal property in any way they saw fit. The summative effect of these laws gave married women the legal right to manage, free from a husband's control, all real and personal assets that she brought to the marriage or acquired in her own name during the marriage. She became free to act as a businesswoman, to acquire and sell real estate, and to bequeath goods as she wished.

Critics of the 1870s legislation decried what they perceived to be the rending asunder of the notion of marriage as a community: by creating "two authorities in the same household ... it held up a sort of premium to the wife to commit acts of insubordination. ... savoured of 'Women's Rights' [and] was calculated to revolutionize the whole household system," John Robson, a disgruntled British Columbia politician, exclaimed on the eve of the passage of that province's first MWPL. The Married Women's Property Law, "Observer" wrote to the Victoria *Colonist* in January 1873, gave to married women "no more responsibility than a single woman living in concubinage with a man."[13] Contemporary supporters disagreed and argued that families would be strengthened in that women would be protected from "bad husbands."[14] Moreover, as the Victoria *Standard's* editor wrote in January 1873, British Columbia's first MWPL "is not by any means a one-sided measure extending protection only to wives, but aims as well to protect the interests of husbands, where the law now exposes them to loss and inconvenience ... for the recovery of debts contracted by wives prior to the date of marriage," and it made them solely liable for any debts contracted on their separate estates "in the way of business" after marriage.[15]

Few historians argue that the MWPLs were primarily designed to augment the economic and social rights of married women. Chris Clarkson, in a nicely contextualized analysis of the evolution of MWPLs in British Columbia, posits a twofold process.[16] The 1870s legislation was designed to strengthen the economic independence of a nuclear family headed by an independent yeoman. By allowing a married woman control of some wealth, the legislation could better protect a woman and her family from a dishonest or overly speculative husband, or from the grasping hands of creditors, and thus enable the woman to continue her essential reproductive role. The protection of family stability in a very uncertain economic environment ranked higher than the interests of creditors in British Columbia in the 1870s. The MWPL was a measure designed to ensure the economic and reproductive functions of the nuclear family. This perspective allowed space for a patriarchal state to step in and protect women and their children in contexts where husbands had by their abusive behaviour, fraudulent actions, or simply unsuccessful economic speculations forgone that right.

By the 1880s the priorities of the legislators had changed. The 1887 MWPL in British Columbia no longer privileged the maintenance of a yeoman-headed nuclear family. In a new emerging economy that was increasingly propelled by big capital and corporate organization, the ideal of the yeoman family began to fade from view.[17] Instead, the rights of creditors took centre stage. Opponents of the 1870s MWPLs had argued that men could protect themselves from creditors by transferring property to their wives since the legislation was far from precise as to what constituted a fraudulent transfer. In British Columbia, "as the legislature became increasingly dominated by lawyers, speculators and businessmen supporting and dependent on oligarchic capital, legislators looked ... to correct the problem."[18] The MWPLs of the 1880s in both British Columbia and Ontario did precisely that, and they made it more difficult to transfer property in an attempt to defraud creditors.

In her consideration of the impact on families of the MWPLs in the United States, Carole Shammas favours a variation of this argument. She too sees the MWPLs as a protective measure intended more for creditors than for women. Yet "from a political standpoint," she suggests, "the acts were testimony to the extent to which the U.S. political system promoted individual property rights." What was breaking down, she asserts, was the traditional family economy. Capitalism was in the

process of changing from a structure centred on "family based manage-
ment to [one based on] corporate based management." It was easier
for men to cede stocks and bonds to their wives because those assets
could be managed more cheaply by others than could land and busi-
nesses. Moreover, by giving women control over wealth, she provoca-
tively suggests, many men (and women) would no longer be interested
in marrying. Divorce was now more economically feasible for women.
Since men could no longer control their wives' assets, there was less rea-
son for them to contest divorce, and divorce rates accelerated accord-
ingly. In sum, the family was becoming "a less reliable organizational
unit for capital formation."[19]

Some historians argue that these laws were potentially enabling for
women, but only for the relatively few who had access to property to
protect.[20] Moreover, it is often pointed out that a conservative judiciary
qualified and muted married women's rights to property throughout
much of the late nineteenth century.[21] By the end of the century, the
legal historian Constance Backhouse writes, "the law would ... appear to
be egalitarian and even handed ... [but] property allocation would con-
tinue to be gender-imbalanced. It leaves one to wonder whether the
battle to obtain formal property rights for married women, a struggle
that engaged so many for so long, was the best choice that feminists
could make."[22] Backhouse's query is the departure point of this book;
the central question is: What do we know about the independent eco-
nomic activity and wealth-holdings of married and other women in late
nineteenth-century urban Canada? Were middle-class women espe-
cially in a sphere separate from the activity of men, a zone within which
activity focused only on domestic issues: caring for husbands, raising
children, and keeping house? Or did many women through their man-
agement of various types of wealth, from household goods to land to
stocks and bonds to business affairs, demonstrate the connectedness of
private and public and, in so doing, render the notion of separate
implausible and the idea of spheres problematic. Until we can provide
credible answers to those questions, we cannot begin to answer Back-
house's query.

A closer consideration of the notion of spheres is appropriate here.
Few historians now argue that women were tightly contained in a
domestic setting separate from the more worldly setting of men. Even
one of the more influential statements of the spheres paradigm, that
made by Leonore Davidoff and Catherine Hall, emphasizes the porous
nature of the boundaries between public and private.[23] It is not my

intention to demolish a caricature. Rather, this work builds on and extends a historiography, international in scope, that increasingly recognizes the permeability and interconnectedness of public and private.[24]

Perhaps a useful way to visualize this interconnectedness is to employ a continuum rather than spheres as a metaphor for examining women's participation in the world of capital at the turn of the twentieth century. Depending on the activities under investigation, private might extend somewhat further along the line; public might begin at an earlier point. Where one shaded into the other depended on the nature of the activity and the context within which that activity occurred. The division between public and private was variable, contingent, and changing. The notion of a continuum encourages thinking of connections and meeting points and seems a particularly appropriate way to "see" capital at work. If, as I seek to demonstrate in this book, women were active participants in the affairs of capital, then the ideology of spheres cannot capture the essence of behaviour in such affairs. Conduct in matters relating to capital implies relationships: interactions between borrowers and lenders; between purchasers and sellers of land; between renters and owners of property; between customers and merchants; between landladies and boarders. Such interactions do not imply equality; behaviour in the capital sphere often depended on and promoted dependencies and inequality. Yet even from the perspective of power, the notion of a continuum has merit. As will be noted throughout this book, agency was never the *sole* prerogative of the "monied": the lenders, owners, or sellers. Those women (and men) who borrowed, rented, and purchased acted in their own interests and could and did adopt strategies at odds with the wishes of those with whom they bargained.

Recognizing power imbalances and emphasizing relationships, this work demonstrates that in many of these affairs of capital, women acted in a surprisingly public way, and they did so in the face of strong public notions prescribing the contrary. Indeed, it is interesting to note that one close observer of the "woman question" in the United States felt that at the turn of the century "the old idea of two separate spheres for men and women has been rejuvenated and commands the assent of many persons, both men and women, who are capable of thinking out the solution of other problems, but have given up this one."[25] Whether such proscriptive views simply ignored reality or were an increasingly shrill response to activities that some felt could not be condoned is difficult to know, although throughout the book some (it is hoped, well-considered) speculations are presented.

While I argue forcefully that women were far more autonomous in matters of finance and general economic activity than many historians and most especially many historians of Canada have as yet argued, I do not suggest that, as a group, women became the equal of men in these sectors. Throughout the work, close comparative attention is given to male and female enterprise, and without reifying either, comments concerning the relative power of men and women are made. To be perfectly clear, this work does not present a whiggish account of women's triumphs over adversity, of their collective rise to a level of parity with men in matters of finance and general economic endeavour. While the activity of some individual women surpassed in measurable ways the enterprise of most men, women on average fell short, often far short. A pessimistic reading would be that inequalities, often substantial, remained. A more optimistic reading highlights the very substantial and surprising gains made by women in sectors commonly perceived to be more public than private, more male than female.

I seek to provide in this book a detailed picture of women managing their own capital as investors, as inheritors and bequeathers of wealth, as landowners, as mortgagees and mortgagors on the basis of land, as borrowers and lenders on the basis of chattels, and as businesswomen on their own account. Their presence in each of these areas has received some attention from historians, and their comments will be referred to at the appropriate places in the chapters that follow. As yet, however, no study has included all the sectors mentioned above, nor has any study adopted a systematic comparative approach to the analysis of such material.[26] It may be that the MWPLs had no impact on such behaviour. It may be that other factors operative at various local levels filtered these laws in ways that current historiography has yet to test. In order to pursue a rigorous comparative approach, this book focuses on various levels of unit of analysis. Where sources allow, a national urban picture will be presented, most extensively, but not only, as in chapters 7 and 8, which consider women in business, and more briefly in chapter 1, which examines general wealth-holding, in chapter 4, which looks at landholding, and chapter 5, which considers mortgages. As well, proscriptive and other commentaries on women's proper behaviour are drawn from a wide range of often national written sources, including newspapers, magazines, novels, parliamentary debates, and more private correspondence. Within this general context, the book focuses most directly on the activity of women and men within two cities – Hamilton, Ontario, and Victoria, British Columbia – in late nineteenth-century Canada, in part because assessment rolls, wills, and mortgage and chattel records are generated at the local level. But that analysis, too, is situated within a comparative urban and gender frame in order to provide context for understanding the activity patterns uncovered, and moreover, in chapter 3 context is provided for investment behaviour in Hamilton via comparisons with investment behaviour in the province as a whole.

Chapter 1 provides a broad template within which the more finely focused analyses offered in subsequent chapters can be situated. By drawing on a large run of women's and men's probates spanning a half-century, the chapter provides an overview of the relative size and composition of women's wealth compared to that of wealth held by men in Victoria and Hamilton and comments on the changes in the investment portfolios of men and women within and between the two cities over time. The impact of legislation, especially the MWPLs, on wealth accumulation and investment is carefully considered. While women could invest from the private "sphere" of their homes and thus were not as apt to be seen in conflict with their prescribed "proper role" in society, the investment behaviour of women charted in this chapter raised much discussion in late nineteenth- and early twentieth-century Canada. The variability of that gender discourse and the interplay between discourse and behaviour is noted. As well, the significance of women's investment activity for general economic development and for demonstrating the interdependence of private and public is highlighted.

The general parameters of women's wealth and their actions in the investment sphere having been established in chapter 1, chapter 2 focuses more closely on a related aspect of wealth management: inheriting and bequeathing assets. How did the inheritance process enable or restrict women's agency in material affairs? What was the relationship between bequeathment practices and the investment behaviour of men and women uncovered in chapter 1? Essentially, the chapter provides a comparative study of the inheritance process in Victoria and Hamilton over some fifty years and suggests that women increasingly benefited from that process. Wills, however, supplied more than simple instructions as to the disposition of material wealth. They were themselves discourses, and discourses made all the more poignant and significant because they were, in a real sense, last words. Accordingly, the chapter attends carefully to the attitudes and messages left by men and women in the course of writing their last wills and testaments and points to the assertiveness and independence displayed by many women.

In terms of wealth management, chapters 1 and 2 focus mainly on an older group of the general population, although in their inheritance strategies this group could and did, it is suggested, enable a younger group. Chapters 3 through 6 focus more closely on particular aspects of wealth management that our discussion of the probate data introduced and at the same time broaden the focus to a wider-aged group of men and women.

Chapter 3 looks at men and women as investors in financial stocks, specifically in the fields of banking and insurance in Ontario.[27] While some nineteenth-century analysts advised women to steer clear of stock-market activity, chapter 3 demonstrates that, far from doing so, women became significant players in the purchasing of financial stocks, and it underlines that many young women were so involved. By comparing the investment activities of Hamilton women with those in the province as a whole, the chapter establishes the representivity of women (and men) in that city. Indeed, one could legitimately speak of the feminization of that financial market in Ontario over the course of the last half of the nineteenth century and the first years of the twentieth.

Those who, in the late nineteenth century, offered financial and investment advice to women, invariably pointed to the importance of land. Chapter 4 provides an in-depth examination of women and men as landholders in Victoria and Hamilton in the late nineteenth century, based on linked assessment and census data for each city. As in chapters 1 and 2, the comparative focus on men and women in two cities allows one to better appreciate the significance of trends across space, time, and gender. The similarities and differences between the landholdings of men and women in these two cities are carefully explored. In order to understand those differences, a central discussion of the ways local economic and demographic realities filtered general legislation such as the MWPLS is provided.

The next two chapters build on and extend that analysis in several ways. Chapter 5 compares the behaviour of women and men as mortgagors (borrowers) and mortgagees (lenders) on the security of land in Victoria and Hamilton over a forty-year period spanning the late nineteenth and early twentieth centuries. The impact of provincial laws, especially those concerning dower, on and local economic contexts for this behaviour is highlighted. The significant extent to which female-controlled capital underwrote urban and general economic development in this time period is suggested. Perhaps just as significant, and generally overlooked in the historical literature, is the extent to which women were borrowers in their own name from both corporations and other individuals and productive spenders of such money.

Chapter 6 examines borrowing and lending by men and women in a slightly different context. Most studies of mortgaging focus on land as a security. But men and women also borrowed and lent on the basis of chattels, often household goods under the management of women. Chapter 6 examines this behaviour as it took place in Victoria over the last forty years of the nineteenth century.[28] In studies of bequeathments, household goods owned by women are often noted for their sentimental and symbolic familial importance. This chapter demonstrates that such goods also had significant material value in the context of both consumption and production. Yet as is noted in chapter 1, women increasingly owned more than household goods. A trend toward the participation in the chattel market of women borrowers and women lenders on the security of business assets is highlighted, as is the overrepresentation of women entrepreneurs compared to their male counterparts in this market. The chapter in part argues that any easy distinction between the consumptive and productive spheres of economic activity is unwarranted. Seeing women as consumers and men as producers separates household and family from productive enterprise and perpetuates the notion of separate spheres. In fine, this chapter focuses on the symbiotic nature of production and consumption and suggests that women stood at the convergence of both.

Chapters 7 and 8 build on the evidence presented in chapter 6 concerning the presence of women in the world of entrepreneurship. In these chapters the discussion moves more centrally to an analysis of women in business, an activity that some have argued was relatively the most visible economic endeavour engaged in by women and that, as a result, most dramatically challenged the precepts of the separate spheres ideology.[29] Chapter 7 provides national estimates of the degree to which women and men in the workforce owned and operated businesses. Patterns of business behaviour in Victoria and Hamilton are situated within this general context. Finally, a further comparative frame is provided via a systematic comparison of the business activity of women and men at the beginning and end of the twentieth century. For those in the workforce, the chapter argues, women in urban

Canada were more apt to be self-employed than men in 1901 and were
at least as likely to be self-employed as were similarly situated women
some ninety years later. In many ways this single finding best indicates
the assertiveness of women in economic matters at the turn of the twen-
tieth century. Many women, including married women, ran businesses
situated within and outside their homes. Many of these women, too,
were demonstrably middle-class, the group presumed to be most con-
strained by separate spheres ideology.

In a related way, by focusing on the role played by women in family-
run businesses, chapter 8 provides further evidence of the interplay
between home and entrepreneurial activity. Via a systematic compari-
son of the characteristics of male- and female-headed family businesses,
the chapter points out that home and family were sanctuaries for the
"exercise [of women's] gentle sway" in ways that would have dismayed
separate spheres ideologists.[30] Home provided many women entrepre-
neurs the opportunity to engage in and manage their own enterprise
free from direct male control. In fine, the chapter suggests that family
business was firmly and often profitably situated within the "woman's
sphere," and in so doing, it qualifies Shammas's argument concerning
the breakdown of family capitalism.

In the conclusion, the arguments previewed in this introduction and
developed throughout the book are reviewed. Special attention is given
to the ways in which the book demonstrates the importance of the
MWPLS in enabling economic agency on the part of married and unmar-
ried women. At the same time it is noted that underlying social and cul-
tural changes certainly contributed to the increase of such economic
behaviour, perhaps most importantly ones related to the emergence of
a liberal middle-class order in society generally. The roles that histori-
ans have argued women played in the furtherance of that middle-class
project are reassessed in light of the evidence of their economic behav-
iour presented throughout this study. Avenues for further exploration
are suggested.

Victoria, British Columbia, and Hamilton, Ontario, two urban com-
munities with different economic structures, investment opportunities,
and demographic characteristics, are the primary sites for this study.
Founded as a fur trade centre in the 1840s, Victoria experienced a
short-lived spurt during the Gold Rush era of the early 1860s, but it was
not until the decade of the 1880s that significant economic expansion
and population growth took place. By the end of that decade Victoria
was the eleventh largest Canadian city by population, having increased

by 184 per cent to 16, 841 people. It ranked fifth in per capita value of industrial output among the twenty Canadian cities with a population over 10,000. The bubble burst in the 1890s. "The signs of improvement in business are few and far between," C.A. Holland, the manager of the city's largest mortgage and investment company, wrote in May 1896, a lament he reiterated throughout much of the decade. Indeed, a year later he wrote to his London board of directors that he had gone to the extreme of "investing in a bicycle, second hand, $45" in order to better apprehend and collect from outgoing tenants![31]

By 1901 the city had dropped from the top 25 per cent to the bottom 20 per cent in per capita value of manufacturing output, and while its population had grown to over 20,000, so too had that of its principal rival, Vancouver. Possibilities for local investment shrank in this period. Banks and insurance companies were for the most part owned by outsiders and eastern-based capitalists were quickly picking off other potential investment opportunities in manufacturing and shipping. Victoria, then, provides an excellent micro-environment for examining how women investors, entrepreneurs, and general wealth-holders fared in a context of rapid growth and severe decline.[32]

Compared to Victoria, Hamilton was an old city: it celebrated its seventy-fifth anniversary in 1891. Situated at the head of Lake Ontario, it competed with its larger urban rival, Toronto, for control of a common commercial hinterland. In terms of population, it was the fourth largest Canadian city in 1891 and the fifth in 1901, with 49,000 and 53,000 residents respectively. By the last quarter of the century, the city's entrepreneurs focused intensely on manufacturing: metal production, cotton mills and men's and women's clothing expanded in this period. Often called the "Birmingham of Canada," the city had, in 1891 and again in 1901, a greater proportion of its workers employed in manufacturing than was the case in either Toronto or Montreal. In contrast to Victoria, Hamilton represents a heartland city that had made it as an industrial centre. Investment opportunities, relative to Victoria, were many and varied.[33]

Demographically, the two cities represent an even greater contrast. In 1901 only 13 per cent of Hamilton's population had been born outside Canada, and almost all of the 6,800 immigrants came from the British Isles. By contrast, one-half of Victoria's residents had been born outside Canada and a good percentage of them came from Asia. In the period under review, there were considerably more men than women of marriageable age in Victoria. While the latter city exhibited a sex ratio generally associated with frontier communities, Hamilton's resembled that of relatively longer settled regions. As late as 1901 there were 144 men of marriageable age for every 100 women in Victoria; in Hamilton the ratio was 82 men for every 100 women.[34] Scholars have speculated on what effect imbalanced sex ratios might have had on women's agency, and the possible impact of these different "marriage markets" on the wealth-holding patterns in each city will be looked at closely in this book.[35]

Since the interaction between practice and ideology is a central focus of this work, the central records utilized in this study are of both a qualitative and a quantitative sort. Novels, poems, newspapers, legislative debates, private correspondence, wills, and sundry other qualitative sources have been examined in an attempt to provide a sense of the ideological discourse that characterized the period under investigation. Systematic analysis of the social data embedded in such routinely generated sources as censuses, assessment rolls, mortgage records, probates, and wills is the only way that a broad picture of women's economic behaviour can be sketched. Such an approach can uncover what Bernard Bailyn has termed latent tendencies: trends and processes that contemporaries did not recognize but which were, nonetheless, occurring. "When seen in connection with the clarifying latent landscape," Bailyn notes, public events "appear to occupy different positions than heretofore."[36] Once we have such a context, the activities of individual women can be better appreciated. Indeed, this work provides many close studies of individual women active in matters of finance and business in order to offer insights into motivation, provide a more evocative sense of personal context, and point to the particular ways that gender ideology, while constraining, was nonetheless variable – dependent on a variety of local and personal contexts, class, and other structural factors. There is no fundamental contradiction in approach or method here. The first approach searches out averages in order to make useful comparisons across space, time, and gender. The second, by adopting a more micro-perspective, provides space for a fuller appreciation of human experience, even while, given the context provided by the first approach, recognizing in specific ways the constricted and bounded nature of that experience.

Did, then, the MWPLs tend to "revolutionize the whole household system," as Robson feared? Or did they, as Backhouse and others have averred, promise more than society was willing to deliver? Read on.

Gender, Wealth, and Investment: Victoria and Hamilton, 1869–1931

Catherine Kreamer, a widow, died in Hamilton in October 1891. Her will, handwritten by herself twelve years earlier, decreed that her daughter should receive "$125 and the bedding and equipage in the bedroom ... and a fashionable bedstead shall be bought for her ... Also a breakfast table, rocking chair and six common chairs, the center table, the Looking Glass, the musical instrument, the Bureau, two sofa pillows and a vase of flowers. She is also to have the classic dishes out of the cupboard and the silver spoons likewise some cheap dishes, knives and forks and a cow." Mrs Kreamer's grandson received a "common bedstead and a straw bed, four blankets and feather pillows and a chest large enough to hold all his wearing apparel." Mrs Kreamer continued with her itemized bequest, carefully listing clothing and jewellery for sundry other people. Harriet Pounder, a married woman, died in Hamilton in July 1891. Her will, written two years earlier, left fifty-eight separate items to eighteen different women and three men. The items ranged from a "small ring" to gloves, handkerchiefs, cases, and "Phrenological Heads." A similar list of domestic items was enumerated by Mary Helen Baillie, who wrote her will in July 1889 in Victoria, British Columbia. She bequeathed household items to ten different women and two men. "As I have had my share with my late husband in furnishing the house with furniture," Sarah Finlayson, of Victoria, wrote in her 1905 will, " it is my wish that after my death the said furniture with everything belonging to the home is not to be sold but to be divided equally between my sons and daughters." Asenath Sharp, a spinster of Hamilton, went so far as to leave her "dresses and underwear" to her sister.[1] Wills such as these, and there were many of them, seem to support the notion that women were at home in the domestic sphere:

the goods they owned testified to that orientation, and the people to whom they bequeathed those goods were more often than not women like themselves.

Women more than men were, in the words of the British historian R.J. Morris, "'things' people."[2] Yet although women owned and clearly treasured domestic goods, they owned and treasured more than those. The probate of Katherine Kreamer's will revealed that only 12 per cent of her wealth was in household goods: land accounted for 38 per cent, and debts owed to her a further 36 per cent of the estate. Household goods represented only 3.5 per cent of Mary Pounder's estate; bank stock (83 per cent) and cash in the bank made up the rest. Sarah Finlayson's personal property was listed as $500, a mere 2.2 per cent of her total estate. Similarly Asenath Sharp's clothing was but a tiny part of an estate worth $11,659. These assets suggest that women had interests of a material sort that took them outside the home. Moreover, in this era household goods were themselves changing. In her 1915 will Hermiena Lyons of Victoria bequeathed a piano, household furniture, and books, goods often owned and bequeathed by women to other women, to her daughters. But she also left another "household good," her "automobile the Hudson 37 car 1913 License number 7258 ... to be used as at present while my daughters or either of them shall remain at home with their father."[3]

This chapter explores the relationship between gender and wealth-holding via a comparative analysis of the probates of men and women in late nineteenth-century Hamilton, Ontario, and Victoria, British Columbia. The intent is to provide comparative measurements of the extent and types of wealth owned by women and men in these cities; to compare the patterns of investment engaged in by those women and men; and to situate their behaviour within the dominant and relevant gender discourses of that era. The first part of the chapter discusses the relevant historiography concerning women and investment. The second examines the strengths and weaknesses of the central source material: wills and probates. The last two sections address the following questions: Did women's wealth increase over the time period of this study? Did women's investment practice differ significantly from that of men? In subsequent chapters the bequeathment practices of women and men in these two cities will be compared, and the holdings of specific assets and the behaviour of women in specific financial and economic markets and in specific cities will be analyzed in more detail.

The historiography relating to the Married Women's Property Laws has evolved over the last twenty years from charting and accounting for the passage of such legislation – although the explanatory part of that process continues – to a focus on the impact of those laws on women's lives. The first generation of impact studies based their conclusions on close analysis of court cases and qualitative commentaries drawn from press, personal correspondence, and similar types of sources. Their conclusions were mixed. Some argued that the judiciary was a conservative and negative weight that contained and limited the potential for women's agency implicit in such laws. While agreeing that the judiciary was conservative, other scholars suggested that judges protected rather than controlled women in their encounters with the marketplace.[4]

More recently, studies have focused on women's actual behaviour in the market prior to and following the passage of the MWPLs. These studies have taken a number of tacks. Especially in Great Britain, studies of consumption have demonstrated that married women were active in their own names as buyers and sellers long before the MWPLs made such behaviour legal. Studies of patent registrations in the United States have charted a marked increase in women's participation following the MWPLs. Using quantitative data drawn from wills and probates, historians in many countries are finding that the MWPLs led to increased activity on the part of women as will-makers and as wealth-holders. Margaret Coombs has demonstrated that following the 1870 British Married Women's Property Act, married women "seized the opportunity" to "make choices about their wealth-holding." Carole Shammas has noted that following the MWPLs in the United States, women "were at least in a position to make some decisions about their and their family's own consumption, investments and wealth transmission."[5] Similar studies are only just emerging in the Canadian context. Susan Ingram and Kris Inwood provide a carefully constructed study of wealth-holding by women in Guelph, Ontario, in the second half of the nineteenth century and conclude that the MWPLs contributed to a sharp increase in "the female held share of all property and the female share of all owners in the town." Work by Livio Di Matteo and Peter George on Wentworth County, Ontario, in a similar time period has also pointed to increased wealth-holding by women in the era of the MWPLs.[6]

Currently, historians are attempting to gain a clearer picture of the nature and significance of the wealth that women increasingly owned.

David Green and Alastair Owens have focused on single women as wealth-holders in Great Britain in the first half of the nineteenth century and concluded that these gentlewomen capitalists were significant owners of government securities throughout the period. Using company records and qualitative data drawn from the financial press and investment advice literature, Janette Rutterford and Josephine Maltby have argued that, despite contemporary nineteenth-century male attitudes that saw women as helpless and inept victims in the financial world, some British women were actually quite active and successful as independent financiers, investors, and speculators. Focusing more closely on attitudes rather than behaviour, Susan Yohn has emphasized the restrictive impact that a dominant ideology which viewed women as angels of the hearth had on women's investment behaviour in the United States in the same period. Contrary to Rutterford and Maltby, Yohn argues that women were in fact "crippled capitalists" who, even if they had wealth, lacked the agency and possibility of exercising power commensurate with that wealth. In essence, she sees women entrepreneurs and investors as silent and passive bystanders, and argues that a similarly restrictive ideology remains powerful in the United States at the turn of the twenty-first century.[7]

Most of the literature mentioned above has focused on the late nineteenth century, and we know relatively little about wealth-holding of women in the first half of the twentieth century. As well, much of the literature that examines specific investments of women is based on qualitative and/or single-asset information. What are required are studies over a longer time period that include analysis of as much of the women's portfolio as possible and that can then comment more fully on investment diversity and degree of speculative behaviour. While such analyses should certainly be situated in the context of male investment behaviour, they should avoid essentializing the woman investor and instead be sensitive to the fact that all women – and indeed, all men – did not invest in similar ways. Such studies should also be sensitive to the fact that gender ideology, while an important context within which to situate investment behaviour, was itself always evolving. Ideology interacts with, rather than simply restricts, behaviour. Using probate evidence from two Canadian cities, this chapter situates wealth-holding of men and women in a comparative context with special attention on the type of investment behaviour, the gendered ideological context within which such behaviour occurred, and the nature and reasons for changes overtime.

There is a substantial literature from both a Canadian and an international context on the merits of probate records.[8] That literature almost unanimously concludes that there is no better available source for studying the nature and distribution of wealth-holding in the nineteenth and early twentieth centuries.[9] Probate records are the result of a court-administered process designed to assess systematically the worth of a deceased person's assets. The state required that probates be undertaken for tax purposes, and executors or appointed administrators carried out that task.[10] The detail provided in these reports cannot be found for as many people in any other nineteenth- or early twentieth-century Canadian source. At a general level that literature also warns of several important biases in probate data. The age cohort is older than that of the general population; those whose wills were probated had something of value to bequeath, so that on average they would probably have been wealthier than individuals not probated; in almost all jurisdictions only a minority of those who died left wills. Probates and wills, then, might be expected to be representative of an older, wealthier, and perhaps more sickly minority of the population at large.

Moreover, there are reasons to question the extent to which such data reflect the actual wealth of that supposed minority. In the first place, wills should be seen as the last phase of a process of bequeathing that often commenced well before a person died. Testimony from many wills indicates that property had already been given to various family members, and as a result, other individuals received more in the will. As Isabella Black, a Hamilton widow, noted in her 1897 will, her son "Arthur has had his share already." In 1881 John Robertson, a gentleman living in Victoria, left his wife and two daughters the major part of the estate because, he explained, "I have already paid [my son a] considerable sum of money." Hannah Briggs of Hamilton went to the unusual length of detailing what she had distributed before death: all her personal property and $10,000 in bonds to her daughters, leaving an estate of $5,807 to be distributed after her death.[11] Diaries and some extant correspondence also point to bequeathing before death in order to provide a form of life insurance in old age. It is difficult to know the extent of these *inter vivos* transfers. Nor was appraising an exact science, and consistency across time and place could be problematic. Taxes could encourage people to transfer assets before death and/or to (fraudulently) devalue the stated worth of the ceded property. We might expect the probated values, then, to be lower-bound estimates of the surveyed population's total worth.

In these ways, therefore, wills and probates provide a glimpse of property relations at one point in the life course of the individuals involved, and this point may not be reflective of the whole life course of property owners. For that reason some historians, such as Alastair Owens, argue that inheritance should be studied "as a distinct life-course stage rather than a more general window onto the social relations of property." Yet even Owens admits that this was one of the "key moments of transition within families."[12] It was a process that had long-term impacts on the property-holding patterns of family members. While wills were enacted at a particular life-course stage – death – their impacts, it can be argued, extended across the life course of those who did and did not inherit. Their provisions enabled and restricted the property-holding possibilities of many at different stages in the life course from the deceased. Moreover, the writing of a will was an opportunity to make a final and perhaps summative normative statement and disposition of one's remaining material wealth. The seriousness of the moment should not be lost sight of. There would be no second chance. Perhaps some parts of that wealth had already been transmitted – at times of marriage or births or a child's "coming of age" – and in that sense the final types and amounts may not reflect the wealth of the bequeather in years past. But no study has yet suggested that *inter vivos* transfers differed systematically according to some set of social characteristics. It is just as likely that men and women, situated within similar legal and general social contexts, engaged in *inter vivos* transfers in a generally similar fashion. Thus if the "box scores" relating to wealth-holding of individuals at death differ from what may have earlier been the case, the *relative* holdings may be assumed to be similar to those of past "moments." At one level this chapter operates on that assumption; but of course the study as a whole also goes beyond wills and probates and examines as well landholding patterns, land and chattel mortgage investments, and general business endeavours in order to offer as wide a picture as possible of the gendered nature of wealth-holding in late nineteenth-century urban Canada.

Two further challenges in the use of wills and probates for this study require mention. The first concerns the comparability of probates across legal jurisdictions. Succession duties were higher in British Columbia than they were in Ontario: in British Columbia all estates under $5,000 were exempt from taxation; in Ontario estates under $10,000 were exempt. In British Columbia and in Ontario exemptions were made to relatives for estates under $25,000 and $100,000 respectively. As well, the rates of taxation were somewhat higher in British Columbia. To the extent that taxation encouraged *inter vivos* transfers and fraudulent under evaluations, then, one might expect that British Columbia probates underestimated wealth to a somewhat greater degree than Ontario probates.[13]

More frustrating is the fact that before 1907 British Columbia probates tended to be less fulsome in the depiction of personal assets than was the case in Ontario. The Estates Devolution Act, passed in Ontario in 1887, required probates to report on real as well as personal assets. Similar legislation was not passed in British Columbia until 1894.[14] Data that will permit reasonable comparisons – reasonable in the sense that we can at least be aware of possible biases – across jurisdictions are only fully available for the period following 1894. Even then compliance came more slowly in British Columbia than in Ontario: between 1894 and 1901, 63 per cent of Victoria's probates broke down asset distribution; for Hamilton after 1888, the percentage was just under 100.[15]

Tables 1.1 through 1.3 provide an introductory overview of trends in women's wealth-holding in the era of the MWPLs. Carole Shammas has assembled a comparative group of American studies of women's wealth based on probate data. Table 1.1 summarizes the relevant part of that information and compares it with the number and worth of probates for Victoria and Hamilton in the late nineteenth and early twentieth centuries. Several points can be drawn from the data in that table. The most significant is that following the passage of the MWPLs, women's probates as a percentage of all probates increased, and in almost all jurisdictions so too did women's percentage of probated wealth. Women's probated estates represented 23 per cent of all probated estates in Hamilton in the 1869–71 period. Twenty years later the share increased to 43 per cent of all probates, and by the end of the third decade in the twentieth century fully 54 per cent of all probates were in women's names. The increase in the percentage of probated estates held by women in Victoria might at first glance seem less dramatic than that for their Hamilton counterparts. In fact, however, the increase reflects the skewed sex ratio in that city. In both cities more women had assets in their own name, thus necessitating having their estates probated even if they neglected to write a will.

Table 1.1 also provides a glimpse at the structure of women's wealth in the two cities under particular investigation in this study. In both cities the wealth owned by probated women fell far short of that owned by

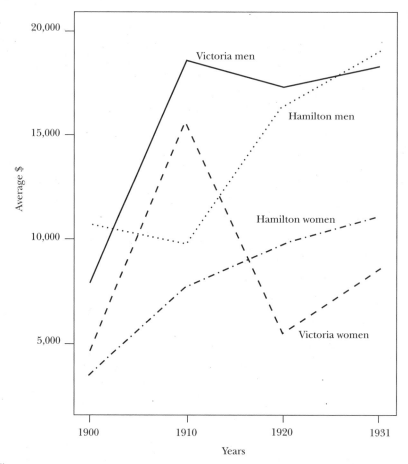

Figure 1.1
Average probated wealth for men and women: Hamilton and Victoria, 1900–31

probated men. Just how far short is nicely illustrated in figure 1.1. As Carole Shammas has noted, wealth inequality is best seen as a measurement of economic power, and in that sense figure 1.1 underlines the dominance of men in late nineteenth-century urban Canada.[16] Yet the nature of the spread in average probated wealth differed across cities. The spread was much narrower in Victoria in the late nineteenth and early twentieth centuries but widened fairly dramatically after 1913. In Hamilton the spread between male and female average probated wealth narrowed somewhat as the period progressed. In 1900 men in Hamilton, on average, owned two-thirds more than women; at the turn of the century men in Victoria owned on average only two-fifths more than women. By 1930 the figures had virtually reversed: on average, Hamilton men owned two-fifths more than Hamilton women; Victoria men owned just over half again as much as Victoria women. In other words, women in Hamilton were (slowly) moving to a position of wealth commensurate with their proportion of probates; while the opposite was the case for Victoria's women. The post–World War One Victoria data stand in apparent contrast to the findings reported by Shammas for a series of American cities, on the basis of which she concluded "that over the last century the wealth holding of women had dramatically increased."[17] Data for the Canadian cities do not extend as deeply into the twentieth century as those for the American cities reported in Shammas's study, and so Victoria's decrease may have been of a temporary nature. The relative downward trend in wealth-holding for Victoria women will be explored more closely following a more in-depth examination of investment strategies and asset composition in several Canadian urban communities.

As table 1.2 demonstrates, will-making, too, became more common for women in the late nineteenth century. The incidence of will-making by probated women in both cities increased sharply in the years following the passage of the MWPLs, further evidence of the positive impact of the legislation on women's agency in matters of finance. Yet the percentage of women in these two Canadian cities who wrote wills seems to have stabilized around the turn of the century. Women were taking advantage of the legal opportunities provided them by the MWPLs. In most jurisdictions in the United States, MWPLs had been passed earlier than in Ontario and British Columbia. Since the legislation in both Canada and the United States was not retroactive, one would expect that there would be a delay of about one generation before its full impact occurred.[18] Despite the later passage of the MWPLs in Canada, the extent of wealth-holding and will-making by women in Canadian jurisdictions in the late nineteenth century closely resembled that in the United States, thus underlining the significance of that legislation for Canada's female urban middle class.

Table 1.3 demonstrates that married Canadian urban women became more active as testators and as owners of wealth following the passage of the MWPLs. The first MWPL in Ontario to mention explicitly the right of a married woman to bequeath her assets as if she were a *femme sole* was the 1884 act; British Columbia followed suit in 1887.[19] In the pre-1887 era it was not uncommon for husbands to oversee the writing of their wives' wills. Bartholemy Ferrand of Victoria wrote on the will of his wife,

Marie, in October 1880: "I hereby consent to the above will." Ralph Ingham, also of Victoria, assured the probate court that on 25 June 1877 his wife, Catherine, had "during her coverture with me by and with my consent made and executed her last will and testament."[20] The MWPLs freed women from such controls. Legal recognition that they could write wills represented a significant expansion of a married woman's individual civic rights. Many took full advantage of that freedom, and none more so than in Victoria. That city's married women were exceptional in terms of their high percentage of women's probates, wills, and probated wealth in the late nineteenth century and the first thirty years of the twentieth. Sixty per cent of women's wills in Victoria in the late nineteenth century were written by married women, a figure which not only exceeded that for Hamilton but also outpaced the highest known proportion for communities in the United States, 40 per cent in California, in the same time period. The California comparison is significant at least in part because the laws governing a married woman's right to own property in that state – known as the community property system – allowed a married woman to bequeath half the property acquired by her and her husband during marriage as well as to exercise that right for any separate estate she might have.[21] In other words, married women in that state had been for a long time relatively free to bequeath separate from their husbands' control, a right only recently granted to Victoria's married women.

Women in both Canadian cities, then, clearly benefited positively from the passage of the MWPLs. Nevertheless, women's share of wealth did not increase evenly and, as we have seen, in Victoria even declined after 1913. As well, women in all jurisdictions owned far less than men. Women made significant gains, but measured by probate wealth-holding, they did not become the equal of men.

A closer look at wealth-holding by women and men in Victoria and Hamilton underlines the fact that they lived in a society characterized by severe inequalities in wealth. At the turn of the century, the top 10 per cent of wealth-holders (men and women combined) in Victoria controlled 71 per cent of all probated wealth, and those in Hamilton controlled 78 per cent.[22] Comparisons of wealth distribution across nations and regions are fraught with problems as a result of different data sources, legal regimes, and reporting methods, to name a few, but context can be provided via rough comparisons to wealth distribution in other regions. Victoria's and Hamilton's figures are similar to those found for eight countries, including Australia, New Zealand, England,

and four European nations in a similar time period, where the top 10 per cent held between 70 and 90 per cent of all wealth.[23] For Hamilton, the Gini coefficient, a standard measure of wealth inequality was .84, and for Victoria, it was .80, figures that also fall within the range of those reported for the other eight jurisdictions.[24] The extent of wealth inequality in Victoria and Hamilton can also be compared to that found in other North American areas. The Gini values for Ontario (1872), Nova Scotia, (1899–1902), Massachusetts (1889–92 and 1899–1902), and Ohio (1899–1902), for example, fell between .72 and .90.[25] Wealth was distributed more unequally among men than among women in Victoria and Hamilton. The Gini values for Victoria and Hamilton men were .82 and .86 respectively, and for Victoria and Hamilton women the values were .65 and .64.[26]

Tables 1.9 through 1.11 confirm in a more detailed way the unequal distribution of wealth within and across genders in Hamilton and Victoria. Wealth distribution for both genders was remarkably similar in both cities (tables 1.9 through 1.11, rows 5 and 6). Men dominated the top 20 per cent of probated wealth-holders in both Victoria and Hamilton. In 1900 Hamilton men were 2.5 times more likely than Hamilton women to make the top 20 per cent; the comparable ratio for Victoria was 1.7 times. Thirty years later the difference had narrowed somewhat to 1.9 for Hamilton males, while it remained at 1.7 for their Victoria counterparts.

Whatever the reasons for the different spread in total average wealth across gender between the two cities (see figure 1.1), perhaps the most striking finding related to wealth-holding by gender is suggested in figure 1.2. At the turn of the century, the difference in average probated wealth between women and men only became starkly in favour of men in the top wealth category; below that group the average probated wealth of Victoria women exceeded that of men by a factor of 1.5, and the average probated wealth of Hamilton women was nearly the same as that of the men. Twenty years later the figures for men and women were virtually the same in both cities.[27] Put another way, the average probated wealth of all but a third of Hamilton's men in 1900 and less than a quarter in 1922 could not be differentiated by gender. In the case of Victoria, probated women in both eras, on average, owned more than all but a little under a quarter of their male counterparts. By the eve of the Depression the average probated wealth of women in this category in Hamilton had begun to slip but in Victoria women in this category owned on average 8 per cent more than did men. Moreover,

Figure 1.2
Average probated wealth by gender for all but the top 20 per cent of
wealth-holders: Hamilton and Victoria, 1900–31

as a comparison of figures 1.1 and 1.2 suggests, even for Hamilton the
differences were much smaller than when the top 20 per cent of wealth-
holders are included.

The last set of observations conflate the bottom 20 and the middle 60
per cent categories, as presented in tables 1.9 through 1.11. Arguably,
it might not mean much to have a higher average net worth when the
size of the "pie" is small relative to that shared by the top wealth quintile
and especially when that worth situated one near the bottom of the eco-
nomic ladder. Yet it is precisely at that point that "every penny counts";
so the measurable difference in average net wealth in favour of women
in the bottom wealth category probably had real meaning for those who
struggled to live with meagre assets. Moreover, at the turn of the cen-
tury in both cities and especially in Victoria, proportionately fewer
women than men occupied the very bottom wealth level. In both cities
men were far from dominant in the middle 60 per cent category: in
both cities for most of the period between 1898 and 1930 women
bulked in the middle group. In Hamilton, female middle-group wealth-
holders on average owned between 10 and 14 per cent less than men in

the late nineteenth and the first third of the twentieth century. On average, Victoria's female middle-group wealth-holders were as rich as were the men in the middle group in 1900 and richer than men in 1921, but during the 1920s they fell seven per cent below men's average probated wealth in the middle wealth quintiles.[28]

The main point is clear: despite some important differences between the two cities in the gendered distribution of wealth – throughout most of the period Victoria women were closer to Victoria men in average wealth below the top quintile than Hamilton women were relative to Hamilton men – in both cities from the 1890s into the third decade of the twentieth century, the very wealthy tended to be men; below that top strata of wealth and power, women, as measured by probated wealth, were close to if not the equals of men as potential economic/financial actors.

Because of the complexity of these trends, it is easy to forget the simple but very significant fact that in both cities more women were probated wealth-holders as the twentieth century progressed, even if, as was the case in Victoria, women's average probated worth declined in relation to that of men while in Hamilton women's average probated wealth moved closer to that of men. The increase in women wealth-holders is important for a number of reasons. More women were acquiring in their own names the means for the exercise of some financial/economic agency. Indeed, in Hamilton the percentage of female probated wealth-holders mirrored that of women in the city as a whole. In Victoria the relative percentages were not significantly different. As women wealth-holders became more commonplace, one might expect to find changes in society's expectations concerning the relation of women to financial issues. One might even expect to find women themselves exercising such potential agency in an increasingly public and aggressive way.

Up to this point we have predicated our notion of equality and inequality on a simple relationship between extent of net wealth and sex. The broad assumption is that if a man and a woman were located in the same wealth quintal, then they could be considered to have access to relatively similar amounts of prestige and power. In the nineteenth century some thought that argument had merit. Allowing a married woman more control over money, the Toronto *Globe* believed, would lead her husband to treat "her with more real respect and with greater justice" even if "he may feel a little hard about her independence at first."[29] In a debate on the British Married Women's Property Act in

1870, Septimus Hansard commented that when a woman received the legal right to some property in marriage, it would instill in her husband a "general feeling of respect towards the woman ... [and he] would feel that woman was not the mere drudge that she is now ... if she was a woman who had an independent existence and independent rights." John Westlake, a British lawyer with much experience in issues concerning family and property agreed. "I can," he affirmed in the same debate, "state ... that the possession of a separate estate does really give the wife a very independent position, and causes her to be more consulted in matters which concern the management of the household, and putting out in life of the children, and gives her in the family a position of real importance corresponding to that separate estate."[30] Some older work in sociology supports such a relationship: access to more resources leads to increased bargaining power by women and diminishes male dominance.[31] At the turn of the twenty-first century, it is difficult to rest content with such a baldly materialistic argument. Wealth may indeed be enabling, but how one uses or is allowed to use that wealth might be more a function of what Pierre Bourdieu has called habitus, "a set of structuring dispositions" that guide everyday actions.[32]

With particular reference to the notion of gender, much scholarly literature has characterized the late nineteenth and early twentieth centuries as a time when a crisis of masculinity occurred. Others eschew that portrayal, arguing that gender is never fixed but rather evolves as social and economic environments change.[33] In the context of the financial and investment sector, the later hypothesis has merit. As we noted in the introduction, the separate spheres ideology was only one of several "dispositions" or discourses within which women and men managed and understood their lives. The structuring dispositions that helped guide the action of many middle-class folk in this era were far from set in stone. The following reading of popular and financial literature points to the existence of a range of opinion and attitudes concerning women and the investment world.

Nineteenth-century women were often seen as angelic mistresses of the home necessarily absent from the worldly rough-and-tumble of business and financial matters. Even in the late twentieth century financial analysts often saw investing as "a task that falls in the 'masculine' realm."[34] Not surprisingly, such an attitude was much more deeply entrenched a century earlier. Much popular literature taught that a woman should "use her highest powers at home/To train, to touch, but not to roam." A married woman in an 1895 novel, *Geoffrey Hampstead*, came "to believe that she had something of the financier about her and even told her husband that she was beginning to quite understand all about money matters, at which, Joseph [her husband] smiled an ineffable smile." Jokes about women's bookkeeping habits abounded: a husband, on asking his wife what the recurring entry "G.K.W." in her household accounts meant, received the following reply: "Why, that isn't anyone," she said "You see every now and then there is a certain sum for which I cannot account and so I put down G.K.W. – goodness knows what. Don't you see?" The "mismanaging widow" was a common stereotype in the late nineteenth century. In *Pen and Pencil Sketches of Wentworth Landmarks*, Mrs Dick Lauder lamented the manner in which a widow "proved herself an unjust steward": having been left "full control of his property ... [s]he, as might have been expected, made a calamitous hash of the things committed to her charge." "Didn't you say her husband made his will all in her favour?" enquired Mrs Lunt in Elizabeth Fairbairn's 1878 novel *Nothing Like Black on White*. "Why yes," replied Mrs Parly, "but that nasty old scheming father of hers was so very determined to buy up all the shares in the brewery. He borrowed money, and I can't tell you all he done. The house she is in is mortgaged. He got her own daughter to sign some papers, by which she has as good as lost all."[35]

As the historian Mary Ryan has demonstrated, women's role in the home was essential for the training of the appropriately independent middle-class man.[36] As the poet quoted above put it, her function was "to train, to touch, but not to roam." If women roamed, left the home for other pursuits, what then would be the chances of success for the emerging male middle class? One defence against such a development was to praise certain "female" characteristics and disparage others. Many male financiers had no time for "He-She[s]." "What a gay scene," Robert Smith, a British Columbia politician, joked in 1873, "it would be to witness ladies on 'Change' bobbing around in their Dolly Vardens, speculating on Stocks." Henry Clews, a veteran nineteenth-century Wall Street trader, felt that women "are not qualified by nature for the speculative and financial operations in which so many men have made their marks." Women lacked the necessary "mental qualities" for investment, were "comparatively helpless," "without compass," and "too impulsive and impressionable," and, if successful, they benefited from "extraordinary luck" or, more likely, the sage advice of men. "It is probably only," he concluded, "in the matrimonial line that women can become successful speculators."[37]

Clew's catalogue was pretty common.[38] By generally ignoring the possible activity of women as investors and financiers, historians have implicitly accepted that they were unimportant in this field.[39] Yet Clew's catalogue can be best understood as a defensive reaction, rather than self-satisfied gloating. This suggestion gains force at two levels: a second foray through the popular or prescriptive literature available to and often written for (and sometimes by) women demonstrates the emergence of a countervailing set of options for women as investors and financiers. Popular literature and, indeed, more specialized commentary from the financial and investment community was not all of a piece. The task then becomes one of linking behaviour to two competing sets of "structuring dispositions." As Heidi Gottfreid points out, "Bourdieu sensitizes researchers to trust people's conduct as a guide to understanding practice."[40] Gender historians focus closely on such "structuring dispositions," and that literature remains alive to the probability of multiple, overlapping influences on people's behaviour.[41]

Women of Canada: Their Life and Work, a publication of the National Council of Women of Canada, emphasized how unmarried women have "from time immemorial ... collected their rents, made their investments, sued their debtors, [and] compounded with their creditors." But married women, too, had rights. Commenting on the "legal evolution of married women in Canada," a columnist writing in the Woman's Realm section of *Massey's Magazine* in 1896 averred that the law had given married women "equal, if not greater, legal rights than their husbands."[42] Robert Barr, a prolific Canadian novelist, essayist, and reporter, often privileged "the new woman of bright wit and aggressive accomplishment" in his writing. Edith Longworth, in Barr's novel, *A Woman Intervenes*, lives up to her name and, despite resistance from some family members, proves herself to be an astute investor of her own money and a crucial adviser and lender to her father at a time of financial crisis. Indeed, her father "often ... referred to her as his man of business." Edith agreed. "I have a head for business," she declared and was willing to take "risk" and speculate in mining stock.[43] In Mary Denison's novel *That Wife of Mine*, published in Robertson's Cheap Series and advertised as "Popular Reading at Popular Prices," Lissa's husband, Charlie, was surprised by "her accomplishments in the way of business. I never knew that she was an expert in culinary purchases, a bookkeeper in a small but expeditious way, a person with experience in letting and subletting; in fine a whole bureau of expedients and experiments." Given these accomplishments, Charlie was compelled to treat her, "not as a child to be petted, encouraged and guided," but "as an equal."[44] Thomas Webster, an itinerant Methodist clergyman, "was," in the words of his biographer, "vigorous in advocating equal rights for women." In *Woman Man's Equal*, he concluded that "erelong [women] shall occupy the position to which they are entitled, as man's compeer – the position of equality with him in all the relations of life." One can only assume that this message was a central part of his many sermons delivered throughout Upper Canada/Ontario from the 1830s to the mid-1880s.[45] Mrs Parley, in *Nothing Like Black on White*, used her story of the bilked widow to make a bigger point. "I guess," she affirmed, "neither father, mother, brother, sister, no, nor husband either, would get me to sign my name to any paper of their dirty transactions that I didn't thoroughly understand, you bet. I don't care what any person says to the contrary, every woman, married or single, should know enough of business so as not to be tools of others. There, I've been pulling too hard and broke my needle. Wouldn't I be a good advocate of women's rights?"[46]

Manuals designed specifically to provide women with practical knowledge on the ways of business and investment existed.[47] *Women in Their Business Affairs*, a two-volume work published in 1894, edited and written by a prolific novelist, William O. Stoddard, was advertised in Canada. The book promised advice on "Keeping Accounts, Rights of Married Women, Real Estate, Business papers, Personal Property, Banking, Building and Loan Associations, Investments, Insurance and Wills." A manual on "Etiquette for women," published in Toronto and Montreal in 1871, listed a number of possible careers for women, including brokers. "Already we have firms of women brokers. This is wise and right," Dio Lewis, the author of *Our Girls*, concluded.[48] Articles on successful women investors, such as "How a Lady Investor Has Made Twenty-Five Hundred Percent" or "Notable Women Financiers," appeared in popular magazines, as did advice on "Investing for Women."[49] Financial institutions courted women's business, assuring them that they would deal with them independent of their husbands. From at least the mid-1870s federal post office savings banks advertised, "Deposits may be made by married women, and deposits so made, or made by women who afterwards should marry, will be repaid to any such women." In 1894 the Birbeck Loan and Savings Company of London, Ontario, set up local boards for women in Toronto and Ottawa. By 1913 brokerage houses such as Aemilius Jarvis and Company, a member of the Toronto Stock Exchange, openly advertised for the business of "The Woman Investor." "We are always glad to have women investors consult with us either personally or by letter," the company promised, "no matter how small the sum may be that they have to invest." As well, the company offered complimentary copies of "our booklet, specially written for women investors."[50] Clearly, competing visions of the appropriateness of women as investors and financiers existed in the public discourse of late nineteenth- and early twentieth-century Canada.

In June 1912 "Another Business Girl" contributed an article to *Saturday Night* titled "The Business Girl as Speculator." "It is said," she wrote, "that conversations, as carried on between men and men, and women and women, are classified under two heads: Men – 'property and stocks,' women – 'fashions and the latest pink tea' ... [but] now-a-days we find another key note has been struck ... stocks and bonds and property have become part and parcel of [the business girls'] life ... You will hear [mining stocks] discussed with such a familiarity as would make our grandmothers rise up in holy horror and wonder to what a pass the gentler sex has reached when they mingle with business men with a freedom unthought of in their day of obscurity and modesty. Sheltered as the women of the past have been from all business ventures, it is surely a strange statement of affairs, and so it must seem to our mothers and grandmothers."[51] This article is interesting for at least two reasons. It sheds light on the financial activities of primarily young, single women who worked in business offices and/or as professionals and makes the point that many of these business girls were alert to the possibilities of investment and speculation. It is also interesting for its generational perspective. In the author's eyes these young women were a new breed, easily differentiated from their "mothers and grandmothers." A systematic examination of the assets left by those mothers and grandmothers in their wills suggests that far from rising "up in holy horror," many mothers and grandmothers would have nodded in quiet acquiescence at their daughters' conduct in the sphere of finance.

Before we look intensively at the types of assets women and men held, as indicated in their final estates, it is possible to provide a broader picture of the number of potential women investors in urban Canada in the late nineteenth and early twentieth centuries. In England in the later nineteenth century, censuses often identified women "of rank and property," who in 1871 represented 2.2 per cent of women over the age of nineteen.[52] Canadian censuses of this period do not provide similarly categorized information on wealth. The 1901 Canadian census, however, does supply several types of information relative to money and property.[53] Two are particularly suggestive in the context of women and investment.

The first relates to a series of questions designed to determine one's relationship to the means of production.[54] Whether one lived on one's own means was one of those questions. The enumerator was to record a positive answer "for persons who do not carry on any remunerative calling and live on their own means, as from incomes, superannuations, annuities, pensions etc." Women over the age of nineteen living on their own means in cities with 5,000 or more people represented 3.8 per cent of all women in that age category in those cities. The comparable figure for men was 3.9 per cent. Women were as likely as men to be living on their own means: women were 52.2 per cent of the population and 51.7 per cent of all people on their own means.[55] In addition to their means of income, they differed from other women by being on average older and more often widowed and single. They also stood out in another, and from the point of view of finance, important way.

The 1901 census provides information on an individual's property holding: the most important data concerned the number of acres, number of lots, and number of houses owned. While the census severely undercounted the property holding of women, the information is nonetheless useful. Women living on their own means were more likely to own real property than, taken as a group, all other women.[56] In fact, urban women living on their own means were more than twice as likely to own property than were urban men who were employees, and more likely to own than, taken as a group, all men who did not live on their own means.[57] Women on their own means who owned property were also likely to own more property than other women owners and to own, on average, more property than all male property owners who did not live on their own means.[58] Women such as Sarah Finlayson of Victoria, who owned eighty lots, three stores, two barns, and one house, and Lizzie Brown of Toronto, who owned sixty-four houses and sixty-five lots, were among the most active property owners among those who lived on their own means.

More than most other women and most men not living on their own means, women on their own means were in a position to be investors and financiers. It is the case that not all women living on their own means were wealthy by any standards. But it is also the case that the property proxies we are using for wealth hardly take into account all types of wealth that might be in the hands of those living on their own means. Nor should it be forgotten that other women who were employees, employers, and self-employed and, in terms of numbers, those who, most significantly, declared no relationship to the means of production and thus were counted as not in the workforce also owned property. Just relying on the census, which undercounts women owners of real property, there were some 17,500 women in urban Canada who owned land and or houses. There were another 10,000 women living on their own means who were not recorded as owning real property but may well have had substantial other assets. Taken together, these women represent 6.8 per cent of all women over the age of nineteen and might be regarded as the outer limit for the number of potential women financiers in urban Canada at the turn of the twentieth century.[59]

Tables 1.4 and 1.5 present data that shed light on the investment activities of women and men in Victoria and Hamilton following the passage of the MWPLS. We will focus first on the situation circa 1900, and in the following section we will chart change over the next twenty years. The data point to several interesting comparisons and convergences between the investment activities of men and women in these two cities. A primary point to note is that circa 1900 the place of residence mattered and that differences in investment patterns between men and women within cities pale in comparison to the contrast in general investment behaviour between cities. Over half the investments of men and women in Victoria, for example, were in land: in Hamilton, by contrast, land represented only a quarter of male and two-fifths of female assets. Measured by percentage of investors and of total wealth, Hamilton men and women were much more involved in income-generating financial investments than were their counterparts in Victoria. Hamilton's men and women invested more intensively in a broader range of financial sectors – mortgages, bank stock, bonds, promissory notes – than did Victoria's residents. Interestingly, too, more of Hamilton's men and women invested more of their capital in life insurance than did their western counterparts. At a broad level, the contrasting investment activity reflected the nature of local capital markets. Hamilton was an older city and was situated within a much more densely populated area than Victoria. The economic and financial infrastructures of longer settled communities were usually more complex than in regions of more recent settlement and offered a wider variety of investment opportunities. The investment patterns displayed by the probate data reflect the contrasting opportunities available to residents of each city.

The fact that Victoria underwent significant deindustrialization in the decade of the nineties further contributed to the funnelling effect of investment in that city. A number of locally owned enterprises began to be "picked off" by eastern interests in this period. Several of Victoria's wealthiest entrepreneurs aided and abetted this process. Indeed, they might be said to have led the way in terms of the investment profiles displayed in the probate data. Thus R.P. Rithet, a prominent Victoria businessman, began to sell his holdings in salmon canneries and the Albion Iron Works even as he increased his holdings of Victoria area land from $43,420 in 1891 to $98,020 in 1901. The Dunsmuirs, arguably the wealthiest entrepreneurial family in Victoria, followed suit, increasing their investment in Victoria area land from $78,000 to $244,630 in the same decade.[60]

The inter-city comparison highlights the broad similarity of investment patterns by men and women within their respective locales. To a degree, the investment patterns and type of wealth-holding of men and women within each city converged in the late nineteenth century. The wealth of middle-class women cannot be neatly summarized as household goods: in Hamilton men and women had virtually equal and minimal wealth in such goods; indeed, Hamilton men were more apt to own household goods than were Hamilton women. In Victoria more women invested more of their capital in household goods than did men, but the overall worth of household goods for women was less than half that of cash in bank, mortgages, and other financial investments and less than a quarter of that invested in land. Fewer Victoria men and women used savings banks than did their Hamilton counterparts. Yet those Victorians who put money in banks did so at a relatively intensive level compared to the more widespread but seemingly more casual usage of Hamilton residents.[61]

It would be wrong, however, to push the notion of convergence too far. In matters of wealth-holding and investment, gender still mattered. In both cities women put more of their cash in banks, invested more often in mortgages, had little capital invested in business stock, and owned less life insurance. In both cities they were more apt to concentrate their investments in one sector; men were more apt to diversify their investments. Eighty-eight per cent of Victoria women who owned land and 50 per cent of Hamilton's landed women had only a bank account or household goods as other assets; the comparable figures for Victoria and Hamilton men were 52 and 33 per cent respectively. Finally and most dramatically, women, on average, had much less money to spread around than did men. In Victoria the average man owned 1.6 times and in Hamilton 3 times the probated wealth of the average woman (last row, tables 1.4 and 1.5). It seems reasonable to think that these relatively limited financial resources restricted the spread of financial investments by women and encouraged investments in more conservative and traditional sectors of the economy.

It might be tempting to characterize the investment profile exhibited by women in these two cities as traditional and conservative. As tables 1.4 and 1.5 indicate, in both cities fewer women than men invested in what are commonly considered higher risk sectors: owning stocks, businesses, and farms. At the turn of the century, only 4 per cent of Victoria women invested in the higher risk sector, compared to 15 per cent of men. In Hamilton 16 per cent of women and 38 per cent of men put money into the riskiest sector. Within each city almost identical percentages of men and women invested in the moderately risky sector comprised of mortgages, bonds, debentures, promissory notes, and book debts.[62] In each city women were as likely as men to lend capital and in Victoria to lend a higher proportion of their capital than men. Nor were women reluctant to invest in land: the probate data suggest that more Victoria women were apt to invest in land than men and that Hamilton women put more of their capital in land than did Hamilton's men.

Does the relative lack of financial diversification and stock-owning by women emerge, then, from a conservative and relatively sheltered household-bound focus of late nineteenth-century middle-class women? Many middle-class married women had only recently gained the legal right to manage their own money via the passage of the MWPLs in the late nineteenth century. It is safe to assume that their education and general upbringing rarely provided them with the tools for investing such capital. Most investment advice for women in this era counselled caution and conservative behaviour. "Especially avoid mining stocks and bonds," one counsellor wrote. Women should concentrate instead on municipal and national state bonds.[63]

Interestingly, many studies of women and investment in the late twentieth century have identified similar conservative tendencies. Gallup surveys conducted in 1996 and 1997 concluded that American "women are unlikely to take many chances with their savings ... and this conservative slant makes for a notable breach between the genders." Similarly, a Female Investor Poll of nine hundred Canadian women investors conducted by Toronto Dominion Bank in 2001 concluded

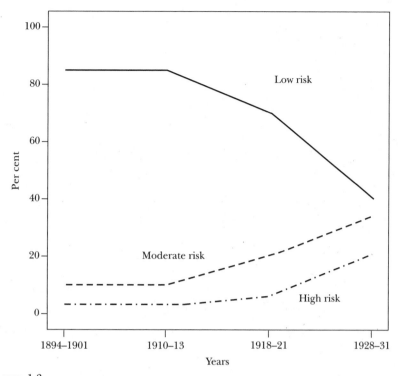

Figure 1.3
Female investment patterns as a percentage of total investment by degree of risk:
Victoria, 1894–1931

that "almost all ... categorize their investment style as low-risk or
medium-risk."[64]

Yet the trend in the first decades of the twentieth century was towards
more aggressive investment behaviour on the part of men in Victoria
and women in both cities. These trend lines are most easily seen in
figures 1.3 through 1.5. Up to the early 1920s Victoria's women con-
tinued to put over half their capital into land, and in the boom years
of the pre–World War One era, over three-quarters of their capital
was invested in real estate (see table 1.4). Qualitative sources suggest
that land investment was a widespread practice for the generation of
women coming of age in the immediate pre-war era. "More than once,"
Another Business Girl wrote in *Saturday Night* in June 1912, "I have
come in contact with girls, teachers, nurses, business girls who are
investing in small houses or lots in their own city." Women as well
as men asked financial or real estate columnists for advice: "Would
I be wise," L.A. wrote to the editor of Gold and Dross, *Saturday Night's*

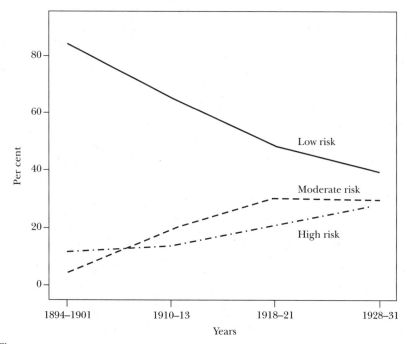

Figure 1.4
Male investment patterns as a percentage of total investment by degree of risk:
Victoria, 1894–1931

investment section, "investing my savings in [land in Port Edward]?"
She was advised to exercise extreme caution in investing in "undeveloped" land, albeit land that in this case "appears a reasonable purchase." Katherine Roberts, a married woman living in Victoria, detailed
in her 1920 will the numerous lots she owned in Victoria and
Shawnigan Lake, a resort centre just north of the city. Her will indicates
that she was an active buyer and seller of such land. Land and housing
is often classified as a consumption rather than an investment item, but
even in the twenty-first century, financial consultants such as Cheryl
Broussard have urged women to "buy their own homes or invest in
some type of property ... Having your own home is a form of wealth
building." As Gwen Sheridan, a successful Canadian investor, put it in
October 2003, "It's really comforting to have something concrete. But
it's also part of diversifying, to include real estate in your portfolio."[65]
    But women investors in Victoria were not wedded to land investment.
As real estate values decreased in that city during and after World War
One, women (and men) moved their money to other financial sectors.

In fact, the decline in land values following the boom era in Victoria may have pushed investors to look for different opportunities. At a time of expanding communications and increasingly effective interconnections between the city and the wider investment world, Victorians, male and female, invested in a more geographically dispersed array of companies and associated ventures than had been the case in the late nineteenth century.[66] In 1917 Emma Leech, a married woman in Victoria, for example, had 45 per cent of her assets invested in the Staverly Coal Mine Company of England. The probate of Clarissa Sellick, a married woman who died at the age of fifty-four, listed holdings in the Marconi Wireless Company, the Stewart Mining Company, and the Electric Steel Pole Company of Minnesota. This trend continued throughout the 1920s. In 1924 the probate of Mary Cox of Victoria listed stock worth $29,400, $15,000 of which were stocks and shares in Great Britain and the rest in American railroads, India securities, and sundry Canadian-based enterprises ranging from the Bell Telephone Company to the Canada Cement Company. In 1930 Agnes Auld, a married woman living in Victoria, had close to $10,000 invested in such companies as B.C. American Oil, Imperial Oil, Goodyear Tire and Rubber Company, Commercial Securities Company of Winnipeg, and C.H. McFayden and Company of the same city. In 1926 Lillian A. Restall of Victoria left a portfolio composed of a loan to the city of Capetown, South Africa, some British War Stock, and, among other items, investment in a Japanese government loan. In 1926 Annie Elizabeth Beaumont, a widow living in Victoria, had money invested in bonds and debentures and/or stock of the following states and companies: Denmark, Argentina, the state of São Paulo, Canadian National Railways, the Pacific Great Eastern Railway, the Canadian Pacific Railway, and the British Columbia Telephone Company.[67] Victorian investors, female as well as male, were becoming players in the global capitalist world.

Women especially moved to other financial investments and, along with men, to other stock. By the 1930s over two-fifths of Victoria's probated women put money in bonds, debentures, and promissory notes, up from under a third in the early 1920s. A similar pattern was evident in stock investments: one-quarter of Victoria's women investors put money into stocks other than banks, up from a tenth in the early 1920s (see table 1.4). Indeed, on the eve of the Great Depression in Victoria, 44 per cent of men invested in the risky, non-traditional sector, up from 15 per cent at the turn of the century, as did 28 per cent of women, up from 4 per cent in 1900. In Victoria male and female investment

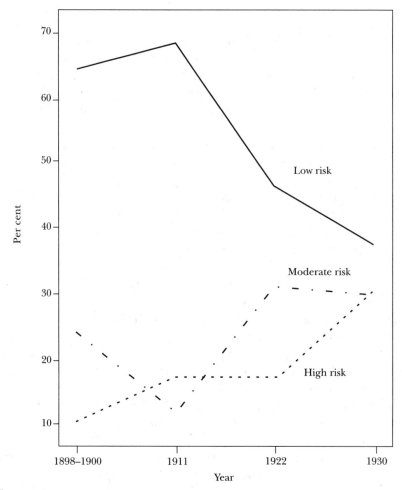

Figure 1.5
Female investment patterns as a percentage of total investment by degree of risk:
Hamilton, 1898–1930

behaviour converged as the twentieth century progressed. As figure 1.5
indicates, a similar trend to more aggressive or non-traditional invest-
ment was apparent in the conduct of Hamilton's women investors.
Indeed, by the 1920s there were relatively small differences in invest-
ment behaviour between the two cities. Hamilton men and women
were still slightly more aggressive than their Victoria counterparts, but
the gap was closing. In both cities the tendency to own household
goods was the same, and gender made no difference. The use of savings

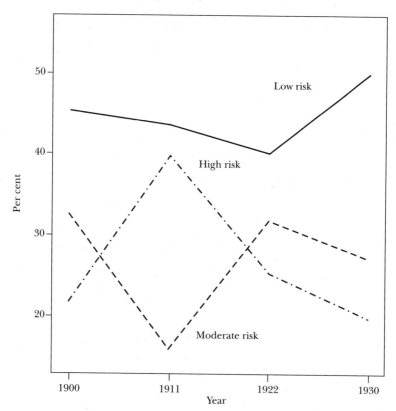

Figure 1.6
Male investment patterns as a percentage of total investment by degree of risk: Hamilton, 1900–30

banks had equalled across the two cities, and women continued to put more of their assets there than did men.

But what are we to make of the data presented in figure 1.6? Up to the early 1920s the investment practice of Hamilton's men closely resembled that of women in that city. For reasons that are not immediately apparent, that behaviour changed sharply sometime in the 1920s. By 1930, as a comparison of figures 1.5 and 1.6 indicates, Hamilton's women were more aggressive investors than its men. During the twenties, male investors in that city put a higher percentage of their investments in life insurance than ever before (see table 1.5) and lowered their positions in general financial investments in the moderate sector and in other stock in the high-risk sector. By contrast, relatively little of women's capital was put in life insurance; mortgage investment increased, but the most dramatic change was the increased investment

in bank and other stock in the high-risk sector. The onset of the
Depression may have been a factor in the changed direction of invest-
ment by Hamilton's men. But such a supposition begs the obvious ques-
tions as to why only men changed their investment practice and women
did not and why was there not a similar reaction in Victoria?[68] Whatever
the answers to these questions (and a different perspective on this issue
is provided in chapter 3), the most interesting finding remains unchal-
lenged. It was not always and everywhere that men were the aggressive
investors. As the twentieth century progressed, differences in invest-
ment behaviour between men and women in Victoria narrowed signifi-
cantly. By 1930 in Hamilton, women, not men, were the aggressive
actors in the field of investment.

The probate data certainly suggest that many women in Victoria and
Hamilton were actively building wealth. We know at a broad level from
our discussion of the data presented in table 1.5 that men tended to
invest more often than women in riskier financial ventures. We do not
know whether or how such behaviour was qualified by one's wealth
category; or put another way, whether one's wealth standing or one's
gender was a better predictor of investment behaviour. From our dis-
cussion of the data presented in tables 1.4 and 1.5 we also know that
where one lived – Victoria or Hamilton – affected one's investment
practice in 1900 and seemed less of a factor twenty years later. But,
again, we do not know what the effect of wealth was on the relationship
between investment practice and place of residence. It may also have
been the case that whether a woman was married or not might affect
her investment strategy. If a woman was married, it is possible that her
husband exercised influence over, if not control of, her investment;
such a potentially controlling influence might not be as significant
for widows and single women, and their investment practice might
differ from that of married women. Ideally, one would like to assess the
influence of these variables in the presence of all such variables. Simple
cross-tabulations do not permit these distinctions. The most common
procedure in social science for analyzing a context of overlapping influ-
ences is multiple regression. When one is examining a dependent
variable with only two values – risky investor or not – and when the dis-
tribution of values is uneven – fewer risky investors – then the best form
of multi-way analysis is logistic regression.[69]

The figures reported in table 1.6 are the log odds of one's chances of
investing in the riskiest category, measured in the context of all vari-
ables in the table and compared to the reference category within each

variable. In 1900 Hamilton residents, for example, were 3.5 times more likely to invest in the risky category than were residents of Victoria, after controlling for gender, wealth, and marital status. Wealth made a difference, but only in Victoria and then only for those in the top wealth bracket. In Hamilton wealth was not a significant predictor at the .05 level.[70] The apparent effect of age on investment behaviour in Victoria is intriguing.[71] In the presence of the other variables, those under age forty in Victoria were somewhat more likely than those over forty to invest in the risky sector. One is tempted to suggest that the relatively young were more open to the emerging market in stocks than were their elder counterparts. Too much, however, should not be made of this conclusion because age squared was not significant, and when age was run as an interval variable, the log odds result was .970 with a significance level of .06, suggesting that any tendency for the "young" to be riskier investors was small indeed.

As an indicator of investment behaviour, marital status was not significant with women and men in the equation. And most interestingly, marital status was not significant when the regression was run with only women. Whether a woman was single, married, or widowed had no measureable effect on her investment behaviour. The set(s) of "structuring dispositions" that marked the contours of women's investment practice extended beyond that of spousal control. Clearly, of all the variables available for analysis in 1900 other than residence, gender was the most consistent predictor of the chances of investing in the risky sector. In Hamilton *only* gender significantly affected the odds of so doing, with men being 2.9 times and in Victoria 4.5 times more likely to engage in relatively risky investments. The gendered pattern of investment suggested by the data in tables 1.4 and 1.5 is underlined by the more intensive analysis reported in table 1.6. At the turn of the century the risky category comprised of stocks and other owned assets was "male" territory. Yet a cautionary note is appropriate here: men dabbled in stocks; relatively few men were involved in that sector – 36 per cent in Hamilton and 15 per cent in Victoria– and fewer still were intensively involved.[72] One might then ask whether gender affected the pattern of investment outside the relatively rarified business of stock-owning? Put another way, did the majority of women invest differently from the majority of men in these two cities? And, a related question: were the investment strategies of those in the mid wealth range, where women, as we have seen from table 1.4, bulked large in numbers and were close to men's average wealth, affected by gender?

The answer to the first query is that the majority of women did not invest differently from the majority of men. A logistic regression run with the dependent variable whether or not one was a moderately risky investor – that is, invested in the second investment tier as indicated in tables 1.4 and 1.5 – and all variables the same as in table 1.6 removed gender from the list of significant variables. Only place of residence, Hamilton, and whether one was in the top wealth quintal positively affected the odds of investing in that sector.[73] Gender was also not a significant predictor of the odds of investing in the conservative category of assets. Nor for those in the broad middle range of wealth-holding was gender a significant predictor of investment behaviour. Logistic regressions including only moderate wealth-holders and run on risky/ not and moderately risky/not both excluded gender as a significant variable. Place of residence was in both cases the strongest determinant of investment patterns: those in Hamilton in the mid wealth range were 5.7 times more likely than their Victoria counterparts to invest in the risky sector and 3.4 times more likely to invest in the moderately risky sector.[74]

The data in table 1.7 confirm that by the 1920s the investment patterns of men and women were similar in both cities.[75] One's gender was not a good predictor of the odds of investing in the risky sector in Hamilton and only a moderately significant predictor of the odds of so doing in Victoria. As in 1900, gender was not a significant predictor as to who would invest in the moderately risky sector, nor was it significant in terms of predicting the investment behaviour of those in the middle range of wealth-holding. Place of residence was not a significant predictor of investment behaviour. Finally, as in 1900, a logistic regression run with just women determined that marital status and residence were not significant predictors of investment behaviour.

On the eve of the depression, as table 1.8 indicates, place of residence continued to have no impact on one's tendency to invest in risky sectors. If one knew the gender of an investor, that also would be no help in predicting whether that person invested in risky sectors of the economy. The more wealth one had, the greater the odds of investing in stocks. The findings were the same for the odds of investing in the moderate sector: gender was unimportant, as was place of residence. Wealth was the best predictor. It was also the most important determinant of investment behaviour with just women in the logistic regression. For the first time, however, a women's marital status was of some significance: married women tended to invest somewhat more than widows in the risky sector.

We have talked much about convergence of investment behaviour across genders and across cities in the half-century covered in this study. But two somewhat contrary trends need to be underlined. The first is best put in the form of a question. Had women become men's equal in the investment world? The simple answer is no. Despite a general convergence of investment practices between men and women during the first several decades of the twentieth century, the difference in probated wealth held by women and men in both cities remained substantial. By the early 1920s the gap in Victoria had, in fact, increased: Victoria men owned on average 3.1 times more probated wealth than did women, up from 1.6 in 1900, and this gap diminished only slightly over the next ten years (see table 1.4). For Hamilton the trend was in the other direction: by 1922 men owned on average 1.7 times more probated wealth than did women, down from 3 times in 1900.

The second query arises from the discussion of the first and has been touched on earlier in this chapter. Why did women's wealth, relative to men's, trend downwards in Victoria after 1913 and trend upwards in Hamilton? Livio Di Matteo has noted in his study of probated wealth-holding in northwestern Ontario between 1885 and 1920 that women's share of that wealth fell dramatically after 1913. He suggests that women in the Thunder Bay area were heavily invested in land and especially in mortgages and that, following the collapse of the wheat boom in the post-1913 period, they suffered economically to a greater degree than did men. "The potential existence of a national setback in women's wealth accumulation and property holding in the wake of the boom," he proffers, "is a particularly intriguing question."[76]

Di Matteo's question is an excellent one, yet the contrast in the gendered wealth trends between Hamilton and Victoria following World War One cautions one against generalizing too broadly. Sets of local demographic, cultural, and economic conditions determined contours for women's empowerment or lack thereof. Fuelled by general prosperity linked to the wheat boom in western Canada, by substantial regional immigration, by increased American investment in local timber resources, and by anticipation of a commercial upswing following the completion of the Panama Canal (opened in 1914), a boom that "astonished old timers and ... the Province at large" engulfed

Victoria in the pre–World War One era. In just two years – 1911 and 1912 – the city spent close to $8 million in upgrading its infrastructure. As a result of these and other expenditures, the city by 1917 owed some $23 million to sundry British and American investment banks.[77] This influx of financial capital was meant (almost literally) to pave the way for industrial expansion. Yet between 1907 and 1913 only 14 per cent of $23 million in building permits related to industrial pursuits. Forty-three per cent went towards the construction of private residences, and the rest was split between government and commercial buildings. The gross value of manufacturing production in Victoria in 1911 in fact fell short of the amount produced in 1891, and per capita value of production did not reach the 1881 figure.[78] Many of Victoria's residents and especially its women put their money in land. Indeed, between 1910 and 1913 over three-quarters of women's probated wealth was invested in land, a figure much higher than that for any previous or subsequent period covered in this study, as table 1.4 shows, and much higher than that invested by either Victoria's men or men and women in Hamilton. With the commencement of war and, in the case of Victoria, the non-arrival of industry, the bottom fell out of the land market.

But this is not the whole story. Local infrastructural development in Victoria in this time period was most often initiated by the city council. If three-quarters of the members of that council, most of whom were contractors or realtors, voted for a particular local improvement, the affected residents could not overturn it and were liable for regular repayments amounting to 75 per cent of the total cost. Moreover, money raised in this manner was not counted as part of the city's legal borrowing limit, that being 20 per cent of its assessed tax value. As the respected economist from Queen's University, Adam Shortt, concluded in his 1922 report,

> In some of the most heavily burdened portions of the City, so anxious were the speculative subdividers to get their attractively improved property [improved via the passage of improvement by laws] on the market, that they were quite willing to saddle their prospective customers with the whole cost of the local improvements, the amount of which was not revealed to the new owners until some considerable time after the lots had passed into their possession. The civic authorities, on their part, some of them being considerably interested in the sale of the newly improved properties, had little hesitation in incurring very heavy obligations, the repayment of which, it was

claimed, would not fall apon the City, which was acting merely as agent of the property owners in expending the money and collecting from individual owners their assigned proportions.[79]

In 1911 the city council passed a revenue-raising tax that further jeopardized landed investments. It opted for a single tax on the assessed value of land and no tax on improvements. Since land was to be taxed at its market value, this policy encouraged the development of vacant lots in advance of tangible demand in the hopes of rendering the land remunerative. In short, the tax fuelled speculative development. During the period of greatest speculation, however, assessed value of land was well below market price. Only when the market began to collapse did assessed values increase. Commencing on the eve of World War One, Victoria's ratepayers found themselves burdened with varying and often onerous local improvement taxes, along with a high general mill rate levied on an artificially high assessment value. Tax arrears reached $3,400,000 in 1918 and only began to decline the following year because the city repossessed property it could not sell at tax sales.[80] If the probated records for Victoria in this period are any guide to wider practice, women suffered disproportionately in the ensuing economic and financial downswing, a blow from which they had hardly begun to recover on the eve of even more massive economic troubles in the Depression years of the 1930s.

But was the situation in Hamilton substantively different? Like Victoria, Hamilton experienced a major boom in land development. Between 1911 and 1915, subdividing activity reached a pre–World War Two peak. The city council facilitated such development in part by the use, as in Victoria, of local improvement taxes. As John Weaver and Michael Doucet have noted, "Charging citizens for improvements was raised to the level of a science in most municipalities." One result was a surplus of lots and a decline in the land market. But there were differences. Hamilton's ratepayers assumed a smaller proportion of the improvement costs than did those in Victoria. As well, Hamilton did not impose a single tax. Vacant lots were not therefore taxed as if they were the equal of developed lots, and owners could ride out a flattening in the land market with lighter financial consequences than could owners in Victoria. Finally and most importantly, the boom in Hamilton was fuelled by industrial growth, whereas the boom in Victoria was driven by the *anticipation* of such growth. Financial capital facilitated Victoria's boom; industrial capital underwrote Hamilton's. Hamilton experienced, in Weaver's words, "an industrial boom." In 1903 there were two hundred industrial plants in the city. By 1913 there were four hundred. And, unlike in Victoria, the downturn in Hamilton was eased by the acquisition, through the Imperial Munitions Board, of substantial industrial contracts during World War One.[81]

Probate records underline the difference in investment behaviour during the pre–World War One boom period in both cities. It is true that in both cities women invested more of their wealth in land than did men. But Hamilton women demonstrated only a small tendency to invest more in land in 1911 than they had at the turn of the century, and male investments in Hamilton land varied hardly at all from 1898. Such was far from the case in Victoria. As we have noted, Victoria women had over three-quarters of their investments in land in 1911, up from 56 per cent at the turn of the century, and men, although down from the turn of the century, had 55 per cent of their capital in land (tables 1.4 and 1.5). The setback in women's wealth-holding following the pre–World War One boom, then, was greatest in western cities, where land speculation significantly exceeded similar behaviour in longer settled and more industrialized communities such as Hamilton.

For the most part, what we have measured in this chapter is the growth of legal ownership of various types of wealth by women. It is certainly true that formal ownership may differ from control over assets.[82] The decision-making processes within households remains a difficult nut, both for social scientists interested in current trends and for historians interested in past trends, to crack. While we cannot know how influenced women were by male others in their investment decisions, evidence exists that many women were financially knowledgeable, bought and sold stocks, and instructed their heirs as to how their estates should be invested. Lavina Guerney, a Hamilton widow, noted in her will that she and her sister had been joint purchasers of Dominion Power and Transmission Company shares worth $3,500. Hilda Emma Sellers of Victoria referred in her will to the joint purchase by herself and her daughter and a female friend of shares in the Langley Syndicate Investment. Elizabeth Ann Jacques, a married woman living in Victoria, bequeathed ownership of the Kallappa Mine in Tofino to her five eldest children. Since, Sara Knights-Bayne of Victoria wrote in her 1931 will, "I have spent much of my own income from my father on the said group of mineral claims," she asserted the right to bequeath ownership of those mining certificates to her sister. Many other

women, married, widowed, and spinsters, bequeathed what the' cor-
rectly referred to as "my" shares in companies to heirs.[83]

Some women felt confident enough to dictate even to their husba.1ds
on matters of investment. Mary Walsh of Victoria instructed her hus-
band and son, as co-trustees, to liquidate her estate and put the money
in "investments authorized by law for the investment of trust funds" or
invest in "first mortgages of improved real estate ... not exceeding 50
per cent of the improved value." Hermiena Lyons in her 1915 will cau-
tioned her husband as trustee to invest in only "first mortgages on good
revenue producing and improved property" and to do so with an eye to
"conservative valuation as a revenue producer and not on a basis of
speculative value." Alma Mason of Hamilton left her estate in trust to
her husband and directed her executors – her husband and brother-
in-law – to sell the estate and invest the proceeds in mortgages to raise
her "infant children." Ada Harrington of Victoria instructed her execu-
tors – a male and a female – to invest in railway stock only if a dividend
of 4 per cent had been paid for the last ten years and not to invest in
municipal stock in any city with a population less than 200,000. Jane
Galletley, also of Victoria, left instructions to her husband and daugh-
ter, the co-executors, to invest the estate in municipalities "of the Brit-
ish Empire" with over 50,000 people or in the stocks of railways,
insurance companies, and industrial banks "of the British Empire" that
had for the last seven years paid a 3 per cent dividend. With the excep-
tion of Turkey and the Balkan states, Galletley also allowed her heirs to
invest in national stocks.[84]

If women were not men's equals, it is nonetheless wrong to conclude
flatly that investment was a man's game. Certain types of investment
may have been, but the investment field in general was populated by
male and female players. Gender did matter, but not absolutely.
Indeed, for most types of investment, it was not a good predictor of
involvement. The historian R.J. Morris has distinguished between male
and female investors in England in the 1830s by describing the former
as putting to work "active male risk capital" and the latter as guardians
of "passive capital." In the late nineteenth and early twentieth centuries
in urban Canada such a characterization would only perpetuate gender
stereotypes.[85] Even in the late 1890s the majority of women with assets
in Victoria and Hamilton invested in ways similar to the majority of
their male counterparts in each city. In this context the notion of sepa-
rate male and female spheres breaks down. At the turn of the twentieth

century, gender most often mattered only in the context of investment in the relatively risky sector of stocks and other owned assets, and even in that category in 1900 some women were active. As the various logistic regressions demonstrated, over the first third of the twentieth century, gender became an insignificant predictor of investment behaviour. Women became increasingly aggressive investors, and by 1930 in Hamilton they were more aggressive than men, all of which suggests that there was no one sphere for all women, just as there was no single sphere for all men.[86]

Investment in stocks as opposed to bonds and other securities is nevertheless often contrasted as active versus passive investment behaviour.[87] The former can confer some degree of managerial authority; the latter is often thought to be without such control and more at the mercy of the decisions of others. While an argument can be made that such a dichotomy is overly simple – there are many examples of bondholders with managerial powers – it nonetheless points to where maximum potential power lay, and in that domain a minority of men dominated in 1900 even as they dominated the top level of wealth-holders. Even by 1930 more men than women invested in stocks, although the relative difference was narrowing significantly. In some ways stock purchases fuelled the future. Risks were high and potential investment returns greatest in that sector. As we have seen, many late twentieth-century commentators have remarked on the "risk averse" nature of women investors. While more women than before are investing in stocks, they remain as a group less likely than men to do so, and they tend to invest more in what are termed conservative rather than risky stocks. The persistence of this trend worries some commentators. "Women can't afford to be too conservative," one woman financial adviser has warned. "Higher risk means higher projected return."[88] The implication is that for the gap between male and female wealth-holding to close, wealthy women may need to change their investment tactics.[89] The evidence presented here suggests that such a change was indeed fast occurring in the first third of the twentieth century, even as the relative wealth owned by men and women remained fairly constant.

If modern commentators are correct that women in the late twentieth and early twenty-first centuries are more conservative investors than men, then research needs to focus on the Depression and post-Depression eras in order to see what constellation of factors led to changes in the trends outlined in this chapter. Perhaps conservative societal expectations concerning appropriate behaviour for women became more powerful. Yet such proscriptions were strong in the early years of this study. In March 1900 Hetty Green, a successful American capitalist, answered the question "why women are not money makers" in the following way: "the blame – or credit, if you like – for this condition of affairs rests more with the training that has been given women from the beginning of time than from any design on the part of creation." Women were expected to curb male excesses, not participate shoulder to shoulder with men in the riskiest sectors of finance. Women were homemakers, not money-makers. As Henry Clews asserted in 1888, "women who aspire to [invest] are not usually endowed with the self-respect, the modesty and the independence of masculine favor which characterize all high minded women." Certainly one would not have to look very hard to find similar attitudes throughout the twentieth century. A century later, for example, a successful woman financial adviser in the United States could remark that "many women, especially in their 40s and 50s, were raised not to talk about money. It wasn't ladylike."[90]

One might have thought that, given the relatively bounded financial behaviour of women in the twenty-first century, such behaviour must have been much more constricted a century ago. Yet the evidence presented here suggests that women were surprisingly active and increasingly aggressive as investors in late nineteenth- and early twentieth-century urban Canada. Ideological proscriptions were not all of a piece. The fictional Mrs Longworthy had many counterparts in the real world. In an era of much more restricted expectations concerning the proper roles for women, many women with assets were actively investing in ways indistinguishable from the investment patterns of most men. Investment firms such as Birbeck Loan and Savings Company and Aemilius Jarvis attempted to capitalize on this activity. Given the recent passage of the enabling MWPLs the prevalence of this behaviour is quite noteworthy. The investment behaviour of women in late nineteenth-century urban Canada speaks to the existence of women's agency. Yet the mothers and grandmothers of the "Business Girls" of pre–World War One Canada bequeathed more than their daughters ever acknowledged. It is perhaps at this point that proscriptive gender ideology exerted its greatest power. While, if the data from Hamilton and Victoria probates are any guide, it is true that those daughters themselves became increasingly active and aggressive players in the investment world, they perceived themselves as different from those who came before them. The fact that they so easily and quickly overlooked past behaviour underlines the insidiously circumscribing power of Bourdieu's "structuring dispositions." Confronting similar proscriptions, each new generation of potential women investors may have seen themselves as the real pioneers, never encouraged to seek strength from past practice – in fact, generally discouraged from thinking that they had shoulders on which they could stand, past behaviour from which they could draw strength, confidence, and encouragement. Instead, perceiving themselves as pioneers, they may have spent too much time reinventing the wheel.

2

Inheriting and Bequeathing: Women and Men in Victoria and Hamilton, 1880–1930

Clearly, women had assets that they could bequeath: 32 per cent of those who owned probated property at their time of death in 1900 were women in the two cities examined closely in this study. By 1930 that percentage had risen to 42. What, then, do bequeathment trends in wills by both men and women indicate regarding women's empowerment? A study of inheritance patterns can add to our understanding of the social relations of property. Probates provide detailed enumerations of wealth-holding at a specific point in a person's and a family's life cycle. Wills supply a context within which to appreciate the social significance of assets and the roles of individuals within family, kinship, and friendship groups. As Stobart and Owens write, a study of inheritance "offers a window onto the mechanisms of social and economic reproduction."[1] It is important, however, to reiterate that wills, like probates, reflected a particular stage in a person's life. Property was conveyed at other points in an individual's and a family's life cycle. Yet arguably, bequests through wills rippled more widely through social spheres than did gifts at weddings and births and other such occasions for the redistribution of forms of wealth. And death was special if only because of its finality. Wills existed as the last accounting, a summing-up, a reordering amidst loss. Wills were the last words and therein lies their ultimate significance.

The specific focus of this chapter is on how the wills of men and women enabled and/or restricted women's agency in material affairs. Did they simply recreate existing social relations, or did they contribute to the making of something new? To whom were men and women most likely to bequeath their wealth, and what might such practices mean for economic agency within the context of family and broader kinship

relations and for activity in the public realm of industry and finance on
the part of those who inherited? Did, for example, bequeathment prac-
tices facilitate and underpin the investment practices of men and
women as detailed in chapter 1? In this sense it is important to uncover
trends in bequeathment practices by men and by women. It is impor-
tant, too, to be attentive to the way wills were written or, better, to be
sensitive to the tone and phrasing employed by men and women in
conveying their property to others. The act of conveyance was itself a
reflection of personal ownership, and attitudes to such property and to
wider social relations are often palpable in the rhetoric employed in
the writing of wills.

In the Canadian context, previous studies of the place of women in
men's wills have generally focused most closely on an earlier time
period and on rural areas. The general conclusion is that relatively few
women inherited free of controls and that a substantial proportion of
widows were left dependent on their sons for future sustenance.[2] To
the extent that these studies have extended their analyses into the era
of the MWPLS, little change in bequeathment patterns have been noted.
Indeed, one study concluded that "wives' position with regard to inheri-
tance seems to have deteriorated by the end of the century."[3]

Such was not the case in Victoria and Hamilton in the late nineteenth
and early twentieth centuries. Many wills written by men suggest that in
urban Canada in the last quarter of the nineteenth century, women's
sphere extended well beyond the domestic homestead and did so with
their husband's full support. In November 1880 George Trumbull, a
Hamilton tavern keeper, "having full faith and confidence in my
beloved wife," ceded his business to her. In the same year John Barr, a
Hamilton stonecutter, left most of his wealth to his wife "because she
materially, economically and otherwise aided and assisted me in acquir-
ing most of my property and in keeping and holding intact the remain-
der while none of my children in any way helped me therein." "I make
no provision of any kind for my children," Francis Wise of Victoria
wrote in his 1904 will that "as I have full confidence in the business
capacity and good judgement of my wife and am satisfied that in her
final disposition of the property that shall by this instrument fall to her
... she will do exact justice to all our children."[4]

The data presented in tables 2.1 and 2.2 from men's wills suggest a
trend towards empowerment for women. Since wives tended to outlive
husbands, it is perhaps no surprise that they were usually the prime
beneficiaries in men's wills. This was the case in both Victoria and Ham-

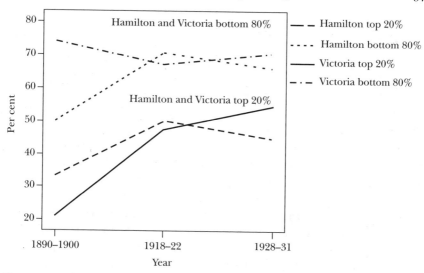

Figure 2.1
Wives as sole executrices in men's wills by wealth cohort: Hamilton and Victoria, 1880–1931

ilton and was so before and after the passage of the most enabling MWPLS. It is interesting to note, however, that especially in Hamilton, women were more often prime beneficiaries in the later than in the earlier period and in both cities they, as a percentage of prime beneficiaries, peaked in the pre–World War One era.

A key indicator of empowerment is the degree to which the inheritor controlled the bequeathment. In the early 1880s, prior to the passage of the most important MWPLS in each province, about two-fifths of women who were prime beneficiaries in both cities were subjected to various controls. Even as more women became prime inheritors, so too more women in both cities by the end of the century were receiving that inheritance free from controls. In Hamilton women prime inheritors under some control remained constant at a quarter after 1900. In Victoria the figure was closer to a fifth during the first third of the twentieth century. Relatedly, it would make sense to think that women inheritors would require less protective language in an increasingly liberal era of MWPLS. That supposition holds true for Victoria, but in the case of Hamilton, where the use of such language was never widespread, legislative changes to property laws seem to have had little impact.

Historians have often used the gender of executors as an indicator of women's agency in will-making and bequeathments.[5] In both cities in the first thirty years of the twentieth century, women exceeded or were close to 50 per cent of the executors (sole and co-executors combined) appointed by men (tables 2.1 and 2.2). In both cities and especially in Victoria, these figures tended to be higher than was the case in the pre- and immediate post-MWPL period. Historians have also found a strong positive correlation between wealth and the use of male executors.[6] Broadly speaking, men in Hamilton and Victoria were no exception. As figure 2.1 indicates, in both cities the wealthiest men were the least likely to appoint their wives as sole executrix. Shammas has argued that as the economy became more sophisticated, assets came to be held and managed by non-family members (trust companies and corporate managers) and in that context allowing a wife to control family assets was less threatening to the patrimony's future.[7] It is hard to test this plausible conclusion. Certainly, trust companies became more active players as executors as the twentieth century progressed. But this was a gradual process, and the evidence suggests that women and men gave up control to trust companies only reluctantly. In the opinion of Bartholemew Partington, the chief gardener for the provincial government buildings in Victoria, executors were totally unnecessary. "I do not wish to appoint any executors or trustees," he wrote in his 1926 will. "Everything without any reservation I wish to leave to my wife."[8] In Victoria men appointed no trust companies as executors in the 1910–13 period and only four (in one of which the deceased's widow was co-trustee) in the 1918–21 period. By the 1930s trusts were more active, and some men, such as William Webb of Victoria, gave great latitude to the Royal Trust Company to invest as it saw fit "without being limited to investments authorized by law for trustees" and to have the final say as to the sale of his widow's home and purchase of a new one.[9] Yet trust company involvement remained limited to a small number of estates: 35 out of 267, and 7 of those were trust companies co-appointed with a wife or other family member. A similar trend was evident in Hamilton: 5 of 118 estates in 1922 and 11 of 125 estates in 1930.[10]

It may have been that the heirs of men looked to trusts and other professionals for advice in the management of the estate, but male will writers did not seem overly concerned with such management issues in the period covered in this study. Charles McAnally of Victoria nicely reflected this attitude in his 1912 will. His wife was to be sole executrix and trustee during her lifetime with "absolute and uncontrolled" power to implement his will. If and only if she wished, she was free to "personally employ" any professional to assist her. In 1930 Burt Richards, a dental surgeon in Victoria, appointed his wife as sole executrix and, "without in any way restricting her absolute power," recommended that she seek advice from "some dependable investment trustee."[11]

Moreover, many executrices, such as Margaret Hirst, exhibited perseverance and determination in looking after their estates. Hirst, the sole executrix of her husband's will, went to court in Victoria in 1895 to claim, as it turned out successfully, the money that her late husband, Thomas, had deposited in the Dominion Government Savings Bank "in the fictitious name of James Miller." Margaret Smith of Hamilton, sole executrix of her husband's estate, hired a collection agency in an attempt to collect money from some one hundred individuals who owed the estate. Apparently, the agency attempted to defraud her; so in March 1881 she sued the agency for $4,500. We do not know the outcome of the case, but we do know that Margaret Duncan and Matilda Hounsley, both of Hamilton and both executrices of their late husbands' estates, did successfully sue men who owed their estates.[12]

In fact, the data from these two Canadian cities suggest that women, and most especially wives, gained more control as executors as the period progressed, not less (figure 2.1). This trend was true for both those in the top wealth percentiles and for those in the lower wealth cohorts. As women in both cities became more aggressive investors, so too they became more active as executors. The trend is clearest in Victoria, where married women in the top wealth cohort increasingly gained control as executrices as the twentieth century unfolded. This finding nicely parallels the fact that, as we saw in the previous chapter, married women in Victoria held a far higher percentage of women's assets than did their Hamilton counterparts.

A more precise picture of women's place in men's wills would emerge if one were able to control completely for the presence of wives and children. Information on surviving children is spotty, but our knowledge of marital status is more fulsome. A closer look at how men treated their wives in their wills underlines the trend suggested by the data in tables 2.1 and 2.2 and figure 2.1. Under the custom of dower a married man was required to grant one-third of his landed estate to his widow. Such a stipulation did not bother Phil Woollacott, an unemployed married man who wrote his will in Victoria in 1882. Ignoring his wife and four children aged one to twelve, he elected instead to leave his estate in trust for the use of Jenny Florence, "with whom I am now living." In 1880 Robert McElvy, a gentleman living in Hamilton, clearly felt that a deed of separation dated 27 December 1875 would protect him from possible dower claims by "the Woman McElvy." While other men such as John McGregor, a Hamilton gentleman, decreed that his wife would get what he bequested "in lieu of all dower to which she might in any event be entitled,"[13] most married men, as tables 2.3 and 2.4 indicate, routinely bequeathed the bulk of their estates to their wives. Indeed, it is noteworthy that in both cities wives who were prime inheritors were increasingly likely to be the executor as well, and the use of protective language for wives declined in both cities after the passage of the MWPLS.

Many wives were nonetheless restricted in dealing with bequests by provisions in their husbands' wills. While the trend was toward fewer impositions of control over wives after the passage of the MWPLS, in both cities wives remained somewhat more likely than other women to experience such control even by the end of the period covered here (compare tables 2.1 and 2.2 with tables 2.3 and 2.4). Some historians have seen the existence and persistence of such controls as evidence of a dominant patriarchal culture, the exercise of "patriarchy from the grave."[14]

The most common controls stipulated that the inheritor could use the interest on the estate for life or for as long as she remained unmarried or a combination of the two. In every case for the types of control listed in tables 2.3 and 2.4, the husband also listed to whom the assets were to be bequeathed after the wife had died or remarried. While there were exceptions, such as William Berney, a Hamilton merchant, who allowed his wife, Nancy Jane, "to continue and carry on for her own use and benefit the grocery business ... during her widowhood," most of the prime beneficiaries subject to control were also restricted to acquiring only the interest off the estate.[15] The estate itself was reserved for future heirs. Husbands may have had several motives for controlling their wives' access to assets after remarriage. Such stipulations may reflect the desire of men to control their wives' bodies and sexuality even from the grave. Such an assumption is certainly consistent with much literature on the attitude of the judiciary to woman and sexuality in the late nineteenth and early twentieth centuries. In this context women were often seen as chattels.[16]

The imposition of controls by husbands over their wives can also be understood from a more thoroughly familial, if no less a patriarchal, perspective. Before the introduction of the MWPLS a husband would have thought that when his widow remarried, the new husband might assume the inheritance, and young children from the first marriage

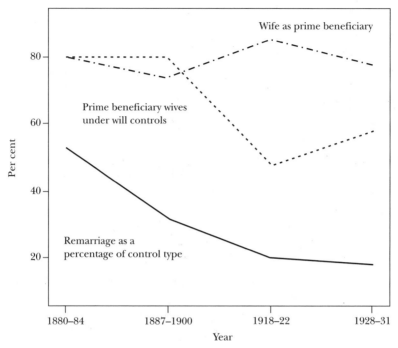

Figure 2.2
Position of wives in the wills of men with children: Victoria and Hamilton
combined, 1880–1931

might be less of a priority to the stepfather.[17] Thus the remarriage stip-
ulation made sense as a way to protect that inheritance for the children
or other relatives. In this context wives became what Owens, writing of
Lockport, England, in the first half of the nineteenth century, called
"property custodians" rather than owners of capital. In the context of
the emerging middle-class family the task of widows was to protect and
oversee the ultimate transmission of wealth to children. Widows were
the agents "for the material and ideological reproduction of middle-
class domesticity."[18]

The evidence presented in figure 2.2 suggests that times were chang-
ing. With the passage of MWPLs, controls on widows' access to bequests
altered and gradually diminished. The most dramatic difference was in
the use of the remarriage condition. One would expect to see less use
of the remarriage stipulation since married women could now legally
maintain control of their own property. This assumption is consistent
with the data presented in tables 2.3 and 2.4 but can be most clearly
appreciated by selecting for analysis only the wills of married men with

children and examining the status of wives in those wills. Our information on family composition at the time of the writing of the will is insufficient to bear the weight of detailed statistical analysis, but combining information from the two cities as in figure 1.2 yields some interesting insights.

Husbands who died with children were slightly less likely to name their wives as primary beneficiaries (figure 2.2) than were all husbands as reported in tables 2.3 and 2.4. More significantly, husbands with children were much more likely to impose controls on their wives even when they granted them prime beneficiary status. In effect there was a strong preference among married fathers to engage in a two-step transmission process. Their wives were given interim use of some assets, usually in the form of yearly interest from a trust account set up after the liquidation of the deceased's assets, the proceeds from which were reinvested in conservative ways. After their widows' death or remarriage those assets remaining in the trust account became the direct property of children designated by the father.

Nevertheless, in the years following the passage of the MWPLs, even married fathers altered their will-giving practices. While the designation of wives as primary beneficiary remained high, controls eased and, as figure 2.2 demonstrates, remarriage restrictions were increasingly seen as unnecessary. Although there were exceptions, such as George Carey of Hamilton, who appointed his wife sole executor only until she remarried and then his son was to take over, and Alexander Mayberry, also of Hamilton, who in his 1924 will bequeathed his house and real estate to his wife "during her lifetime or until such time as she should remarry," in both cities married men resorted to the remarriage control less frequently after the passage of the MWPLs.[19] The drop in the general use of controls in each city is explained by the declining use of the remarriage provision. Widows who remarried were now less of a threat to the deceased husband's patrimony. Life provisions were sufficient to the task.

Many widows with children still performed the task of custodian and agent of middle-class domesticity, but the enforcement of that traditional niche in the male inheritance process was, in the late nineteenth and early twentieth centuries, under going change. At some level the easing of restrictions on widows' access to bequests parallels the increased activity of widows and other women in the wider fields of finance and, as we shall see, business in general. In fact, these changes mirrored the many public acknowledgments and statements of support for women's presence in matters of finance and investment, as we detailed in chapter 1. At the same time it is entirely probable that many widows who received their bequests without controls continued to act in the broader interests of family obligations. As Owens, among others, notes, capital is always embedded in obligations and rights of a social sort.[20] What women, whether married, single daughters, or widows, were gaining was the right to exercise those obligations in their own ways free from direct supervision by a male other.

Mary Baker is a case in point. Her husband, Richard, the owner of a flour and feed business in Victoria, died in September 1886 leaving his whole estate to his wife free of all controls. He had other options. He might have bequeathed the business to his forty-two-year-old son, who worked in the firm and lived next door to him in Victoria. But he gave everything to his widow. Doubtless Richard expected that Mary would bequeath the business to their son on her death. And demonstrating her adherence to family interests, she did just that. Yet she took her role seriously and exercised some significant agency in the process. "I give to my son Michael," Mary Baker wrote in her will, "all my share and interest in the goodwill, stock in trade, furniture, fittings ... and book debts of the firm ... together with all the moneys at the Bank of British North America at Victoria standing to the credit of the firm." Then came the "but": "subject to the payment and discharge by my said son of all the debts and liabilities of the said firm due and subsisting at my decease." Richard did not require that of Mary but she required it of her son. Nor was her son an executor: two employees of the Dominion Government Savings Bank fulfilled that role and presumably were expected to see that Michael did indeed liquidate the debts. This case suggests that it should not be assumed that widows were simple transmitters of family property. Rather, it is just as possible that many, like Mary Baker, took their role as custodian of family assets seriously and in so doing, imposed their stamp on the proceedings.[21]

The case of Mary Baker McQuesten, a widow living in Hamilton, suggests the care that widows who were free from restrictions on bequeathments put into the writing of their own wills. McQuesten's husband had clearly given her the freedom to do as she wished with her assets, which included a house, a rental property, some stock, and household items. On 5 February 1902 she sent a draft of her will to her son Calvin for his advice. Mary was particularly concerned to give her daughters enough to be comfortable. Several further letters were exchanged and by the end of February the will was finalized. "[M]other's mind," one of her daughters wrote, "is at last at rest for her Will is signed and witnessed by Mrs. Mullen and Mrs. Irving, one thing off her mind."[22] Women exercised their agency with care. For many if not most women with wealth, writing a will was serious business.

In the period following the passage of the MWPLs, many of the men who continued to worry about their widow's remarriage imposed only a watered-down version of the traditional control. In both cities before 1887, all the men who invoked the remarriage clause denied their widows any share of the estate. As John William Williams, a Victoria stable keeper, declared in November 1882, his wife could use the interest on his estate for life "provided she remains a widow, but not otherwise." Writing his will in 1895, Henry Hancock, a tobacco retailer in Victoria, felt more confident: he granted his wife life interest in the estate, and if she should remarry she could enjoy the rights to half the estate, the other half to go immediately to his son, who would receive the remainder on her death. Clark Watson, a retired farmer living in Victoria, gave his wife $2,500 a year, which was to be reduced to half that amount should she remarry.[23] Perhaps not surprisingly, the use of simple life-control provisions remained strong and, expressed as a percentage of all controls, increased or remained high in both cities. In the early 1880s just under one half of all wives who were primary beneficiaries were subjected to some control by their husbands' wills. In Hamilton the percentage of wives under some form of control levelled off at about a third after 1900. In Victoria the number dipped to a fifth in the years surrounding the war and then jumped to over a quarter in the late 1920s. The relatively few wives who inherited a secondary portion of the estate were more likely to be subject to controls, whether of the type of relying on a son for maintenance or of receiving the interest of a partial estate for life or widowhood. Excluding unknowns, after 1887, 45 per cent (14 of 31) secondary inheritors enjoyed their inheritance free of control.[24] Clearly, despite the continuing desires by some men, most especially fathers, to set limits on their widows' control of bequeathed goods, widows were increasingly afforded greater agency over an important part of the rest of their lives.

It is hard to assign an absolute significance level to the gradual movement towards empowerment of women in men's wills in these two Canadian cities. Yet as we have seen from our examination of probate data, will-making, and investment behaviour, Canadian women in the late nineteenth and early twentieth centuries were far more than passive recipients of wealth from men. A close look at the content of

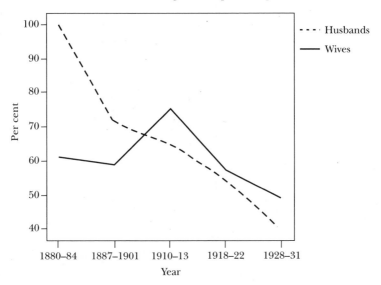

Figure 2.3
Wives and husbands as executrices/ors: Victoria, 1880–1930
NOTE: There were only four married women in the 1880–84 cohort. Numbers for women and men for the other dates are at least twenty and usually well in excess of that.

women's wills provides further evidence of assertiveness and the exercise of a bounded agency by Canadian women in this period.

One of the more obvious differences in the data presented in men's wills (tables 2.1 and 2.2) and in women's wills (tables 2.3 and 2.4) relates to the relatively few women appointed executrix by other women. Was this an example of dependency by women on men to run their financial affairs? In fact, the marital status of the will maker explains much of the difference. Widowed and especially single women were far more likely to appoint another woman as executrix than were married women. Single women looked most often to female relatives or female friends, and widows were most apt to rely fairly equally on daughters and/or sons. Married women looked most often to their husbands as executors (as did husbands to their wives), and that is the main reason why there are relatively few women executrices listed in women's wills compared to men's wills.

Yet in both cities throughout much of the early twentieth century women were less apt to appoint their husbands executors than were men to appoint their wives executrices. While the trend lines, as indicated in figures 2.3 and 2.4, are different in the two cities, by the end of the period covered, married women were increasingly looking to

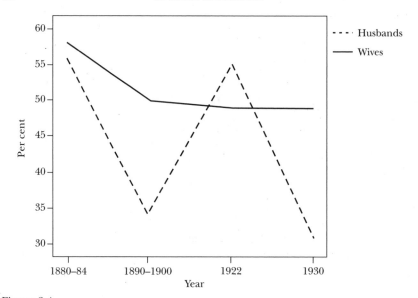

Figure 2.4
Wives and husbands as executrices/ors: Hamilton, 1880–1930
NOTE: There were eighteen married women in the 1880–84 cohort. Numbers for men and women in the other periods were always well in excess of twenty.

people other than their husbands to superintend the distribution of their assets after death. Most often the alternatives were the sons and/or daughters to whom women were bequeathing their goods. In Victoria married women had been moving in that direction since the passage of the MWPLs. In Hamilton the trend is far from straightforward, but it is clear that one cannot predict the extent to which married women would appoint their husbands executor from one year to the next. Such behaviour hardly points to dependency on the part of married women in that city. That married women showed little hesitancy to bypass their husbands as executors is suggestive of independence and agency on their part.

Women were also less likely than men to grant the bulk of their estates to another woman (compare tables 2.3 and 2.4 with tables 2.5 and 2.6). It is the case that for both cities and most time periods widows and single women were far more likely than married women to designate a woman as their primary beneficiary. Married women were always more apt to grant their estates primarily to their husbands (as were husbands to their wives) than to any other category of inheritor. This might seem a surprising finding given that much of the literature has stressed the tendency for female legatees to leave more of their estates to women than men did. It is logical to think that the apparent change in bequest behaviour by the women profiled here may reflect the fact that it was now possible for more married women to leave estates and that those married women who did so would usually grant their estates to their surviving husbands. These findings fit well with the paradigm of separate spheres: women both interacted with other women and were subordinate to men, and their bequests reflected that social behaviour; men concerned themselves more with the protection and promotion of the next generation.

The reality is somewhat more complex and interesting. A close focus on the nature of bequeathments to primary beneficiaries points to a convergence of behaviour and motive between men and women. The separate spheres perspective is an inappropriate paradigm for understanding inheritance patterns in the post-MWPL era. Compare, for example, the extent to which women imposed controls on men with male controls on women (tables 2.5 and 2.6 with tables 2.3 and 2.4). While the numbers are small for the male inheritors in women's wills, the relevant percentages in the tables are fairly close for most years, and for Hamilton in 1900 and Victoria in 1910 and 1918 women were more apt to impose controls on men than men were on women. It is true that generally more wives than husbands were subjected to controls, but a comparison of tables 2.3 and 2.4 with 2.5 and 2.6 points to a surprising number of wives who *did* impose controls on their husbands. A fluctuating but noticeable number of women who granted their estates primarily to their husbands did limit control to a life interest and decreed to whom the remaining assets would go. Indeed, in both cities at the end of the 1920s women were about as likely to put their widowed husbands under some control as men were to do so for their widowed wives.

While Mary Walsh and Sarah Blake of Victoria both co-appointed their husbands and sons as trustees, they only allowed their husbands access to interest on the estate and/or the right to live in the house until death, after which the women decreed how the assets were to be divided amongst their sons and daughters. Mrs H. Des Biens of Victoria appointed two women as executrices and left the bulk of her estate to her six children: "To my Husband, Louie Des Biens [I leave] the sum of one hundred dollars if there is any money in the Bank and a home on the property as long as he lives." Mary Bulwer, in her 1907 will, allowed her husband to buy her house and property for $7,000, the money to be paid to the estate for the use of her daughter when she became of age. Margaret Connelly of Hamilton wrote her will in January 1882 and allowed her husband rights to household goods and real estate for "his natural life," after which the estate should be sold and the money divided between her three children.[25]

David Weber Corbin's wife, Caroline, died in Victoria in 1889. Caroline owned and managed a clothing store which she had inherited from her first husband, William Jeffries. That business she ceded to her son, who was to be employed in the store by her trustees at the salary of $60 a month until he reached twenty-one years of age. Her husband was to have no part in the business, but he did receive $5,000 "free of duty." David remarried and his second wife, Mary, died in 1902, granting David life interest in her residence and all that was in it as long as he kept it in good repair and well insured. He also received, for no longer than twenty-one years, interest from the estate at the "uncontrolled discretion" of the trustees, who could "act according to what they consider to be the best interest of my said husband and not withhold the said income from him unless they see good reason." At the end of that period the estate was to go to a nephew. Sarah Donovan of Hamilton granted her estate to her husband, "absolutely recommending" that he divide all between her children on his death. Mary Davidson of Victoria and Sarah Harris of Hamilton were more controlling. In January 1895 Davidson granted her husband life interest in the estate, decreeing that her sister and children were to get all equally after his death, an interesting example of providing for family on her side (a not uncommon disposition) rather than her husband's. Harris put her estate in trust for her husband to use the interest to look after her children.[26]

Indeed, some men argued that restrictions such as these were too onerous. "I wish," Elizabeth McKay wrote in her 1926 will, "Hugh McKay, my husband, to live in this house after I am gone ... and at his death all I leave to be given back to my own relations." Hugh had the right to the interest on the estate during his life, but during the probate hearings he claimed that he had "very little income and was unable to secure sufficient money to pay for the necessities of life." On that basis he requested the right to the whole estate. The situation confronting Lillian Edgington's husband, who claimed he was disabled and penniless, was somewhat different but nonetheless speaks to women's agency. Most of Edgington's estate, worth just over $2000, was in the form of cash in the bank. William, her husband, argued that all the money was his. He had, he said, given the cash to his wife to put in a joint account. Instead she had put it in an account in her name only. That, according to William, only occurred because she had "practically no banking or

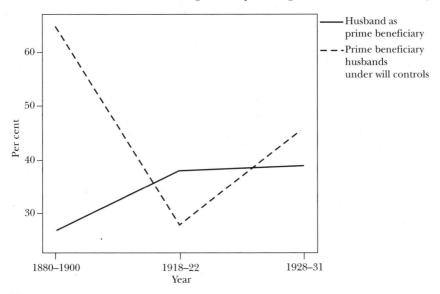

Figure 2.5
Position of husbands in the wills of women with children: Victoria and Hamilton combined, 1880–1931

business experience"! The estate was ultimately divided equally between himself and his son.[27]

Three further examples suggest that some women, like some men, imposed more than simple life-interest conditions. In September 1892 Isabella Aubin of Victoria gave everything to her two daughters, subject only to allowing her husband use of the personal estate "with them" as long as he remained unmarried. Eliza Willis of Victoria stipulated in her 1914 will that her husband could have the interest off the estate and live in her home "during his lifetime or until he remarries." In March 1881 Margaret Charlton of Hamilton "being of sound, disposing mind, memory, judgement and understanding, but knowing the uncertainty of life," stipulated that her "beloved" husband, a farmer, could enjoy equal interest with her daughter in all real and personal assets "for so long as he may remain single and unmarried after my death and no longer being only to him a life interest and no more unless terminated as above." She died a scant seven months later, leaving two children and her forty-three-year-old husband, Joseph.[28] These women had their own ideas as to how assets should be transferred to future generations and were not willing to subordinate those ideas to those of their husbands.

As the data in table 2.7 demonstrate, married women were far more apt to ignore entirely their husbands in their wills than were husbands to ignore their wives. This tendency was always high in Hamilton and increased steadily in Victoria in the late nineteenth century. Selecting only married women with children for analysis underlines this trend.

Married women with children were less likely than married men with children to impose controls on their spouse (compare figures 2.2 and 2.5). Should one conclude that they were more trusting of their spouses and/or that they were willing to leave it to their widowed husbands to transmit goods to their children and thus not practise the two-stage transmission process so favoured by married men? In fact, married women with children adopted a simpler strategy. They tended to ignore their husbands. About 80 per cent of wives became the primary beneficiary in the wills of husbands with children: for the period as a whole, well under 40 per cent of husbands received that designation from wives with children.

It may well be that married women took advantage of the fact that their husbands, as wage earners, could look after themselves, and thus these women were in a sense free riders in the inheritance process. They had, as some studies have noted with regard to bequeathment patterns in the early nineteenth century, "the luxury of granting favours to specific children."[29]

Yet this "coddled woman" interpretation seems less apt for understanding behaviour in the post-MWPL era. Many women bequeathed goods to their children despite the existence of their husbands, rather than because husbands in some way made such an action possible. In her 1906 will Anne Maria Leeming of Victoria granted most of her substantial estate to her children but did offer her husband the following proposition: she would cede him $60 a month for the rest of his life if he granted all rights to his life insurance to her children within sixty days of her death. If he failed to do so, he was to receive nothing, and should he interfere in any way with the will, all payments to him were "null and void." Annie Cooper, in her 1905 will, allowed her husband use of the house for as long as he lived and granted all else "absolutely" to her daughter, and to ensure that no trouble would occur, she appointed her daughter sole executrix. Helen Glide, in her 1896 will, was equally protective and assertive. She appointed her daughter sole executrix and granted her husband the right to interest off the estate for life, and then her daughter was to enjoy similar rights; on the daughter's death, all was to go uncontrolled to Helen's granddaughter.

The following examples suggest that the assumption on the part of men that trustees could protect their assets for their children's use, as proposed by Shammas, was a double-edged sword. In 1929 Margaret Bolseth of Victoria left $90 to her husband and $1,300, the bulk of the rest of her estate, in trust for her young son. Her firm wish was for her son to receive that bequest "intact" when he came of age. She desired that her husband provide for the "maintenance and education of my said son" and cautioned her trustee (the Royal Trust Company) "to take every reasonable precaution to ascertain that any sums that may be requested for [the son's] maintenance and education ... are actually needed for such purposes." In her 1929 will, Mary Louise Ross, also of Victoria, warned her trustee "that under no circumstances" was there to be "any dealings with my divorced husband" and all her estate was to go to her daughter.[30]

Daughters and sons appeared in women's wills as prime beneficiaries (sole and equal to others) more often than they did in the wills of men, in part because men died earlier than women; thus husbands were more apt to bequeath most of their assets to their widows rather than directly to their children.[31] Throughout the period, daughters appeared in mothers' wills more often than sons. But after the passage of the MWPLs, the tendency of mothers to reward daughters more often than sons lessened: in the early, pre-MWPL era mothers in both cities were about twice as likely to mention daughters rather than sons in their wills. After 1887 in Victoria 38 per cent of women's wills mentioned daughters and 34 per cent mentioned sons; for Hamilton the respective figures are 41 and 30.[32] A more precise indicator of the tendency of mothers to favour daughters can be seen by selecting only those wills where we know that both sons and daughters were alive.[33]

The trend suggested in table 2.8 is similar to the figures from all wills presented above. In both cities, but more so in Hamilton in the later period, mothers favoured daughters over sons as prime beneficiaries. Some have explained this behaviour as partly a result of the type of assets bequeathed by women: personal goods that would only be of interest to other women.[34] This interpretation fits well with the separate spheres paradigm and may have merit in the pre-MWPL era, but in Victoria and Hamilton in the early 1880s and in the late 1890s over 75 per cent of primary bequests from married women included cash, bonds, and land as well as personal property, and the figure was higher for all women in both eras. In the post-1900 era the figure was just under 100 per cent. The diversity of the bequests suggests that women,

including married women, had goods to give that had utility outside
the parlour and home, goods that were of equal material interest to
sons and to daughters.

In fact, the goods that women left their sons and daughters did not
differ significantly by type. In both cities there was a small tendency for
women to give land more often to sons than to daughters: after 1887 in
Victoria, 80 per cent of sons received land from their mothers and 71
per cent of daughters did; in Hamilton the figures were 67 and 64 per
cent respectively. As we saw in chapter 1, women who left estates had
for sometime gone outside the home in search of remunerative invest-
ments. From this perspective it is more difficult to understand women's
behaviour as emanating from a culture separate from that of men.
Like men, women too were interested in the economic impact their
bequests could have on households in the next generation.

Indeed, there is a gradual convergence of bequeathment patterns of
fathers and mothers to children in the late nineteenth century. While
women continued to mention their children in their wills more often
than men, by the turn of the century men and women in both cities
mentioned daughters as the prime beneficiary as or more often than
sons (compare tables 2.8 and 2.9).[35] This is a significant trend, perhaps
suggestive of changing perceptions of women's place in financial and
economic affairs. Treating daughters differently and less well than sons
has been termed the "productivity ideal" of bequeathment practices.[36]
The trend toward equalization of bequests suggests that daughters were
increasingly being considered as "productive" in a sense similar to that
of sons. And even if this was not a conscious rationale for equal distribu-
tion, such distributive practice nonetheless had the effect of creating
the potential for increased activity on the part of women in financial
matters. As we have seen in chapter 1, many women, including "busi-
ness girls," did not hesitate to take advantage of that opportunity.

Some women, and undoubtedly some men, privileged daughters for
reasons similar to those of Sarah Hutchinson, who admitted, "I would
have liked to have done more for [my son] but with my small means I
feel I ought to leave my daughters all as being more needy." Often, too,
unmarried daughters received priority, as in Annie Deans's 1889 will
and Elizabeth Oates's 1919 will; both ceded personal and real goods to
two daughters as long as they remained unmarried, after which time all
was to be divided equally amongst all the children.[37] The MWPLs pro-
vided legal security for daughters, and fathers increasingly made
bequests to daughters in the seeming confidence that after marriage

their daughters would retain control of their inheritance. This point is also suggested by the fact that only a minority of men and women in either city couched their bequests to daughters in protective language of the sort used by Isabel Askew of Victoria in 1899: "I declare that the shares hereby given to each of my said daughters shall be for her separate use from the debts, control and engagements of her present or any future husband with whom she may intermarry." Or, and perhaps the most extreme in this regard, that used by Clara Wilson, a married woman of Hamilton, in her 1927 will specifying that her daughter "shall not take a vested interest in my estate until the death of her husband."[38] Nonetheless, after 1887, only a few more than 25 per cent of men in both cities who bequeathed goods to their daughters used protective language, while 28 per cent of Victoria women and only 10 per cent of Hamilton women did so.[39] It should be noted, however, that men were much more likely to use protective language for daughters than they were for their wives in the period after 1887 (see tables 2.3 and 2.4), and Hamilton men were far more likely to do so than were Hamilton women.

David Green and Alastair Owens have noted the "active way" that single women "disposed of their assets" in England in the first half of the nineteenth century.[40] Similarly, it is worth emphasizing here the strikingly assertive and independent tone of women's wills, and most especially married women's wills, in these two Canadian cities. In May 1888 Esabella Sheriff of Hamilton explained why she bypassed her husband, appointing her son and daughter as co-executors and dividing the estate between her three children: "all my property herein devised and bequeathed is my own separate property and that no part thereof has come to me by or through my present husband, and I do not consider that he has any moral right to any part thereof." Sheriff understood her rights under the MWPLs and was determined to exercise those rights. Eva Pawley of Victoria was equally determined to exercise her rights, although for reasons of a different sort. "It is with great regret that I make this will," she wrote in 1919, "and exclude my husband's name from it." We had "many very happy hours together before sin and sorrow touched our lives so deeply."

Sarah Pawson of Hamilton, after bequeathing her estate to her sister and another woman, had a second thought: in a codicil she granted her husband the right to "carpets, bedstead and other articles of my household furniture which were purchased by him at the time of our marriage." She too had a firm sense as to who owned what within the marriage and exercised control over *her* property. So also did Elizabeth Conway, the owner of a tavern outside Victoria. In 1890 she declared "with respect to the business of an hotel and saloonkeeper carried on by me ... or any other business in which I may be engaged at my decease I empower my trustees to continue the same for as long as they shall see fit ... with liberty to employ my husband." Her husband received nothing else: her five daughters and son shared the bequest. A similar sense of propriety and concern for the welfare of the next generation is clear in the wills of Catherine Baughman of Hamilton and Harriet McKay of Victoria. "My husband," Baughman noted, "having received considerable money from me during my lifetime," was to receive only part of the estate, the rest to be divided between four relatives. McKay went a step further: not only did her husband receive nothing, but she instructed her trustee to call in at any time "the monies lent to my husband John ... on mortgage of the chattels used in his business" and give the proceeds to her daughter.[41]

There were other possibilities. More women, like Susan Elliston of Victoria, might have left all to their husbands, "in perfect confidence that he will carry out my requests and wishes, known to him, in regard to my daughter."[42] But as table 2.10 demonstrates, married women – and, for most years, especially Hamilton's married women – were wary of leaving their assets in the uncontrolled hands of their husbands. It was more often the case that they ignored them or controlled them.

The patterns of bequeathment in men's and women's wills supported and facilitated the general investment behaviour of women uncovered in our analysis of probate data in chapter 1. In this context the following point deserves emphasis: the movement was towards convergence of bequeathment practices between genders. As men loosened traditional controls, women exerted more and more agency in their disposition of material assets. Women took advantage of their individual civic rights and in that sense exemplified a characteristic often attributed only to middle-class men: an assertive sense of self-worth and self-regualtion. The overall trend in bequeathments was for more women, irrespective of marital status, to receive assets relatively free of patriarchal control. The MWPLs made it more feasible for men to grant assets free of control to their daughters and even to their widows. As the period progressed, daughters and sons were as likely to inherit equally and similarly with respect to types of assets. In this way bequeathment practices helped to underwrite the growing investment by "business girls" and other women in stocks, bonds and land.

We saw in chapter 1 that while wealth was undoubtedly enabling for women, measuring the degree to which they were free actors in investment decisions – that is, free from control by men – is a difficult task. Evidence from wills presented in this chapter shows that in many cases women did make financial decisions free from a husband's control and in the process exerted a controlling influence on their spouses. Even women who, like Mary Baker, inherited with controls attached exercised a significant degree of independence in the way they bequeathed those assets. While the number of women who gained real autonomy in the management of material assets cannot be known, indications of the possibility of such independence have been presented. Moreover, the increasingly aggressive behaviour of women in the field of investment is nicely reflected in the assertive and confident tone that characterized so many of women's last words. Women demonstrated a keen sense of proprietorship and, in many cases, understanding that extended beyond household goods to stocks, bonds, and debentures. Finally, perhaps most evocative is the spirit of independence that emanated from many women through words like those written by Annie Heard in 1905: "I hereby declare it is my intention to dispose of my property without reference to my husband ... the same having been earned by me ... without consideration of or making any provision for my said husband."[43]

3

The Gender of Shareholders: Investment in Banking and Insurance Stocks in Ontario, 1860–1911

The probate data that we analyzed in chapter 1 suggested that women were active as holders of stocks in financial and a range of other companies. We then looked, in chapter 2, at how women and men bequeathed their wealth. One of the arguments put forward in that chapter was that bequeathment patterns increasingly enabled younger, single women as well as married women in this time period. The probate data already examined are suggestive and generally supportive of that contention in the sense of the changing nature of assets owned by women and in the sense that the general asset composition came to resemble that of men over time. But probate data, as we noted, have limits, an important one being that the sample is drawn from a generally older segment of the overall population. Perhaps, then, what we found with wealth-holding and asset composition, as indicated by probates, did not reflect well the holdings of a wider age group of men and women in urban Canada. Indeed, perhaps women only acquired such wealth as the probates have revealed on the eve of their own deaths, most obviously from recently deceased husbands or other relatives. This chapter is the first of four that seek to widen our investigation of potential women wealth-holders, in this case by looking at women and men who invested in stocks via an analysis of published shareholder lists. Subsequent chapters examine women as real property owners and as mortgage borrowers and lenders both of real property and of chattels.

"There are many different kinds of stocks," John Howard Cromwell advised American businesswomen at the beginning of the twentieth century. They varied "all the way from the stocks of old and substantial financial institutions, which, year after year, have paid to their shareholders handsome dividends, to those of far-off gold mines or silver mines, which may in fact exist only in the minds of gullible shareholders." But, Cromwell warned, "only a fortunate few are in all respects competent" to discriminate between good and bad stocks. He would have none of them: "The conclusion ... must be that all kinds of stocks, without exception, are to be regarded as dangerous, and are to be avoided always and entirely." Not all advice offered to women by investment experts was this negative. Writing in 1896, William. O. Stoddard, argued that "investment is the mother and father of the economy." "Hoarding is a bad practice and does not, after all, provide the safety which is its only attractive feature." Nonetheless, he warned women, stock investments must be "strictly measured, defined and limited ... and require watching and the adoption of protective measures provided for by existing laws."[1] With a close focus on investment in bank and insurance stocks, this chapter compares the participation of women and men in the stock market. After a quick review of what the probate data reveal, our focus then turns to an examination of the changes in the gendered pattern of holders of bank shares in Ontario from 1860 to 1911 and in insurance stocks from 1880 to 1900 and finally to a closer look at women and men in Hamilton who invested in banks and insurance companies in this period. Where possible, I have linked bank shareholders from Hamilton to the censuses of 1881 and 1901, to permit an analysis of their personal characteristics over time.

By international standards, the institutional structure for investing in Canadian stocks was, for much of the late nineteenth century, fairly rudimentary. The Toronto Stock Exchange incorporated only in 1878, four years after the Montreal exchange. Banks dominated business: in the week ending 7 May 1883, for example, 6,716 shares had been traded on the Toronto exchange, and 5,854 of those were bank stocks. Banks were relatively popular investment opportunities: as one brokerage company put it, "No other form of investment pays such rapid profits as first class bank shares." Dividend payments from these banks were fairly steady in the period under review and doubtless proved attractive to many investors.[2] In 1890 the Canadian Bank of Commerce paid a 7 per cent dividend and the Bank of Hamilton 8 per cent, and according to the Toronto *Globe*, Canadian banks paid out $10.6 million in dividends in 1900. The dividend rates were probably a percentage or so lower than what could be realized on mortgages, but of course a further attraction for investing in stocks was the possibility of their increasing in value over time. As the brokerage firm of Wm Walkerton and Company

Figure 3.1
Assets of women and men in stocks from probate data: Hamilton, 1900–30

advertised in the 1880s, "If You Want to make money on [banks] write
for our pamphlet which explains how investments are managed. As
high as three hundred per cent profit was made last year in this way by
ordinary investors who put up from $100 to $500 or $1000, and were
guided by our advice when to buy and when to sell and what shares
were most likely to advance in price."[3]

By the eve of World War One, Ontario's and Canada's economy had
greatly diversified and the securities market had expanded, although
financial issues continued to be important. Yearly trading on the
Toronto exchange in general stocks (excluding mining and bonds)
grew from 22,000 in 1879 to 1.6 million in 1902, but that volume
dropped to an average of 646,000 shares a year between 1903 and
1911. One estimate of the total number of shareholders in Canada in
1913 puts the figure at 114,125, or 4 per cent of the population aged
twenty and over. This percentage can be compared to what one scholar
has termed "serious shareholders" in Great Britain, who represented
2.2 per cent of the population in 1913. In that year some 38 per cent
(42,800) of Canada's shareholders invested in banks.[4]

As figures 3.1 and 3.2 indicate, women and men in Hamilton were
no strangers to stock markets. While, according to probate data, men

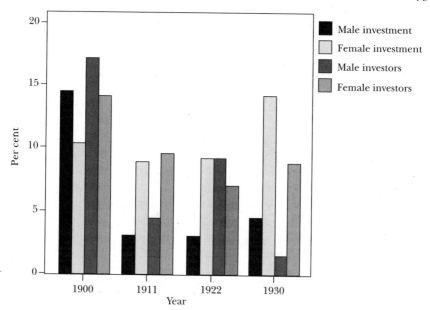

Figure 3.2
Investment by women and men in bank stock from probate data: Hamilton,
1900–30

generally invested more of their total capital in shares than did women,
the gap had narrowed considerably by the early 1920s, and as we saw in
chapter 1, the reverse was the case by the end of that decade. Women
were especially attracted to investment in bank stocks (figure 3.2). As
the probate data for Hamilton women indicate, the percentage of capi-
tal invested in bank stocks by women fluctuated around 10 per cent
from 1900 to the early 1920s and rose to just under 15 per cent by
1930. By contrast, the percentage of capital invested by men in banks
declined from 14 per cent in 1900 to just under 5 per cent thirty years
later.[5] If the Hamilton probates are any guide, then, investment in bank
stocks was increasingly a women's sphere of activity.

   Figure 3.3 provides a revealing look at the gendered nature of invest-
ment in bank stocks in Ontario in the late nineteenth and early twenti-
eth century. Three banks were chosen for this study. The Bank of
Upper Canada, the province's pre-eminent bank, was selected for 1860
(Upper Canada became Ontario after Confederation). That bank went
bankrupt six years later. The Canadian Bank of Commerce started busi-
ness in 1867 with its headquarters in Toronto and quickly grew
to become one of the province's most successful banking institutions.

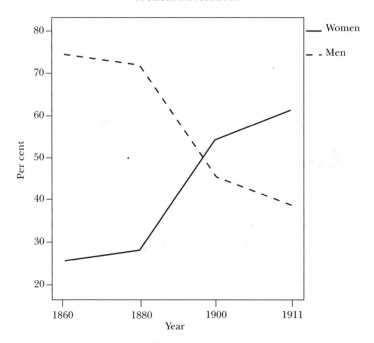

Figure 3.3
Gender of bank shareholders: Ontario, 1860–1911
NOTE: The data are from Canada, House of Commons, *Sessional Papers*, for the years indicated. Only investors who lived in Ontario are included. Only those with known gender are included, and corporations are excluded. Total shareholders sampled for 1860: 1,116; 1880: 886; 1900: 1,083; 1911: 864. Unknowns for each year are small in number, and even if all of one sex, they would not significantly affect the trends in the figure.

The third was the Bank of Hamilton, an institution with a strong regional clientele and one that allows for an analysis of bank shareholders who lived in Hamilton. It was established in 1872 and taken over by the Canadian Bank of Commerce in 1923. The Canadian Bank of Commerce and the Bank of Hamilton were surveyed for 1880, 1900, and 1911.

Women moved from 26 per cent of shareholders in 1860 to fully 61 per cent in 1911.[6] Their profile changed little over the first twenty years. The big shift occurred after 1880 and before 1900, precisely the era of the MWPLs. The trend after 1880 was almost identical for both banks: women increased their participation in the Commerce from 29 per cent in 1880 to 62 per cent in 1911 and their representation in the Hamilton bank from 22 per cent to 58 per cent. It is true that men tended on average to invest more money and to hold more shares than women, but even in these areas, as table 3.1 indicates, women's participation increased significantly during the era of the MWPLs and continued to grow after 1900.[7] Moreover, in all years the standard deviations for men were considerably higher than those for women, indicating that a relatively few men held a large number and value of shares. Women's holdings tended to be more evenly dispersed. There is no doubt that men controlled more capital than women in these years, but the activity of women investors in the area of bank stocks strongly suggests that many women were willing and able to invest to the extent that their relatively limited means permitted. It is appropriate at this point to recall that measured by percentage of personal wealth, as the Hamilton probate data indicate, women may have invested *more* of their total capital in bank shares than men and in that sense cannot be seen to be necessarily more conservative in this sphere than their male counterparts. In fact, some investment manuals encouraged women to invest in financial stocks, pointing out that those investments tended to be relatively safe and to yield relatively consistent dividends.[8] Over the course of the late nineteenth century, what might be termed the era of the Married Women's Property Laws, many more women than men came to invest in bank shares and may have invested more of their total capital in that sector than men. From those perspectives, investment in bank stocks was clearly a gendered affair, a sphere dominated by women.

Perhaps the pattern of gendered investment in the banking sector did not correspond to investment in other areas of the stock market in this time period. Shareholder lists for fire and life insurance companies were, like those of banks, published annually by the federal Parliament. Four insurance companies, among the largest in their sectors, were surveyed for 1880 and 1900, two fire insurance companies and two life insurance enterprises. The British America Assurance Company, founded in 1834, and the Western Assurance Company, founded in Toronto in 1851 represented the fire insurance business, and the Canada Life Assurance Company, founded in Hamilton in 1847, and the smaller Toronto-based Confederation Life Association, founded in 1871, represented the life insurance business. Information on dividend payouts is incomplete, but the Western Assurance Company generally paid 10 per cent annually, and the British America about 7 per cent annually. The Canada Life Assurance Company paid consistent dividends around 10 per cent.[9] The Confederation Life Association advertised that it paid out "large dividends" which seem to have been around 7 per cent in the late nineteenth century. An article in the *Globe* in 1901

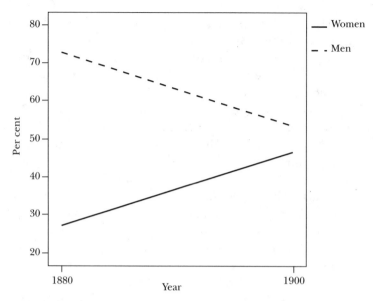

Figure 3.4

Gender of insurance company shareholders: Ontario, 1880–1900

NOTE: The shareholder data are from Canada, House of Commons, *Sessional Papers*, for 1880 and 1900. Only those with known gender are included, and corporations are excluded. Numbers are 1880, 346 cases, and 1900, 534 cases.

noted that there was "a growing tendency among all classes to invest" in that company.[10]

The pattern of gendered investment, as indicated by figure 3.4, is very similar to that for banks, although women were a little less dominant in terms of numbers as investors in insurance companies, moving from 28 per cent in 1880 to 48 per cent in 1900. As with banks, men dominated in terms of the value of stock held, holding 78 per cent in 1880 and dropping a little to 73 per cent twenty years later, slightly higher than their relative holdings in banks in that year. Some individuals, especially men, invested in more than one company. Since, as with banks, the intent here is to obtain a picture of the gender of shareholders in the insurance sector as a whole and not simply for an individual company, multiple holdings (for men and women) were combined, and multiple company shareholders counted once only. The gendered holdings of the individual companies are shown in table 3.3. There shareholders who invested in more than one company are counted as they appear. The result is that men are a little more dominant than exhibited in figure 3.1, but the trend is the same. Three of the four companies had similar gender distributions in 1880, varying from 72 to 69 per cent men. Men constituted 94 per cent of the Confederation Life Association's Ontario shareholders, the newest and smallest of the companies. By 1900 there were somewhat wider variations between the four companies, although in three of the four, women substantially increased their numbers. Sixty-one per cent of the British America Assurance's Ontario stockholders were male, as were 53 per cent of the Western Assurance Company's. By 1900 the two life companies had in a sense exchanged positions: only 58 per cent of the Confederation Life's shareholders were male, but men had increased their percentage in Canada Life from 69 to 73.

Not only did more women enter the investment field by purchasing bank and insurance stock in the late nineteenth and early twentieth century, but many of those women who did so also increased the intensity of their activity. In both areas more women invested in multiple companies in this era. Of the forty-three multiple investors in banks in 1880, only eight were women (19 per cent). By 1900 the number had increased to twenty-eight, or 48 per cent of multiple investors, and by 1911, 54 per cent of those who invested in more than one of the banks in our sample were women (forty-seven). The trend was the same, although less dramatic, in the insurance sector. Women who invested in more than one company in the insurance sample represented 16 per cent of multiple investors in 1880 (three) and 31 per cent in 1900 (twenty-three). Indeed, some women invested in both sectors: Cynthia Fuller, a sixty-five-year-old married women living with her husband in Hamilton in 1880, had subscribed for $6,800 in shares in the Canada Life Assurance Company as well as owning shares in the Bank of Commerce. Mrs Winnifred Sewell, a forty-five-year-old widow who lived alone as a lodger in Hamilton in 1901, owned no real property but did hold $1,700 in the Commercial Bank and had subscribed for $800 in stock in the Western Assurance Company. She, of course, may have owned other stock as well. The 1901 census recorded that she was living on her own means, as were, it will be recalled from chapter 1, some ten thousand other women in urban Canada who owned no real property. Indeed, one out of every eight women insurance company shareholders also invested in bank stock in 1880, and that number rose to one out of five in 1900. The comparable figures for men were one out of six in 1880 and one out of 4 in 1900.

Since historical literature in this area is fairly thin, it is hard to situate these figures in a larger context. Recent work on women and investment in Great Britain, however, yields some relevant comparisons.[11] In the late nineteenth century, women investors in three banks – the Bank of Liverpool, Martin's Bank, also in Liverpool, and the Ulster Bank – represented between 31 and 48 per cent of shareholders and 16 and 41 per cent (Ulster Bank, 1914) in value of shares. These figures are very similar to what the Ontario data reveal: Ontario's women bulked somewhat larger as a percentage of shareholders and, compared to the Ulster Bank, a little less in terms of percentage of share value. The authors of the Ulster Bank study also point to the increased presence of women as shareholders between 1877 and 1914 and attribute that increase in part to the passage of the MWPLs in England. The major point is clear: if banks and insurance companies are any guide, women in Ontario in the era of the MWPLs invested in ways similar to their sisters in Great Britain, despite the obvious and dramatic differences in the size of the two capital markets.[12]

But who were the women who invested in banks? Were they like Lydia Payne, who in September 1866, worried about the collapse of the Bank of Upper Canada, wrote to the bank in some distress since she "depended on my stock invested in it for support in my old Age." Or were they more like the "business girl" who assured the readers of *Saturday Night* in 1912 that "stocks and bonds ... have become part and parcel of [the business girl's] life"?[13] The shareholder lists by themselves provide little information about the personal characteristics of investors. In an attempt to answer this question, then, I have linked Hamilton investors in bank shares in 1880 and 1900 to the respective nominal-level census returns for those years.

At first glance the numbers – 38 women investors in 1880 and 111 in 1900 – might seem too small to bear the weight of much analysis. Certainly, one has to be cautious in one's conclusions, but it should be noted that these women do not represent all Hamilton women who invested in banks in this time period. In the period covered there were at least six other banks listed on the Toronto Stock Exchange, and more were listed on the Montreal exchange. Companies in other financial sectors were also listed, as were mining and some industrial stocks.[14] The numbers, then, should be seen as reflective of a larger whole.

The first point to note is that the shareholders resident in Hamilton exhibited behaviour very similar to that in the province as a whole. Hamilton women increased their proportion of all Hamilton bank shareholders from 26 per cent in 1880 to 56 per cent twenty years later, and their percentage of shares owned from 8 to 30 in the same period. In 1900 women in Hamilton owned 26 per cent of the value of bank shares held by people resident in that city, a figure that compares to 28 per cent in the province as a whole.[15] These comparisons give one some confidence that investors in Hamilton may reflect the profile of at least the rest of urban Ontario.

A good indication of the degree to which Hamilton women increased their participation in the sector of bank stocks is the number of women investors as a percentage of women twenty years and older in the city as a whole. This measurement controls for population change. Table 3.2 presents the results for all women and for women in each marital category. All women, no matter their marital category, became more active as bank investors in the era of the MWPLs. How did this pattern compare with men? In 1880 there were 107 male shareholders in the Hamilton and Commerce banks living in Hamilton; that figure represented 1.2 per cent of the twenty-and-over male population. By 1900 the number of male bank investors had dropped to 87, or .6 per cent, the same ratio as for women. It will be recalled that the Hamilton probate data recorded declining interest amongst Hamilton men in bank stocks in the twentieth century. Perhaps that trend started earlier.

The explanation for this movement by Hamilton men out of bank stock is not immediately obvious. Certainly, much of the 1890s was a time of economic slowdown if not recession in Hamilton, and perhaps the troubled economy prompted more men than women to dispose of stock. Relatedly, perhaps the unstable economic conditions encouraged men to transfer their stockholdings to their wives for safe keeping from potential creditors. It is hard to test for this hypothesis in any definitive way, but available evidence does not seem to support it. If such a strategy was widespread, one would have expected a greater increase in married women stockholders than in fact took place. As table 3.2 indicates, the increase was modest compared to the decrease in male participation. As well, we would expect that that strategy would lead to a significant drop in the percentage of married men who were participants in the stock market. In fact, married men bulked large in both years: 81 per cent of male investors in 1880 were married, and 76 per cent in 1900.[16] Another possibility is that men were investing more in other securities in this period. While we cannot test for this possibility in a comprehensive way, we can add those who invested in insurance stock to the individuals who invested in banks, and when we do so, we find the ratios for men in 1880 and 1900 to be 1.3 and .7 respectively.[17]

The comparable figures for women are .5 and .7 respectively. In both the insurance and bank sectors male participation declined even as female participation increased.

What these dual trends reveal is, in the context of existing literature on women and investment in the late nineteenth and early twentieth century, quite remarkable. In Hamilton at the turn of the twentieth century, one could not predict on the basis of his or her gender whether a person over the age of nineteen invested in the stock market. Women were as apt to invest in stock as their male counterparts. A closer look at these women investors is warranted.

Married women increased in absolute numbers and in relation to their numbers in the population of the city, but their gains were over-shadowed by those of widows and single women. How might one account for this phenomenon in the era of the MWPLS? One explanation is that married women had already increased their presence following the passage of the 1872 MWPL, which allowed married women to own and dispose of shares and to maintain any dividend or sale income separate from the control of their husbands.[18] After 1880 they continued to increase their holdings (on average, the number of shares owned by married women increased from 18 to 26), while their presence in the market grew at a slower rate, but increased nonetheless.

Relative to their population in the city as a whole, widows were the most active investors, and that should come as no surprise. On average, they owned the greatest number of shares (twenty-two in 1880 and thirty in 1900). In 1901, twelve of the sixteen widows for whom we have information about the relation to means of production in the census were living on their own means. Fourteen of the twenty widows were head of their households in 1901. For Mary Bower, the income from her two Commerce Bank shares was minimal compared to her rental returns from one house and one store, although she continued to own the shares in 1911. But she was not typical. In 1900 over half the widows owned shares worth in excess of $1,000. Emily Moore, a sixty-year-old widow who lived with her unemployed eighteen-year-old daughter, owned the most: $15,000 worth of Commerce Bank shares. The dividends from that investment plus the rental income she received from three stores permitted a comfortable living.[19]

What is perhaps most interesting is the significant increase in single women investors. They became the largest group of women investors, rising from 23 per cent of women shareholders in 1880 to 42 per cent in 1900.[20] As table 3.2 indicates, they also exhibited the greatest increase relative to their numbers in the city as a whole. In 1880 married women owned, on average, twice as many shares as single women, the average number of shares owned by widows was 2.4 times that held by single women. By 1900 single women were closing the gap. On average, they owned almost the same number of shares as married women, and widows owned only 1.3 times the average number held by single women. The average age of women investors remained steady at forty-eight, but reflecting the increased numbers of single women, the proportion under forty increased from 22 per cent in 1880 to 30 per cent in 1900. These trends suggest that the business girl who wrote to *Saturday Night* had, as it were, "her finger on the pulse." In the era of the MWPLS, younger, single women entered the stock market, for bank shares at least, in proportionately greater numbers than did women who were married or widowed.[21]

There are at least two primary and overlapping explanations for this trend. The first relates to how the MWPLS operated. As we have noted in earlier chapters, married women were not the only beneficiaries from the passage of these laws. The granting of more control over wealth to married women allowed fathers and mothers to bequeath wealth to single daughters with more frequency since they had less to fear from acquisitive behaviour of prospective husbands. The increased investment profile of single women might be a reflection of that bequeathing behaviour. Certainly, the timing of their increased presence in the bank share sector is consistent with that hypothesis. Fathers and mothers might have been more willing to bequeath shares to single daughters following the passage of the 1872 MWPL. By the late 1880s and 1890s it is reasonable to think that that bequeathment process would have begun to have an increasing effect on the fortunes of single daughters. As we shall see below, many of the single women investors were indeed daughters or sisters who lived at home, generally with one parent or other relatives in the house.

A second and related possible explanation for increased wealth-holding by single women is of a demographic nature.[22] A contributor to the Toronto *Globe* in February 1887 was concerned with what the writer saw as the rising age of marriage for women. One reason for that apparent trend, "Garth Grafton" (journalist and novelist Sara Jeannette Duncan) thought, was "the increased independence of women. Girls to-day are earning money enough to support them in comfort who twenty years ago would have been compelled to choose between dependence upon father or husband." "We cannot doubt," Grafton

continued, "that the alternative of supporting herself or being sup-
ported by somebody else she can exist perfectly well without, presents
itself very often to the women wage-earners of the present day." "Nei-
ther," she concluded, "can we doubt that their choice in the matter
often contributes directly to the state of things which it is the business
of this article to deplore."[23]

If we put aside the fact that Garth Grafton believed "dependence
upon father or husband is the ideal relation of all womankind," this
writer had stumbled on a significant demographic trend in late nine-
teenth-century Ontario. Women *were* marrying later or not at all, and
more single women were in the workforce. In Hamilton in 1881 there
were 1,095 more women than men of marriageable age (eighteen to
forty) and that number had increased to 2,123 by 1901. Not sur-
prisingly, the percentage of women who were single in that age
group increased from 47 in 1881 to 52 in 1901. That proportion also
increased for women over the age of forty from 9 per cent single in
1881 to 13 per cent in 1901.

As Grafton noted, single women were also increasingly apt to be earn-
ing their own money. In Hamilton 52 per cent of single women of mar-
riageable age had an occupation in 1881, and 61 per cent had an
occupation in 1901. Nor were those jobs always menial in nature. In
1899 the Toronto *Star* lamented the demise of housekeepers and ser-
vants. Working girls "worship the God that has his throne high over the
department store. They prostrate themselves before the noisy chitte-
ring god of the typewriter. Upon the altar of the cruel sewing machine
god they shed their blood. But the poor homely god, whose symbols are
the frying pan and the dust brush, goes a begging for followers."[24] In
1901 single women had more job choices than had been the case
twenty years earlier. Indeed, some 9 per cent of these women were self-
employed or employers, a group we examine more closely in chapters 7
and 8. Nor were all single women struggling to make ends meet. Many
may have been, and most earned far less than their male counter-
parts,[25] but if one takes out the 9 per cent who earned less than $100
and were probably part-time workers, single working women in Hamil-
ton earned, on average, $230 a year in 1901, and fully 40 per cent
made more than that sum. In that year some 4 per cent of the single
women in Hamilton (159) who were earning money also owned land.
The trend towards more women than men of marriageable age, cou-
pled with the liberating aspects of the MWPLs and the increased employ-
ment activity of single women, helps us to understand why those

women stood out by their numbers as investors in bank stock in late nineteenth-century Hamilton and very likely in urban Ontario as a whole.

While the average age for single women investors was five years younger than that for married women and seventeen years younger than the average for widows, not all single investors were young. Twenty per cent were fifty years of age or over. These women would have had different reasons for investing than younger, single women, and in most cases their investments comprised the sole or major part of their income. Half the under-forty-year-old single women had occupations in addition to their dividend income. Only one of the eleven over that age had employment, and she was a boarding-house keeper. On average, they owned thirty-four shares, compared to twelve for the under-forty-year-old group.

It is interesting that most single women bank stock investors, whether they had an occupation or not and whether they were under or over forty, lived with family and thus shared living expenses, a fact that may have made it easier for them to invest in the stock market. Nine were daughters, eight were sisters, two were sisters-in-law, and one was an aunt. Only five of the twenty-five for whom we know the relation to head of the house headed their own households. Two of those rented their homes, and one owned the residence she lived in. Several examples help to put a more human dimension to these trends. The Harris sisters – Augusta, Frances, and Mary Ann – pooled their resources and lived in a house owned by Augusta, who also owned a store, although the census did not list an occupation for her or her sisters. Whether they operated or rented a store, the sisters certainly pooled their investment income. Between them they owned ninety-eight shares worth $9,800 in the Bank of Hamilton, which in 1900 would have yielded $784 in dividends. These women were aged between fifty-one and sixty-five, and they probably represented a not uncommon living arrangement. Certainly, the shareholder lists for Ontario investors indicate that many women with the same family name who lived in the same city invested in stock. Bertha Savage, a thirty-seven-year-old schoolteacher, lived at home with her widowed mother and two sisters, both of whom also worked. She owned twelve Canadian Bank of Commerce shares worth $600. Her mother, Elizabeth, owned three Commerce shares worth $200. It is very possible that Bertha and her mother inherited those shares from her deceased father, a possibility that, if true, underlines the willingness of parents to bequeath wealth to unmarried daughters in the era of the MWPLs. Whether she initially inherited them or not, we find Bertha Savage on the 1911 shareholder list as the owner of three more shares worth a total of $750. Since her mother was sixty-eight years old in 1901 and does not appear on the 1911 shareholder list, it seems clear that Bertha inherited her mother's three shares sometime after 1901. While the dividends paid out by the Bank of Commerce fluctuated somewhat, a conservative estimate is 7 per cent per year, which would in 1901, give her another $42 in yearly income to add to her salary of $525 from teaching.

At the other end of the earning spectrum, Emily Martin, a thirty-six-year-old who "shed [her] blood" on a "cruel sewing machine," also lived at home with her parents. She worked six months a year in a factory as a dressmaker and still managed to own ten Canadian Bank of Commerce shares worth $500. These shares in 1901 generated $35 to add to her employment earnings of $100. The fact that she had acquired one more share by 1911 suggests that the dividend income was important to her. Jessie Macdonald, a self-employed dressmaker, lived at home with her widowed mother and two sisters, one of whom was also a dressmaker and worked with Jessie out of their home. Jessie earned $175 a year and owned $5,000 worth of Bank of Hamilton shares. She was the oldest daughter and may have inherited these shares from her father. Whatever the case, since the Bank of Hamilton generally paid 8 per cent yearly in dividends, the payout from those shares would have amounted to $400 in 1901, well in excess of her earnings as a dressmaker!

Indeed, the 585 women investors in the Bank of Hamilton and the Canadian Bank of Commerce generated some $75,000 in dividend revenue in 1900 (assuming a conservative 7.5 per cent return), for an average addition to earnings of $128. If we take the estimate mentioned earlier of 42,800 shareholders in Canadian banks in 1913 and assume, conservatively, that half were women and that, on average, they owned $1542 worth of shares (the average for Ontario women in the Bank of Hamilton and the Commerce Bank in 1911), then a conservative 7.5 per cent dividend would yield just under $2.5 million in a single year. Whether looked at in the aggregate or in the context of an individual women's familial and personal financial situation, investing in bank stocks was an important enterprise for a significant number of women in Ontario in the late nineteenth and early twentieth century. Moreover, there are indications that women were far from passive holders of this stock. We know that 238, or 41 per cent of the women who owned in 1900, still held stock in these banks ten years later. One hundred and twenty-five had increased their holdings, 51 had decreased theirs, and 62 had stayed the same. Clearly, the earnings from these shares meant a great deal to those women. We do not know whether the other 347 shareholders sold all their stock, died, changed their name through marriage, or moved out of Ontario, but even on the basis of those we do know about, women were far from inattentive shareholders. Many definitely did change the composition of their portfolio over time.[26]

It is important to remember that our knowledge of the investment practices of these and other women is only partial, bounded as it is by time constraints and by the small slice of possible investments analyzed in this chapter. The experience of Anne McCullough makes the point. In 1900 she lived with her husband, John, and son, also John, in Hamilton. She owned $1,700 in shares of the Commerce and Hamilton banks, and her seventy-two-year-old husband, who was living on his own means, owned $1,400 of Hamilton bank shares. Anne died a widow in July 1922 and left $30,876, most of which went to her son. Half of that bequest was in bank and financial stocks: $5,100 in the Hamilton bank, $3,874 in the Commerce bank, $2,170 in the Bank of Montreal, and $4,692 in the Hamilton Provident Loan and Savings Company. But she also owned $980 in stock of the Steel Company of Canada, $790 in shares of Commercial Canners Ltd, $1,700 of Dominion Power and Transmission Company stock, and real property worth $4,560.[27] Undoubtedly, Anne McCullough had inherited some of these assets from her deceased husband, although she was an owner of stock in her own name as a married woman twenty years before her death. Small wonder that brokerage companies such as Aemelius Jarvis took the time to write and distribute booklets "specially written for women investors."[28]

This analysis of the gender of shareholders in a representative selection of Ontario's major financial institutions confirms the observation made in the earlier chapters that the MWPLs enabled more than simply married women. As well, the age distribution of women bank shareholders underlines the fact that the relatively young as well as the relatively old participated in these capital markets. While single women were increasing in numbers in Ontario in the late nineteenth century, their participation in the stock market reflected more than that demographic trend. Even as their numbers increased, their collective participation as stockholders outpaced that increase. In part as a result of the participation of single women, women, by the end of the century in Hamilton and probably in the rest of urban Ontario, were as apt to invest in stocks as were their male counterparts. From this perspective, the Hamilton probate data underestimate women's presence in capital markets. Younger women, many of whom would have been enabled by the changes in inheritance strategy made possible by the MWPLS, invested in significant numbers, numbers that the probate data could not reflect. This observation allows us to better understand the fact that the Hamilton probate data point to women owning more shares than men only in the late 1920s. In fact, this was not a phenomenon simply of the 1920s: during that decade many of the women who were active as shareholders in the late nineteenth century were dying. The 1920s Hamilton probate data, as indeed the case of Anne McCullough suggests, reflect a trend that had its origin some thirty years earlier.

4

The "fountain-head of all production": Land and Gender in Victoria and Hamilton, 1881–1901

In 1994 Royal LePage, a large Canadian real estate company, trumpeted in its issue of the *Homeowner* that single women had moved ahead of their male counterparts in home buying. "Clearly," the article concluded, "women believe in home ownership as a solid investment." Ten years later the company noted that women were becoming "an increasingly significant part of the market ... [They] are using their purchasing power to invest in real estate and have little trepidation about doing it alone."[1] Yet such activity was hardly as revolutionary as these and other similar reports imply. A century earlier, in one of the most comprehensive advice manuals written for businesswomen at the turn of the twentieth century, John Howard Cromwell had argued unequivocally that "real property ... owned and controlled by the single investor" fulfilled "to an exceptional degree all the requirements of the rules of investment." Indeed, he continued, "the direct ownership of real property may ... be considered to be the *most* advantageous general form of investment."[2] Accordingly, he devoted just under two-fifths of his 418 pages to a discussion of the advantages of real property as a home and as an investment for businesswomen.

Women (and men) living in Victoria and Hamilton in the late nineteenth and early twentieth century agreed. Probate data indicate that more investors put a larger proportion of their money in real property than in any other single investment sector in the time period covered in this study. As figures 4.1 and 4.2 demonstrate, rarely fewer than three-fifths of investors had landed assets. It is true that the value of those assets relative to other investments declined over time (often, especially in the case of Victoria, because property values declined in this period), but throughout the years studied real property continued to bulk large

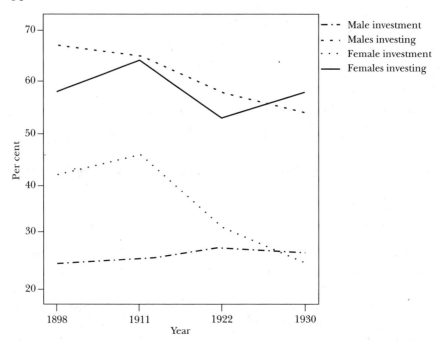

Figure 4.1

Investment in land by gender: Hamilton, 1898–1930

NOTE: Data are from table 1.5.

in a majority of probates in both cities. As we saw in chapter 1, the probate data also suggest that, even relative to men, women were very active as property owners. In fact, these data indicate that in the late nineteenth century probated women in both cities were more apt to invest in land than were probated men, and throughout the period women were more apt to invest a greater part of their capital in land than were men.

Indeed, it probably never would have occurred to a person walking in a Canadian city in 1901 that, according to the census of that year, a woman owned nearly every fifth lot, house, and store in the city (see table 4.1). For those cities over 5,000 in population, the incidence of female ownership varied only marginally. In the two largest cities in Canada, Toronto and Montreal, women owned 18 per cent of all real property; similarly, in cities with 5,000 to 20,000 population, women owned 17 per cent of all real property. This was a dramatic change from thirty years earlier, before the introduction of the MWPLS. Gordon Darroch and Lee Soltow, from their analysis of property ownership in Ontario in 1871, as indicated by the census of that year, esti-

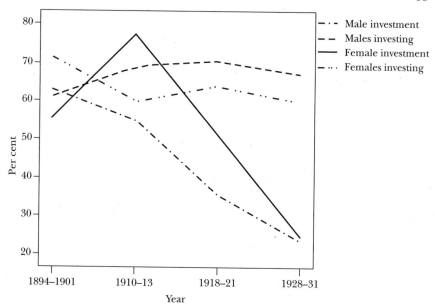

Figure 4.2
Investment in land by gender: Victoria 1894–1931
NOTE: Data are from table 1.4.

mate that "just 5 per cent of Ontario's adult women owned property in their own right."[3]

This chapter takes a closer look at the activities of women and men as land- and homeowners, paying particular attention to the interrelationships between gender, age, and city of residence. The data for much of the ensuing discussion consist primarily of assessment rolls for Hamilton and Victoria linked where possible to census returns primarily for the period 1881 to 1901. An extensive discussion of some of the challenges encountered in using these sources can be found in appendix 1.

We first provide some context for the distribution of property ownership in both cities. At a general level, historical literature yields two hypotheses concerning inequalities in urban property distribution. The so-called nostalgia interpretation posits that the smaller and more recently settled a community, the more equal the distribution of real property. A second perspective suggests that during a period of early industrialization property-holding will be relatively unequal, tending towards greater equality as the city enters a more mature and stable industrial phase. Canadian historians have considered both hypotheses. The work of Doucet and Weaver on Hamilton and Burley on Winnipeg has cast substantial doubt on the validity of the nostalgia perspective. Gordon Darroch, in his study of wealth-holding in Toronto in the late nineteenth century, has provided some support for the second hypothesis.[4]

The data presented in table 4.2 provide no support for the nostalgia or frontier thesis of relative equality. Severely skewed property distribution characterized both cities, most especially Victoria. Land sales for the four years prior to 1863 in Victoria had been under the virtual control of the Hudson's Bay Company. During that period the company sold nearly a third of all lots in Victoria to 182 buyers, in the process realizing close to $300,000.[5] Despite this substantial devolution of property, property-holding remained markedly unequal throughout the period covered. It is true that between 1863 and 1891 there is some indication of more equal distribution: if the bottom fifth experienced little change, the top fifth did lose control of close to 6 per cent of the value of city property. This gradual trend, however, did not continue in the 1890s. Both the increase in inequality signalled by the Gini coefficients and the increased share of the top 20 and 10 per cent of propertied holders point to a sharp increase in inequality during that decade. In a period of declining industrial output, the propertied elite increased their grasp of the city's real property assets at the direct expense of the other four-fifths. "We think," the manager of the British Columbia Land and Investment Company informed his superiors in London, England, "you would do well to recommend any of our clients to purchase real estate here ... careful buying should show a good result." During this period of deindustrialization, the moneyed elite liquidated much of their industrial related assets and transferred substantial capital to real property.[6]

The trend in property distribution in Hamilton lends support to the Doucet-Weaver and Burley position and some support for Darroch's findings on Toronto. The data for Hamilton in table 4.2 are from samples; so we might expect that the holdings of the wealthiest groups would be undercounted because of their tendency to own multiple properties, not all of which would be caught in the sample. Yet even allowing for some bias in that direction and, more importantly, assuming that the bias is constant across the period surveyed, it would seem that property distribution in Hamilton was somewhat less skewed than was the case in Victoria. Moreover, and consistent with the findings of Darroch for Toronto in a similar period, there is evidence of a small decline in inequality in the late nineteenth century. Hamilton also suffered an economic downturn in the 1890s, and as in Victoria, the top landholders during that period increased their control of property in the city. Yet property concentration remained substantially lower than in the more economically troubled city of Victoria and lower than had been the case in Hamilton in 1871.

Despite some fluctuation in the pattern of ownership evident in table 4.2, the overwhelming impression is of the constancy of inequality. This is especially the case for Victoria, where the top 10 per cent of property owners never owned less than half of the city's landed wealth. And in both cities, it should be noted, more than 80 per cent of the population over nineteen years of age owned no real property at all. Nor should these figures be particularly surprising, they fall – Victoria closer to the top, Hamilton closer to the bottom – within a range of inequality uncovered by researchers in other North American cities in this era.[7]

We have seen from our discussion of probate holdings in chapter 1 that the MWPLs made a positive difference to probated women's wealth-holding. Given the somewhat skewed age/life course position of those probated women, the question arises as to whether a more age-inclusive population of women experienced similar positive benefits. An examination of landholding by women in Hamilton and Victoria in the last quarter of the nineteenth century suggests that, as with participation in the stock market, the answer is a clear yes.

The highlights from table 4.3 are depicted in figures 4.3 and 4.4. Those figures point to the continuing wide gulf between the share of landed wealth held by women and that held by men. Clearly, parity of landed wealth-holding remained a pipe dream for women in the late nineteenth century. Yet unprecedented change was occurring. The figures nicely illustrate the upward trend of women's share of assessed wealth in both cities and especially in Victoria. That the trend commenced in Victoria even before the 1870s reflects the extreme gender imbalance in the small city in the 1860s. Indeed, the city fathers even organized immigration schemes whereby women were sent to the colony via ships from England in 1862, 1863, and 1870 in an effort to rectify the imbalance. Of more importance is the fact that in both cities women's share of assessed wealth increased in the 1870s, a time when married women were still restricted in their ability to own and dispose of real property. The MWPLs of the 1870s gave married women the right to dispose of and acquire personal goods outside their husbands' control, but they did not grant the same freedom to them in terms of selling real property. To sell land, married women required the signed

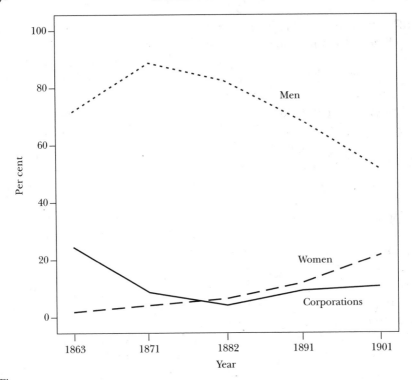

Figure 4.3
Assessed wealth by ownership shares: Victoria, 1863–1901

assent of their husbands. Nevertheless, this early upward trend suggests
that single and widowed women, and perhaps some married women
with the consent of their husbands, were increasingly entering the land
market. For some of those women, the 1870s legislation may have whet-
ted their appetites for more.

   Whatever the effect of the early MWPLs on land acquisition, it is evi-
dent that more substantial gains took place after the passage of the leg-
islation in the 1880s, which gave married women the right to buy and
sell land free from any legal restriction on their husbands' part. The
1880s legislation was most definitely facilitative and catalytic in effect.
Victoria women moved from owning one in every twenty-nine dollars of
landed wealth in 1871 to one in every five dollars of landed wealth at
the end of the century. The trend was similar for Hamilton women:
they owned one in every twenty-two dollars of landed wealth in 1871
and one in every seven dollars in 1899.[8]

   The trend was different for men in both cities. As women gained,
men lost. In fact, if the male share of landed wealth had stayed the same

Figure 4.4
Assessed wealth by ownership shares: Hamilton, 1871–99

at the end of the century as it had been in 1881, Victoria's men would
have held $4.7 million more and Hamilton's men $3.5 million more.
But their share declined, and the increase in women's share of landed
wealth accounted for 45 per cent of male decline in Hamilton and 47
per cent in Victoria. Corporate holdings accounted for much of the
rest of male decline in landed wealth-holding. Some might consider
that corporations, controlled as they were by men in the late nine-
teenth century, ought to be counted on the male side of the ledger.
Even if we do that, the share of landed wealth owned by "men" declined
from 91 per cent in 1881 Hamilton to 81 per cent in 1899; the respec-
tive decline for Victoria's "men" was 85 to 62 per cent. Women made
the biggest gains, and if we combine corporations and men, women
made the only gains.

Did those women who owned real property own lower-valued prop-
erty than men? In other words, relative to men, were the minority
of women who entered the market fringe players? The complete count
assessment data we have for Victoria allow a clearer answer to this

question than the gender-specific (women) complete count data for Hamilton. As the data in table 4.4 indicate, Victoria women were hardly fringe players. Yes, their average assessed value was always lower than that for men, but that average value increased from 50 per cent of men's in 1871 to 66 per cent of men's in 1901. In 1871 women numbered one in fourteen propertied individuals; by 1901 they numbered one in three, only fractionally under their proportion of the adult population as a whole (1 in 2.7 individuals over age nineteen was a women). Indeed, it can be argued that 1901 was a symbolically important moment for women landowners in Victoria. Women, as a proportion of all individual owners, increased from zero representation in the top fifth of landed wealth-holders in 1863 to 31 per cent of individuals in that category in 1901, only slightly under their proportion of all individual wealth-holders (33 per cent). And for the first time, women in the bottom two-fifths of wealth-holders in 1901 were under their proportion of all individual wealth-holders (women were 32 per cent of individuals in the bottom two-fifths of all wealth-holders, compared to 33 per cent of all individual wealth-holders), while, again for the first time, men bulked larger in the bottom two-fifths than they did as a percentage of all individual wealth-holders.

Moreover, the kinds of property owned by women closely approximated the type owned by men. After 1881 the proportion of property held by women with buildings was close to that held by men, and women tended to invest more of their wealth in buildings than did men, suggesting that they did not routinely enter the market via the purchase of relatively cheap unimproved lots; at least, they did not do so to any appreciably greater extent than did their male counterparts. Indeed, by 1901 women were almost as likely as men to own more than one property and more than one building.

What did Victoria women do with the property they owned? Table 4.5 suggests that they used their landed property in much the same ways as their male counterparts. Like men, most women who owned property owned their own homes. For those who did own their homes, the odds of their renting out other property did not vary by gender. Similarly, roughly equal proportions of men and women who did not own homes were active in the rental market. And finally, table 4.5 confirms that women were not markedly more likely than men to own unimproved lots. They had a palpable presence in Victoria's land market.

Hamilton women, too, were an increasingly significant presence in that city's land market. On the basis of sample data, it would seem that the average value of women's property was closer to that of men's than was the case for Victoria women. Indeed, by 1899 the average holding of a woman in Hamilton exceeded that of a man by some 20 per cent.[9] The number of propertied women increased in the twenty years after 1881 by a factor of 2.7, a growth rate lower than that for Victoria women (6.6) but impressive nonetheless.

We cannot compare the landholding patterns of Hamilton women with those of Hamilton men but we can compare them with the behaviour of Victoria women. In both cities over half the women who owned property owned their own homes, and only a minority of women homeowners also rented property. The similarities end there. In Hamilton, women who owned property but not a home were, like Mary Ford, who received $30 a month from the rent of four houses, heavily into the rental market, much more so than their counterparts in Victoria (tables 4.5 and 4.6).[10] The reason is clear: Victoria women were five times more likely to own only vacant lots than were women in Hamilton. In contrast to Hamilton women, a significant number of female landowners in Victoria entered the market via the purchase of vacant lots. Fewer Hamilton women exercised that option, probably because in 1901 there were fewer vacant lots to be purchased in that city.[11]

Kris Inwood and Sarah Van Sligtenhorst, in their careful study of the positive effect of the MWPLs on women in Guelph, Ontario, raise an interesting possibility. They wonder whether the increase in women's property holding in this period was to some extent simply an artifact of demographic recomposition. A number of studies have documented that the likelihood of owning property increases with age. Perhaps, they speculate, "an aging of the Canadian population ... may have contributed to the patterns visible in assessment-based studies."[12] Tables 4.7 through 4.10 have been designed in part to explore that proposition. The tables demonstrate the incidence of real property ownership for those twenty years and older in Victoria and Hamilton by marital status, sex, and age in the late nineteenth century. They are designed to be as comparable as possible with the relevant tables presented in the Inwood and Van Sligtenhorst study of Guelph in the same era (see appendix 2 for further discussion of the tables).

The tables exhibit a lot of data. For ease in comprehension, the discussion will be centred on the following proposition. Local demographic regimes were of fundamental importance in structuring the social patterns of landholding in late nineteenth-century Canadian cities. The contrasting landholding patterns exhibited by men in Victoria and Hamilton are a case in point. As table 4.8 indicates, the incidence of property ownership for Victoria men dropped dramatically during the decade of the 1880s (from 29.6 to 19.7 per cent). A combination of economic and demographic factors account for this decline. We have already noted that Victoria in the 1880s experienced significant economic development. The city's per capita industrial output increased dramatically, as did its population. The sharp decline in the incidence of property ownership is closely related to the changing age and marital status of Victoria men in this decade. Although the incidence of property ownership declined for all marital groups and most age categories, the decline was most dramatic for single men. Young single men flocked to the city in search of work. The average age of men twenty years and older fell from 39.4 in 1881 to 35.6 in 1891. Moreover, the proportion of single men in the twenty-and-over population rose from 47 per cent in 1881 to 57 per cent in 1891. The increased numbers of men put pressure on the availability of land, and prices shot up throughout the decade, peaking in the early 1890s. Younger men could not afford to buy. As prices declined in the 1890s, land was disproportionately acquired, as we have seen, by already wealthy property owners.

Why would Victoria men have had a lower incidence of ownership than Hamilton men in 1901 (19.7 compared to 23.4 per cent; see tables 4.8 and 4.10)? The question is on the surface puzzling because the incidence of ownership by married and single men in both cities is similar and the incidence of ownership by widowers in Victoria is higher than that of their Hamilton counterparts. A good part of the answer lies in the fact that fully 46 per cent of men aged twenty and older in Victoria in 1901 were single, compared to only 32 per cent of Hamilton men. Moreover, 37 per cent of all men 20 and over in Victoria were single and under the age of thirty-nine. The comparable figure for Hamilton men was only 28 per cent. In both cities in the 1890s single men struggled to obtain decent employment during severe economic downturns. One result was a similarly low incidence of property ownership by these men in both cities. In the 1890s young single men had to contend with a declining economy; they had few savings, and landowning remained outside their grasp. In both cities, then, single men had the lowest likelihood of owning property, in part because they tended to be much younger than married and widowed men. The fact that in Victoria there were simply many more younger single men than in Hamilton helps to account for the lower overall incidence of property ownership by men in the western city.

More generally, the incidence of male property ownership, as expected, did increase with age for most marital groups in most years in both cities. But, as we noted above and as was indicated in the sharp drop in percentage of assessed wealth owned by men in Victoria (see table 4.3), the overall incidence of male property ownership plummeted for all age and marital groups during the last twenty years of the nineteenth century. Our data for Hamilton is not as fulsome as that for Victoria, but on the basis of the significant decline in share of assessed wealth for Hamilton men between 1891 and 1901 (see table 4.3), we might suggest that a similar drop in the incidence of male ownership occurred in that city in the 1890s.

The data presented in tables 4.7 and 4.9 confirm what table 4.3 pointed to: women's experience in the land market in both cities differed considerably from that of men. The incidence of women owning property increased. Nor can these gains simply be attributed to an aging population. Married, widowed, and single women showed gains in the incidence of property ownership across virtually all age categories throughout the last two decades of the nineteenth century.[13] The incidence of property ownership by women in Victoria increased from 6.5 per cent of all women twenty years and older in 1881 to 12.3 per cent in 1901, a significant narrowing from the gap between men and women in 1881.[14] The gain in Hamilton was significant, if less impressive: from 4.7 per cent in 1881 to 6.5 per cent in 1901. In Victoria by 1901 the incidence of property ownership by single women exceeded that of single men, and in Hamilton the incidence of ownership by widowed women exceeded that of widowed men. While the incidence of male property ownership for Victoria men under thirty-nine declined from 13 per cent in 1881 to 9 per cent in 1901, it increased for similarly aged Victorian women from 3 per cent in 1881 to 7 per cent in 1901.

There is much to explain here. Why would single and widowed women in both cities have benefited from legislation aimed at married women? A substantial part of the answer has already been suggested in our discussion of changing inheritance patterns in chapter 2. Fathers and mothers were increasingly likely to pass on land and other wealth to their daughters in the confidence that the MWPLs would protect their inheritance from greedy husbands. Moreover men were less apt to exercise control over the inheritance they left their wives than had been the case before the legislation. Indeed, widows might have been able to protect their property more effectively during their marriage thanks to the MWPLS and might have been more willing to remarry, given the protection the laws provided for their assets. We might expect, then, that land ownership, a favourite asset of women in both cities over this time period, would increase for younger married women and for older married women, many of whom might have recently entered their second marriage. This supposition is strengthened because of the fact that the MWPLS were not retroactive to a time before their passage. They directly enabled women who married in the period and only indirectly those already married.

In fact, the data in tables 4.7 and 4.9 lend some support to these suppositions. Older married women in Hamilton experienced the largest gains in property ownership within the married women group. In Victoria the pattern was even more dramatic: under-forty-year-old married women increased their incidence of property ownership from 1.9 per cent of all married under forty in 1881 to 8.3 in 1901. The next closest rate of increase was that experienced by married women sixty years and older. What makes the Victoria case more dramatic is the fact that the rate of increase for married women at all ages was greater than that for widows and single women. In Hamilton – and, indeed, in Guelph – not only did the rate of increase for married women lag behind that for single women, but in each city married women were a minority of women property owners. Widowed women dominated in the two Ontario cities; married women dominated in Victoria (see table 4.11). The intercity contrast in the marital distribution of women property owners echoes the pattern found in the relative probated wealth-holding by women in both cities, and the probate data, as figures 4.5 and 4.6 indicate, suggest that that differential lasted well into the twentieth century.[15]

Why would Victoria women have a higher incidence of real property ownership than Hamilton and Guelph women, and why would married women in Victoria stand out as property owners and owners of probated wealth compared to their counterparts in the two Ontario cities? Clearly similar property law legislation could impact local communities in different ways. The MWPLS were enabling legislation, we must look more closely at local environments to understand the extent to which women were able to take advantage of those laws.

Can one account for this contrast by arguing that Victoria was in some sense a "frontier zone" that provided women greater possibilities

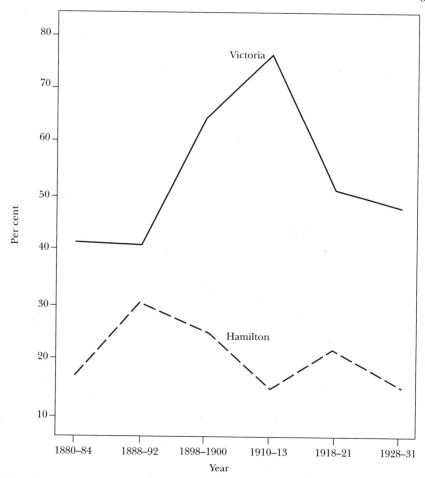

Figure 4.5
Women's probated wealth held by married women: Victoria and Hamilton,
1880–1931
NOTE: The figure is constructed from data in table 1.3.

for independent economic activity in the land market?[16] To do so, one
must proceed cautiously. Against any such argument are the simple
facts that in economic and chronological terms, the city was not a sim-
ple frontier zone. It was just short of fifty years old in 1891, and more
important, it was an industrial city of some complexity. Yet in the 1880s,
as we have seen, the city experienced the most dramatic population
increase of its history. By 1890 most of the people living in the city had
arrived in the previous decade. This was a boom period. Moreover as

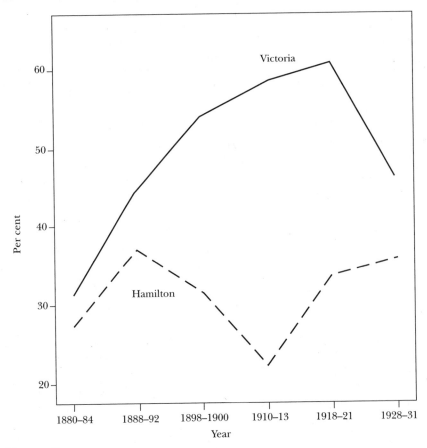

Figure 4.6
Married women probated as a percentage of all women probated: Victoria and
Hamilton, 1880–1931

table 4.12 suggests, the city's population density was less than that of
Hamilton, and especially so in the early 1880s.

The notion of open spaces is, of course, a central tenet of the frontier
thesis. Certainly, some well-placed contemporary observers were fond
of pointing to what they considered the very different environment for
property development in British Columbia compared to Ontario. The
solicitor for the Union of British Columbia Municipalities referred to
British Columbia as "a new country, where speculation in real estate is
rife ... where half the properties are usually vacant lands."[17] Perhaps
Victoria's relative openness, together with the MWPLs, helps to account
for the contrasting patterns of landholding by women in Victoria and
in Hamilton.

In fact, as we have seen, Victoria women, to a degree very like Victoria men, did take advantage of the city's relative openness and had a substantial number of undeveloped lots as part of their real estate holdings. By comparison, and very likely because undeveloped lots were not as easily available or, if available, not attractively situated, Hamilton women included relatively few undeveloped properties in their real estate holdings (table 4.13). It makes sense to think, then, that the entry costs into the land market favoured women in Victoria more than their counterparts in Hamilton. Certainly, developed land commanded, on average, a much higher assessed value than vacant lots; in Victoria in 1901, for example, the average assessed value for a vacant lot owned by a woman was $1,590, and for an improved lot, $3,951.

Yet there are several reasons for thinking that the relative openness of Victoria is by itself an insufficient explanation for the greater numbers of women landowners. In the first place, a substantial number of women in Victoria owned developed as well as undeveloped land. They could afford both (table 4.13). Secondly, given the extent of undeveloped land owned by Victoria's women, one would expect that the average cost of their properties would be considerably lower than that for Hamilton women, who primarily owned land with buildings. In fact, that does not seem to be the case. The average assessed value for a property owned by a woman in Victoria in 1901 was $3,334, and for a Hamilton woman, $2,660. It is true that salaries were higher in Victoria than in Hamilton, as was the general cost of living. Indeed, one would like to be able to translate these values into constant dollars, but interregional comparisons that would permit that conversion do not exist. Nevertheless, on the basis of the available data, it is hard to mount a case for cheaper land in the western city. Finally, it should be noted that men in Victoria were less, not more, likely to own land in 1901 than were their counterparts in Hamilton (tables 4.8 and 4.10). If the greater availability of vacant land in Victoria could be expected to account for greater ownership by Victoria women, why would the effect not be the same for men? It seems clear that other factors were at work.

One possible explanation argues that the frontier may have attracted people of a particular character: hardy souls who could fend well for themselves. The migration process may have selected women with characteristics suited to independent activity in financial and economic spheres. Yet there would seem to be difficulties with this formulation. In the first place, it is hard to test in any meaningful way. There are no significant differences in ethnic background (birthplace and nationality) between women who did and did not invest within and across cities. Moreover, such a formulation tends to demean the agency or spirit of those women who for whatever reason did not or could not trek west. Simply because Hamilton women did not invest to the same extent as those in Victoria does not mean that they did not wish to. It simply means that local factors militated against such activity to a greater extent in the eastern than in the western city.

Some American historians have pointed to more liberal laws in the west than in the east in the United States as an indication of a more egalitarian culture on the western frontier. This variant of the frontier thesis has been offered as a key factor in accounting for more female property ownership in Victoria than in the east. Chris Clarkson, in an insightful study, has suggested that a relatively more egalitarian culture in British Columbia may have been a factor in the greater gains achieved by Victoria's married women.[18] His argument is intriguing. He points to one clause in the 1887 British Columbia MWPL that was not in the 1884 Ontario MWPL as being of significance in this regard. That clause explicitly allowed husbands to transfer real and personal property to their wives "without the intervention of a trustee or trustees."[19] Clarkson privileges the actions of a prominent lawyer, rising politician and soon to be chief justice Theodore Davie, as the prime force behind this change. He argues that Davie's "understanding of the act was cultural, rooted in equitable practices and the aims of earlier British Columbia legislators."[20] Specifically, Clarkson suggests that this difference from the Ontario MWPL and the passage of other laws, most notably legislation to allow a husband to assign life insurance to his wife and children free from creditors' claims, reflected Davie's "desire to continue to allow husbands to transfer property to their wives, thereby preserving it from market liabilities ... unless the transfer was specifically made to evade creditors." In sum, Clarkson takes Davie pretty much at face value. He sees him as Davie wished to be seen: as one who believed that, in Davie's words, a "middle course should be adopted between debtor and creditor" and that the legislature would use, as Davie put it, "every means in its power to prevent fraud."[21]

A somewhat different explanation for Davie's actions, one which puts more stress on self-interest, is also possible. On the insurance bill, C.A. Holland, manager of the British Columbia Land and Investment Company (BCLI), a company to which Davie was behind payment on a very large loan, had this to say: "Davie's assets are practically nil with the exception of a large amount of life insurance which is ceded apon [*sic*] his children. Some three years ago whilst he was Attorney General he (no doubt simply for his own protection) passed an act which makes life insurance policies payable to wife or children absolutely unassailable by creditors though it permits of the insured making a change during his lifetime."[22] Correspondence in the BCLI papers refers to Davie as "a highly representative man," one who was looked to as an example for others to follow, one who had standing in the community. That correspondence also refers to Davie as a sharp operator, one who "all through this business ... has shown himself capable of acting in a very undesirable way," a view shared by the manager of the Bank of British Columbia, to which Davie also owed a large overdue sum about which "they are anxious ... chiefly because they do not trust him."[23] All of this is not to deny that Clarkson may have a valid point concerning the enabling part of those acts for women. Rather, it is to suggest that the motives lying behind those acts were rooted less in some fine notion of an egalitarian culture or even in a desire to protect creditors and more in the needs of an elite composed of, to a significant extent, men in debt. If a cultural explanation is to be offered for the different patterns of women's involvement in land and wealth more generally, then that culture might emanate from the degree to which British Columbia was a region of debtors compared to Ontario as a region of creditors.

In fact, however, it is difficult to know what impact this one clause had on actual behaviour. In the same MWPL, in phrasing identical to the 1884 Ontario MWPL, women were explicitly not allowed to transfer property for the purposes of defrauding creditors. On Clarkson's own evidence, British Columbia's judiciary disapproved of marital property transfers; "all transfers between husband and wife were treated as suspicious until proven otherwise," he concludes.[24] Clearly, the judiciary stood apart from this "egalitarian" culture.

But if courts commonly overturned transfers intended to avoid creditors, Clarkson shows that they upheld transfers by husbands to their wives when the purpose was to avoid inheritance taxes. The property so transferred would, while the husband was alive, be held in trust by his wife. After the husband died, the property would be hers to do with as she wished, free from any administrative or succession duties. Clarkson has uncovered an interesting inheritance strategy. Whether, however, one can then suggest, as he does, that the existence of such a strategy "may provide insight into reasons why married women held greater amounts of property in British Columbia than elsewhere" is more problematic. In the first place, there was nothing to stop women in Hamilton from employing the same strategy. The 1884 Ontario MWPL did not preclude property transfers between spouses unless they were deemed to be an attempt to defraud creditors. That married women in Hamilton did at times transfer property they owned to be held in trust by a third person is indicated by a court case involving Hortense Phelps, a married woman living in Hamilton in 1891. The land in dispute, Phelps explained to the judge, was "held in trust for me and belonged to me , but the deed was taken in the name of my ... father owing to the fact that I was a married woman and my husband was living apart from me , and it would encumber the title if the land were taken in my name as when I wanted to sell objections might be raised to the title owing to the fact that my husband did not join in the deed with me."[25] While the property transfer was occasioned by reasons different from those outlined by Clarkson, the point remains that such transfers in trust could and did take place in Ontario as well as in British Columbia.

Secondly, one has to wonder, as Clarkson himself does, about "the extent of these practices."[26] An individual would have to own a very large estate to be worried about avoiding inheritance taxes: property under $25,000 was exempt from any tax if bequeathed to a relative. Only 35 of 761, or 4.5 per cent, of probated estates filed by men and women in Victoria between 1880 and 1901 exceeded $25,000.[27] Either this practice was exceedingly common and thus kept estates in the non-taxable range, or, more probably, there were simply too few families with wealth of a level that would encourage widespread use of such a strategy in the first place.

While helpful, spatial and egalitarian notions of the frontier seem insufficient explanations for the differences in women's wealth-holding. A third characteristic, one related to the demographic structure of frontier communities, has greater explanatory power. If Victoria approximated the classic picture of a frontier settlement, one would expect to find a high ratio of men to women, high in absolute terms and high compared with the sex ratio of a more settled community such as Hamilton. As table 4.14 indicates, such was indeed the case.

Historians have not written much concerning the potential impact of sex ratios on social behaviour, and in the Canadian context at least, much of what has been written has been rather severely critiqued.[28] Economists have paid closer attention to the possible significance of unbalanced sex ratios. Ethel B. Jones has argued that in the United

States, states where men outnumbered women were more apt to support suffrage legislation, if only because men in those states were less at risk of losing their voting majority. Rick Geddes and Dean Lueck have explored the relationship between the passage of MWPLS in various American states and the sex ratios in those states. The null hypothesis was that "the gender makeup of a state does not influence women's rights." Geddes and Lueck have presented the argument that states with more men than women might have been more apt to favour MWPLS in an attempt to attract more women to their communities. Their results were somewhat inconclusive.[29] At a more general level, two social psychologists have been less reticent. Using a wide-ranging review of anthropological and historical literature, Marcia Guttentag and Paul Secord have argued that sex ratios "considerably above 100" for a sufficient period of time can have "dramatic social consequences."[30] They contend that high sex ratios give women more agency in their social interactions with men. They do acknowledge that "each situation is conditioned by a variety of other factors," factors that they subsume under the term "structural." Moreover, they warn that too high a sex ratio can lead men to take extraordinary measures to contain and control women.[31]

Were there any particular structural conditions in Victoria that might have restricted women's bargaining power with men? Adele Perry has argued that indeed there were. Non-heterosexual and non-white liaisons were severely proscribed. Moreover, she points out, married women in British Columbia were, on average, ten years younger than their husbands (the largest age differential of any Canadian province) and that this disparity in itself would have made it difficult for women to act with much independence.[32] In Victoria, however, the age differential was much less: in 1891 married women were, on average, only 4.6 years younger than their husbands, and married women with property were 5.7 years younger, only a slight difference. Importantly, the age difference was virtually the same in Hamilton (4.2 years). In this sense Victoria did not reflect the social structure of a frontier community. Perry's point concerning non-white liaisons is, however, quite relevant. Victoria throughout the period under review contained a very large number of single Chinese males. Given prevailing social proscriptions, these men, should be removed from the potential marriage market, and Victoria's sex ratio should be recalculated to reflect that fact. As table 4.14 indicates, even with the Chinese excluded, the sex ratio remains significantly high and much higher than in Hamilton.

It is important to look more closely at one aspect of the family living arrangements of the married women who owned property in both cities. Specifically, were these women more or less likely to live with their husbands than all women in each city? If they were significantly less likely to live with their spouses, what might that mean for their married state? As well, we want to know whether these living conditions varied across cities. Perhaps it is the case that the high number of "married" women property owners in Victoria compared to Hamilton can be accounted for by a relatively larger number of women living without their husbands in the house. In this sense they may have been married in name only. In fact, from this perspective the results are somewhat surprising. In Victoria 6.8 per cent of all married women did not have a spouse in the house in 1901. In Hamilton the proportion was similar: 8 per cent of all married women did not have a spouse in the house. What is surprising is that in Victoria 7.6 per cent of married women with property did not have a spouse in the house, close to the proportion for all married women in that city. By contrast, in Hamilton the spouses of 20 per cent of married women property owners were not in the house in 1901.[33]

Whatever the reasons for the differences, the central point to note for this chapter is that the greater number of married women with property in Victoria compared to Hamilton cannot be accounted for by the presence or absence of a spouse. Rather, if one is inclined to think that married women without spouses should be put in a separate analytic category from married women with spouses, then the difference in the chances of married women owning property in Victoria would be increased relative to Hamilton, not decreased.

Did the high sex ratio condition the Victoria marriage market in such a way that married women were able to participate in the land market with more frequency than their Hamilton counterparts? Such an inference is plausible. One might expect that market to operate at two levels: that of initial entry and that of re-entry. Young never-married women might be in a position to acquire some financial independence via marriage to men of property. In some cases the prospective bride might be able to convince her husband-to-be that some of his property or at least any property she might have inherited should be in her name only. Given the unbalanced sex ratio, widows, especially those with property inherited from their first husbands or from parents, might be expected to have greater opportunities for remarriage in Victoria than in Hamilton. At a general level, marriage patterns are not inconsistent with these possibilities. In fact, women did marry more quickly in Victoria than in Hamilton: in 1891, 60.7 per cent of women between the ages of twenty and thirty-four in Victoria were married; the comparable figure for Hamilton women was 45.3 per cent. In 1901 the respective figures were 55 and 42 per cent. Widows remarried more easily as well. Between 1880 and 1900 Victoria widows were involved in 11 per cent of all marriages that were registered in that city; the comparable figure for Hamilton is 6.9 per cent.[34]

To what extent did the marriage patterns of married women with property reflect these general trends? In the first place, married women in Victoria with property were older than married women without property (42.5 years compared to 36.3 years) and, indeed, were older than married women with property in Hamilton (42.5 years to 39.8 years). This pattern suggests that widows played a prominent role in marriages involving propertied or about to be propertied women. An analysis of marriage registrations for the city of Victoria between 1880 and 1900 confirms this supposition: as we have seen, widowed women were involved in 11 per cent of all marriages; by contrast, 25 per cent of all married women with property who married in Victoria in those years were embarking on at least their second marriage.[35] Many, if not all, of these women brought property with them to their second marriage, and, most importantly, they maintained that property in their own names. While there are instances of younger women marrying much older propertied men, this was not the norm. As we have seen, the average difference in age between married women with property and their husbands was not very different from that of all married women and their husbands. Nevertheless, the data in the marriage registrations do support the notion of a two-tiered marriage market in Victoria. The 75 per cent of propertied women found in the marriage registrations who were marrying for the first time did so at an average age of twenty-six, twelve years younger than that of the widows who remarried. Moreover, the difference in age between a propertied woman marrying in Victoria for the first time and her husband was six years, identical to that between the remarrying widow and her new husband. Put crudely, Victoria's marriage market made it possible for a woman who desired security and property as well as love to marry a man close to her own age.

The contrast in the marriage markets in the two cities is also an important context within which to understand the relatively larger land and general investment activity of widows in Hamilton and married women in Victoria. Hamilton's widows may indeed have benefited from the MWPL while married, but given the nature of the marriage market, they would have found it relatively more difficult to remarry than did widows in Victoria. Such a supposition also helps to account for the relatively larger number of married women in Victoria who left wills than in Hamilton.

Attractive as this line of reasoning is, it has its limits. As table 4.15 indicates, when one combines married and widowed property owners, the incidence of ownership was, especially after the passage of the most enabling of the MWPLS, much higher in Victoria than in Hamilton. In other words, the difference between the investment activity of different marital groups in Victoria compared to Hamilton cannot simply be attributed to the overlapping effects of marriage market and life cycle. Given the different sex ratios in the two cities, women in Victoria may have remained in a married state for a longer time than did women in Hamilton. But the point remains that whether married or widowed, more Victoria women were landowners and general investors than was the case in Hamilton.

For Victoria women, at least, land acquisition depended on more than opportunistic first or second marriages and/or inheritance as widows. Forty-one women who owned land in Victoria in 1891 or 1901 and did not own city land in 1882 were married in the city between 1872 and 1880. In all likelihood all of these women acquired land after the passage of the 1887 MWPL. By the time they acquired land, twenty of the forty-one were widows, four had remarried, and seventeen were still married to their first husband. Clearly, a significant number of women not actively in the marriage market benefited from the passage of the MWPLS. It may be that the combination of those laws and local economic and especially demographic conditions created a climate more conducive to property ownership by women in Victoria than for their Hamilton counterparts. Although it is difficult to document, it may well have been the case that potentially advantaged women (women who might have some opportunity of property ownership) observed what others in their class were doing and at some level followed suit. It may well have been that a form of networking between women took place and thereby helped to attract others to participate. Testing this hypothesis requires close attention to possible interaction between women and/or their husbands, research difficult to do and beyond the scope of this book.

Yet from a different perspective, the issue of relations within families cannot be easily ignored in a study that examines women's ownership and, by implication at least, control of property. The legal documents that point to the patterns of behaviour outlined above are for the most part silent on the issue of decision-making. Were, for example, married women who rented properties in their own name simply owners in name only? Were they able to spend their returns independent of spousal influence? Was such revenue more often considered to be part of the family's income? If the last was most likely the case, does this mean that women's autonomy was significantly diminished? Or was the ability to make an independent monetary contribution to family welfare in and of itself a source of pride and independence? It is also quite possible that married women were "hiding" property from their husband's creditors. It is very difficult to tease out answers to these questions from census and assessment data alone. What an analysis based on such evidence does provide, however, is parameters within which some women had at least the potential to act independently in areas of wealth management. Qualitative evidence can suggest the range, if not the frequency, of such behaviour.

Undoubtedly, some found themselves in the position of Catherine Worrell of Hamilton, who in 1882, at the age of eighteen, had married her husband, Harry, after he had verbally promised "to make me well off." Two weeks after the marriage he gave her a present of a lot and house in Hamilton for which she signed the deed of ownership. But her husband soon ran into financial troubles and commenced drinking heavily. He put the property up for auction and ordered his wife to appear at the lawyer's and sign the necessary conveyances. "I had to go and sign the deed when he told me ... I signed it. I had to because I was scared to getting abused, to get licked. I had to do just as he said. I would get it if I did not ... He had licked me before for no reason that I know of." It is hard to know just how representative this behaviour was. But beyond that issue Catherine Worrell's is a tale that operates on at least two levels. At one level it provides a window into a sordid domestic situation, one that scholarship has documented in many other instances.[36] At another, the Worrell case can be read as an example of a woman coming to understand her rights in the era of the MWPLs. We know of Worrell's plight because she had the courage to leave her husband and institute a court case in 1886 to overthrow the sale on the twin grounds of signing under threat and signing underage. As she admitted to the court, when the sale took place she did not understand that she was legally underage. By 1886 she had acquired a firmer sense of her entitlements under law, and despite her vulnerability as a woman living apart from her husband, she went to court to realize those rights. While the legal issues in the case were not directly related to the MWPLS, the sense of entitlement that underlay Worrell's actions nicely reflected the enabling implications of those laws. Although we do not know how the case was resolved, one point is clear: in her view, "My husband has no claim on the property. He said he would buy it for me and did do so," and she was determined to retrieve it.[37]

Harriet Vint, also of Hamilton, evinced a similar attitude. With her own money she had bought property on which she wished her husband, a carpenter, to build a house. As she put it, "My husband did my business for me ... did work for me." She granted him a general authority to order supplies, and he, in effect, acted as her agent. "I let him look after my business for me." But she drew the line at working with a Mr Ripley, who, she claimed, was living with his housekeeper in sin while his wife was in an asylum. Vint therefore refused to pay Ripley's claim and asserted that her husband had exceeded his instructions in this case. She lost the case, but her strong proprietorial attitude rings clear.[38]

Mary Howard, who lived near Victoria, did not own any property in her own name. She realized her vulnerability. "John has not made a will in my favour," she confided to a friend. "He always says I am alright." Mary, who claimed she worked "like a nigger" and wanted "John to pay off some of the mortgage on the house," expressed an anxiety that must have been felt by many married women in this era. For those who already owned some property or other security, the ability to preserve its worth without sacrificing ownership to another, even if that other was a husband, was an empowering development in their lives.[39]

Other sources also speak to women's involvement in the acquisition and management of properties. Moore and Davis was a successful real estate and property management firm operating in Hamilton in the last half of the nineteenth century. The firm placed mortgages, collected rent, saw to property repairs, and bought and sold property on behalf of a wide range of clients. In the words of the company's biographers, the operations of firms such as Moore and Davis "allow insight not only into business cycles and structural changes in capitalism, but also into important social relationships."[40] Indeed they do. In particular, the outgoing correspondence of the firm managed by William Pitt Moore and John Gage Davis points to the importance of women to their business. A simple tabulation of the gender of those who received letters from Moore and Davis between 1871 and 1901 highlights the growing

importance of women to the firm's affairs.[41] Letters sent to men, of
course, may have concerned women; so this is an underrepresentation
of the importance of women to the firm's business. For the whole of the
period, women received 304 of the 2,315 letters that the company sent
to individuals with a known gender, or about 1 in every 8 letters written
by the company. This measure of women's involvement in its business
indicates that they became increasingly prominent over the later part
of the nineteenth century. Women received 1 of every 14 letters sent
between 1871 and 1875 and 1 in every 6 between 1898 and 1901.

The correspondence indicates that propertied women paid extremely
close attention to the management and disposition of their financial
assets, no matter how modest those assets might have been. Moore and
Davis was generally quite careful to communicate at length with its
female clients. Rarely did it attempt to dictate. Rather, the firm gener-
ally adopted a deferential tone, as in its correspondence with Mrs E.
Byrne in May of 1880. After explaining that a fence was down on a
rental property of hers, it advised fixing it, concluding with "don't you
think you had better do it? Please let us know." After outlining the pros
and cons of a possible sale, the letter concluded with the query "don't
you think it would be as about as well to accept?"[42]

The firm's advice, however, was not always accepted. Although we
only have outgoing letters from Moore and Davis, its correspondence
with Mrs Eliza Thompson points clearly to her determination to mange
her property with close care. Thompson, a married woman who in
1881 owned two rental properties with a combined assessed value
of $1,720, for example, would only rent her property by the year,
despite the recommendation by Moore and Davis to let by the month.
As well, she steadfastly refused to insure her property with the company
suggested by Moore and Davis, arguing that she had heard that
the insurance company was in financial trouble. The land company
undoubtedly received a commission from the insurance company for
each policy issued so Moore and Davis tried hard, but failed, to change
Thompson's mind.[43] Moreover, the correspondence suggests that she
and other women closely scrutinized charges and expenditures. Miss
Kate Stamp received an apology in July 1883 for an "oversight" by the
firm in not sending $4.87. In this instance, apparently, someone else
did the accounts, "which is why we missed it." After a successful trans-
action in June 1883, Moore and Davis wrote to Eliza as follows, in
a clear attempt to head off any complaints: it would charge regular
commission, to "which we are sure you will not object as it was hard

work to get it in that shape." The firm only charged commission, as agreed, at 1 per cent less than it usually charged, Moore and Davis wrote with reference to another transaction later that same year; "there is no law to govern that; it is of course as may be agreed between parties." The firm in the same letter had to justify its commission on property sales as well.[44]

The company's correspondence with both men and women also reveals that many renters were women and that these women were well aware of their rights. In April 1889 a Mrs Hartley, who ran a small business in rented premises, offered to pay part of her overdue rent and made it clear that "the counter, shelving and awnings" belonged to her.[45] Women seemed to routinely bargain for better rental rates: Mrs Givens wanted a yearly, not a monthly, rental, as did Mrs Counsell, Moore and Davis informed the owner, James Beaucroft, in January 1880. Later that same month the company told Thomas Beasley that the "woman who wanted to take the shop on King Street for a Confectionary" desired a better deal. Miss Ross, Moore and Davis wrote to Mr J. Gillespie in April 1880, would only take the house for four months and indeed threatened to "leave May 1 if the sewer is not connected." Women valued well-maintained properties. In April, Thomas Woodruff was told that Mrs Burns, who lived next door to his property, wanted the fence repaired immediately. In May, Mrs James Kelley demanded that a fence on her rented property be repaired. In May 1882 Moore and Davis informed Eliza Thompson that Mrs Hodson would not take the house for $13.52 plus the water tax but might take it for $14 if Thompson paid the taxes and water rates. In addition, she wanted some wallpapering and whitewashing done. A year later, when Thompson attempted to transfer the water tax to her tenant, Hodson refused to renew.[46]

In fact, the correspondence strongly suggests that Moore and Davis routinely conducted its rental affairs with women. The company informed Mrs Byrne that "Mrs. Doyle in No 11 owes two months rent and says her husband works out of the City and that she will pay it on Saturday, which is the best we can do." "We have tried," Moore and Davis wrote to Eliza Thompson in September 1881, "to get the rent from O'Donnell and she says her child is sick and her husband absent – so that she cannot pay until the first of next month." The phrase the "tenant's wife was in" recurs throughout the correspondence.[47] Clearly, there was a class difference between women who owned and those who rented. But agency was not the perquisite of owners only. Nor was property management simply a man's world. Whether as owners or renters, women were actively involved in negotiating rents, maintaining property, and protecting their rights to that property.

Our examination of women's wills has underlined the meticulous care with which items to be bequeathed were enumerated and given to descendants.[48] In this context the delight with which women cared for the items they owned is quite clear. More generally, scholars have been quick to equate property ownership with some, however qualified, degree of independence. Indeed, the sufficiency of the notion of a "modest competency" underlines a great deal of social and economic analysis into the lives of nineteenth-century families.[49] The following cases suggest that propertied women – those who owned property, however "modest," in their own names – certainly enjoyed and carefully nurtured that sense of independence.

In June 1886 R.G. Tatlow, a real estate and insurance agent, and his wife were boarding in British Columbia, pending the construction of a new home. His wife was especially tired of living in someone else's residence and awaited moving day with an impatience sparked by the fact that "the house is going up on her lot." She would never again board she assured her husband, although as Tatlow went on to write, "she has already hinted at 'board' [for him]."[50] Mrs Tatlow's satisfaction and psychological contentment on owning her own home is obvious.

In 1891 Sarah Hayward, the wife of a local coroner, was one of the top ten women landowners in Victoria. She had acquired most of the land in the 1880s. Scattered correspondence in her family papers suggests that her husband, also a substantial landowner, did not presume to act on her behalf in land transactions. On receiving an offer to purchase a lot owned by his wife, Mr Hayward warned the prospective buyer that "it must be understood that this must be subject to confirmation by Mrs. Hayward." While he was willing to advise his wife, "The property is no good to us," he stopped far short of dictating the answer: "will you let me know as soon as possible what you think about it?" And so she did, agreeing with her husband that the property should be sold but setting terms different from those proposed by him.[51] Clearly, Sarah Hayward managed her own property, and her husband respected that authority.

In this period, mortgage companies, as we shall see in the next chapter, were cautious in granting loans to married women. The manager of one large mortgage and loan company in Victoria advised against granting a mortgage to one married woman, despite the property being "very desirable," because the husband was "very undesirable."[52] Press reports and politicians echoed the fear that the new MWPLS facilitated fraud, and certainly, as Lori Chambers has demonstrated, Ontario court cases indicate that many married couples attempted to use those laws to defraud creditors. Yet it should be noted that the laws passed in Ontario and British Columbia in the 1880s made it much more difficult for married couples to practise fraud with impunity. Judges in Ontario, in British Columbia, and, as Shammas has noted, in many jurisdictions in the United States became increasingly strict in their decisions and protective of creditors' rights.[53]

Indeed, in unintended ways, attempts by married men to defraud creditors by transferring property to their wives actually opened up opportunities for some wives to gain greater economic independence. We noted in the introduction the case of Mrs Dieckman, who fought a claim by her husband to repossess a business he had signed over to her. She claimed that her husband was "perfectly sober" when the transaction occurred "and that she took the business, paid all the debts, and saved it from ruin." She had no intention of giving it up.[54] In 1904 Mr Cammell of Hamilton sued his wife for recovery of a hotel that he had deeded to her two years previously. He said both had agreed that the transfer of title would be simply temporary and that he could reassume ownership whenever he pleased. Mrs Cammell, however, refused to give up her newly acquired property. She informed the court that she had been married to her husband for twenty-two years and that for the last four or five her husband had taken to drink and she was worried about providing for her two children. Her husband, she said, had refused to pay two creditors and did not want her to pay them, since the transactions had been conducted under his, not her, name. Ignoring him, she paid the debts, upgraded the furnace and roof of the hotel, and began to collect the rents even though, as she admitted, she had had no part in the running of any business since she had married. She was determined, she stated, to provide for her children, and since she could not trust her husband in his present state to do so, she would not give up the property. The court, recognizing Mr Cammell's attempt to use the MWPL to defraud creditors, dismissed the suit.[55] In a wonderfully ironic way, Cammell had provided his wife with a real chance for economic security and financial independence. And in a determined and even courageous manner – he was at times very aggressive, if not abusive – she seized the opportunity.

Clearly, women were actively involved in property issues in Hamilton and Victoria. The increase in their incidence of ownership, in both absolute terms and relative to the holdings of men, was significant in both cities. Clearly, too, the MWPLs enabled more than married women to participate in the land market. Younger single as well as older widowed women owned and rented properties in greater numbers over the course of the late nineteenth century. While we cannot know the degree to which all women who had legal title to property also exercised real control over their assets, we can suggest that the expectation was increasingly that women should have such control. Yet the patterns of ownership varied across the two cities. Whether one favours the cultural/frontier interpretation put forward by Clarkson or the demographic argument focusing on dramatically different sex ratios or on a combination of the two, a more general and significant observation can at this point be made. The MWPLs had a variable impact, filtered and perhaps conditioned as they were by customs, economic structures, and demographic regimes at the local level. Much of the historiography on the presumed impact of the MWPLs has focused on courts, newspapers, and provincial or state units of analysis. These sources tell us what some contemporaries thought. As Bernard Bailyn argued two decades ago, routinely generated sources of the type used in this book allow one to uncover latent trends, processes that contemporaries did not recognize but which were nonetheless occurring.[56] Their excavation permits us to see how many women, albeit still a minority, were accessing the tools of capitalism and were quite happy to use those tools in many of the time-honoured ways pioneered by their male (and some female) predecessors.[57] In this sense, just as the first wave of women's rights advocates were in many ways conservative, so too were the less voluble, but perhaps more powerful, late nineteenth-century wave of women capitalists. It is to their activities in the areas of mortgaging, consumption, and business that we now turn.

5

Stretching the Liberal State: Legal Regimes, Gender, and Mortgage Markets in Victoria and Hamilton, 1881–1921

Mortgages were key financial instruments in the late nineteenth and early twentieth century. Stock markets were only just emerging; so land and mortgages were convenient and generally well-understood markets for the investment and raising of capital. To the extent that land was the major part of most families' wealth-holding, the mortgage market probably represented the major source for credit for most families in this period. Clearly, purchasing property was the single biggest pursuit underwritten by mortgage capital. Yet, as the Toronto *Globe* averred in 1870, "there may be twenty very cogent reasons why a man should [take out a mortgage]." Indeed, studies of mortgaging in the urban United States in the late nineteenth century have emphasized that mortgage money was used for a wide range of purposes. One comprehensive study of mortgaging in Detroit during the last two decades of the nineteenth century has concluded that the financing of property purchases accounted for only 30 per cent of mortgage investment.[1] People employed mortgage money to improve property, facilitate business ventures, acquire personal property, pay off other loans, and more generally, simply to enhance their immediate standard of living.

In the time period covered in this study, individuals dominated the mortgage market. As Doucet and Weaver have noted, institutional "share of the mortgage market may have remained smaller than that serviced by individuals until as late as the 1960s."[2] In part, the dominance of this market by individuals reflects the ease with which small investors could amass knowledge of local reality possibilities compared with the difficulties of so doing for the "more daring stock investment."[3] Perhaps because mortgages touched the lives of most people, popular attitudes towards them were decidedly ambivalent, if not invariably negative. "A curled knot of snakes," as one saying went, "is not as deadly as the signature to a mortgage."[4] Few wished to be seen as money-lenders: nearing the end of his illustrious public career and blithely overlooking his less public business career, Sir John A. Macdonald assured the House of Commons, "I would never be" a moneylender.[5] Mortgagees were commonly depicted as grasping and mean-spirited, as in Joanna Wood's 1894 novel, *The Untempered Wind*. "His father and he went that day to see the old man who held the mortgage. He was a shrewd old miser, and was fain to secure himself in every way against anxiety and loss." "Nick Perkins, the Money Lender," in Paul Gardiner's 1900 collection, *The House of Cariboo and Other Tales from Arcadia*, could not wait to foreclose on his mortgages. "Almost daily now since the beginning of the month which marked the end of the two years of the mortgage [he] and his horse and buggy drove along the [mortgaged property] ... he would deliberately look about him with that insolent proprietary air so common among men of his class."[6]

Women were often deemed to be no match for men of that sort. A "mortgage on their home," Amelia Barr wrote in her novel *A Knight of the Nets* in 1896, "was a dreadful alternative to these simple minded women; they looked upon it as something of a disgrace." Hard labour was a better alternative for these two spinsters. "'A lawyer's foot on the threshold,' said Janet, 'and who or what is to keep him from putting the key of the cottage in his own pocket, and sending us into a cold and ruthless world? No! No! Christina. I had better by far lift the creel to my shoulders again. Thank God I have the health and strength to do it!'" Barr depicted the classic stereotype of women pitted against the heartless lawyer, the embodiment of a cold and ruthless world. And in those rare instances where women were themselves the mortgagees or, more usually, the wives of the mortgagees, they were seen as "would-be" women. "His [the mortgagee's] upstart wife had long been urging him to foreclose the mortgage," Mrs James C. Thompson wrote in her *Sketches from Life: Being Tales on the Ten Commandments and Various Texts of the Scriptures* (1876), "as she was ambitious to show off her newly-acquired dignity by playing the lady of the manor, and her husband, a coarse, narrow-minded, uneducated man, very much under the dominion of his would-be lady wife, intimated to Mr. Maitland [the mortgagor] this intention, unless he were not paid his money immediately."[7]

Yet there was another perspective. John Howard Cromwell, in his book of advice to American businesswomen, considered mortgages to be good investments for women, as that type of investment was "long-established and well-known." He felt that "a mortgagor will, if necessary, refuse to pay other debts in order to pay the interest upon a mortgage which is a lien upon his property, because, otherwise, he may lose the house which shelters him and his family". "It must be remarked," he concluded in his fifty-three-page chapter on mortgages, "that search and investigate as diligently as we may, no form of loan investment which, in points of safety, simplicity, certainty of income, and freedom from the demands of an arduous and irksome vigilance, will be found to be equal to loans which are secured by satisfactory bonds and mortgages upon real estate."[8] Did women listen to and act on the advice of people such as Cromwell? Little is known about the role of women as either mortgagees (lenders) or as mortgagors (borrowers). We do know from scattered studies of individuals that women participated as lenders, but only two published studies appear to have to a greater or lesser extent systematically compared the behaviour of women and men as mortgagees.[9] Examining women in rural mortgage markets in nineteenth-century Michigan, Charles Heller and John Houdek claim that their analysis was the first to differentiate between men and women lenders. They discovered that women held one of every six mortgages in their study area between 1841 and 1899 and that that participation increased to one in five during the last two decades of the century. Heller and Houdek concluded that women seem to have been as knowledgeable as men and that they did not fill a specific niche reserved simply for women.[10] As part of their article on the impact of the MWPLS on women in Guelph, Ontario, Kris Inwood and Sarah Van Sligtenhorst briefly charted the rise of women's participation in the purchase and sale of land and the taking and giving of mortgages in that community during the latter half of the nineteenth century, and they concluded that by 1901 women's participation in these financial transactions was nothing short of "remarkable."[11] The MWPLS may well have encouraged women to participate in their own names in this financial sector to an unprecedented degree. Moreover, given the importance of mortgage debt to household and other finance in this era, it might very well be the case that women were significant underwriters of general economic growth in a period when they have most often been seen as limited to facilitating household matters.

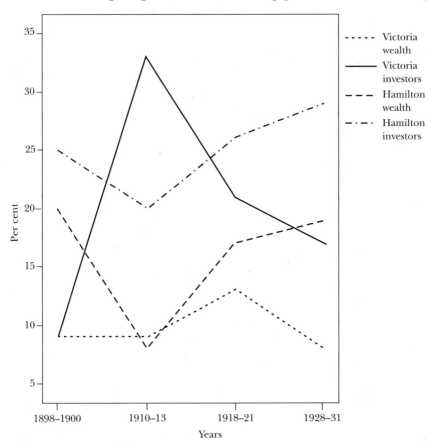

Figure 5.1
Women as lenders in the mortgage market from probate data: Victoria and
Hamilton, 1898–1931

This chapter seeks to chart and understand the significance of the
roles played by women in this central capital market. The following sec-
tion provides a first look at women's roles as mortgagees and mortgag-
ors and as buyers and sellers of property in Victoria and Hamilton. An
explanation for the at times similar and at times contrasting profiles is
offered by situating the activity patterns in the context of different legal
regimes in each province. The analysis then moves to a more detailed
examination of women as actors in the mortgage sector and demon-
strates the extent to which female controlled capital facilitated urban
and general economic development in this era.

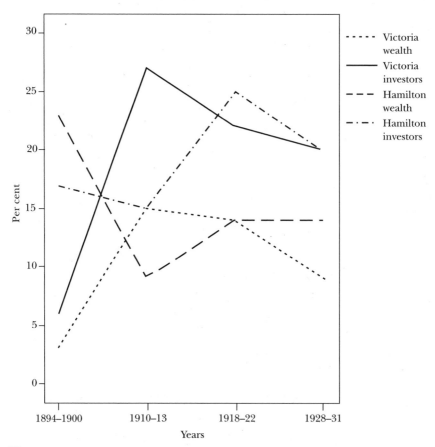

Figure 5.2
Men as lenders in the mortgage market from probate data: Victoria and
Hamilton, 1898–1931

We have seen from our examination of probated wealth that women
were not strangers to the mortgage market (figure 5.1). Mortgage
investment was an important part of the portfolio of many women in
this period. Interestingly, for Victoria women (and men), that interest
seems to have declined, especially after the pre–World War One boom.
The reverse was true for Hamilton women. After 1911, their investment
in mortgages increased. Very likely, these contrasting investment pat-
terns reflect the harsher land collapse in Victoria compared to Hamil-
ton in the postwar era. Land prices stabilized more quickly in Hamilton
than in Victoria and most likely than in other western cities in this
period. While the pattern is different within each city, it is nonetheless

true that, according to the probate data, women in Hamilton were always more apt to invest in mortgages than were men, and Victoria women either exceeded or were only slightly less likely to invest than were Victoria men (figures 5.1 and 5.2). Throughout the period, single and widowed women in both cities invested in mortgages more often than did married women. Those non-married women who invested in mortgages were often living on their own means, and for them, mortgage investment was a major part of their portfolios (usually in excess of one-third of their total investments for women in both cities) and generated a significant amount of their income. The probate data do not yield much more information than that. Only rarely were the outstanding mortgages actually detailed as to number held, specific amounts, interest rates, and to whom the money was lent. For that information, one has to look elsewhere.

The abstract deeds to property for Hamilton and the mortgage and sales books for Victoria provide information on credit transactions and sales transactions with property as the unit of analysis. I have collected all transactions for Victoria in 1881, 1891, 1901, and 1921. Given the intense real estate activity in that city in the pre–World War One boom period, I have collected all transactions for Victoria in 1911 only for the months of February, June, and November.[12] There are seventeen microfilm reels at the Archives of Ontario detailing property transactions for Hamilton between the years circa 1799 and 1911. Each reel provides data arranged chronologically by survey areas. I have taken all the information from nine of the reels for 1881, 1891, and 1901.[13]

Figures 5.3 and 5.4 provide a first look at the place of women in the mortgage markets of Victoria and Hamilton in the late nineteenth and, for Victoria, early twentieth century. In both cities the presence of women mortgagees and mortgagors acting alone or with other women increased significantly following the passage of the MWPLS in the 1880s. Women's participation as mortgagees in Victoria rose from one in eleven in 1881 to a little under one in four in 1901 and declined somewhat to just under one in five in 1921. In Hamilton, women's participation rose from one in five in 1881 to one in three in 1901. Women mortgagors in Victoria increased from one in twenty-four borrowers in 1881 to one in five in 1901 and just under one in four in 1921. In Hamilton, women mortgagors rose only from one in fifteen in 1881 to one in ten in 1901. While women's participation rates as mortgagees and mortgagors increased in both cities, they did not rise at the same rate. Interestingly, in Victoria, women's participation as mortgagors

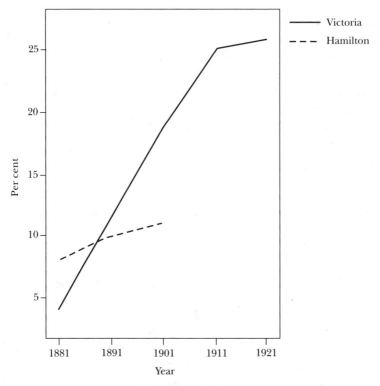

Figure 5.3
Women mortgagors as a percentage of all mortgagors: Hamilton and Victoria,
1881–1921

increased even after the pre–World War One boom, suggesting that
some, at least, of that debt was carried over into the postwar era. In a
finding that confirms that suggested by the probate data, women mort-
gagees in Victoria shied away from the mortgage market following the
collapse of the boom. Yet in that city the difference in the involvement
of women as mortgagees and as mortgagors pales in comparison to the
contrast between the profile of women mortgagors and women mort-
gagees in Hamilton. Whereas in Victoria by 1901, women constituted
over a quarter of all participants as mortgagees and a fifth of all mort-
gagors, by the same date in Hamilton, women accounted for more than
a third of all participants as mortgagees and only a tenth of all partici-
pants as mortgagors.

The same participation pattern as that for women mortgagors is evi-
dent for women acting singly or with other women as sellers of prop-
erty. In Hamilton between 1881 and 1901 these women fluctuated at

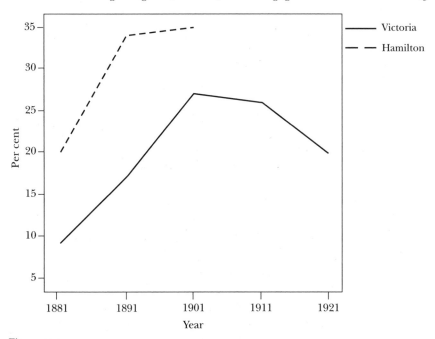

Figure 5.4
Women mortgagees as a percentage of all mortgagees: Hamilton and Victoria,
1881–1921

between 7 and 15 per cent of all sellers, whereas in Victoria in 1911 and
1921 women sellers represented between 21 and 34 per cent of all sell-
ers. As with mortgagees, women buyers of property in Victoria were
close to the percentage of women sellers (20 and 26 per cent in 1911
and 1921). Such was not the case in Hamilton. Women buyers as a per-
centage of all buyers far outstripped women sellers as a percentage of
all sellers (buyers fluctuated between 18 and 32 per cent between 1881
and 1901).

How can one account for the contrast between the two cities, espe-
cially in activity as mortgagors and sellers, and how can one explain the
wide spread in women's involvement in Hamilton as mortgagees and
buyers compared to their participation as mortgagors and sellers? The
primary explanation for the differences is fairly easily stated. The chal-
lenge lies in assessing the implications of that explanation for under-
standing the role played by women in the land and mortgage markets.
The explanation is found in the different laws regarding dower in both
provinces. Dower was an ancient practice probably dating from the
Roman Empire and adopted by England in the early medieval era. It

granted a widow the right to some portion of her husband's estate, usually a life interest in a third of all realty. Thus if a husband sold real estate and his wife had not renounced dower, his widow after his death could claim one-third interest in that property from the buyer. This right was granted in recognition that under common law married women were *femme couvert* and basically without property rights. "The reason, which our law gives for adopting it," the eminent British jurist William Blackstone wrote, "is a very plain and sensible one; for the sustenance of the wife, and the nurture and education of the younger children."[14]

When Upper Canada adopted the laws and statutes of England in 1792 (more formally known as "the date of reception" of English law), this was the state of the dower provisions, and in substance they remained so throughout the period under investigation here. In the early 1830s, husbands were allowed to bar dower, but only with their wives' consent. In a sense, a wife retained the right to renounce a right. And as Robert Baldwin noted in 1845, "at present there was never any difficulty for a prudent man to get his wife to release her dower."[15] In the pre-MWPL era, the debate on dower turned on the need to sell specific properties that could easily be seen to be free of encumbrances versus the general right of a widow to enjoy, as Baldwin put it, "the pitiful provision secured to her by the right of dower."

The nature of the discourse surrounding the issue of dower is nicely indicated in a debate on a bill to abolish dower in Upper Canada in 1847. Some pointed to the "wickedness" of certain widows such as "Tierney [who] ... had walked into possession of her fat third of property after property, broad and rich, until she had gathered the respectable figure of between three and four hundred estates!" "For one ill behaved wife," the Toronto *Globe* countered, "there are twenty bad husbands, and this is the only frail protection which a woman has against the conduct of her lord." It would be wrong to abolish dower, Robert Baldwin believed, because "in England property is generally held in large and profitable estates, on which the rights of the wife are secured by marriage settlement. In this country it rarely or never happened that there was a marriage settlement, and the wife had no protection whatever but her dower."[16] That bill was defeated, but in 1868 the Ontario legislature passed an amended dower act which allowed the barring of dower by husbands on the sale of unimproved land, in the hopes of better facilitating the opening of land in the northern areas of the province.[17]

Still, in Ontario the dower law had teeth. "The question of dower is a vexatious one," Assignee wrote to the Toronto *Globe* in January 1880. It was a law, he thought, that "it would be well to regulate if possible. The real estate of a married insolvent comes into the hands of an assignee and he finds the sale impossible at anything like a fair price. Only a speculative purchaser would buy ... others not wanting to purchase a possible law-suit and *trouble with a woman*." As David Mills, an eminent lawyer and the member for Bothwell in Ontario, informed the federal House of Commons in April 1884, for the most part in Ontario "it is not in the power of a proprietor to devise [property] in such a way as to deprive his wife of her dower."[18]

But in British Columbia, husbands did have that power. As was the case with much common law, dower rights in England changed over-time. In 1833 a British act was passed that allowed husbands to bar dower in their wills and leave women without any estate rights. More-over, that law also made it possible for a man to mortgage or sell land while his wife was alive and bar any subsequent claim to that property. This act was implemented to better protect creditors and purchasers. If a husband did not leave a will, if he was intestate, then the rights to a life interest in a third of the real property still accrued to the widow. The laws adopted from Great Britain by British Columbia were as of 1858 and thus included this revised dower legislation.[19] In the mid-1860s British Columbia passed a Homestead Law which did require husbands to get their wives to agree to any sale or mortgaging of prop-erty. But this stipulation only applied to homesteads that were regis-tered, and they could only be registered by the husband. Available evidence suggests that only a small percentage of homesteads were ever registered.[20] Arguing that married women deserved "an interest in the real estate of their husbands," Arthur Bunster moved a bill to strengthen dower rights in the province in 1872. He pointed out that current law did not provide married women that right and thus allowed "cases where great hardships and injustice had been done to women by reckless and cruel husbands." His proposal got nowhere. Those opposed argued, incorrectly but revealingly, that the 1833 English legislation had done "away with the question of dower." In fact, the 1833 act had amended and restricted dower but did not abolish it. More importantly, Bunster's opponents maintained that ease of prop-erty transfers would be impeded by the re-enactment of such an act.[21] These arguments resurfaced in the early twentieth century to once again defeat attempts to establish a stronger dower measure in British

Columbia. Indeed, by the 1920s the province was the only provincial jurisdiction in Canada without a dower measure strongly protective of a married woman's or widow's property rights.[22]

In British Columbia a husband could sell and mortgage property without consultation with his wife. His wife's signature was clearly not required. In at least some instances this power led to scenarios of the sort predicted by Bunster. On 17 June 1908 the *Prairie Farmer*, published in Winnipeg, printed a letter from "An Old Woman" from British Columbia. The woman recounted a story concerning her married neighbour. The neighbour's husband had fallen into bad company, spent too much time in bars, and was persuaded by his drinking friend to sell his homestead. He and his friend "went to a lawyer and agreement was made and a part of the money paid before the wife heard anything about it ... This poor woman found she could do nothing but take her children and walk out ... and they are now scattered all over, while the husband still hangs around the hotel spending the money as he gets it by instalments, but the poor wife got nothing."[23] From the women's point of view, then, dower laws in British Columbia hampered hardly at all their husbands' autonomy in matters of property transactions.

A more fulsome discussion of dower, one that provides further context within which to understand the issue and underlines the frontier-oriented concern for ease of property transactions evidenced in the British Columbia debate, took place in the federal Senate as part of a debate on the proper land registry system for the North-West Territories in 1885–86.[24] The proposal was to adopt the Torrens system, a land registry system that British Columbia had already adopted. Under this system, local registry offices were established where a mortgagee or purchaser could check a title to see if there were any encumbrances on it. If nothing was registered, then the property was held to be unencumbered. This approach simplified property transactions, making them the equivalent, in a sense, to chattels and giving confidence to mortgagees and buyers that no hidden "blots" on the property existed.[25]

Dower was one potential blot that needed to be eliminated to better facilitate the liberal pursuit of efficiency within an emerging capitalistic environment. "The dower," Senator Kaulbach of Nova Scotia asserted, "is precarious and uncertain, and it hampers land and destroys its value in the market largely." "No one regrets more than I do," Senator Girard of Manitoba lamented, "the provision to do away with the old custom of dower and courtesy, which were pledges of love and mutual affection"; but in the end he could see the need for the measure. David

Macpherson, a prominent senator from Ontario, did not believe that the abolition of dower diminished in any significant way traditional rights held by wives. In fact, he doubted that there were "many instances where the wife succeeded in preventing her husband from mortgaging his land or selling it if so disposed" even under a system of dower.[26] Indeed, several senators held up the British Columbia system as the model to be followed.[27] A minority, like Senator Plumb of Ontario, argued that abolishing dower weakened the fabric of family. "I believe," Plumb asserted, "that in many cases the existing law saves families from utter destruction and destitution ... where men are dissipated, extravagant or otherwise squander their properties, the resolute conduct of the wife, who is not necessarily controlled by her husband, may save the family from ruin." "We are legislating not for people of wealth," he continued, "... but for the humble householder and his family, and we are trying if possible not to take away any safeguards that are thrown about the sanctity of the household and the safety of the family and children." "This law should be amended," Senator Trudel from Quebec succinctly stated, "in such a way as to preserve the rights of the wife."[28] Yet as in New South Wales and in British Columbia, the proponents of an unfettered market in land carried the day, and dower was abolished in the North-West Territories.

Different dower regimes affected the legal processes governing land transfers by married men and women. In Ontario a person granting a mortgage on the security of land to a married man invariably required the signature of the man's wife on the mortgage contract. Only in this way could the mortgagee be sure that he or she had full rights to an unencumbered security in the event that the mortgage was not repaid. Similarly, a person purchasing land from a married man invariably required the signature of the man's wife on the deed of sale. Only in this way could the purchaser be protected from any subsequent dower claims. Such guarantees were not necessary in British Columbia. Figures 5.5 and 5.6 indicate how these different dower regimes affected the profile of participants in the mortgage and land sales markets.

As these figures make clear, a husband and a wife acting together in a real estate transaction as a mortgagor or seller of property were a rarity in Victoria, while in Hamilton husband-wife partnerships were commonplace. In Victoria the minority of husband-wife mortgagors were probably related to transactions involving registered homesteads. Interestingly, the abstract deeds for Hamilton did not always list the husband first. In the years covered in this study, one of every eight

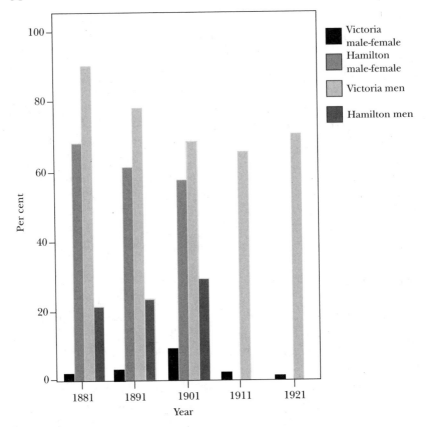

Figure 5.5
Male-female partnerships and men as a percentage of all mortgagors: Victoria and
Hamilton, 1881–1921

married mortgagor partnerships listed the wife first.[29] This pattern may
reflect the fact that, should a wife die intestate, her widowed husband
was entitled to what was termed "his tenancy by courtesy" out of his
wife's lands, usually a one-third interest in the real estate for his life-
time. The astute mortgagee or purchaser might therefore have
required the husband's signature to any transaction involving property
owned by a married woman in her own name.

Did dower laws empower Hamilton's married women to a greater
extent than they did married women in Victoria? Certainly, Ontario's
Chancery, Queen's Bench, and Appeal reports and newspaper reports
of court proceedings were peppered with cases concerning dower. As a
review of a new book on the law of dower in Upper Canada asserted in

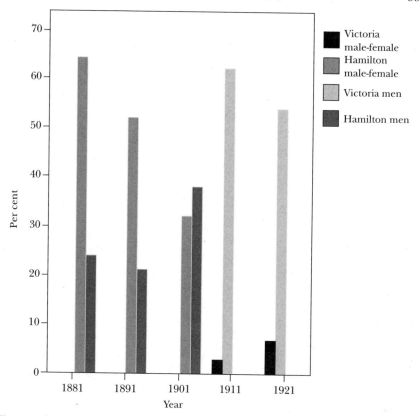

Figure 5.6
Male-female partnerships and men as a percentage of all sellers: Victoria and
Hamilton, 1881–1921
NOTE: The Victoria data do not separate selling and mortgaging properties in a clear way
until 1911.

September 1863, "a large share of litigation arises from the assertion of
this right, guarded and strengthened as it has been by our legisla-
tion."[30] No such cases were reported in the published law reports of
British Columbia. Not all cases were decided in the married woman or
widow's favour, but it is clear that dower rights were prized by women,
and many went to court in an attempt to attain what they considered to
be their rights under the dower legislation.[31] It is also clear that we are
not privy to the negotiations that may have occurred within households
prior to transactions that barred dower. One might argue that at least
Ontario's dower laws required that a husband acquire his wife's signa-
ture. How he may have achieved that we do not know.

Some formal protection against potential abuse did exist. In Ontario and British Columbia and in most jurisdictions in the United States throughout much of the nineteenth century there remained in place a traditional protective device designed to ensure that married women who wished to sell or mortgage property which they owned fully or partly understood the transaction and were free of any coercion from their husbands.[32] A product of medieval English common law, the protective procedure was known as the privy or separate examination. As Justice Spragge stated in a case involving this procedure in Ontario in 1870, "It was the manifest intention of the Legislature to afford to married women protection against the alienation of their real estate except with their free and voluntary consent."[33] An example from British Columbia is illustrative. In May 1891 Isabella Perrin, a married woman who lived in Victoria, desired to borrow $2,250 from John Liarks giving as security real property that she owned in her own name. Before she could do so she had to sign a form titled "For Married Women," swearing before a local notary "apart from and out of the hearing of her ... husband ... that she knows the contents and understands the nature [of the transaction and] that she executed the same voluntarily without fear or compulsion or undue influence of her said husband, that she is of full age and competent understanding, and does not wish to retract the execution of the said instrument."[34] The MWPLs had given to Perrin the right to sell or mortgage property in her own name, but the need for a privy examination, at once protective and paternalistic, remained in place. This was independence of a constrained sort. The examination, as Stacey Braukman and Michael Ross conclude in an analysis of its impact in the United States, "was a barrier to women's progress."[35] Married women were *femme sole* almost.

Clearly, the privy examination was a paternalistic device. What is less clear is the amount of protection it provided married women. Unlike in the United States, there seems to have been few court cases in nineteenth-century British Columbia and Ontario that focused on the privy examination. One Ontario case that did concerned the issue of whether the husband's solicitor could act as the examiner without fear of undue conflict. Justice Spragge was clearly troubled by such an action. "Consider the position of the woman," he said. "Can she feel as free to disclose her real feelings and wishes when one of those to whom she makes answer ... is her husband's professional agent?...she will almost certainly apprehend that any appearance of disinclination on her part would be reported to her husband."[36] Yet he and his fellow justices condoned the action simply because it seemed to them that English jurists condoned it. Such a ruling reflected the tendency of Ontario's judges to follow English precedents far more often than adapting law to the needs of a new society.[37] And of course, of more relevance here, such a judgment could hardly inspire confidence on the part of married women in the privy examination system.

The matter of a private examination did come up during the senate debate on the Torrens system. Most felt that the process was a form of legal "fiction," a right without power. Senator Alexander Campbell wondered if anyone had "ever known a case" in which a magistrate stopped a transaction: "I have never known of it in my experience. It is a mere form. The wife goes to a magistrate and she is asked 'Do you make this transfer through fear or coercion?' And the woman never says she does." Senator James Gowan agreed: "Thousands of cases have come before me in my capacity as judge, and I do not remember at this moment a single case in which any objection was made."[38] Several senators, somewhat more cynically, felt that married women always had their price. "A married woman would hardly sign a deed without getting a silk dress. In fact the title was almost considered impeachable by her unless she got it." Campbell concurred: "The silk gown suggestion ... is the ordinary remedy for any difficulty on the part of the wife."[39] Whatever the norm, the Ontario laws regarding the privy examination and dower were potentially enabling for women to the extent that they facilitated discussion of property issues within families and provided some support for widows. Married women could not be summarily ignored in matters of property, although whether this consideration made them equal in any sense to their husbands in these areas is a moot point concerning which the available evidence remains slim.

There were other possible options designed to protect married women's property. George Gillespie, a wealthy Hamilton merchant, left an $80,000 estate to be divided equally between his two sons and one daughter. His sons received their share without controls. His daughter received hers as income from a trust for life with a limited right to bequeath. As he explained in his will, Gillespie had arranged these terms "so that if and while she shall be under coverture the same shall be for her sole and separate use and she shall not have power to dispose of the same in the way of anticipation" but could bequeath it to her husband and children in trust. By putting the money in trust, Gillespie went beyond the formulaic statement "for her own and separate use" and created a form of marriage settlement in anticipation of such an event in the future.[40]

Formal marriage settlements would seem to have been fairly popular in Lower Canada, but not, as Robert Baldwin noted, in Upper Canada/ Ontario.[41] Those few who did take advantage of this option were members of the wealthy elite. A nice example of the negotiations underlying the creation of such settlements follows. On 12 June 1889 Adam Brown, a prominent merchant and politician from Hamilton, noted: "I gave my consent to [my daughter's] lover Mr. E B Smith of London provided he woes her. He has a good grocery business in London retail and jobbery does $160,000 his brother supplies him with most of his goods. He puts $3000 in Daisey's name and $7000 he has yet to get from his father's estate also in her name he insured his Life for $10,000 and puts that in her name."[42] Daisey Brown was a privileged woman.

Lucy Ronald's marriage to George Harris of London, Ontario, in 1867 provides a rare look at a marriage settlement in operation. From the start Lucy and George had opposing ideas as to how the settlement should be structured. George did not want the settlement to be managed by trustees, arguing that "the law gives the woman the entire control of her own property". He wanted "Lucy to keep control of hers and not place it in the hands of trustees to manage well or ill as they may think, but without her being able to interfere."[43] George's position seemed at one level admirable: married women should have agency in financial matters. Lucy had other ideas. She wanted trustees to have control, very likely in order to protect her money from her husband and allow her to will it to her children or to whomever else she wished.[44] If George disagreed, she threatened to end the courtship. As a member of the federal House of Commons noted in March 1878, "it had been found in many cases where marriage settlements depended on the action of the wife, that, when the husband became involved, he got the trust in his own hands." Lucy Ronald got her way, and in the course of what was an unhappy marriage for her, she often consoled herself by thinking,"One thing I am glad in my heart [is] that a settlement was made at my marriage." While George did not like the settlement, "I am thankful it was made."[45] In November 1875 Lucy confided to her diary that "George and I think so differently on many subjects that it is difficult to avoid rocks in doing anything. The marriage settlement is one source of trouble. I am convinced that it is a good thing for the children, he thinks not."[46] Even though the lack of control often frustrated her – she worried that the trustees were not sending a large enough payment, that payments did not come on time, and that she was always short of funds – she remained ever appreciative of the service her trustees performed.[47]

A.R. Buck, in a study of the abolishment of dower in New South Wales, has argued that historians have for too long ignored the implications of this action for women's rights, preferring instead to concentrate on the enabling qualities of the MWPLs. His primary point is that both sets of laws were implemented to facilitate ease in property transactions in order to, in his words, impose "the logic of the market on social relations." In this context the abolishment of dower has to be seen as "regressive" for women's rights, he believes, even as the MWPLs can be seen as progressive.[48]

Buck is helpful as far as he goes. One can agree with him that the desire to commodify land underlay the abolishment of dower, but one needs to go beyond his conclusion that the rescinding of dower was regressive and the MWPLs progressive examples of legislation affecting women's rights. Rather, we should be sensitive to how these laws interacted together to promote and impede actual practice in the conduct of property matters by women, and especially by married women. We know that married men in Victoria invariably sold and mortgaged property without their wives' signatures. But the reverse was also true. Married women sold and mortgaged their property without their husbands' signatures. Not only did more women operate as *femme sole* as mortgagors in the mortgage market in Victoria than in Hamilton (figure 5.3), but those who did were generally married. Indeed, over 75 per cent of women in Victoria who mortgaged properties without a partner in 1881, 1891, and 1901 were married.[49] In Hamilton the comparable percentage in 1901 was 33. This is a suggestive pattern.

The behaviour of married women in matters of property in Victoria suggest the need to look at dower and the MWPLs not as separate and, in Buck's view, seemingly contradictory pieces of legislation. Clearly, a weak dower law such as that in British Columbia and no dower protection such as the cases of New South Wales and the North-West Territories allowed husbands to profit from their wives' contributions to the acquisition and improvements of real property. They could sell that property with or without their wives' consent. Yet could it be that the weak dower regulations in British Columbia – weak, that is, from the wife's point of view – encouraged married women to own property in their own names since they could not rely on dower to protect their property rights within the family?[50] Conversely, might it be the case that the more enabling dower provisions operative in Ontario muted the need by married women to own property in their own names? We saw in chapters 1 and 3 that Victoria's married women were significantly more directly involved in investment and especially in landownership in their own names than were married women in Hamilton. They were also, as we have seen in this chapter, more directly involved in the mortgaging of property as *femme sole* than were their Hamilton counterparts. The comparative perspective employed in this study allows one to think that the weak dower law in British Columbia might have acted as a spur to that involvement, and a stronger dower law in Ontario might have blunted the need.[51]

The debate on dower and the Torrens system in the Senate and the earlier debates in British Columbia and Upper Canada/Ontario demonstrate that some men in public life feared for the rights of women and argued that if dower were abolished, women would have no power in the family and to that extent the family – and indeed, the nation – would be irretrievably weakened. Yet others in British Columbia and in the Senate predicted that the legislation would go far towards stimulating behaviour of the sort exhibited by married women in Victoria. Charles McKeivers Smith, the editor of the Victoria *Daily Standard*, wrote in 1872 that those who opposed dower seemed to view women as "useful domestic animals whose office it is to minister to the daily appetites of man [rather than seeing them] as his social or intellectual equal."[52] Thirteen years later Senator Campbell of Ontario expanded this point, and in so doing, he chipped away at the boundaries of nineteenth-century liberal thought. Campbell pointed out that the tendency of legislation in the British world "certainly has been to cease to regard the wife as one with her husband – to cease giving him control over her property, and [instead] habilitating her with all the power and authority which is necessary or should go to an unmarried woman with reference to her own property." In his view, that was "a course which recommends itself to most men of liberal minds – that the wife should be considered in every way, quite as capable of taking care of her own property and as having a full right to deal with it – to mortgage or sell or to do what she likes with it – as if she were not married ... It seems to me that is a more liberal way to treat a woman, and a safer way with reference to her character and habits and formation of her mind and the chances of her being entirely the head of the family, that one would desire to see in her."[53]

Campbell's comments attain significance at least in part because he was at pains to link them to what nineteenth-century liberal men should believe. The liberal set of "structuring dispositions," especially as they related to appropriate "gendered" roles, was far from fixed. Ian McKay, in a path-breaking article, has argued that in Canada in the nineteenth century liberal-minded men valued the individual ownership of property above all else, even while denying such a possibility to women. Alice Kessler Harris has characterized "America's version of liberal theory [as] a deeply rooted gendered prerogative." Mary Dietz, in a wider study of liberalism, feminism, and citizenship, has written that "in early liberal thought, the ethical principles that distinguish liberalism – individual freedom and social equality – were not in practice (and often not in theory) extended to women, but solely to 'rational men' whose rationality was linked to the ownership of property."[54] And at an even more general level Carole Pateman has argued that the practice of contracts signalled the beginning of a new form of patriarchy, one in which men dominated and women were subordinate or absent.[55] Yet Campbell evoked the principles of liberalism and allowed married women a central place in the ownership of property. For him, this did not signal the breakdown of family. Rather, allowing a married woman to manage property in her own name was useful training "for her character and habits and formation of her mind." In his view, such experience would fit her well for "being entirely the head of the family." In his depiction, women were not simply part of the "other" that defined the liberal rule. The MWPLS and the restrictive dower laws, in their different but linked ways, facilitated a rethinking of the role of married women within an emerging liberal state. This reworking allowed that, at least in some matters, married women could be viewed as an inherent part of the liberal rule. In Victoria many middle-class married women took advantage of that opportunity.

Intriguingly, in Ontario, as we have seen, married women behaved differently. One could easily think that the province's married women had the best of all available worlds. Campbell certainly never suggested that a married woman should have equal share with her husband in property each had contributed to the development of during their marriage. Yet in Ontario such a view was just about within reach, even in the nineteenth century. As early as 1860, a member of the Upper Canada Legislative Council favoured a liberal dower law because "in many instances [a wife] contributes just as much to enhancing [family property] as the husband."[56] Some thirty years later a writer for the Toronto

Globe argued that the retention of dower and the enactment of the
MWPLS were linked by a common understanding that women possessed
"inalienable rights." The MWPLS allowed married women to "accumu-
late property by their own individual exertions, industry and economy,
and why should they not be permitted to deal with it as they chose, with-
out consulting their husbands?" In the writer's view, "that was the con-
clusion arrived at by the Legislature." The anonymous author then
depicted dower in contractual terms. No longer was the measure
explained as a protective, paternalistic device, as it might have been
understood in early times. Now it was to be understood as a quid pro
quo. Ontario's dower law was "another name for compensation which
she receives for the aid given her husband in accumulating property ...
In Ontario the presumption is that every farmer's wife, and in fact every
property owner's wife, has a vested interest in her husband's lands;
because, be it ever so little, she must have done something towards
accumulating the savings which the lands represent."[57] The *Globe's*
editors agreed. Arguably, so too did Ontario's legislators. They did,
after all, pass a series of MWPLS even while retaining a form of dower
protection for widows in the face of examples to the contrary in
England, Manitoba, the North-West Territories, New South Wales, and
British Columbia.

The question nonetheless remains: if Ontario's property laws were
more permissive towards the rights of married women in the area of
property than those in British Columbia, why did proportionately so
few married women in Hamilton own property in their own names
compared to their Victorian counterparts? It remains possible that at
some level the retention of dower did indeed blunt the need, if not the
desire, for married women to own land in their own name, and the
absence of a strong dower law in British Columbia acted as a spur to
married women's property acquisition in Victoria. Yet it is only when
these contrasting legal regimes are situated within a broader social con-
text that the different behavioural patterns can reasonably be fully
explained. As argued in the preceding chapter, the contrast in the sex
ratios in the two cities remains the most economical explanation for the
different ownership patterns. The fact that there were fewer women
than men of marriageable age in Victoria gave to those women a bar-
gaining space not available to their Hamilton counterparts. The
absence of an effective dower law may have acted as an incentive to
acquire property in their own names; the unbalanced sex ratio
provided the necessary condition for the realization of that desire.

Hamilton's married and intending to be married women operated within a more constricted social environment even as they lived within a more, in the context of property rights, permissive legal environment. They could of course remain as spinsters, and many did.[58] But more often than in Victoria their bargaining powers within courtship and marriage itself seemed weaker than those enjoyed and used by women in Victoria. Once again Senator Campbell's views are instructive. When chided by another senator who suggested that "although the relative positions of husband and wife are altering, I think that always, or at least for a long time, the average wife will be very considerably under the influence of her husband," Campbell responded immediately. He certainly hoped "the average wife will continue to be considerably under the influence of her husband."[59] In the area of property ownership such seems to have been the case in Hamilton.

The play of "influence" is of course precisely the most difficult factor to assess. When married women barred their dower rights in Hamilton, were they acting under undue influence, or can we understand such action as an example of agency and empowerment? Clearly, there is no simple answer to this question. Clearly, too, influence could be a subtle process and extend to financial dealings beyond that of dower. We will return to this point in our conclusion to this chapter, but first we look more closely at women in action as mortgagees and mortgagors. In the ensuing analysis the activity profiles of Hamilton women will be charted with and without the involvement of married couples. In that way the question of influence concerning the issue of dower is left open, and trends can be appreciated from various perspectives. We look at the general social characteristics of lenders and borrowers and then at the activity pattern of especially women in the mortgage market, and finally we comment on the importance of women in this financial sector.

What separated a mortgagee from a mortgagor besides the fact that the former had money that the latter desired? Did mortgagees exhibit a set of social attributes that distinguished them from mortgagors? From a set of personal characteristics, is it possible to "predict" who would most likely be a mortgagee or a mortgagor? As we have seen in chapter 1, the most common procedure in social science for analyzing a context of overlapping influences is multiple regression. When one is examining a dependent variable with only two values – mortgagee or mortgagor – and when the distribution of values is uneven – fewer mortgagees – then the best form of multi-way analysis is logistic regression.

The list of social variables that are significantly associated with being a mortgagee or a mortgagor is very short, and it did not change over the late nineteenth century. Of interest is the fact that gender is not among them. In other words, if one only knew the gender of a person active in the mortgage market, one could not predict whether that person was more likely to be a mortgagee or a mortgagor. Nor could one predict the nature of a person's involvement on the basis of his/her religion or birthplace.[60] If one knew a person's age, occupation, and marital status, then one stood a good chance of predicting whether that person was a mortgagee or a mortgagor. In both cities the younger a person was, the higher the odds that that person borrowed in the mortgage market, and the older he or she was, the higher the odds that that person lent money. Professionals, those in sales, especially realtors, and, in Victoria, white-collar workers and retired people were most likely to be lenders, while in both cities those in the manufacturing class were most likely to be borrowers and least likely to be lenders. In Victoria, but perhaps not in Hamilton, single and widowed individuals were more likely to be mortgagees and married people more likely to be mortgagors.[61] A regression run with just Victoria women and all other variables the same, as in table 5.1 resulted in even higher incidences of widowed and single women as lenders and married women as borrowers.[62]

Annie Calder of Victoria was one of the more successful of women mortgagees. Born in Ireland, she had accompanied her father and sister to Victoria, probably arriving before 1874. She never married and lived with her father until his death in the 1890s. By 1891 she was the owner of their home, and her younger married sister and her family boarded with her. In the 1901 census the sixty-one-year-old spinster said she was living on her own means and had a yearly income of $600. She also owned real estate with an assessed value of $8,100. Calder lived in comfortable circumstances and maintained her lifestyle primarily via an active mortgage business and conservative investments in bonds and debentures. In her mortgage account book covering transactions between October 1884 and December 1892, she recorded loans to twenty-five different people for a total of thirty-one transactions involving $38,590, charging an average 10 per cent in interest. Her investments from 27 January 1885 to 2 August 1886 generated $1,386.05 in interest payments. At her death in 1903, mortgage money owing her amounted to $7,000 equal to 28 per cent of an estate worth $24,756, a percentage, as we have noted at the beginning of this chapter, close to the average for those unmarried women active in the mortgage sector.[63]

While Annie Calder maintained a formal account book to manage her mortgage investments, Frances Gay Simpson, a sixty-year-old widow living in Hamilton with her twenty-nine-year-old unmarried daughter, recorded her mortgage affairs in her diary. And her affairs were substantial. In 1881 she had eleven mortgages outstanding, of which we have values for nine. Those nine mortgages totalled $21,777, loaned at an average rate of 7.3 per cent interest, for a return of about $1,633 for the year. Typical of most Hamilton women mortgagees, she showed no bias towards women: seven of the mortgagors were men, two were women, and two were a man and a woman. Her average loan was much higher than that for Hamilton men and women in 1881.[64] One further point is also of note, and it relates to Annie Calder's activity as well. Both of these women lent to people outside their city of residence. The general data that we have collected for mortgage activity in both cities (see tables 5.2 and 5.3, for example) relate only to mortgages in the city of reference. Thus some of Calder's and Simpson's mortgage business and undoubtedly that of many others is not captured in this file. Put simply, the activity patterns depicted below must be seen as underestimates of total activity.

For the most part, the nature of the social separation between borrowers and lenders is not surprising. Young, often newly married men and women needed capital for down payments on houses or for a range of other needs. Older, often widowed individuals had accumulated capital to invest, and the mortgage market facilitated that desire. We might expect that those in the skilled and unskilled manufacturing sector, the classic blue-collar workers, would on average earn less that those in the professions and general white-collar enterprises and thus require credit. In the end, perhaps the most surprising finding is that women could not be distinguished as mortgagees or mortgagors simply on the basis of their sex. Much of the limited literature dealing with mortgage investment in the nineteenth century accords a place for women, usually widows, as lenders of capital. The data from Victoria and Hamilton underline the presence of women as lenders but also point to their prominent role as borrowers. We will return to this point later in the chapter after we have looked more closely at the activity patterns of women as mortgagees.

What space(s) did women occupy in the mortgage market? Tables 5.2 and 5.3 provide a general overview of the activity of mortgagees, people and companies who lent money on the security of land, in Victoria and Hamilton. When one compares the data in these tables, several points stand out. In both cities women's participation in terms of percentage of lenders, transactions, and value increased significantly after the passage of the MWPLS in the 1880s. In both cities their involvement seems to have levelled off after the 1890s. These trends are comparable to what we found in our analysis of the probate data in chapter 1. As well, in both cities and especially in Victoria, men dominated the market. The exception to this statement is Hamilton in 1901, when women were involved in only 11 per cent fewer transactions than men and numbered one in three of all mortgagees.[65] But the narrowing participation is primarily counted for by the increased activity on the part of companies. Companies cut into male, rather than female, involvement in Hamilton. Women held their own; transactions by men declined by some 8 per cent from 1891. A somewhat similar pattern seems to have occurred in Victoria. Female transactions increased even as corporations flexed their muscles. By comparison, male transactions declined by nearly 30 per cent between 1881 and 1901, before stabilizing in the pre– and post–World War One era. Interestingly, in both cities married couples rarely acted together as mortgagees. In the absence of legislation compelling joint action, men and women went their separate ways.

Tables 5.2 and 5.3 point to a contrast in degree of women's activity as mortgagees in both cities. Hamilton women participated in a greater proportion of transactions than did Victoria women, lent a greater proportion of capital, and represented a higher proportion of participants. How might we understand this different activity pattern? One way is to take into account the different sex ratios in each city. In other words, it may be that in proportion to their numbers in the cities, just as many women participated as mortgagees in Victoria as in Hamilton. Figure 5.7 depicts women as a percentage of the population over nineteen in Victoria and Hamilton and as a percentage of mortgagees. In 1881 the gap between the proportion of women in the city and their proportion as mortgagees was 26 per cent for Victoria and 29 per cent for Hamilton. In 1901 the respective gaps were 4 and 12 per cent. When the sex ratio in each city is taken into account, then, the activity profile of Victoria women as mortgagees in 1881 was very similar to that of Hamilton women. In 1901 Victoria women, in proportion to their numbers in the city, participated to a greater degree than Hamilton women.

Women increased their presence in the mortgage market such that by 1901 that participation came closer to reflecting their proportion of over-nineteens in each city. They were also closing the gap between the probability of a man being a mortgagee and that of a women being one.

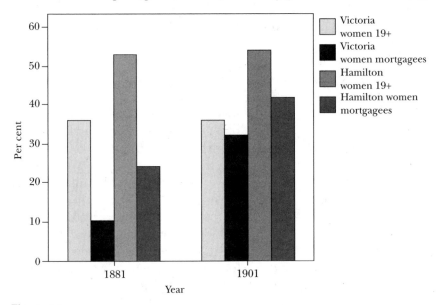

Figure 5.7
Women as a percentage of over-nineteens and as a percentage of men and women mortgagees: Victoria and Hamilton, 1881–1901
NOTE: Population figures for each city come from machine-readable files of compete-count nominal-level census returns for each city in 1881 and 1901.

If we control for their proportion in the city's population, Hamilton men in 1881 were 3.2 times more likely than Hamilton women to be a mortgagee. In 1901 that probability had decreased to 1.9 times more likely. In Victoria in 1881 men were 4.7 times more likely than women to be mortgagees and in 1901 that ratio had shrunk to 1.2.[66] Knowing the sex of a person was an increasingly less useful indicator as to whether or not that person was a mortgagee. This is an interesting finding that raises several broader questions. If the probability of a woman being a mortgagee was becoming closer to that for a man, was it also the case that women's activity in the market resembled men's? Or did women occupy a special niche? Or did each city exhibit a different pattern?

The possibility that women occupied a special niche, a separate sphere, in the mortgage market can be explored in several ways. One is by examining what we might call the participant's intensity level: number of transactions per mortgagee and average size of loans. A second approach is to look at lenders' preferences: what were the characteristics of those to whom mortgagees lent? A third perspective relates to the lender's managerial skills: interest rates charged, repayment terms, and foreclosure rates.

We look at the intensity level first. Measured by average number of loans, participation by women did not differ greatly from that by men. In both cities they were equal to or just under the averages for men.[67] Measured by average size of loan and average amount invested, women's participation fell short of men's. In Hamilton the average size of loans made by men exceeded those by women by 27 per cent in 1881 and 20 per cent in 1901. In Victoria the comparable spread was 19 per cent in 1881 and 16 per cent in 1901.[68] Sixty per cent of Annie Calder's loans, for example, were $1,000 or under. Her average loan was $1,245, compared to an average of $3,197 for Victoria men in 1891.[69]

The difference in average size of loans raises the possibility that women dealt with a different segment of the mortgage market than did men. The signals are mixed. Such might have been the case in Victoria: men were much more likely to be in the top 25 per cent in terms of size of loan and even in the top 50 per cent.[70] In Hamilton there was no such tendency. In fact, in 1891 and 1901 women were more likely to be involved in the top 50 per cent of loans than men and only slightly less likely to be in the top 25 per cent.[71] The measures for intensity employed here suggest, then, that women did not inevitably lend to a clientele significantly different from that serviced by men.

Perhaps women lent more often to family or to other women than men did. If we use same last name as an admittedly crude indication of familial loans, Hamilton women lent to family in only 4 per cent of transactions in the late nineteenth century, just slightly more than men. Victoria women were even less likely to lend to family: between 1881 and 1921, slightly over 1 per cent of all loans went to a person with the same last name, a percentage very similar to that for men in Victoria. There is no evidence that Annie Calder or Frances Gay Simpson lent to any relative. Clearly, women mortgagees stepped well outside the boundaries of family when conducting mortgage business.

Heller and Houdek, in their study of women mortgagees in rural Michigan, found that "women did not lend to other women inordinately."[72] A useful way to test for the tendency of women to lend to other women is through a variation of the standard labour quotient, designated here as LQ (loan quotient), where

$$LQ = \frac{L1/L}{M1/M}$$

L1 is number of mortgages granted to women by women, and L is total number of mortgages lent to women; M1 is total number of loans made by women, and M is the total made by all mortgagees. The resulting quotient is an indication of probability: a quotient of 2.5, as in Victoria in 1881, for example, indicates that people in that category – in this case, women lenders – were 2.5 times as likely to lend to women as one would expect given the proportion of women in the mortgage market. Taken on a year-by-year basis, the results presented in table 5.4 are variable. In some years, women did lend disproportionately to other women, and in other years they did not. Annie Calder seems typical here. In 1885 two of the five people who borrowed from her were women, but women numbered only one of the twenty-five who borrowed from her over the next seven years. If one looks at the period as a whole (1881–1901 and 1881–1921), however, women in Victoria were more likely to lend to other women than were their counterparts in Hamilton and were more likely to do so than one would have expected given the proportion of women in the mortgage market.

Women's behaviour as mortgagees in Victoria, then, differed in at least one way from that of Hamilton's women mortgagees: they tended to lend more often to other women. It is possible that the smaller average loans made by Victoria women compared to Victoria men and the fact that Victoria women lent disproportionately to women were linked: women mortgagors may have borrowed on average smaller sums than male mortgagors and thus were more attractive clients for Victoria's women mortgagees. Or, if it was the case that Victoria's women mortgagees actively sought out female clients, then that factor would help to explain their smaller-sized loans. Whatever the causal direction, the relationship between the two patterns of activity remains to be explored.

It is the case that in Victoria in the late nineteenth century, women, on average, borrowed smaller sums than men. It is also the case that women consistently lent relatively smaller amounts than men to both men and women, and since women tended to want smaller sums, there may have been some meeting of needs between women lenders and women borrowers in the city's mortgage marketplace.[73] In Victoria, women mortgagees had relatively fewer funds at their disposal compared to male mortgagees, and their behaviour in the mortgage market reflected that fact. It is therefore tempting to suggest that the tendency of women to lend to other women in the city should not be interpreted simply as an example of female ghettoization, of a separate spheres mentality operating in the mortgage market. Many men also lent small sums, and some women lent large funds. That too was the situation in Hamilton. Indeed, it is at this point that the comparison of women's behaviour in Hamilton compared to that in Victoria is instructive. In both cities women had less money to lend than men and on average lent in smaller amounts. In both cities they generally borrowed smaller amounts than men. It would not, then, be a surprise to see more women lending to other women. Yet this did not occur in Hamilton.[74] In contrast to the situation in Victoria, the desire for smaller funding by Hamilton women failed to attract women lenders in a disproportionate way. Does this pattern suggest that women in Victoria may at some level have consciously sought out women borrowers? Perhaps, but the Hamilton case also points to the fact that such behaviour was not predictable and cannot be explained as some inherent aspect of the gendered makeup of women. Moreover, in 1891 and 1911 Victoria women mortgagees did not lend disproportionately to women borrowers. Nor did Annie Calder. The probable explanation is more prosaic: in both cities women mortgagees acted as rational money managers, lending according to their means and, as we shall show later in this chapter, borrowing according to their needs.

We do not have nicely comparable data from both cities concerning the manner in which women managed their loans. The best data is that for Victoria, and it is presented in table 5.5. In terms of contractual requirements, female-initiated loans did not differ noticeably from male-initiated loans. Interest rates were similar, and the rates charged by female and male mortgagees did not vary on the basis of the mortgagor's gender.[75] Annie Calder may have been an exception to this general practice: she charged women an average 8.5 per cent in interest and men an average 10.3. On balance, however, men and women charged what the market would bear. The time stipulated for repayment in the contract also did not differ across genders.

If contractual requirements were gender-blind, collection strategies were less so. Although not shown in table 5.5, there was variance in actual repayment time. In 1881, 45 per cent of female-initiated loans were repaid after the contracted due date, compared to 40 per cent for male-initiated loans. In 1891 the respective figures were 50 and 42 per cent. Gender may have been a factor in accounting for the difference in repayment times. It is suggestive that in 1891, the year for which we have a suitable number of cases for analysis, women were much more apt to grant renewals to or suffer late payments from women than they were from men. Almost two-thirds of loans granted to women by women were not paid at the due date, compared to under half of those granted to men. The respective figures for male-initiated loans were just over two-fifths for each group. These are indications that gender might have played a role in the transactions entered into by those who were active in the mortgage market.

As mentioned, some of the "late" payments may have been renewals and not simply delinquent loans. Nonetheless, the different collection rates hint at the possibility that women mortgagees had more difficulty enforcing repayments than did their male counterparts. This possibility gains further weight when one takes into account a second collection strategy, the use of foreclosure. Women were nearly twice as likely as men to foreclose on their loans. As table 5.5 shows, in 1891 women foreclosed on almost one in four of their loans, while men foreclosed on only one in seven. The rate of foreclosures by women did not differ by gender (nor did the rate of foreclosures by men). Nor were women mortgagees more impatient than men. Both men and women fore-closed on a loan when it had run about four times its contracted repay-ment time. Women foreclosed more often than men primarily because proportionately more of their borrowers reached that point than did those who borrowed from men. The higher foreclosure rate and the larger overdue rate both suggest that women faced challenges that men did not in Victoria's mortgage market. Whether those challenges stemmed from some degree of inexperience on the part of women in their choice of suitable borrowers or whether a borrower thought that he or she could take advantage of a woman more easily than a man are interesting questions.

A closer look at the social characteristics of those who borrowed is instructive. We already know that in both cities borrowers were younger than lenders, had different occupations, and were more likely to be married. Did women lend to a different subset of these borrowers than men? The social characteristics of those who borrowed from men and those who borrowed from women presented in table 5.6 point to some possibly significant differences. Women tended to lend to people who desired smaller loans, who were more likely to be in manufacturing or white-collar occupations, and who were less likely to be in sales and pro-fessional jobs and less likely to be Roman Catholics. Yet perhaps the most telling set of differences relate to age, household status, and mari-tal state. Although the average age was very similar, the distribution of the ages of those who borrowed from women differed in one important respect from the age distribution of those who borrowed from men. Thirty-five per cent of those who borrowed from women were under the age of thirty; only 25 per cent of those who borrowed from men were in that age bracket. Moreover, those who borrowed from women were more likely to be single, less likely to be married, and less likely to be a household head than those who borrowed from men. Could it be that women loaned more often to people who were just starting out in life; people who were not yet running their own households or had only just started to do so; people who may have, in relative terms, accumulated fewer resources than older, better established borrowers?

The social profile of those who defaulted on loans granted by women suggests an affirmative answer to those questions. The tendency of women, rather than men, to lend to younger, less well established borrowers came back to haunt them. Those who defaulted on loans owed to women were disproportionately drawn from the youngest age category, from non–household heads, and from single, never-married individuals, precisely those areas where women tended to place proportionately more loans than did their male counterparts. Interestingly, the one foreclosure that we know Annie Calder enforced was against a twenty-seven-year-old married man with, at the time of the loan, a twenty-three-year-old wife and a year-old baby. Forty-three per cent of those who defaulted on loans owed to women were under the age of thirty, 48 per cent were non–household heads, and 30 per cent were never-married single individuals.

There is a third factor that helps to account for the larger default rate on female-granted loans, and that factor relates to the occupation of the borrowers. Those who borrowed from both men and women were drawn most commonly from workers in the manufacturing area of the economy. The default rate of these borrowers was quite high: 48 per cent of all defaulters on female-granted loans and 46 per cent of those who defaulted on male-granted loans worked in the manufacturing sector. That was a sector under siege in Victoria in the 1890s. During that decade, the city's economy underwent a fairly swift transition from industrial to service-sector employment. Forty-two per cent of all employed males worked in manufacturing in Victoria in 1891. By 1901 that figure had dropped to 31 per cent.[76] In addition to lending disproportionately to young, non–household heads, women lent somewhat more often than men (36 compared to 32 per cent) to people who worked in the most unstable sector of the city's economy.

By 1901 there is some indication that women were learning from past experience. While we lack data on defaulters in 1901, we do have social data on borrowers.[77] While, on average, men continued to lend to older people than did women (41.7 to 39.5 per cent), women were as likely as men to lend to those under the age of thirty (15 per cent in each case) and as likely to lend to those in manufacturing (25 per cent for women and 24 per cent for men). Even though the criteria used by women mortgagees in their selection of borrowers more closely resembled that employed by male mortgagees than had been the case in 1891, the favouring by women of non–household heads continued to be pronounced: 51 per cent of those who borrowed from women in 1901 were non–household heads; only 37 per cent of those who borrowed from men were not heads of households. Women also continued to be more partial to lending to never-married individuals (20 per cent compared to 15 per cent), although the tendency to do so was markedly less pronounced than had been the case in 1891. Finally, women continued to be less likely to lend to married individuals (70 per cent compared to 77 per cent).

In several ways, then, women mortgagees did exhibit different behaviours or strategies than those engaged in by men in the mortgage market. How might we understand those differences? Many seemed to have stemmed from the simple economic fact that, on average, women had less money to invest. Thus Victoria's women lent more often to women and non–household heads and in 1891 to younger borrowers largely because those individuals borrowed smaller sums than household heads.[78] As well, the fact that women had, especially in 1891 in Victoria, greater difficulty collecting on their loans can be seen as an indirect result of their lending smaller sums to a more risky clientele. Victoria women did, it should be noted, tighten up on this practice in 1901. The inference here is that women became more market savvy as they gained experience. It is difficult to be absolutely conclusive on these issues, but the economic argument for women's behaviour as mortgagees seems stronger than the obvious alternative that women lent to other women simply because they were of the same gender. As we noted earlier, that practice did not occur in Victoria for all the years surveyed and almost never in Hamilton. A lack of experience coupled with a relative lack of funds seem more persuasive as general explanations for women's conduct as mortgagees in these two late nineteenth-century Canadian cities.

Up to this point in our analysis, we have emphasized the relative lack
of funds employed by women compared to those invested by men. In
the aggregate, however, women's investment through mortgage funds
in the infrastructure and general economy of the cities of Victoria and
Hamilton in the last two decades of the nineteenth century was surpris-
ingly substantial. If we take the average of the amounts invested in 1881
and 1891 and assume that the result is roughly equivalent to what was
invested in each year between 1881 and 1890, the total for that decade
is $1,749,905. If we do the relevant calculation for the decade of the
nineties, the result is $2,174,905, for a total of just under $4 million.
The calculation for Hamilton women must be more speculative since
we do not have a complete sample of the mortgages. If we assume that
we have caught half the mortgages for each year and employ the same
calculation as for Victoria, then the total amount is $3 million invested
by women in Hamilton's infrastructure in the last two decades of the
nineteenth century.[79] If these funds all went into the construction of
housing, then at an average of $1,500 for a house in Hamilton, women
could have underwritten the construction of 2,000 homes.[80] If we take
the same figure for Victoria, then the number of homes would be in
excess of 2,500. In fact, these rough estimates are for two reasons over-
estimates. In the first place, some of the mortgage money must have
been in the form of renewals, not new money. Secondly, not all mort-
gage borrowing took place to finance land and housing purchases. Nev-
ertheless, even as rough indicators, they make the point that money
invested by women had a substantial impact on city development in
Canada in the late nineteenth century.[81]

It is time now to look more closely at those women who borrowed in
the mortgage market, a sector of economic activity generally ignored in
the historical literature. Tables 5.7 and 5.8 provide a brief recapitula-
tion of the activity of women as borrowers in the mortgage market. We
have discussed and accounted for the major contrast in borrower's pro-
file between the two cities: couples' dominance in Hamilton and the
prevalence of men and women acting on their own in Victoria. Tables
5.7 and 5.8 underline that difference and also, especially in the case of
Victoria, indicate that following the MWPLs of the 1880s, women's par-
ticipation as borrowers increased markedly in terms of numbers, trans-
actions, and amounts borrowed. In a sense, the same was true to a lesser
degree in Hamilton. It should be noted that couples' dominance
declined from 69 per cent of transactions and 73 per cent of value in
1881 to 58 per cent of transactions and 50 per cent of value in 1901.

The activity of sole women increased somewhat in terms of both transactions and value over the same period, but generally those women who participated as borrowers in Hamilton's mortgage market did so alongside their husbands.

Further insight into the activity of women borrowers is possible via an analysis of the records of two land and mortgage companies active in Victoria and Vancouver and one life insurance company headquartered in Toronto. The British Columbia Land and Investment Company (BCLI), operating out of Victoria, and the Yorkshire Guarantee and Securities Corporation (YGSC), based in Vancouver, acted as intermediaries between British lenders (often women) and local borrowers. They concentrated their business on mortgage and land development in British Columbia, primarily in the Victoria-Vancouver region. The two companies issued 1,254 loans between 1889 and 1896. The Confederation Life Insurance Company operated on a national level, with special attention to Ontario, but including, as we shall see, some loans to residents of Vancouver. Although the records for Confederation Life are leaner than those for the two local mortgage companies, they nonetheless provide a possible national frame within which to situate the more intensive discussion of regional mortgage activity in British Columbia.

As table 5.9 indicates, women occupied a prominent niche in the portfolios of the two locally focused land and mortgage companies. Loans granted to women outnumbered those granted to companies and couple applicants. One of every eight borrowers was a woman, and one of every nine loans was granted to a woman. These ratios compare very closely to the one in seven borrowers who were women and one in seven and a half loans granted to women in Victoria's mortgage market for the combined years 1891 and 1901 (see table 5.7). In this sense, professional companies acted toward women in a fashion similar to that of individual mortgagees. In another way they seemed somewhat more cautious. One dollar of every $13.5 loaned by these two companies went to a woman; $1 of every $10 loaned went to women in the wider mortgage market for the combined years of 1891 and 1901. On balance, however, the fact that these companies lent about a quarter of a million dollars to women in this short period indicates that women were being taken very seriously by major actors in the local capitalist marketplace.

If the activity of Confederation Life is any indication, women may not have received similar attention at the national level. In fact, as the data in table 5.10 indicate, women, after a brief jump from one of every seventeen loans in the 1870s to one of every eight in the late 1880s and early 1890,s dropped to only one of every fifteen by the end of the century. How might we interpret these data? It should be noted that the middle period compares closely to the findings for the two local companies in a similar time frame (see table 5.9). Perhaps the activities of those two companies changed in a fashion similar to that of the nationally based company in the late 1890s. We lack detailed data from the mortgage companies' records, but we can provide evidence about company activity in the wider mortgage market in Victoria for 1901, part of 1911, and 1921. In those years, companies registered 103 loans to individuals: women received 1 of every 4.5 of those loans. The BCLI granted 1 in 4 of its 30 loans to women in that time period. Clearly, the Confederation life pattern was not replicated at the local level in British Columbia.

A further indication that women were far from the insurance company's first choice as borrowers is the rate of refusals. Between 1888 and 1894 the success rate for men was 66 per cent and for women 56 per cent. Between 1895 and 1902 men's success rate increased to 83 per cent and women's only to 64 per cent. The reverse was the case in Victoria. Women were successful on 74 per cent of their loan applications and men on only 69 per cent of their attempts.[82] We do not know the extent to which Confederation Life's loan policies reflected the operations of other nationally focused companies in the mortgage sector, but we do know that the gendered operations of that company stood in significant contrast to the practice of the BCLI and the YGSC in British Columbia. And of course, we do have a wider context within which to put this contrast. The greater participation of women in Victoria and Vancouver in the corporate borrowing sector compared to women's participation in the lending activities of the nationally focused life insurance company fits neatly within the pattern of activity of Victoria women compared to that of women in Hamilton in many financial sectors. Simply put, women in Victoria were as a group much more active than their counterparts in Hamilton and perhaps elsewhere in Canada.

It is interesting that, as with Confederation Life, husbands and wives constituted only a small minority of those who borrowed from both BC-based companies (2.8 per cent for the BCLI and 4.3 per cent for the YGSC, table 5.9). This was not for lack of effort on especially the BCLI's part to get husbands to co-sign on loans requested by married women.

The BCLI's managers often viewed married women as simply extensions of their husbands. The company, for example, declined to grant Margarette Boechofsky a $3,000 loan despite the fact that she offered security worth three times the value of the loan (this was well over the average margin, see below). "The house is quite a good one," E.B. Morgan, the company's Vancouver agent, wrote, "and altogether the property is considered to be a very desirable one." The hitch was Boechofsky's husband. "He," C.A. Holland, the company's general manager, quickly responded, "is *very* undesirable, and has made himself notorious once or twice – you could have a great deal of trouble with him ... so it would be as well to decline the business."[83] For Holland, a husband was an inseparable part of his wife's business. Martha Tyson's application for a $2,000 loan was judged satisfactory because her husband "keeps a clothing store in the city. I consider the moral security to be good." Holland urged Morgan to "please get the husbands to join in the mortgages in the case of married women, where possible."[84] He clearly understood that he could only cajole, not compel. He failed to convince the Tysons to co-sign, and the loan was granted in the wife's name only. Some husbands saved the company the trouble of asking: Captain J.D. Warren borrowed $1,000 in March 1893 "for Mrs. Warren."[85] Companies such as the BCLI and some husbands, including J.D. Warren, continued to resist the legal reality that married women could now borrow independently from their husbands' involvement. Patriarchal values still underlay the loan-granting policies of credit companies in this period. In the face of this resistance, it is all the more remarkable that, as we shall see, married women borrowed from them as *femme sole* as often as they did.

The two companies might have discriminated against women in other ways. Not everyone who applied for a loan to these companies received one, and as we have seen, men were refused somewhat more often than women. On average, men and women were charged the same interest rate: the BCLI charged each 9.6, and the YGSC charged men 9.7 and women 9.9. The dollar value of security required was also, on average, very similar: for every dollar a man borrowed, the BCLI expected $1.4 in security; for women the amount was $1.5. The respective figures for the YGSC were higher but did not vary significantly across gender: for every dollar borrowed by a man, the YGSC required on average $2.4 in security; for women, it required $2.2.

Were women good credit risks? Some have argued on the basis of Dun and Bradstreet credit records that women may have been better credit risks than men.[86] The YGSC records allow us to test for that possibility. That company foreclosed on 27 per cent of loans granted to women and 23 per cent of those granted to men. The early 1890s were a time of boom and bust. By 1894 real estate prices were declining fast in both cities, and general economic activity was slowing down. In this context, no separate sphere protected female borrowers more than their male counterparts. In this troubled economic era, the YGSC did not foreclose on women any more quickly than it did on men. It carried most loans during the recession simply because to assume ownership would entail management and tax costs that it did not wish to incur. In 1899, on the eve of an economic upswing and the strong promise of rising real estate prices, the company foreclosed on 50 per cent of its delinquent women creditors and on a similar percentage of its male borrowers. In this sense, at least, the YGSC was gender-blind.

As we found in the larger Victoria mortgage market, and despite the patriarchal attitude of the BCLI, most of the women who borrowed from these two companies were married (80 per cent). Most were also young (60 per cent were under forty and 26 per cent under thirty). The borrowing activity of those women in the credit market was very similar to that of men. While the average-sized loan granted to a man exceeded that granted to a women by a factor of 1.5, 73 per cent of women borrowed $1,500 or less, compared to 70 per cent of men. Most men (80 per cent) and most women (89 per cent) borrowed only once. Some, such as Mary Coombs, whose house had suffered fire damage, borrowed to repair or expand existing homes. Most borrowed to finance the construction of a new home: for a two-storey home in Vancouver the cost was about $1,500. In December 1892 Fannie Beer, for example, co-signed with her husband to borrow $1,100 from the YGSC to construct their first home, and she also received a loan in her own name for $1,000 from Confederation Life.[87]

Most women and most men borrowed without any evident expectation of turning a speculative profit. It might be tempting therefore to characterize women's activity in this market as conservative behaviour and to explain it by reference to neoclassical assumptions concerning the altruism inherent in family economies: families prosper through the joint utility functions performed by their members.[88] Such behaviour is also consistent with the separate spheres perspective concerning the appropriate role for women: selfless and supportive. Yet the fact that married women appear to have borrowed primarily to build and/or improve their family homes does not mean that one can understand that activity as simply altruistic. As we have seen throughout this and previous chapters, women borrowed to secure their long-term economic situations. The ability to finance and improve a home without sacrificing ownership to another, even if that other was a husband, was an empowering development in their lives.

Moreover, some women did, in fact, borrow for speculative purposes. Mary Black, a lawyer's wife and owner of many Vancouver properties, had no trouble obtaining $1,800 from the BCLI.[89] Emma Gold, a wealthy Vancouver widow and "a large property owner," had, however, to be watched with care. "Mrs Gold," Holland wrote, "may be worth a great deal of money, but she is a dangerous customer except on the best of security."[90] The five women who were married to real estate agents tended to borrow large sums, presumably for speculative purposes. Anastasia Clements, a married woman who lived with her mother, made no secret of her reason for seeking credit: she reported her occupation to be a "capitalist." Seven married women borrowed from more than one company, and there is scattered evidence of other women who approached both and signed with the one that offered the best interest rate.[91] These were savvy borrowers.

Few women, however, matched the degree of activity of Mary McKee, the wife of William McKee, a builder, renter, and seller of houses in Vancouver. The McKees operated a nice business. As Holland noted in September 1892, "Mr. McKee builds a very good style of a house and seems to *have no difficulty* in disposing of them – either rent or sale."[92] William built and Mary financed. In 1891 she contracted with the YGSC for two loans at 10 per cent interest. She then approached the BCLI, and over the next two years she borrowed from that company eleven times and turned down three other offers. It is clear that she went to the Victoria firm because it offered, on average, lower interest charges at 8.4 per cent. But she also explored offers from other companies, including Confederation Life. In September 1892 the insurance company offered her two loans, but she turned them down. Very likely she consolidated her financial operations with the BCLI because that company was willing to cut a percentage point off its interest rate if it received "the agency and collection of rents of all the houses."[93] She also received a good rate on insurance from the Victoria-based company. Only one aspect of the business bothered Holland. He urged his Vancouver agent to "get [her] husband to join in all cases possible."[94]

Mary always resisted Holland's pressure; clearly, she considered herself to be an equal partner with her husband: she managed the money and he the construction.

Women were important players in the mortgage markets of late nineteenth-century Canadian cities. They were significantly active as lenders and as borrowers. In this sense, they were rentier capitalists and, in a fashion, entrepreneurs who borrowed capital to create something new. If we adopt the same procedure to estimate the amount of money borrowed by women in late nineteenth-century Victoria as we did for the amount loaned, then we can estimate that women borrowed about $1.2 million during the 1880s and $1.5 million during the 1890s. If all of this money was new funds and put into housing construction, then women who borrowed may have constructed 1,500 homes. Women operating as *femme sole* borrowers were far less numerous in Hamilton, in part as a result, as we have detailed in this and to a degree in previous chapters, of the impact of different legal and demographic regimes. But they were, again as we have seen, a much greater presence as mortgagees.

For the most part, our analysis suggests that women acquitted themselves well in the market. Many, such as Annie Calder and Frances Gay Simpson, maintained a decent lifestyle through investments in mortgages. Married women could also benefit from the passage of the MWPLS and they increasingly acted as mortgagees. Yet, and this is a point often lost sight of in discussions of the MWPLS, married women also benefited from the passage of those acts in a different way. Married women in search of, rather than possessed of, capital took full advantage of the new legislation to become quite visible as borrowers in the mortgage sector. Those laws facilitated the acquisition of new resources as well as the investment of existing capital.

On balance, women's collective activity as lenders and borrowers can be seen to be similar to the activity of men. Even though there is strong evidence that loan companies and undoubtedly some male mortgagees continued to view such activity on the part of, especially, married women as inappropriate, many others recognized the direction of change signalled by the MWPLS and, like Senator Campbell, attempted to integrate married women as economic actors into their wider liberal world view. The emergence of the middle-class liberal world pointed to by Ian McKay cannot be seen as one simply dominated by men. Many women aspired to be and became independent actors in a liberal middle-class world that some have argued had room only for men.

Equally clearly, the exercise of such agency by married women was both enabling and often fraught with tension. We only rarely find evidence that allows us to experience that tension with some immediacy. Two very different cases involving married women and their diligent attempts to maintain control of their assets make the point. The case of Mahaly Parkin of St Catharines, a town close to Hamilton, suggests the dangers in generalizing that women could invariably be easily taken advantage of. Parkin had lent $3,000 to her first husband to invest in his business and took a mortgage on property he owned as security. Soon after that transaction, they ceased to live as man and wife and eventually filed for divorce. Parkin was determined to receive her due payments. Writing, in her semi-literate way, to a lawyer intermediary in June 1881, she warned that "as conserning the morgage I will do as I said must have the interest up until paid so the quicker the money is paid the sooner the interest will be stoped you see the discount at the bank will be abought twelve dollars it is only to relieve you ... that I make the sacrifice as the way we have managed we could do far better with interest ... I must hold you responsible for the 8 per cent interest until I get my money." "I reseived the orders this morning," she wrote two months later. "I see theire is a new git up at the bank so after this you can send the money ... as I shall expect the full amount of interest."[95]

Mahaly Parkin's financial affairs saw the light of day in the course of Senate hearings on a petition for divorce. The affairs of Mary Kough Brown, wife of Adam Brown, were never aired outside the confines of her family. But they were equally real. In January 1880 Mary loaned her husband $3,475 at 7.5 per cent interest for him to invest in his mercantile business, and in return she received a third mortgage on the Hamilton home where she lived and on several other lots. She was clearly concerned but reluctant to talk directly with her husband about the mortgage. Instead she wrote to her brother for advice and for a $50 loan. She got the advice but not the loan. William, her brother, informed her that Adam had restructured the loan, transferring the mortgage to a second mortgage on his store and promising to transfer his $10,000 life insurance policy to her. William reminded Mary that she had agreed to this, but as far as he knew, no transfer of the insurance policy had occurred. It was a delicate matter. "Experience teaches me," he continued, in what seems a masterful understatement, "that money dealings between husband and wife are not always conducive to marital peace and love." "I hope," he warned, "Adam had the Life

Policy properly assigned to you. Will you ask the question straight or would you prefer my doing so?" William's final suggestion must have been of limited comfort to Mary. "Open your heart to your husband tell him how everything stands but when the new money comes remember that I want you to weigh well what disposition is made of it."[96] Marital peace and love were poised precariously between an open heart and a guarded purse. Such may well have been the situation for many married women with property in late nineteenth-century urban Canada.

6

Gender, Credit, and Consumption: The Market for Chattels in Victoria, 1861–1902

In chapter 1 we pointed to the care with which women enumerated their personal belongings in their wills. At the same time we noted that personal belongings made up only a small part of a woman's total wealth at the time of her death. In the late nineteenth century, personal goods constituted 14 per cent of the estates of Victoria women, and they declined dramatically to an overall average of 3.3 per cent of wealth after 1905 (see figure 6.1).[1] The change in the relative worth of personal belongings, of course, nicely reflects the evolving nature of women's wealth in the time period of this study, and it was that fact that we emphasized in chapter 1. In this chapter we look at this trend from a different perspective. The early years of the MWPLS represented a period of transition in the nature of the wealth owned by women. While we do not have data from which we can estimate the worth of personal property owned by Victoria women for the period before 1894, it is highly probable that that percentage would have been higher than for the last seven years of the century, given the trend depicted in figure 6.1. It is also worth noting that for those women who owned personal property in the late 1890s, that property amounted to 18 per cent of the value of their estates and probably more than that in the years before 1894. It is clear, then, that in the last third of the nineteenth century, personal goods represented significant wealth as well as senti- mental value.

This chapter considers some of the uses made of personal property by women. We are concerned here less with affective relations toward property – sentiment, family heritage, and nostalgia – and more with how women used personal objects for the interrelated purposes of con- sumption and production. Much current historiography focuses on

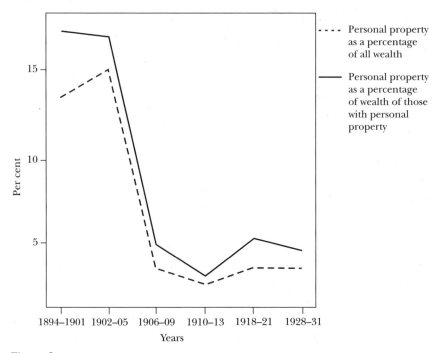

Figure 6.1
Women's personal property wealth as a percentage of all probated wealth:
Victoria, 1894–1931

women and consumption and demonstrates how women as consumers contributed to economic development. Historians have shown that married women were active purchasers of household provisions on credit even before the passage of the MWPLS.[2] Those who have written about "family" borrowing, as well as those who have focused on women and credit, tend to situate such activity within the realm of consumption rather than production.[3] Margo Finn has suggested that such a perspective "is a logical outcome of the development of women's history." It takes as one of its main assumptions the apparent marginality of women to the formal economy.[4] But the notion of marginality can unduly restrict one's understanding of the complexities of consumption. Consumption should not be seen as taking place on the margins of the formal economy. Nor should it be viewed as the opposite of production. In an era of transition from home-based and artisanal to factory-based enterprise, the easy separation of consumption from production seems somewhat ahistorical.[5] But even more generally, such a perspective unduly separates household and family from productive enterprise and, if only implicitly, places women in a separate sphere of household consumption.

Elizabeth Mancke, for example, has shown how "market consumption made household production possible in [pre-industrial] colonial economies." In that era women purchased inputs for the production of household goods: "women consumed to produce and men produced to consume."[6] Each was linked to the market economy, although in different ways. It is suggested here that with the passage of the MWPLs, household property purchased and owned by women continued to straddle the spheres of consumption and production, albeit in ways different from those detailed by Mancke for the colonial era. In the industrializing and urbanizing environment of the late nineteenth century, women householders remained linked to the market economy through the household items many purchased. Initially, such items may have been acquired for their use value within the home. But, for many women, those items often took on a second role, that of facilitating access to needed capital for a myriad of productive and other reasons. "Consumption," as the historian Frank Trentmann writes, "can be about managing familial and social relationships, not merely self-centred acquisitiveness ... Instead of oppositional models of analysis (consumption vs production) ... the challenge [is now] one of integration."[7] Rather than existing in separate spheres, production and consumption ran along a continuum. Women and their goods stood at the convergence of the two.

Chattel mortgage records allow us to pursue answers to some of the issues raised above. Little has been written on chattel mortgaging in Canada. Most studies of rural and urban debt have focused on real estate mortgaging. This lacuna is not exceptional: as the authors of a fine study of chattel mortgaging in a small rural town in Wisconsin in the nineteenth century aptly note: "Scholars have limited their investigations to real estate credit."[8] Yet as this chapter will demonstrate, chattel mortgaging was a very important way not only for rural but also for urban residents to raise short-term capital. After providing the legislative context for mortgaging on the security of chattels and an overview of the extent of such activity in Victoria in the last third of the nineteenth century, the chapter will look more closely at the roles played by women as lenders and borrowers in this market. Where possible, participants will be linked to machine-readable files of the 1881, 1891, and 1901 nominal-level census returns and assessment rolls for Victoria in order to provide greater understanding of their personal and familial characteristics.[9]

Many nineteenth-century financial observers felt that lending and borrowing on the basis of movable property was a risky and unsavoury business. Some saw borrowing on the basis of personal property as an act of desperation. C.F. Ferguson, member for Welland, Ontario, in the Canadian House of Commons, asserted that "if there is one thing more than another which shows the poverty of the people of any country, it is the number of chattel mortgages. When a man gives a chattel mortgage on his household furniture, his cooking stove, his horse with which he has to earn his daily bread for his family, [it] shows destitution in its most marked aspect."[10] Others were extremely wary of lending on the security of personal items. John Howard Cromwell did not mince words in his advice to women: "a loan upon a chattel security, such as horses or livestock ... will not be for a moment entertained by a careful person." Personal property, he continued, "from its very nature, may be removed from place to place, concealed, hidden or destroyed at the will of the persons having the possession." Moreover, he warned, establishing ownership "may be a proceeding of great difficulty." Yet even Cromwell reluctantly recognized that "chattel mortgages may be classed as among the most common methods of securing ... loans, more often than otherwise of small amounts."[11]

In an attempt to regulate and stabilize an oft-used market for lending and raising money, Amor De Cosmos put before the assembly of the British colony of Vancouver Island in 1861 an "Act for preventing Frauds upon Creditors by Secret Bills of Sale of Personal Chattels."[12] At this time the colony was beginning to suffer from the effects of a declining gold rush. Debt absconders were many, and as the act's preamble stated, "frauds are frequently committed upon Creditors by secret Bills of Sale of Personal Chattels." "The bill would provide," De Cosmos informed his fellow MLAs, "that the possession of a bill of sale would give the mortgagee the same power as if he had possession of the goods." It required that the sale or mortgage of any personal property still in the possession of the seller or mortgagor (borrower), thus enabling that person "to keep up the appearance of being in good circumstances and possessed of Property," be "filed with the Registrar General within twenty-one days after the making or giving of such Bill of Sale." "The main object," De Cosmos declared, "was to place charges on personal property in the same position as charges on real property." In this way business people could check the personal assets of a prospective client or loan applicant by exposing what are now known as pocket liens. Personal chattels were any goods "in or upon any House,

Mill, Warehouse, Building, Works, Yard, Land, or other Premises occu-
pied by him ... not withstanding that formal possession ... may have
been taken by or given to any other person." Basically personal chattels
were any goods other than real estate or ships. Over the next thirty
years the Bills of Sale and Chattel Mortgage Act was modified in ways
that made clearer the kinds of property that it encompassed, but its pri-
mary purpose remained that of requiring people to make public the
real state of their personal assets, thus rendering fraudulent transac-
tions more difficult.[13]

Relative to the more organized and institutional structure of banking
and credit and loan activity, chattel mortgage transactions tended to be
personal and local in nature, and as a layer of borrower-lender rela-
tions, existed below that of the banks and mortgage companies. Chattel
mortgaging was a very important way for rural and urban residents to
raise short-term capital, capital being defined as "assets which are capa-
ble of generating income and which themselves have been pro-
duced."[14] In this sense chattel transactions stood at the interstice of
land mortgaging and mercantile credit. Using the device of a mort-
gage, chattels were used as security for promissory note(s) to raise
money for various ends, and from a mercantile perspective, they were
also and quite commonly used as security for their own purchase or the
purchase of other capital goods from hardware merchants, sewing
machine companies, implement dealers or manufacturers, and sundry
other individuals.

Who might have transacted business under the Bills of Sale and Chat-
tel Mortgage Act? The definition of personal chattels encompassed
goods in a home as well as those in a business. Clearly, merchants, those
who sold industrial and household goods on credit, could see this legis-
lation as a means with which to protect their transaction. One would
expect that business people, buyers and sellers on credit, would be
active in the chattel market. One would also expect that buyers of
household items would be present in this market. The expanding liter-
ature on the economic roles of women in the marketplace suggests that
this capital market could serve the interests of women, whether mar-
ried and in the household or active as small entrepreneurs. We would
expect that with the passage of the MWPLs in the late nineteenth cen-
tury, women, married and otherwise, would acquire more control over
money and personal assets. In fact, we know little in the Canadian con-
text regarding the use of personal property by women and especially by
married women. Most queries have focused on reality, but from 1873

on, married women had dispositive rights to personal property not enjoyed with real property until 1887 in British Columbia. They could buy and sell under their own names, free from the direct control of a husband or any other male. We have already seen that MWPLs provided a favourable context for a significant increase in women's activity in local land and mortgage markets, although the exact patterns of such activity were also conditioned by a complex set of local circumstances. Below we will test for the impact of these laws on women's activity in the Victoria chattel market.

Women in the household might have used the chattel market in several ways. They could have used large household items as collateral for the taking out of short-term loans to facilitate household management. In this sense, the chattel loan market can be construed as a kind of pawnshop, only the goods remained in possession of the borrower. Women might also have used goods they owned to raise money for more general productive ends: perhaps to assist their spouse's business. Finally, women in the household might themselves have acted as creditors, lending money to others on the security of sundry chattels.

Not all women who participated in this capital market would do so as household managers. As much recent literature has demonstrated, many women were active as small entrepreneurs in the late nineteenth century, activity facilitated in part by the passage of the MWPLs and examined more intensively in chapters 7 and 8. Many of these small businesses were fragile affairs, often dependent on short-term loans to ward off closure. The chattel mortgage market offered the possibility of acquiring cash by using the fixtures of one's business as collateral. It is reasonable to suppose that women could have been involved as both lenders and borrowers on the basis of small business chattels. After providing a general profile of participants in this market, this chapter will test these assumptions.

Before we move to a general discussion, an examination of the behaviour of several women recorded in these files will shed light on the extent of information available and on the nature of the legal instruments under which these transactions occurred. In August 1888 Mabel Claire, recorded as a "hook" by the registry clerk, contracted with a furniture dealer for what seems to have been the purchase of a mattress, bedroom suite, and household furniture at a total cost of $373. This transaction was conducted under a legal instrument known as a conditional bill of sale, as were close to three-quarters of all transactions found in the Victoria register. Conditional bills of sale allowed for the title to be in the hands of the dealer while the property resided with the buyer. Claire would receive the title only when final payment was made.[15] Slightly less than one in five of all transactions occurred under the terms of an absolute bill of sale. When a grantor (borrower) conveyed rights to property to a grantee (lender) but retained physical possession of that property, and when such a transaction was registered under the Bills of Sale and Chattel Mortgage Act, one can be reasonably sure that the conveyance was done in order to secure a debt.[16] Such almost certainly was the case for Agnes Trachsler, a widow who boarded with a two-year-old son. In June 1889 she conveyed ownership of furniture to Andrew Aaronson, a local pawnbroker, in exchange for $66.

The transactions involving Claire and Trachsler point to the registry's richness as well as its complexities and limitations. We do not have details concerning the timing for repayment or information concerning interest charged. Indeed, the registry only commenced recording the money involved and the nature of the personal property in May 1888. After that date the occupation of the grantor was recorded but not that of the grantee. The contracts also do not tell us what the grantor desired to do with the money raised or goods purchased. For example, we cannot be absolutely sure that the furniture dealer was in fact selling goods rather than lending money to Claire, in return for which she conveyed title to goods she already owned. She, after all, was the grantor of goods, just as a mortgagor grants title of a real property to a mortgagee while retaining physical control of that property. The ambivalence can be further illustrated by an example of another quite common transaction. In January 1891 Annie Anderson, a married woman, conveyed title to household furniture to F.G. Richards in return for $400. Or did she purchase the furniture from Richards, he keeping the title pending final payment? For the purposes of this study the essential point to keep in mind is simply that while property remained in the physical control of the grantor, the title lodged with the grantee and would remain there pending a set of payments. Whether these obligations were incurred as a result of a direct purchase on credit or as a result of a loan on the security of property already owned is a moot point. The effect was the same: women were raising money and/or purchasing on credit using as collateral property in their own name. They were doing so in the context of running their own business, as the case of Mabel Claire illustrates, and in the course of manging their own households, as the cases of Agnes Trachsler and Annie Anderson suggest.

Women were also active as grantees, and as the following example shows, the registry files provide a window into high as well as low finance. Most women, as we shall see, engaged in only one transaction, but between 1888 and 1902 Joan O. Dunsmuir, widow and colliery proprietor, transacted fifteen separate conditional bill of sale arrangements with people in Victoria totalling $360,808. We have comparable evidence for the transactions of men and businesses for 1888–92 and 1898–1902, and during those time periods only the Bank of British Columbia transacted more chattel business. In Joan Dunsmuir's case the nature of the transactions was clear: under the instrument of the conditional bill of sale, she lent money, a great deal of money, to companies and individuals in return for which she received, as security, title to sundry goods. Hotel furniture underwrote a loan of $1,000. A dog, cart, horse, and boat stood as security for a loan of $3,500. Title to the plant of the Electric Tramway Lighting Company warranted a loan of $100,000. It is clearly interesting that a woman was a more active participant in the chattel market that any man. The nature of her activity points to the fact that wealthy widows could and did play significant roles in local economies.[17] But, as the examples of Claire, Trachsler, and Anderson suggest, Dunsmuir, while exceptional, was not alone.

The number of transactions registered in Victoria under the bills of sale legislation reflects the city's changing economic fortunes. Figure 6.2 nicely illustrates the boom and bust of the 1860s, the doldrums of the 1870s, and economic growth in the 1880s and early 1890s, followed by a sharp downturn until the brief pre–World War One boom. During the 1860s and 1870s, 45 transactions, on average, were registered per year. In the first half of the 1880s transactions increased to an average of 66 per year. Between 1885 and 1895 the yearly average rose significantly to 108 before dropping to 65 between 1896 and 1902. The unprecedented boom years prior to World War One saw transactions increase again to some 152 a year between 1910 and 1913. It is clear that people registered more than simply very large business deals. The average size of an individual transaction between 1888 and 1892 was $1,928; for 1893–97, $3,724; and for 1898 and 1902, $2,278. But for each of the three time periods before 1910 the median figure was only $600.

While the various laws governing chattel transactions made it clear that registration was required to protect investors and set strict time limits for the registration of such activity, it is difficult to know the extent to which the files reflect the total transactions of this sort. Very

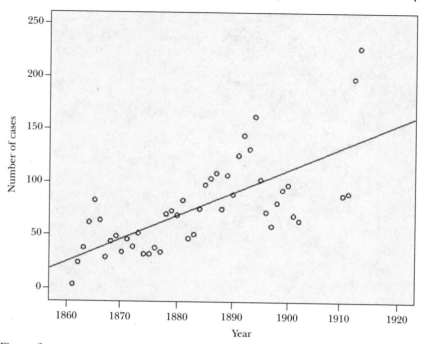

Figure 6.2

Number of transactions per year, 1861–1913

NOTE: For 1861–87, all transactions by women have been counted, as have the total transactions for that time period. Data on money and type of goods are not available for most years before 1888. Complete information on all transactions have been collected for 1888–92 and for 1898–1902. All transactions, broken down by men, companies, and women with money values, have been collected for 1893–97. Names and property types were recorded only for transactions involving women. Only the number of transactions and women's percentage of same have been counted for 1910–13.

likely, they are an underestimation, since buying and selling personal items by married and other women was hardly a new practice. Historians have shown that this activity on the part of married women in England predated the passage of the MWPLs, and there is no reason to assume that the same was not the case in British Columbia. We know, for example, that at least two of the women in the registry files who borrowed money on the basis of chattels before 1873 (the first MWPL in British Columbia) were married and acting on their own. It might be argued that in the context of personal property, the MWPLs were codifying, making customary practice legal. Even if that was to an extent the case, the registry laws and the MWPLs were still enabling if only because they gave to the lender greater security and presumably inspired greater willingness to participate on the part of a wider group of

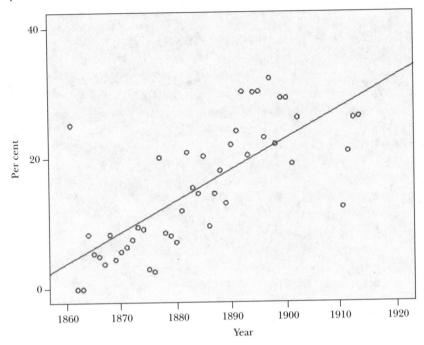

Figure 6.3
Transactions involving women as a percentage of all transactions, 1861–1913

people. In this context it should be remembered that the rationale for
the passage of the chattel legislation arose from the "shady" nature of
the chattel market. Just as that legislation provided for public regis-
tration, so too the MWPLS legally acknowledged the right of married
women to participate in that economic sector and thereby stimulated
such activity.

Table 6.1 and figure 6.3 provide a first look at the relative involve-
ment of women in this market. Measured by the number of transactions
that involved at least one woman, the participation of women in the
chattel market increased in the latter part of the nineteenth century
from one in seventeen transactions before 1874, levelling off at about
one in four of all transactions at the close of the century. The increase
in the 1880s and 1890s and the levelling off at the turn of the century
have been found for women's profile in other wealth-related indices,
most notably the number and worth of probates and women as mort-
gagees. It may be the case that the MWPL passed in British Columbia in
1873 had a positive impact on women's participation in the chattel
market. Following the passage of that act, women's participation did

steadily increase. That legislation permitted married women to buy and sell personal property in their own names. Unfortunately, we lack both good population figures for Victoria in the 1870s and adequate marital status information on the women who did participate in that decade; so the relative increase in women's participation might also have reflected a proportional increase in the number of women compared to men in that city.

The changes in the late 1880s and 1890s, however, cannot be attributed to any significant increase in the relative numbers of women in the city. The proportion of women over the age of nineteen fluctuated around one-third of the over-nineteen population in the city for the last twenty years of the century (36 per cent in 1881, 31 per cent in 1891, and 36.5 per cent in 1901).[18] While the relative participation of individual women remained fairly constant in the 1890s, such was not the case for married women's involvement. Indeed, perhaps the most relevant trend for our purposes *is* the increased participation of married women in the chattel market. Even as the proportion of married women in the city declined from 69 per cent of women in 1881 to 63 per cent in 1901, the proportion of married women in the chattel market increased from 56 per cent of women in the 1881–87 period to 68 per cent in the 1898–1902 period.[19] That increase is consistent with the proposition that the MWPLs did enable increased activity by married women as *femme sole* in this market.

As figure 6.4 indicates, married women increased their activity as grantees to a proportionately greater extent than they did as grantors. In fact, married women's participation at the end of the century as borrowers or purchasers was close to what it had been in the 1880s. By contrast, their participation as lenders or sellers increased by 21 per cent. These contrasting trends suggest that married women were accustomed to participating as buyers and perhaps as borrowers even before the passage of the MWPLs. A similar trend is evident in the landed mortgage sector. In chapter 5 we noted that married women were more apt to borrow than to lend on the basis of landed mortgages. Yet as with chattel market participation, so too with activity in the landed mortgage sector: married women in Victoria increased their presence as lenders and maintained their presence as borrowers over the last twenty years of the nineteenth century. Eighty-five per cent of the women who borrowed on landed security in 1881 were married, as were 85 per cent of those who borrowed on the security of land in 1901. By contrast, in 1891 only 38 per cent of women who lent on

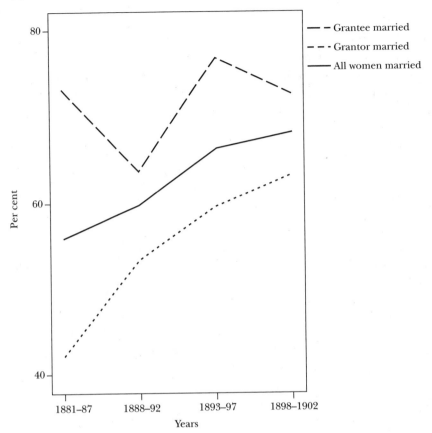

Figure 6.4
Married women as a percentage of all women in the chattel market: Victoria, 1881–1902

the basis of land were married, a proportion that had increased to 54 per cent ten years later.[20] The MWPLs had their greatest impact in freeing up capital for married women, many of whom, as a consequence, became more active as investors, lenders, and sellers in sundry financial markets in the late nineteenth century.

Useful perspective can be provided by further comparing the realty mortgage and chattel mortgage markets. Activity in the chattel market fell short of that in the realty mortgage market. As table 6.2 indicates, more mortgage transactions and more money were exchanged in the realty mortgage market than in the chattel market. Yet what is most interesting here is the fact that while the average size of transaction was higher for the chattel than for the realty sector, the median value was significantly lower. Clearly, as the standard deviation figures suggest, the chattel market was much more bifurcated in nature than was the realty market. Most participants in the chattel market, like Agnes Trachsler and Mabel Claire, borrowed small sums on the security of modestly valued personal property, and most lent small sums on similar collateral. At what one might term the top end of the market, several large firms raised money on the strength of their corporate chattels and borrowed that money from other companies, from financial institutions such as the Bank of British Columbia, and as we have seen, from wealthy individuals such as Joan Dunsmuir.

Indeed, perhaps the most dramatic difference to note is the significant involvement of companies in the chattel, as compared to the reality, mortgage market (compare tables 6.3 and 6.4 with tables 5.2 and 5.3). In the 1890s especially, companies dominated the chattel market in terms of the size of their transactions, lending some 50 per cent of the capital in that market and borrowing only a little less than that. By comparison, companies were participants as borrowers in transactions with a total value of only 8.4 per cent of the reality market in 1891, and in that year women borrowed more than did companies. Company profile was higher as lenders, reaching 20 per cent of the reality capital loaned in 1891 and 13 per cent in 1901. But even in 1901 women lent and borrowed more than did companies in the reality mortgage market. Banks were, of course, forbidden to invest in the reality market at this time; so it makes sense to see more companies as mortgagees in the chattel, rather than reality, mortgage sector. But the contrast is true for both borrowers and lenders. After 1892, companies – primarily banks, general mortgage companies such as the British Columbia Land and Investment Company, and some insurance companies – lent large sums on the security of chattels. Other businesses in such sectors as salmon canning, shipping, lumber, and import and export borrowed large sums on the basis of such chattels as silk merchandise, cannery equipment, brewery stock, and, in one instance, 12,569,875 logs at Cowichan Lake.

By comparison with companies, women's participation in the chattel market seems flat and relatively insignificant. Yet as tables 6.3 and 6.4 show, there were always more women participants as mortgagees and mortgagors than companies, and in the late 1880s and early 1890s women as mortgagees invested more capital in that market. Nevertheless, women at first glance seem much more significant as actors in the reality than in the chattel market. Such an observation might seem counterintuitive. One might expect women to be more active in a market that privileges things rather than a market that privileges real estate. After all, traditional historiography has certainly not seen women as significant players in the reality sector and that historiography has characterized them as fond owners of things personal. As chapters 4 and 5 have demonstrated, however, a significant number of women were active in the reality sector as property owners and mortgage investors. Still, at a broad level the differences between women's participation in the mortgage field and their participation in the chattel area remains puzzling, if not startling. How might one explain the fact that in 1901 women counted for 20 per cent of the capital invested by mortgagees in the reality market and, for a similar period, only 5 per cent of that invested in the chattel market?

The answer lies in the nature of what is being compared. Note that the participation of men in the chattel market also pales in comparison to their activity in the mortgage field: men counted for just under 70 per cent of capital invested by mortgagees in the reality sector in 1901 and only 24 per cent in the chattel market in the comparable period. If one puts the activity of companies in each sector in brackets, then the comparison of men's and women's activity across sectors looks dramatically different from what we have seen thus far. As mortgagees in 1891, women accounted for 15 per cent of investment in the reality sector and, for the comparable period, the same in the chattel area. In the chattel field they increased their investment profile to 26 per cent of the market in the middle 1890s, a share that fell to 11 per cent by the end of the decade. In the mortgage area a similar drop-off did not take place until 1911, and by 1921 women's participation had increased once again. Without companies as mortgagors, there was also a narrowing of activity across sectors by women, although they tended to be more active as mortgagors in the reality than in the chattel field. Despite a possible difference in trend line, the more important point is that with companies out of the mix, the relative activity of women and men in the chattel market compares closely to their relative activity in the reality market. Companies were the wild cards and were clearly much more attracted to the chattel than to the reality financial area. But in their shadow, individual men and individual women continued to borrow and invest, though with less capital than companies and less than they tended to invest in the reality mortgages, in a very similar way in terms of their proportionate presence in each market.

With whom did women transact business? Literature on the market activity of women in the pre-industrial era has pointed to the tendency of women to act with and transact with other women.[21] Literature on the business activity of women in the industrial period has documented a similar tendency towards ghettoization. Women operated in business areas that served the needs of other women. We have already explored this potential activity in the context of the realty mortgage market and found mixed results. Is a similar pattern evident in the chattel market? There was a slight but declining tendency for women to lend to or borrow from other women. Given the number of women and men in the file, women in the early period were about two times more likely to deal with other women than with men. For the period following 1898, although the number of cases is small, this tendency disappeared.[22] While comparative studies of chattel market behaviour in other regions are required, it may be the case that, following the passage of the MWPLs, women gradually became more accepted as legitimate market participants.

In terms of type of participation, women were somewhat more likely to lend than to borrow. Tables 6.3 and 6.4 also hint at a tendency for them to act, at least formally, on their own in this financial market. To a greater degree than their male counterparts, women participated as individuals rather than in partnerships, and when they did participate in partnerships, they generally acted with a man, rather than with another woman. Moreover, and again in contrast to men, when women acted in a partnership, it was almost always as a grantor and only rarely as a grantee. When women wished to lend money or sell goods, they tended to do so on their own, and this pattern includes married women, eight out of ten of whom participated as grantees separate from their husbands. This behaviour was also evident in the reality mortgage sector, as we have noted in chapter 4. These women might well have agreed with Senator Campbell from Ontario, who viewed such activity as consistent with his liberal view of society: a woman, including a married woman, had "full right" to manage "her own property ... [as] she likes with it." It is a further indication that the liberal world described by Ian McKay and others contained more than men as prime actors.

The associative patterns exhibited by women borrowers and lenders raise a larger question: did the social background of the first group differ from that of the second? One body of literature, best exemplified by Craig Muldrew, argues that credit, far from a divisive force in capitalist society, was one means that linked different social groups in communities together.[23] Did men's and women's activity in this market reflect such a pattern? Alternatively, it may be the case that the backgrounds of the two groups differed little. It may be that entrance to the market itself, whether as a borrower, a lender, a seller, or a purchaser on time, depended on certain social criteria, the result being that the two groups reflected a more or less homogeneous whole. If such was the case, then the ties of credit did not bind different classes; rather, to continue with a positive view of credit relations, they strengthened internal class relations.

The first question that the data in tables 6.5 and 6.6 allow us to consider is the degree to which those who participated in the chattel market differed in social characteristics from Victoria's total population. The data suggest that in important ways the market players were a special subset. This is most pronounced in terms of class status. Participants in this market were more likely than the general population to own real property. Employers and the self-employed were more likely to participate than were employees. So too, and especially for men, were those who were married and household heads. If the Chinese male population is taken out of table 6.6, then the ratios of foreign-born participants to foreign-born in the total population (and for Protestants) resemble the figures for women in table 6.5. The bills of sale market attracted a special subset of the total community: compared to the general population, participants tended more often to be foreign-born, married, household heads, propertied, and employers or self-employed.

The differences between grantors and grantees were not as pronounced as the differences between the general population and both groups. In terms of birthplace and religion, the differences between female grantors and grantees and those between male grantors and grantees were not dramatic. Clearly, both male and female grantors were less likely to own property than male and female grantees (tables 6.5 and 6.6). It is also the case that the average value of the property owned by grantors was less than that owned by grantees.[24] At a broad level such distinctions make sense. One would expect that people who owned no real property or even real property worth relatively little would be more likely to rely on the security of other assets, in this case their chattels, to raise money.

Class differences are somewhat more complex in nature. At first glance the differences seem clearer in the case of men. Grantees were more often employers and self-employed than were grantors. With women the opposite seems to be the case. A closer look at the distribution by relation to means of production is provided in table 6.7. For both women and men, employers tended to be grantees more often than grantors. But, and especially for women, the self-employed tended to be more often grantors than grantees. For both women and men, self-employed grantors were less apt to own real property than their grantee counterparts. Thus self-employed men and most especially self-employed women turned to the chattel market to raise funds for the conduct of their business affairs.

Indeed, from the perspective of the self-employed, the chattel market served the interests of women proportionately more than men. Forty-six per cent of female grantors were self-employed, compared to only 27 per cent of male grantors.[25] By documenting the variety of ways that businesswomen employed to finance their operations, the chattel registry provides a window into entrepreneurial activity by women in the late nineteenth century. Twenty-nine women grantors self-identified on the chattel mortgage and/or census that they were boarding, lodging, or hotel keepers, at least eleven of whom were married. Women purchased furniture on time from the Hudson's Bay Company and beer from a local brewery, pledging stock as security. Ellen Johnson, a hotel owner, acquired a capital infusion by granting half-interest in her business. Other women raised money on goods and fixtures from private investors and local investment companies.

Undoubtedly, many of these twenty-nine women did indeed run boarding houses. But for a significant number of others, boarding houses often shaded into bawdy houses. Between 1890 and 1892 six of these women grantors were arrested and charged with keeping a bawdy house or house of ill fame in Victoria, and two more were charged in the 1900–01 period. Three of the nine self-described dressmakers noted below were also arrested for keeping a bawdy house in these years.[26] Minnie Butler, a self-styled dressmaker, was twice arrested for keeping a bawdy house. She kept her business going by pledging her furniture to a pawnbroker for $250. May Fox, who called herself a boarding-house keeper, was charged three times, and the second time she missed her hearing; so a warrant was issued for her arrest. She was fined over $100, a very large amount for a bawdy-house keeper in this era. Fox was almost equally active in the chattel mortgage market. Between 1892 and 1899 she transacted eight business deals, varying in size from $155 to $310. At least six were conditional bills of sale entered into with pawnbrokers. Clearly, to maintain her enterprise and perhaps to pay her fines, she required fairly constant recourse to borrowing, and pawnbrokers were quite happy to oblige her and most of the other prostitutes who borrowed on the basis of their chattels.

But pawnbrokers were not the only lenders to bawdy-house keepers. Most bawdy-house keepers in the chattel market do not appear to have owned land. They were generally listed in the census as boarders. But Theresa Bornstein could and did offer land as security for a loan from the staid and respected British Columbia Land and Investment Company.[27] In 1894 the company lent her $3,000 on the security of land. Three years earlier Bornstein had pleaded guilty to running a house of ill fame. Did the company know with whom it was dealing? It seems clear that it did. Its loan files demonstrate time and again the care the staff put into examining the backgrounds of loan applicants. There is no reason to doubt that they were equally vigilant with regard to Theresa Bornstein. Why else would the company have charged her the exorbitant rate of 18 per cent interest?

Obviously, our data allow for only a partial linkage between women in the chattel market and the business of prostitution and thus undercounts the number of bawdy-house keepers who might have used the chattel market in these years. As well, it is very likely the case that many loans to bawdy-house keepers remained unregistered in this period, as they would have been in the period before the passage of the chattel mortgage legislation. What is clear is that the chattel market acted as a bridge between the formal and informal or underground economy, at the intersection of which prostitutes and their madams conducted their affairs. Nor should it be surprising that pawnbrokers were prominent actors in these transactions. As Beverly Lemire has shown, pawnbrokers in England before and during the nineteenth century provided loans to working-class women and men and in so doing, met a need that more formal credit institutions such as banks were unwilling to address. Lemire's evidence demonstrates that women were quite active in negotiating these loans with pawnbrokers, more active at the boundaries of the formal and informal economy than in the more central and institutionalized credit processes employed by more affluent groups in society.[28]

The ten merchants and nine dressmakers and clothiers, including a gents outfitter (at least eight of whom were married), exhibited an equally extensive set of relations with a variety of creditors. Elizabeth Williams, a local clothier, secured a $5,000 transaction with David Spencer, owner of a large department store, with a pledge on stock-in-trade. The eight women involved in stock and horse dealing and farm produce ranged equally widely in their pursuit of credit. Mary Florence, a stock dealer, raised money on a stallion named Richard the Third from a local businessman. She financed the purchase of or raised money on the security of at least six horses in the early 1890s.

The class differences pointed to by Muldrew are evident in the chattel market. Such differences are, however, hardly startling. One would expect that employers would be in a better position to sell on credit or lend money on personal chattels than employees. The fact is, however, the self-employed and employers were more apt to transact business in this market with people of their own class than with those of the employee class.[29] In a double sense, then, this credit market cannot be viewed primarily as one that bound classes together. While some of that might certainly have occurred, in general terms employees were dramatically underrepresented in the market as a whole, and employers and the self-employed were more apt to deal with non-employees than with those of the employee class. If any "binding" of the sort referred to by Muldrew occurred, it took place more within than across classes. Viewed in class terms, this market offered more possibilities for its business class, and especially for its women entrepreneurs, than for the city's working class.

Participants in the chattel market also exhibited demographic differences. Demographic differences tended to be more important in the case of women. Women who borrowed or purchased were younger than those who sold or lent. While those who borrowed were close to the average age of all Victoria women, those who lent were, on average, much older. Women grantees were twice as likely to be widowed as were grantors and less likely to be married.

Demographic differences suggest that for men, and especially for women, borrowing and lending were tied to life-cycle processes. The data in table 6.8 confirm this pattern. In the case of borrowing, the pattern has been pointed to in a number of studies, most recently by Rotella and Alter.[30] Yet few studies have compared borrowers and lenders across life cycles, and still fewer have pointed to gender differences in borrowing and lending behaviour across the family life cycle. In fact, life-cycle differences were more pronounced for women borrowers and lenders than they were for their male counterparts. While male borrowers bulked in the first three stages of the family life cycle, so too did male lenders. For women, the contrast was more dramatic. Two-thirds of women grantors were in the first three stages of the family life cycle; only two-fifths of women grantees were in those categories. Moreover, three-fifths of women grantees were in the last two stages of the family life cycle; only a third of male grantees were in those stages. At the early stages of the family cycle, women were active as borrowers and purchasers. As the family matured, many widows certainly became active investors and moneylenders. So too, as table 6.8 indicates, did many married women, who, as we noted earlier (see figure 6.4), increasingly moved into lending on the basis of both real and chattel mortgages, thanks to the MWPLS.

The use of logistic regression helps to sharpen some of the above analysis. The following variables were included in a run to test the log odds of being a grantee in the chattel market: occupation, birth, religion, age, relation to means of production, marital status, gender, whether one owned or rented property, and family cycle (see table 6.9). Only a small number of characteristics help us to distinguish between grantees and grantors in the chattel market. Gender is the most important of those characteristics: men were 2.4 times more likely to be a grantee or lender than were women. Women were far more likely than men to be purchasers or borrowers in this market. This finding is consistent with the results for relation to means of production. The regression sharpens our understanding of class differences. The self-employed were about as unlikely to be grantees as were the employees. Only employers and those on their own means were more likely to be a lender than a borrower. It will be recalled that a significant percentage of women grantors were self-employed, and this concentration helps to account for the high odds of men, rather than women, being grantees. It is also possible to consider that women would have been the traditional purchasers of household items, so that their participation as buyers in this market could also help to account for the higher tendency of women to be grantors as compared to men.

Occupation is significant, but the findings here cannot be considered surprising: the professional/managerial sector had the highest odds of being grantees, and those in the service industry the lowest. Again, this result seems consistent with that for gender: women were often boarding bawdy-house keepers, and as we have seen, people in that category were quite visible amongst the ranks of the grantors. Next to gender, whether one owned or rented real property was the most important indicator of the odds of being a grantee. Those who owned were twice as likely as those who rented to be lenders in this market. This finding confirms our analysis up to this point: those without real

property were the most apt to borrow using personal chattels as secu-
rity. One might be tempted to think that this finding, too, might help
us to make sense of the gendered odds. After all, we might suppose that
women as a group would be much less likely than men to own real
property. But as the discussion in chapter 4 has demonstrated,
gendered differences in real property ownership were fairly small in
Victoria in the late nineteenth century. The same finding is true for
men and women in the chattel market: men were slightly more likely to
own property, but the result of a cross-tabulation between gender and
own/rent was insignificant.[31]

The results for family cycle and for age might seem surprising. In the
case of family cycle, the different pattern for women noted above in the
discussion of table 6.8 is not visible in the regression because of the rel-
atively small numbers of women in the file.[32] The finding, then, reflects
male family life-cycle patterns, not female, and to that extent it is not
inconsistent with our earlier findings that life cycle was less important a
determinant for men's behaviour in this market than for women's. Age
is perhaps more intriguing. It was also run as a non-categorical variable
and as age squared and without family cycle. In each run the backward
step process discarded age as not significant. One might have thought
that the older one was, the higher the odds of being a lender rather
than a borrower.[33] Our earlier comments based on the data in tables
6.5 and 6.6 suggested as much. In the presence of the other social vari-
ables, however, age is not a useful predictor as to whether one would be
a grantee or a grantor in the chattel market.

As figures 6.5 and 6.6 indicate, the average size of grantor and
grantee transactions did not differ dramatically by gender. Women
tended to borrow somewhat smaller sums than men and to lend some-
what larger sums. If, however, we take Joan Dunsmuir out of the lender
category, women lent on average much less money per transaction than
did men. In the latter part of the nineteenth century, women in Victo-
ria lent to other Victoria residents $520,787 on the security of chattels.
Men lent just over $2,000,000. Women borrowed on the security of
chattels some $235,000, and men borrowed $2.1 million. Women, rela-
tive to men and to companies, were small participants in this market.
Yet women such as Annie Calder did lend small sums on the basis of
chattels, and the returns contributed to her personal livelihood. As
well, measured by ability to raise money for personal entrepreneurial
endeavours, as we have seen, women's involvement in this market was
quite significant.

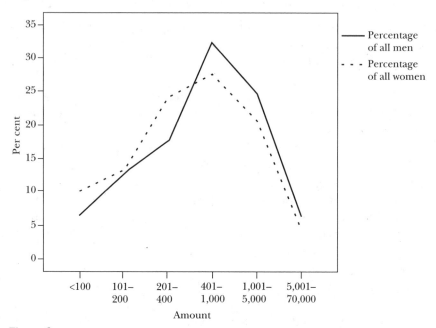

Figure 6.5

Female and male grantors grouped by size of transaction: Victoria, 1888–1901

NOTE: There were 163 transactions for women and 1,090 for men. Partnerships were excluded, as were all transactions over $70,000.

Some have suggested that the MWPLs would have affected only the minority of women who had capital or at least potential access to capital in the first place. The majority of nineteenth-century women would have remained unaffected by that legislation. At a broad level this commentary is persuasive.[34] A closer look at the activities of women grantors in the bills of sale market, however, suggests that too narrow a class-based interpretation of the impact of MWPLs is not warranted. Laura Travis and her husband, both of whom claimed to be unemployed in October 1892, were clearly struggling to make ends meet when they pledged household goods and furniture to one Tom Macabe in return for $302. Annie Wilkinson secured a $42 transaction with John Mellor, a paint and glass merchant, on general household furniture. Her husband, a miner, worked on his own account. Annie had two young sons and took in two boarders in their rented six-room house. The Wilkinsons lived at 42 Humbolt Street, near the White Horse Hotel and assorted cabins, all of which is suggestive of a lower-working-class environment. At least four other married women who

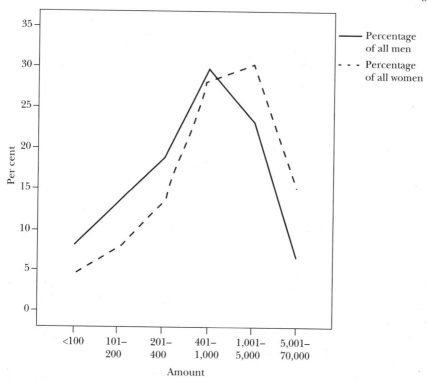

Figure 6.6
Female and male grantees grouped by size of transaction: Victoria, 1888–1901
NOTE: There were 171 transactions for women and 982 for men. Partnerships were
excluded, as were all transactions over $70,000.

borrowed under $200 operated small boarding or lodging houses and
secured their transactions on household furniture. In fact, 70 per cent
of women who engaged in transactions under $200 and for whom
marital status is known were married.

Interestingly, those in the business of prostitution rarely borrowed
such small sums. May Fox averaged $242 per loan, but she was an
exception. The average-sized loan for the other nine women in that
business who borrowed on the basis of chattels was $1,300. Estella
Carrol, a self-proclaimed boarding-house keeper, borrowed $3,900 in
February 1900. A month later she was convicted of operating a house of
ill fame and fined $75. For Carrol, this must have seemed a minor
deterrent: she stated to the 1901 census enumerator that she had
earned $1,100 in the previous year, a very substantial sum for a man or

a woman at that time. The point here is that defining class simply on the basis of size of loan is a very imprecise procedure.

It would be wrong to press the point about multi-class participation too far. Certainly, some of the married women who transacted small business deals were nonetheless in at least middle-class circumstances. Effie Rahy worked with her husband in a seemingly successful fruit and tobacco enterprise. She secured her $200 business deal in 1902 on general stock. Collin, her husband, claimed to have made $1,000 from the business in 1901. The point, then, is not that working-class married women dominated activity in the lower end of the bills of sale market; rather, it is enough to note that they participated at all. The MWPLs provided opportunities to more than simply middle- and upper-class women.

Three-fifths of women grantors had occupations other than housewife, but housewives were also active in this market. No occupation could be found for about half the married women grantors who acted without partners.[35] These women were often identified as the wife of, for example, Mr Pangburn. Many so identified, however, were clearly involved in their husbands' businesses. Indeed, between 1892 and 1899 Clara Haggerty, a contractor–house builder's wife, acted singly once and with her husband three times to raise money on the security of horses (three times) and on household furniture (one time). The time she acted alone, she granted a conditional bill of sale for $3,000 on the security of a number of horses to Ellin Conlin, an American-born Native who had married an Irish-born blacksmith. Gertrude Cunningham, the wife of a dry goods entrepreneur, facilitated the purchase of $100 of soap from a local manufacturer by pledging her household furniture as security. Anne Marie Cook may have been raising money for her husband's mercantile business when she granted a conditional bill of sale for $65 secured on goods and furniture. About 40 per cent of married women with no stated occupation (thirteen of thirty-three) were likely involved in helping to finance their husbands' businesses by raising money on goods they owned. Virtually all of the remaining married women who operated in this market and had no recorded occupation granted conditional bills of sale on household goods and furniture to a variety of grantees, including furniture dealers and general financiers. Very likely these women were outfitting their households and/or raising money on the strength of household items under their control. For these women, household items possessed financial as well as functional value.

More than other women, married women tended to lend to people with the same last name. Thirty-two of the sixty-seven women who we know were married granted a chattel mortgage to a family member, twenty-six of whom dealt with their husbands. Those women who dealt with family members were five times more likely than women who transacted with non-family to grant an absolute, rather than conditional, bill of sale, perhaps suggesting that this was a relatively easy way to transfer ownership of goods between family members, and often the payment exacted was a token $1.[36] In other instances it seems clear that married women were lending money to their husbands in order to help their businesses. Ellen Verrinder seems typical here. She married her husband, Arthur, a dentist, in 1893 and in the same year lent him $3,400 on the security of his "dental effects." Fanny Pitzer granted her husband, William, a farmer, $2,500 on the security of general livestock and farming stock in 1894. Transactions of this sort, of course, can be interpreted in several ways. At one level, the bill of sale provided married women with legal security for the loans granted to their husbands and, indeed, to other family members, loans such women had undoubtedly been granting without such security before the passage of the chattel legislation and may, in numbers we cannot reasonably estimate, have continued to make after the passage of such legislation. In this sense the chattel records, along with memoirs, family papers, and court cases, provide knowledge of the existence, if not absolute frequency, of such transactions. The chattel mortgages may also have represented attempts by businessmen to shield their assets from other creditors. Indeed, in chattel documents registered in Ontario but not in British Columbia, the participants had to swear that they were not engaging in "fraudulent practice."

Fifty-six per cent of the transactions engaged in by women grantors in the time period covered in this study involved household furniture. As the examples above suggest, many of those transactions facilitated productive ends, both within and outside the household. In the industrializing and urbanizing environment of the late nineteenth century, women householders remained linked to the market economy through the household items many purchased. Initially, such items were purchased for their use value within the home. For many women, those items often took on a second role, that of facilitating access to needed capital for a myriad of productive and other reasons. Such items could become, in Sherry Olson's felicitous phrase, "domestic venture capital."[37]

In several ways the activity of women exhibited in this analysis of the bills of sale registry points to transitional processes in play in the late nineteenth century. Overall, women remained linked to the market economy in ways different from men. They tended to be more often than men borrowers or purchasers in the chattel market. Yet especially for married women, the trend was in the other direction. In the time period covered in this study, married women became increasingly likely to be lenders in the chattel market, reflecting, as we noted earlier in the chapter, the positive impact of the MWPLS. Women's participation was more closely linked to particular stages in the family cycle than was the case for men (table 6.8). Throughout the period examined, they relied much more heavily on household goods to raise money, and partly as a result, the average amounts raised were lower than those raised by men. Indeed, only 20 per cent of the transactions engaged in by male grantors included household property.[38] Men relied on goods in the productive sphere to raise capital for further production. For women, it was a case of new wine in old bottles. Household goods, initially acquired for their utilitarian value within the home, had often been used for other purposes. Beds accommodated boarders. Pianos brought in cash as instruments of instruction. Now, however, beds and other household chattels and status items such as silverware, watercolour, and pianos more easily facilitated the acquisition of capital for more general productive ends, to stave off financial ruin, or simply for the attainment of greater prestige and status. With the passage of the Bills of Sale and Chattel Mortgage Act, society codified such activity. With the passage of the MWPLS, society opened the door for women to more easily employ household and other goods for a wide variety of social and economic ends.

There was another, somewhat more gradual change occurring in the chattel market in the late nineteenth century, one that reflects changes in the nature of women's assets that we have noted in several previous chapters. Between 1888 and 1897, 45 per cent of chattel mortgages granted by women were on the security of household goods. For the 1898–1902 period, this proportion dropped to 36 per cent. By contrast, women grantees were increasingly willing to lend money on the basis of business chattels: between 1888 and 1897, 36 per cent of transactions involved business goods, and between 1898 and 1902 that figure increased to 49. A similar trend was evident in the security being offered by women grantors. In the first two periods, 58 per cent of mortgages were secured on household goods. This share dropped to 48 per cent in the final period. Instead, women grantors were increasingly offering business chattels as security, an activity that rose from 15 per cent in the late 1880s and early 1890s to 25 per cent in the mid-1890s and 43 per cent by the turn of the century. These trends point to the increasing prominence of entrepreneurial women in this market. The trend toward lending and borrowing on non-household items also points to the increased diversity of assets owned by women, a finding we noted in our analysis of women's probates, wills, and bequests. Initially, women may well have felt more comfortable dealing with and more knowledgeable about the value of household goods. That knowledge and confidence had extended to other assets by the century's end.

Household goods are multi-purpose items. From the perspective of economic anthropology, such commodities possess social lives that take on special significance at the point of exchange. At such moments, owners are linked to buyers and lenders to borrowers. Arjun Appadurai has argued, "Politics (in the broad sense of relations, assumptions, and contests of power) is what links value and exchange in the social life of commodities." While he does not focus on gender and power and limits his discussion to the "demand side of economic life," his is nonetheless a useful insight.[39] This chapter suggests that the social relations embedded in household commodities were undergoing a slow but important transformation in late nineteenth-century urban Canada. Household goods and women's proprietary interest in them were taking on new values and acquiring new powers in the evolving marketplace. At the same time, women were acquiring and using different assets, often of a business kind, on the strength of which they entered the chattel market as borrowers and lenders. Much borrowing that historians have categorized as one or both of family borrowing (with the implicit assumption that the male head of the house did the borrowing) and borrowing for consumptive purposes in fact was done by women, and done for purposes of production as well as consumption. If, in the words of Mary Douglas and Baron Isherwood, "being fit for consumption means an object being fit to circulate as a marker for particular sets of social roles,"[40] then traditional social roles marked by female-owned chattels underwent change in late nineteenth-century urban places such as Victoria. Women's goods, both those of the traditional household type and those of the emerging business economy, stand as fitting symbols of the permeability of home and market and of women's complex relationship to both.

7

Canadian Urban Women in Business

"Of what earthly use is business life to a woman, anyway," E.B.B.R. mused in the April 1907 edition of the *Financial Post*. The answer, arrived at "after a long time thinking hard," is revealing on at least two levels. First, for this writer, as for many others in the late nineteenth century, "business women" meant white-collar office workers: "a young woman going ... into business life...enters an office [where she] learns early the value of money, of time, of concentration of thought." For E.B.B.R, this step outside the home was positive: "She must take her mind off home affairs and put it right on the work that has been given for her special doing." Yet, and this is the second point, E.B.B.R. did not mean to imply that such activity might connote a change in a woman's proper place or sphere in life. Far from it. The value of being a "business woman" did not lie in any economic contribution a woman might make through her activities as a worker. Rather, as the article's title made clear, the value lay in "Business Women as Homemakers." The real benefit for the woman, for the family, and for society in general came when the businesswoman re-entered the home. "The young woman who enters business...is the woman who will be able to enter a home and give her business training full power in the management of her house." She will appreciate the challenges of making money "and is decades ahead of the allowance-receiving girl who demands the earnings of another as her right." "A wife who understands the worries of a hurried business day will be restful to a man when he comes from town. She will understand that a quiet, unquestioning welcome, a tidy, cosy room, a promptly served and well-cooked meal, take more fatigue from a worried brain than do all the coaxing and fussing that feminine mortal can devise." "[O]ur thorough young business women are unknowingly training themselves to be real home-makers, common-sense mothers, and companionable helpmeets. It cannot be otherwise and the world," E.B.B.R. concluded, "is going to be a better place because of their devotion to business interests."[1]

Despite "thinking hard," E.B.B.R. never entertained the notion that a woman could be in business as a self-employed entrepreneur. Yet many were. What, one wonders, would the *Financial Post's* author have thought about Violet McKee, a married woman who lived in a rented house in Hamilton with her six daughters. McKee was the head of the house, and her husband was not living with her. Along with four of her daughters, she operated a dressmaking business from her home, which earned $1,300 in 1901. Helen Noble, a widow, earned $150 as a furniture manufacturer in Hamilton. Leigh Spencer, a single woman, made $500 as a self-employed real estate broker in Vancouver. Agnes Symonds, a widow, ran a boarding house in Halifax that at the time of the census housed fourteen lodgers and had provided $1,500 in income over the previous year. Mary Humber, a widow who lived in Victoria, was active as a brick maker, a business that she bequeathed to her son and two sons-in-law in 1908.[2]

Moreover, it is clear that many husbands saw nothing wrong with their wives either running a business or participating with them in the management of an enterprise. Louisa Arnold, a married woman, had been running a midwifery enterprise in Victoria since at least 1886; in 1901 the business earned $540. In their wills many husbands freely bequeathed businesses to their wives. William Berney, a merchant in Hamilton, bequeathed his business and all his assets to his wife "to carry on the business as she should see fit." Joe Winslow, a hardware merchant in Hamilton, bequeathed his business, worth over $10,000, to his wife. Joe Kendall, a grocer in the same city, offered his meat and grocery business to his wife at half-price; she had one month to make up her mind, after which the executors were to sell it on the open market. Although George Trumball, a tavern keeper in Hamilton, had a son, he bequeathed his tavern licence to his wife in 1880 for her sole use.[3]

How exceptional was this behaviour? Until recently, women in business have not received much attention from business or other historians. In the late 1950s the direction of North American business historiography was at a crossroads. Seminal work by Thomas Cochran emphasized a broad social and contextual approach; innovative work by Alfred Chandler promoted a narrower and intensive focus on the firm itself, and the Chandlerian perspective, perhaps in part because it was so nicely adaptable to case studies in business schools, came to dominate the field.[4] Times are now changing. Chandler and "Chandlerians" are increasingly under fire, if far from repentant.[5] American historians such as Naomi Lamoureaux, Daniel Raff, and Peter Temin have begun to emphasize a wider, socially embedded' approach to the study of business and to take pains to point to the diversity of business forms and practice. Scholars such as Philip Scranton have made the study of diversity the centrepiece of their work.[6] Historians interested in gender and women's studies are noting that women were a significant part of that diversity.[7] Whereas, for the last decade or so, it has been fashionable and appropriate for historians interested in studying businesswomen to rail against the gender myopia of business historians and historiography and to wonder whether there was any conceptual space for women-centred and gendered studies, such critiques are no longer as relevant.[8] Perhaps encouraged by evidence of emerging conceptual space and perhaps simply forcing the issue, scholarship, especially in the United States, Britain, and Europe, is increasingly focusing on small business, family business, and women in business.[9]

The historiography has moved from a celebratory focus on "exceptional" businesswomen to understanding women in business in the context of the separate spheres paradigm. For women, did self-employment represent a significant reshaping of the women's sphere, an extension of activity into space previously occupied only by men? Historians such as Lucy Murphey have concluded that such women were "on the edges of their sphere, with one foot in the male world of profit seeking, but the other planted in a world of tradition and female culture." This conclusion follows those of studies of female entrepreneurship by Suzanne Lebsock and Glenda Riley. Lebsock writes of the "personalism" that women brought to capitalist affairs, a set of characteristics forged within the traditional sphere of domesticity, and Riley maintains that "women used traditional female values as their guides" in economic matters.[10] Women's familial experiences are emphasized, and market structures given cursory attention. The emphasis on the domestic part of the separate spheres paradigm is gradually shifting. While acknowledging the segmented nature of women's enterprise, Joan Scott has suggested that the market was segmented in other ways as well. Both gender ideology and market structures played roles in the structuring of women's business practice. Pamela Sharpe has argued that, "rather than a confinement to domesticity, we are witnessing a mark of commercial expediency in the sense that women increasingly exploited the opportunities offered by a segmented economy." Edith Sparks, in her study of women entrepreneurs in late nineteenth- century San Francisco, has perhaps gone the furthest in situating and understanding women in the context of business markets. "In short," she notes, "operating a business required capital instincts, not domestic ones."[11]

Canadian historians such as Jane Errington and Brian Young have provided useful studies of female entrepreneurship for the pre-Confederation period. Sources for the early period are, however, scanty, and those that exist do not permit a detailed comparison with the behaviour of women in business in the late nineteenth century.[12] One of the intents of this chapter is to provide benchmark measurements of self-employment by women in the workplace in urban Canada at the turn of the twentieth century. The question is how to provide context for understanding the pattern and extent of such behaviour. Systematic comparison with past activity is not possible. As our discussion of the evolving historiography indicates, understanding such activity within the context of the separate spheres paradigm is insufficient. If we build on that historiography, three ways suggest themselves.

The first is comparing women's activity to that of men in business. The second is to compare women's enterprise in the late nineteenth and early twentieth century with that of women at the end of the twentieth century.[13] Indeed, the late twentieth-century increase of self-employment in the Western world has excited much interest on the part of social scientists.[14] In the waning decades of the twentieth century, North American women were particularly prominent in the creation of new and small businesses. Commentators speak of "today's female passion for entrepreneurship." Much of that literature assumes that such activity represents a "new frontier" for women.[15] While neither of these comparative measures establishes trend lines for the nineteenth century and they thus make it difficult to point to the effects, if any, of such enabling legislation as MWPLs, both are useful contexts for commenting on the extent of women's activity in the business sector. If, for example, it can be shown that Canadian women in the urban workforce were equally or even more likely to be involved in business in the early twentieth century than were men in that era and than were women a hundred years later, then we are encouraged to rethink our view of the possibilities for women's economic agency in that time period.

A third context within which to understand the evidence and analysis presented in this chapter is women's activity in other areas of wealth management, as presented in previous chapters of this study and as presented in a discussion of women and the business of philanthropy in appendix 4. To provide a close comparison with much of the previous behaviour analyzed in this book, this chapter will privilege, where possible, the business activity of men and women in Victoria and Hamilton at the turn of the twentieth century, as well as situating that behaviour within activity throughout the rest of urban Canada.

As will be shown, the extent of women's involvement in business nicely parallels the activity levels of women in general investment, land ownership, mortgaging, and bequeathing, and it thus provides yet another indication of the positive influence of the MWPLs and of the proactive behaviour of women in economic, financial, and business affairs. In fact, it will be suggested that women's business activity constituted perhaps the single most dramatic and visible rebuke to those who continued to advocate a separate sphere for women.

The chapter has two main parts. Evidence indicating the extent of business activity on the part of women in urban Canada at the turn of the twentieth century is compared with similar behaviour on the part of men at that time and is also, where possible, compared to estimates of self-employed Canadian men and women near the end of the twentieth century. Both comparisons point – surprisingly, given the state of current literature – to the strong participation of women in the sphere of self-employment in the early years of that century. Self- employed women and men in 1901 are then compared with regard to selected social characteristics. Did the social characteristics of self- employed women differ from those of self-employed men? For those in the urban workforce, did the odds of being self-employed differ by gender in 1901?

One reason for the relative absence of historical literature on self-employment in Canada is simply the lack of good data with which to measure such activity. It was not until the 1891 and 1901 Canadian censuses that questions asked about relationship to the means of production went beyond that of occupation. Work by David Burley on a small Ontario city from the 1850s to the 1880s and by Michael Katz on the city of Hamilton focus on a period prior to 1891 and thus must rely on occupation information linked to city assessment rolls, newspapers, and directories in order to comment on the extent of self-employment. David Monod, writing on grocers in late nineteenth- and early twentieth-century Ontario, and John Benson, in a wide-ranging study of penny capitalism in rural and urban Canada at the turn of the century, piece together a broad range of sources in providing estimates of such activity over time.[16] While Monod and Benson use the aggregate returns for 1891 and 1901, information on employment status was not aggregated and can only be accessed at the nominal level. Neither makes use of the nominal-level returns of those censuses. Census data, of course, is not without problems, some of which will be addressed in this chapter, but the advantages of using a source that explicitly asked for information on whether one was an employee, self-employed, or an employer avoids both the difficulties in inferring such status from occu- pation name and the pitfalls of data linkage across sundry sources. A major source used for this chapter is the Public Use Sample of the 1901 Canadian census, a 5 per cent sample of households created by the Canadian Families Project at the University of Victoria.[17] Given the richness of this source, it seemed appropriate to shift the focus somewhat from Hamilton and Victoria to urban Canada as a whole for much of the analysis in this chapter. Nevertheless, the place of both cities in the general urban context will be noted, and as mentioned above, illustrative material, wherever appropriate, will be drawn from both cities.[18]

We begin with a discussion of trends in self-employment in late nineteenth century urban Canada. Table 7.1 is based on data from a 10 per cent sample of six cities (Halifax, Montreal, Hamilton, Winnipeg, Vancouver, and Victoria) in 1891 and 1901. By lumping together, as many studies do, employers and own-account employed, these studies miss the complexities of changes in the workforce.[19] Men did become increasingly proletarianized in this decade. So, too, did women such as Mary Fiset. She operated a millinery business in Hamilton from at least 1881 to 1892. Dun and Bradstreet, a credit reporting agency, estimated her worth in 1881 to be between $500 and $1,000, a rating that dropped to under $500 in 1892. Whether she had employees in 1881 is unknown, but according to the 1891 census, she was self-employed with no employees. By 1901 Fiset had closed her business and was an employee in a factory earning $450 a year.[20] This was a large salary for a woman in this era and perhaps points to one reason why self-employment for women declined somewhat in this period: for some women, wage labour alternatives may have promised a more secure and remunerative return than had been the case in earlier years.[21]

The decline in self-employment for men and women in the closing decade of the nineteenth century in part reflected an increased trend to larger business units in that era. Yet even as they swelled the ranks of the employed, men increased their numbers of own-account employed by 50 per cent. Industrialization, along with the growth of a sophisticated communication infrastructure, would seem to have dramatically curtailed participation in the economy as an employer. Growing business concentration meant fewer employers employing larger numbers of workers than ever before. Such processes, in the 1890s at least, had the opposite effect on own-account employment by men. Self-employment became polarized: increasing numbers of small businesses in the own-account sector and fewer but much larger enterprises in the employer sphere.[22]

Like men, women experienced a significant decline as employers. Emma Johnston is an interesting case in point. She was exceptional in that she operated a millinery business in Hamilton from at least 1880 to at least 1902. Few small businesses run by men or women lasted that long. In 1881 Dun and Bradstreet ranked her worth between $500 and $1,000. We do not know whether she was an employer or self-employed in that year. By 1891 she employed four people in her millinery business, and Dun and Bradstreet gave her a "limited" credit rating and did not publish a statement of worth because her "business and investments render it difficult to rate satisfactorily to ourselves." They advised interested parties to come to their office for a "detailed report." Ten years later Johnston operated out of a rented store and received a credit rating of "limited" and a worth of less than $500. In the eyes of Dun and Bradstreet, her long-established business was declining, worth less in 1901 than it had been twenty years before. The credit company may have been correct. Johnston, like many other women and men, was no longer an employer: in the 1901 census she was listed as working on her own account.[23] Overall, however, what may be most interesting about trends in women's employment status is the fairly constant level of their participation in the own-account employment sphere. During a decade of increasing proletarianization in these six cities, women continued to represent over 20 per cent of all own-account employed people.[24]

How confident can one be about these findings? There is a growing literature on the ways that national censuses undercount women's work, especially that performed by married women. It is commonplace to note that the early twentieth-century definitions were ideological in nature, reflecting the notion of separate spheres for men and women. What is more surprising, however, is the tendency of many academics and contemporary commentators to talk of great increases in the participation of especially married women in the workforce in the second half of the twentieth century.[25] Most often, this alleged shift is seen to result from, or at least correspond with, the participation of married women in the workforce during the Second World War. Curiously, far less attention has been focused on the changing census definitions of countable employment in 1951 and after. Even more sophisticated commentators who explicitly recognize the reality of gender bias in labour market statistics fall short of speculating what such changes might mean for "real" trends over time.[26]

Frank Denton and Sylvia Ostry, the most notable of those who have paid some attention to employment trends, apply conversion measures derived from the occupational mix of Canadian men and women in 1951. But the mix of occupations was obviously very different in 1901 – most dramatically in the case of farm workers – so their method is strangely ahistorical.[27] If working women had been counted in 1901 the same way they were in 1951, would one be able to talk of a great increase of women's employment in the second half of the twentieth century? Studies of comparable changing definitions of gainful employment in the United States have suggested that, when such definitions are controlled, women's workforce participation, and more especially that of married women, is seen to be constant rather than increasing.[28]

If more sophisticated conversion methods are required to better appreciate trends in women's general employment, it is equally the case that the subset of women who worked as employers or on their own account, those who are of particular concern in this chapter, were seriously undercounted by censuses in the first half of the twentieth century. This is so for several reasons. Census definitions of gainful employment excluded the work of many women. The Canadian government instructed its census enumerators in 1901 and after that "if married [and other] women ... are only carrying on domestic affairs in a household without wages they are not to be classed as having an occupation," and thus were not to be included in the workforce. Secondly, "regular" work, generally for wages, was the key to being in the workforce or being gainfully employed. But, as Kris Inwood and Richard Reid have noted, many self-employed women worked part-time, keeping house the rest of the time, and since "habitual" and "regular" occupations were the criteria for inclusion in the workforce, such women were more likely to have been labelled homemakers than gainfully employed workers.[29]

Thirdly, not until 1951 did the census recognize unpaid work by family or "blood relatives" in a family-run business such as a grocery store. Up to that point the census ignored unpaid work done by wives and children in such businesses.[30] Some of these workers may have been better classified as employees, but many others should have been recognized as self-employed partners. Three examples illustrate the point. What is one to make of Elizabeth Newman, wife of Thomas, a Winnipeg grocer? Both the Newmans, we learn from the 1901 census, were working on their own account, but only Thomas was given an occupation. Moreover, he worked for six months in a factory while Elizabeth worked for twelve months at home and earned $400 a year, $25 more than her husband. Clearly, she was the full-time operator of the grocery business, at which he worked part-time when he had no factory work.[31] The Newman case is somewhat exceptional in that other attributes of the wife's employment status were acknowledged, even though her primary occupation was not. In untold cases, all of the wife's occupational information would be left blank.

Such was the case of Hannah Maynard, a married woman living in Victoria who started a photography business in the city in 1862. Styling herself "a photographic artist," she routinely advertised her business in the local newspapers. In 1890 Dun and Bradstreet gave her photography business a "fair" credit rating, one above the lowest or "limited" ranking. It also listed her husband's business, a boot and shoe store he had operated since the early 1860s. Such matters did not, however, deter the census enumerator: in 1891 he listed Maynard's husband as owner of the photography business and as the employer of three; she herself was listed as a housewife, as she would again be in the 1901 census.[32]

Margaret Connelly of Hamilton dictated her will in January 1882. Among other assets, she bequeathed to her husband "the stock and trade and goods and chattels of any kind used in carrying on *my business of a grocer*" as long as he paid the debts. Two male executors were to oversee her husband's handling of the debt issue, and "in the event of my said husband failing to make some arrangement satisfactory to my executors, I direct them to sell and dispose of said goods," the proceeds of which were to be given to her husband "for his use absolutely." Obviously, Margaret Connelly ran the business: she referred to it as hers, the debts had been contracted in her name, and she did not hesitate to set limits to her husband's autonomy in the running of that business after her death. Yet even in the face of this testimony, the officials who oversaw the execution of the will referred to her as "the wife of a grocer," not as a grocer herself. Moreover, Dun and Bradstreet had visited the business in 1880 and listed Connelly's husband, James, as the owner. We know that she could not write (she signed her will with "her mark"), and perhaps she and her husband felt they had a better chance of receiving credit if he appeared to be the owner. More likely, her illiteracy was not a factor. They probably simply assumed that a male grocer had a better chance at receiving a good credit rating than did a female grocer.[33]

The Connelly example emphasizes that the census was simply a manifestation of a wider set of cultural proscriptions, a mode of thinking so well exemplified by E.B.B.R. in the *Financial Post* article and an attitude that makes the unearthing of women as economic actors a challenging process for historians. Yet the Newman, Maynard, and Connelly examples also point to what Amanada Vickery, a historian, has noted in the context of England: one should guard against assuming that prescription equals description.[34]

In the absence of detailed census information such as that for Elizabeth Newman, or in the absence of recourse to other complementary files, as in the cases of Hannah Maynard and Margaret Connelly, it is probably impossible to attribute self-employment at the individual level to women who were married to self-employed men. The best one can do is an educated guess at the aggregate level. For the purposes of the analysis offered in this chapter, it is sufficient to note that all figures on the extent of women's self-employment must be seen as lower-bound estimates.

The state, through its census-taking practices, also undervalued the taking in of boarders and lodgers.[35] In 1931, census enumerators were told that "if ... a family keeps a few boarders or roomers merely as a means of supplementing the earnings or income obtained from other occupations or other sources, no one in the family should be returned as a boarding or lodging house keeper." Ten years later a boarding-house enterprise could be counted only if the number of boarders and/or lodgers exceeded the number of family members. Only in 1951, when boarding had been in decline for some years, were such definitions relaxed. In that and subsequent years, boarding and lodging were defined simply as "work in connection with renting rooms or providing meals for boarders."[36]

The business of boarding-house keeping has been given only cursory attention by historians, perhaps in part because it was very much a business run by women, and run by women within the sanctuary of that "non-productive" sphere, the home. Even those historians who do recognize the monetary importance of boarding houses conceptualize such activity as being "non-wage" labour. Bettina Bradbury, for example, sees the taking in of boarders as one of several strategies families developed to supplement wages. Wendy Gamber argues that boarding-house keeping should be seen in the context of labour history rather than simply in the context of the family. Yet even though she recognizes that the process of boarding people involved "entrepreneurial savvy," she never frames that activity as an aspect of business history.[37] At some level, of course, such labelling is obviously artificial: the boundaries between the categories – family economy, labour history, and business history – are clearly permeable. Yet at another level, conceptual framing is important. The frame one uses focuses and limits the queries one is apt to pose. Running a business implies a series of activities that are not implied in labouring for money. Moreover, running a business implies status considerations of a different order from labouring for money. Seeing boarding-house keeping as a business enterprise allows one to emphasize a skill set and a sense of independence that were rarely accorded to women either by their contemporaries in the late nineteenth century or by historians today.

As a business enterprise, boarding-house keeping stood the notion of the private home run by the selfless mother on its head: the home became a public business often inhabited by "strangers."[38] At least 231 women admitted boarders into their homes in Hamilton in 1891, and at the time of the census they had 594 lodgers in their homes.[39] In Victoria in 1901, 374 women had boarders in their home and averaged 2 per household. It was a business that demanded entrepreneurial skills: advertising and promotion – advertisements for lodgers appeared regularly in the newspapers in this period – managing staff – 44 per cent of the 231 women who ran boarding houses in Hamilton in 1891 employed at least one person – collecting rent, and handling finances, to name a few. In the opinion of the Toronto *Globe*, "even 'Board and Lodging' ... mean[s] commercial activity"; "when people take houses, furnish them, and lay themselves out for boarders and lodgers, it must been assumed to be," the *Globe* continued, "because they have gone rationally to work and discovered there was a demand for the accommodation offered." Elizabeth Kingsbury, a British author writing in the late nineteenth century, believed that running a boarding house was a "woman's business," a way for a woman to "develop a little enterprise."

It was an enterprise that required hard work. "No woman in the world," a Toronto *Globe* reporter affirmed, "more utterly wears out her life than she who keeps a private boarding-house." It was an enterprise that had risks: "often her reward is only vacant trunks and base ingratitude." Yet many women facilitated and some, at least, profited from what the *Globe* called "that popular way of living."[40]

Annie Jones, a married woman living in Hamilton, is a case in point. She was listed in the census of that year as a boarding-house keeper. That this enterprise may have given her a strong sense of independence is suggested by the fact that she was also listed as head of the house and that she earned $1,000 a year, compared to her husband's earnings of $500, and finally by the fact that the rented house they lived in was listed under her name rather than her husband's. For some women, boarding-house keeping conferred independence and heightened status both within and outside the home. [41]

It is possible to identify women who had boarders in their household. The 5 per cent sample of the 1901 census yields 1,753 urban women who had boarders in their homes who were *not* recognized as boarding-house keepers by the census enumerators.[42] In the two cities for which we have 100 per cent of the data, the addition of unlisted women boarding-house keepers increased their numbers by nineteen times for Victoria and by sixteen times for Hamilton.[43] Married women were especially undercounted. Elisabeth Guest's husband earned $350 as a labourer in Hamilton in 1901. In addition to six family members under eighteen, his rented home housed no fewer than twelve boarders. Yet her occupation was recorded as housewife.[44] In the 5 per cent sample of all Canadian cities, enumerators identified only 27 married women as boarding-house keepers, ignoring 1,462 other similarly occupied women who were married. While it is true that women identified as boarding-house keepers had, on average, more boarders than those who were ignored, this difference does not fully explain the omissions.[45] Enumerators listed only 20 married women with three or more boarders as boarding-house keepers, ignoring 269 other married women with more than two boarders in their households. A similar pattern holds for widows.[46]

It is far from clear why one would exclude small boarding-house units, those with two or fewer boarders, from the recognition of being run by a self-employed woman. Other enterprises would not seem to have been differentiated along the lines of size. Nor should it be forgotten that the enumerator listed only boarders in the household at the time of the census. This figure did not represent a yearly average; for many families, the number of boarders would fluctuate according to local economic conditions.[47] Finally, as we have seen, after 1950 the census did not assign the occupation of boarding-house keeper on the basis of the number of boarders. A better way to differentiate among boarding enterprises would be by whether boarders took meals, but the census is no help in this regard. It is clear that boarding brought needed cash into the family economy, the enterprise involved risk, women were much more likely than men to oversee such activity, and male census enumerators generally overlooked such enterprise. Indeed, as Wendy Gamber has noted for the early nineteenth-century United States, "boardinghouses [were] vital supports of an urban, industrial economy."[48] Women boarding-house keepers are therefore included amongst the self-employed in table 7.2.

Table 7.2 provides a look at the workforce status of men and women in all of urban Canada in 1901 compared to the employment status of all workers in 1996. As the table indicates, among workforce partici-pants, self-employment was as common for men and more common for women in 1901 than in 1996: just under one in five urban men in the workforce in both 1901 and 1996 were self-employed; the comparable ratio for women is just under one in eight and one in three respectively. Some may think that such a finding is less surprising for men than for women. After all, the historical literature points to a high degree of self-employment in *early* industrializing Canada. That literature argues that as communications (roads, railways, and telegraphs) expanded, small businesses declined and proletarianization increased. By 1901, how-ever, railways criss-crossed a great deal of Canada, and nowhere more so than in Ontario, the country's most industrialized province. Yet even in that province, men in self-employment represented over 20 per cent of the workforce, a figure almost exactly equal to that of Canada as a whole (see table 7.2).[49] Moreover, as we have noted, men significantly increased their participation in own-account employment during the last decade of the nineteenth century. It is true that, for some parts of Canada, the 1890s were far from a time of buoyant economic growth, but for the six cities for which data was collected in table 7.1, combined industrial output increased by 10 per cent.[50]

A closer look at trends in self-employment for Canadian men in the late twentieth century points to important parallels with such trends in the late nineteenth century. The percentage of the male workforce active as employers was the same in 1996 as it was in 1989, and it actually declined by close to 1 per cent after 1993. In other words, as in the 1890s, all growth in male self-employment in the 1990s took place in the sphere of own-account employment. Indeed, men experienced a 38 per cent increase in own-account employment, a rate remarkably similar to that for men one hundred years earlier.[51]

Clearly, the economic context of the late twentieth century differed in many ways from that of the late nineteenth century. Yet even here a point of comparison is worth mentioning. At the turn of the twentieth century, Canada's economy was in the process of a significant structural shift from commercial to industrial capitalism. In the late twentieth century the country was also undergoing important structural change from an industrial to a post-industrial economy characterized by, among other factors, an emphasis on service employment and on technological changes that facilitated decentralization of economic activity, by government downsizing and the increased reliance on self-employed consultants, and by the outward flow of industry to third-world platform economies. In times of significant structural change in the economy, rates of participation in own-account employment would seem to increase dramatically.[52]

For the past twenty-five years, social scientists have been commenting on the rapid increase of self-employed women in the North American workforce. In both Canada and the United States the number of self-employed women has been increasing at a much faster rate than that of men. Between 1989 and 1996 in Canada, for example, that number grew by 45 per cent, over double the growth rate for men.[53] Does such activity warrant Dina Lavoie's enthusiastic designation of a "New Era for Female Entrepreneurship?"[54] It does so in the context of the rate of growth but not when put in the context of degree of participation. More women in the workforce were self-employed in 1901 than in 1996.[55]

It is useful to look more closely at the age characteristics of the self-employed. An examination of both the incidence of self-employment within age groups and the actual age distribution of those who were self-employed underlines the extent and significance of self-employment for women in 1901. Table 7.3 indicates that the higher likelihood of women being self-employed in 1901 holds true for all age groups.[56] It has been noted that over the last twenty years the average age of the self-employed has increased, with the fastest growth taking place in the fifty-five and older group.[57] Yet once again, rather than being suggestive of a new frontier, that trend more resembles a movement to past employment structures. For men and women in the workforce in 1901, those fifty-five and over were most likely to be self-employed. Moreover, during the last ten years of the nineteenth century the average age of men working on their own account increased by a sharp 4.8 years, while that for employees increased by less than a year.[58] The same trend was true of women: the average age of women who worked on their own account increased by 3 years, while that for women employees decreased by almost 1 year.[59] These are noteworthy changes in the course of a decade and parallel changes to the age profile of the self-employed today. Once again it is relevant to note that the two economies are alike in that both were undergoing significant structural change. While these transformations affected various social groups in differential ways, the aged, now and a hundred years ago, adapted, at least in part, through self-employment.[60]

The age profile of the self-employed as shown in table 7.3 is revealing in a second way. The higher incidence of male-over-female self-employment in 1996 (see table 7.2) is true for virtually all age categories. By contrast, working women one hundred years ago participated in self-employment to a greater extent than men at all age levels (see table 7.3), and even without the inclusion of boarding-house keepers, they exceeded the incidence of self-employment by women in the late twentieth century for all but the youngest age level and for men in 1901 for all but the twenty-five to thirty-four age group.[61] Self-employment for Canadian women is far from being simply a late twentieth-century phenomenon.

Table 7.4 provides a look at the age distribution of self-employed men and women in 1901 and indicates a marked difference in their respective age profiles: self-employed women were, on average, four and a half years younger than male entrepreneurs. Fifty-three per cent of women were under the age of thirty, compared to only 36 per cent of men. The contrast in age profile has nothing to do with the participation of single men and women: their average age (twenty-eight) and their percentage under thirty (70 per cent) were identical. The age distribution of those who were married goes a little way towards explaining the variance in table 7.5. Married women entrepreneurs were, on average 1.3 years younger than their male counterparts (43.8 compared to 45.1), but were no more likely than men to be under the age of thirty (13 per cent). The difference in average age is mostly due to a well-known demographic trend in this era: on average, men died before women. Widowed women entrepreneurs were, on average, just over six years younger than their male counterparts (49.5 compared to 55.7). Over a fifth of these women (22 per cent) were under the age of forty and over half (52.2 per cent) were under the age of fifty. For men, the comparable per centages were 17 and 36.

A closer look at marital status is revealing. Although fewer women were in the workforce in 1901 than in 1991, for those that were, the odds were much higher that they would be self-employed no matter their marital status (table 7.5). What is perhaps most surprising is the dramatic difference in the distribution of self-employment among married and widowed women in 1901 and 1991. The contrast is only partly explained by the inclusion of boarding-house keepers in 1901. Even without their inclusion, married and widowed women in the workforce in 1901 were over five times more likely to be self-employed than their counterparts in 1991. The explanation for this contrast lies partly in the different nature of employment opportunities available for married women in 1901, compared to married women ninety years later. Much wage work had to be conducted outside the home, and many married women had children who required their presence. Daycare was not a realistic option in 1901. Moreover, at the turn of the century, many employers would not hire married women, preferring single women or men because of the prevailing notion that a family wage should be provided to the male breadwinner. As a result, married women in the workforce in 1901 were more likely to be self-employed than employees.[62]

A qualification is necessary here. Table 7.5 takes the designation of "married" as recorded by the census enumerators in 1901 at face value. The comments of Elizabeth Wolstenholme, a nineteenth-century British feminist, go to the heart of the matter. "It is assumed," she asserted on the eve of the passage of the 1871 British MWPL, "... that all women marry and are provided for by their husbands." Yet, she continued, the fact is that "of those who do marry, a very considerable proportion are *not* supported by their husbands." Many studies of women in business give only passing reference to whether or not a spouse was in the house of a self-employed married woman.[63] Since the first series of MWPLs were passed to protect the economic rights of deserted women, such a perspective is somewhat puzzling. If women boarding-house keepers missed by the census are excluded, 30 per cent of self-employed/ employer married women did not have a spouse in the house at the time of the census enumeration.[64] This ratio compares to only 7 per cent for all married women in urban

Canada in 1901. Clearly, the absence of a spouse affected married women's relationship to the workforce.

A brief look at the self-employment situation of married women in Victoria and Vancouver in the late nineteenth century provides further and somewhat more detailed support for this observation. Twenty-one per cent of married women in business in Victoria in 1881 and 40 per cent in Vancouver in 1891 did not have a husband in the house. The 1891 figure exceeded by a factor of four the percentage for all women without husbands in the house in those two cities in that year. Nor were these women clustered in the upper age cohorts. Twenty-seven of the thirty "husbandless" women in 1891 were under the age of fifty and they represented one-half of all married businesswomen between the ages of thirty and forty-nine. None owned land, and only two had domestic servants. Some, such as thirty-five-year-old Sophia Bremmer, who supported herself and her three-year-old daughter from her business as a self-employed dressmaker in Victoria, had dependants. Elizabeth Benson, twenty-five years old, and her five-year- old son lived with her brother in Victoria, and with him she operated an insurance company. Most ran boarding houses, as did widows, and a few, such as twenty-eight-year-old Kate Randall of Victoria, combined that occupation with dressmaking in order to earn a living.[65] Perhaps some husbands were away pursuing seasonal occupations, but on the basis of the economic information available to us, few contributed much to the family income. Most married women without husbands in the household worked as employees and as businesswomen because they had few other options.

Yet other women clearly sought out a business career. Isabella Dodds of Dundas, Ontario, recognized such ambition in her daughter. Dodds decreed in her will in 1884 that if her daughter wished to enter business, her executors were to liquidate the estate worth $4,400 and give it all to her in cash to start up a business. Annie Camp, the proprietor of the Prairie Hotel on the outskirts of Victoria, ceded her business to her daughter in 1908. Eva Maude Mary Clarke of Victoria may not have been as fortunate. Her mother died in 1888. With her father's business verging on bankruptcy, the fourteen-year-old attempted to take control of her life. "I have been learning to play the piano for about eighteen months altogether," she wrote to the Supreme Court on the occasion of the probate of her intestate mother's assets. "My present teacher is W. Sharpe of Victoria. It is my intention to qualify myself for a teacher of music of which I am very fond. It is necessary for me to have a piano in order that I may practice. I practice on the piano daily about two hours but it will not be possible for me to continue this practice unless I have a piano in the house where I live." We do not know whether Clarke realized her dream, despite a separate petition from her father requesting control of the legacy to support his children, the court supervised all expenditures from the $800 behest. Yet her ambition suggests the possibility that many young women in the late nineteenth century openly sought independent careers.[66]

Indeed, for some women, what it meant to be married was now under negotiation. For those in the workforce, for example, married women with husbands in the home were more apt than married men to be self-employed. In 1901, 35 per cent of married women in the workforce who lived with husbands were self-employed, and only 26 per cent of married men in the workforce were self-employed. This imbalance was most marked at the younger age groups: 33 per cent of married women in the workforce under the age of forty living with a husband were self-employed, compared to 20 per cent of married men in that age group. In the context of prevailing attitudes in 1901 toward married women in business, the fact that many young married women were entrepreneurs, as were many young widowed women, must be seen as surprising. The entry costs for the type of businesses in which women engaged were probably lower than those for men; so a business career could start earlier for women than for men. But the most significant implications of the age distribution and marital status of self-employed women are best appreciated within the context of prevailing family expectations.

A look at the self-employment situation of married women in Victoria and Hamilton is helpful. If few women sacrificed marriage for a business career, it is not clear that women routinely sacrificed a career in business for marriage. In Victoria one-third and in Hamilton one-quarter of all businesswomen were married in 1891 (and some widows may have been businesswomen before the death of their spouses). Fully one-third of the married women who lived with their husbands in 1891 in Victoria were under the age of thirty, as were 25 per cent of Hamilton's married women with husbands in the house. For some women, marriage may have simply been added on to an existing career in business. Moreover, the percentage of young married women in business in Victoria increased between 1881 and 1891. In 1881, only 6 per cent of married businesswomen were under the age of thirty and most were over forty. In 1891, one in three were under thirty, and over one in two who lived with their husbands were under forty.[67] Nor can this pattern be explained by an increase in marriage of women in that age group: there was no increase. Perhaps the MWPLs help to account not only for an increased proportion of young married women in the land market and for their significant participation in credit affairs but also for their activity in the general business world.

The relationship between self-employment and bearing children is also complex and will be looked at more closely in the next chapter in the context of family businesses. The raising of children was a central tenant of the cult of domesticity. It is often argued that married women chose or undertook a business career because it allowed more flexibility in looking after children. That is a compelling argument, but it does not seem to cover all cases. Bridget Hunter, a twenty-six-year-old married woman who lived in Hamilton in 1891 with her husband, a boilermaker, is a case in point. She had no children and ran a tailoring business that employed two workers. One-third of married business-women with husbands in Victoria in 1891 had no children in the house, and in Hamilton 27 per cent either had no children in the house or had only children over the age of sixteen. Most married women with younger children had older children or relatives who could help them. Anna Barnard, a forty-three-year-old married woman who lived with her husband, a carpenter, in Hamilton in 1891, had six children: one under five, one between five and ten, one between eleven and fifteen, and two between sixteen and twenty. Clearly, the older children could help out in the house while Barnard pursued her business of mat-making.[68] Women with younger children often operated a boarding house or conducted a dressmaking enterprise from their home, thus achieving flexibility in balancing employment and household demands. In the late nineteenth century some businesswomen in Victoria and Hamilton and, indeed, in urban Canada as a whole were reshaping their life course and balancing two roles that society deemed to be in conflict.

Did it make economic sense for a woman to run a business? It is often assumed that waged employment provided "steadier" paycheques than did self-employment and that self-employment generated only "a modest income."[69] The notion that self-employment might have been at least as remunerative as waged employment for women is almost never asserted in the literature. In part this oversight may be because in the late twentieth century, analyses of the earnings of the self-employed suggest that own-account self-employed in Canada made on average close to one-third less than employees.[70] That was not the case in urban

Canada in 1901. The census recorded income for many in the workforce, although the enumerators were primarily concerned with the earnings of employees. The self-employed and the employers were underreported with regard to income. Yet despite the underreporting, the trend lines seem clear. The data presented in table 7.6 indicate that being self-employed and especially being an employer resulted in significantly higher average incomes for both men and women in 1901. Self-employed women earned, on average, 46 per cent more than women employees, and the few women employers earned 98 per cent more than female employees. The differences were even more pronounced for men: 78 and 145 per cent respectively. For many women, self-employment nicely served economic as well as familial needs.

Not surprisingly, men in each employment status took home much higher incomes than their female counterparts. It is interesting to note, too, that, as in Canada in the mid-1990s, the earnings gap between self-employed women and men was higher than that between employee women and men.[71] The relatively high standard deviations for the earnings of the self-employed and employers compared to those for the employees point to a further similarity between the workforce earning patterns in 1901 and the late twentieth century. Earnings were more dispersed for the self-employed and employers, and as a result, one should be wary about generalizing too broadly from averages. It is clear that many of the self-employed were as poorly remunerated as their employee counterparts. The polarized earnings distribution was especially marked in the case of the female self-employed. Their median earnings were only $25 higher than that for female employees, and their modal earnings were the same.[72]

Table 7.6 does not include boarding-house keepers missed by the census. Given that they were assigned no occupation or employment status, few recorded any income. Since in much of the analysis presented in this chapter, women boarding-house keepers are important, it would be useful to have an indication, however rough, of their potential earnings. The 5 per cent sample for 1901 yielded income for sixty women for whom the census enumerator recorded boarding-house keeper as an occupation. These women averaged 3.5 boarders at the time of the census and earned an average of $510 presumably before expenses, over the course of the census year. In Victoria in 1901, thirty-four women who were designated as boarding- or lodging-house keepers had financial information. These women averaged 2.6 boarders and took home an average of $622 a year in income. As a rough measure of potential income, then, one could argue that each boarder generated about $170 a year.[73] Women with boarders in their homes who had no occupational classification and, if they had a husband, he was not a boarding-house keeper averaged two boarders at the time of the census. On average, then, they generated $340 extra income per year, or a total of $596,000.[74] Even if we assume a rate of 50 per cent for expenses, the result, especially for working-class families went beyond the notion of "pin money." As a Toronto *Globe* reporter noted in the late 1880s, "there are many families to whom one or two roomers are a desperate necessity ... too many people are obliged to look to roomers to pay the rent of their houses."[75]

There is no doubt but that the reporter was correct. Jane Stewart, a fifty-five-year-old married woman who lived in Hamilton without her husband, rented to seven lodgers at the time of the 1901 census but declared her annual income to be only $200. If this amount was indeed her gross earnings, then the sum fell far short of what it would have cost her to rent, heat, and outfit the thirteen-room brick house in which she lived.[76] Some women who ran boarding houses looked elsewhere for support. Jane Saunders, a thirty-nine-year old widow with two children aged twelve and thirteen, operated a boarding house in Victoria in the early 1890s. She approached the British Columbia Benevolent Society, a local charitable agency, for aid, as did Annie Glover, a thirty-year-old widow with three children under thirteen who also operated a small boarding house. Clearly, many poor women who headed families shared their homes with others in an attempt to make ends meet, and even then they often fell short.[77] Yet families who were well above the poverty line were as apt as families at the poverty line to have boarders in their homes.[78] The enterprise of boarding was not simply the preserve of working-class married women. On average, husbands of women with boarders in their home in 1901 who were ignored by the census enumerator earned a substantial $570. The average income for husbands who were employees was $515. This is an interesting point because it suggests that middle- and upper-middle-class married women did not hesitate to operate a boarding house, no matter the cultural norms that frowned on such activity. Census enumerators may have taken little notice of this practice, but boarding-house entrepreneurship spanned classes. That middle-class married women, those women at the heart of the separate spheres ideology, transformed their homes into businesses underlines the dichotomy between cultural proscriptions and actual behaviour.

Other measures of wealth are available. The 1901 census provides data on property ownership and rental situations, ostensibly for all people in Canada, although in practice this usually meant household heads. Those data allow one to calculate a measure of individual and family status, if not income. Table 7.7 clearly points to the greater extent of landowning by men no matter the employment status. But it also hints that some self-employed women may have been better off than those who were employed, although the numbers seem quite small: 11.3 per cent of self-employed women owned property compared to 1.7 per cent of women employees. The data are less equivocal for men; clearly, self-employment was more closely associated with property ownership than was the case for male employees: just under 50 per cent of the former owned property, while fewer than 20 per cent of the latter did.

Table 7.7 hides the importance of self-employment for women in at least two ways. For single and widowed women and for married women without a spouse in the house who headed households, self-employment was quite positively associated with property ownership: over two-fifths owned property, while less than one-quarter of similarly situated women employees did. Does this mean that it is safe to state that for those women self-employment was an excellent strategy, one that, on average, resulted in greater security than for employees? Once again one should be cautious. A large number of these women were boarding-house keepers, women who may have inherited their property rather than earned it through self-employment. In other words, the ownership of property may have made self-employment possible rather than the reverse.[79] What the data do suggest is the danger of quick generalizations and of the need for more specific research focused on the lives of self-employed women.

In a second way the data in table 7.7 provide only a preliminary picture of the relationship between self-employment and landed wealth for women. As we have seen, by the measurements used in this chapter, most self-employed women in 1901 were married. According to the census, few of these women owned property in their own names. A more appropriate measure of landed status, then, might be whether more self-employed women than women employees lived in a family of which at least one member owned land. The answer is that measured in this way, self-employment made no difference: 43 per cent of self-employed and the same percentage of women employees were members of such families.[80]

While more work needs to be done on the relationship of self-employment to wealth,[81] the evidence presented here on earnings and landholding suggests that in 1901 many women did increase their material security through self-employment. Indeed, compared to similarly situated women today, the odds were significantly higher that the self-employed woman of a century ago would earn more than her employee counterpart. In some studies, such an assumption has a whiggish hue: women can be seen as economic heroines who competed successfully in the male world of the capitalist marketplace. Even more careful studies praise "the hardy and self-sufficient women [who] stepped out of women's place with few regrets," and one suggests, on the basis of problematic data, that 70 per cent of businesswomen in the American Midwest in the middle to late nineteenth century "should be considered to be of middle class status or better."[82] Yet the evidence also indicates that a significant number of the female self-employed, and many more than for the male self-employed, continued to struggle for material security, often at a level indistinguishable from that of their female employee counterparts. Self-employment in 1901 and a century later brought men greater security than it brought women. In fact, in both eras being self-employed increased, not decreased, the earnings gap between men and women.

It is often noted that in the nineteenth century, self-employed women and, indeed, working women in general found employment in restricted areas of the economy, most generally in pursuits that women might have carried out and continued to carry out as part of their household activities. Boarding-house keeping and millinery work are often cited in this context. Such activity reshaped women's "proper sphere" to some extent. The implication is, of course, that women really entered into the world of business with one foot still in the world of the household. Wendy Gamber has correctly questioned that interpretation for the millinery sector: milliners and dressmakers often learned their trades outside the home in a workshop. Moreover, the identification of millinery as women's work was itself transitory and subject to changing social and economic contexts.[83]

A further perspective on the assumed uniquely gendered and home-linked nature of women's enterprise can be realized by broadening one's unit of analysis. Nancy Bertaux has suggested that for American working women as a whole, the late nineteenth and early twentieth centuries were a time of "widening opportunities" for varied employment and that little has changed in the nature of job segregation since then.[84] She does not, however, differentiate between employees and self-employed. Tables 7.8 and 7.9 focus on women's activity in both the goods- and service-producing sectors of the economy and contrast such activity with that of both men in 1901 and women and men in 1996. Self-employed women in 1901 were much more apt to be in the goods-producing sector than were their counterparts a hundred years later. Moreover, the incidence of self-employment for women in the goods-producing sector was much higher than that for women in 1996 and for men in both 1901 and 1996. Interestingly, it was women in the late twentieth century who were disproportionately funnelled into one of the two general sectors of economic activity, with 93 per cent working in the service-producing area, 10 per cent more than women a hundred years earlier.[85]

One must, of course, be cautious here. It is the case that women who were self-employed or employees who worked in the manufacturing sector in 1901 worked in fewer occupations than did men: 303 occupations for women and 778 for men. And while women had a higher incidence of self-employment, that activity, too, took place over a more restricted range of occupations: self-employed women appeared in 39, or 13 per cent of, manufacturing occupations; for men, the figure is 254, or 33 per cent. And finally, it might be noted that fully 89 per cent of self-employed women in manufacturing worked in five occupations, all of which were associated with the garment trade. Yet even at this point a comparative perspective provides some useful context for understanding this pattern of restricted enterprise. Self-employed men also, albeit not to the same degree, bulked in a few occupations: just under 50 per cent of self-employed men in manufacturing worked in five occupations; almost half of them were blacksmiths, with bakers, butchers, tailors, and shoemakers, all very traditional household endeavours, comprising the rest. The point to note is, that, yes, self-employed women in the goods-producing sector worked in a more limited area of enterprise than their male counterparts, and that enterprise was often related to and capable of being conducted out of the home. But concentration on the part of the self-employed was not unique to women; men, too, often worked in enterprises related to and capable of being conducted out of the home.[86]

At a broader level, the information in tables 7.8 and 7.9 point to what the more detailed focus on the manufacturing category revealed: in both 1901 and 1996 self-employed men tended to be more evenly dispersed throughout the economy than self-employed women. For both years and for both genders, the peaks in such activity generally reflect economic trends particular to each era. In both years self-employed women were prominent in the service category, dominated in 1901 by boarding-house keepers and in 1996 by professionals and other services such as domestics, laundry operators, and hairdressers. Given the movement away from industry in the later era, one might have expected a higher incidence of self-employment in the sales or trade category. For both men and women in 1996, there was a lower likelihood of being self-employed in sales than was the case a hundred years ago, a fact that reflects the concentration of such activity in large department stores that was only beginning in 1901. It should be noted, too, that the contrast in the share of self-employed activity by women in the sales area in 1996 compared to 1901 (25.1 to 2.8 per cent) may be more apparent than real. The *Labour Force Update*, from which the 1996 data is taken, engaged in a much more systematic and intensive process of data collection than did the compilers of the census in 1901.[87] As we have seen, that census severely under-enumerated women's activity in the workplace outside the home and especially missed the extent of self-employed women. It is appropriate, then, to state simply that even though the record of women's self-employment activity in 1901 is severely understated in the census and similar activity in 1996 has been well caught in the *Labour Force Update*, the evidence presented here testifies to the fact that for working women, self-employment was a more common fact of life at the century's commencement than at its close.

In an effort to compare the factors that affect the probability of men and women in the workforce engaging in self-employment, table 7.10 reports the results of several logistic regression analyses on members of the workforce with self-employed/not self-employed as the dependent variable. The results are reported as odds ratios (the exponential [B] statistic) in relation to the reference group within each variable. Thus the information in the city variable for the regression run with only men in the workforce can be read as follows: men living in cities with a population between 1,000 and 5,000 people were 1.2 times more likely to be self-employed than men living in cities with over 200,000 people. This finding is much more persuasive than if simple cross-tabulation had been employed because the regression reports its findings in the context of all other variables in the run. Cross-tabulation can take no account of those other variables and thus can easily lead to misleading conclusions. It is also possible to comment on the relative impact of the city variable as a whole compared to the impact of other variables on the odds of a person being self-employed. The R statistic indicates the "partial correlation between the dependent variable and each of the independent variables."[88]

The regressions in table 7.10 consider locational, individual, and some familial determinants of self-employment. Locational characteristics – city size and industrial and population mix – might be expected to influence the opportunities for self-employment; so the city variable, classified into four population categories, provides an albeit not overly robust measurement of that effect. Individual determinants of self-employment such as marital status have often been pointed to as central influences on the chances of women working. We have already uncovered some of the marital patterns for both self-employed women and men. Yet we do not know how significant marital status is in the context of age and family cycle. It seems reasonable to think that certain occupations were more amenable to self-employment than others. We have already noted differences in the incidence of self-employment in various occupational sectors, both across sectors and across genders. The inclusion of an occupation variable classified into professional, clerical, service, sales, transportation, manufacturing, and general labourer permits a closer focus on the relationship between occupation and self-employment. Similarly, we have seen that cross-tabulations suggest that age and self-employment were significantly related, that for both men and women self-employment increased with age. We would expect that relationship to hold in the presence of other variables.

Literature on entrepreneurship has long pointed to the tendency for the foreign-born – in some sense, the outliers in society – to be over-represented in self-employment if only because normal work channels were less open to them.[89] Yet David Burley has found "an absence of religious and ethnic associations with rates of self-employment" in late nineteenth-century Winnipeg. In the regressions run for this chapter, religion, birthplace, and year of immigration were run separately to avoid collinearity. Property ownership, whether one owned, rented, or neither, is also included, although the relation between ownership and self-employment, is tricky in the sense of the direction of causation: did ownership accrue from the fruits of self-employment, or did ownership, as we suggested for some women boarding-house keepers, facilitate self-employment?

Finally, familial contexts of the self-employed are explored. One such context is whether, if anyone in the family owned property, that made a difference in the degree of participation in self-employment. The answer is not obvious; recall that employee and self-employed women could not be differentiated on the basis of familial property ownership, although they could be on the basis of individual property ownership. More broadly, scholarly exploration of women's workforce participation has keyed on a family economy approach. This model implies that families – generally working-class – coordinated the labour of all members and adjusted participation as a response to variable needs. The literature on self-employment and familial composition is relatively slight. The regressions in table 7.10 provide an introduction to the relationship between family cycle and self-employment. This relationship is explored somewhat more closely in chapter 8. The following life-cycle categories are utilized: wife under 45, no children; all children under 10; some children 10–14, none 14+; some children 14+; wife older than 44, no children; single-person households; not-married female head, with some nuclear family; not-married male head, with some nuclear family.

We begin by focusing on the first two regression runs in table 7.10: men and women with boarding-house keepers. For both groups, location, measured by city size, is not a powerful predictor of the degree of self-employment.[90] Age is quite significant for both groups and confirms that the older age categories were disproportionately likely to be self-employed in urban Canada at the beginning of the twentieth century, as they were at the century's close.[91] Birthplace, while significant, was not powerfully so; the R statistic is relatively low for both men and women. The regression was also run with religion, and the results were very similar. Finally, the regression was run with immigrant year of arrival in four categories, the reference category being born in Canada. The regression with men discarded the immigrant variable as being of no significance.[92] The regression with women yielded a different result: those born outside Canada were less likely than Canadian-born women to be self-employed.[93] Clearly, being a male immigrant did not increase one's likelihood of being self-employed, and being a female immigrant made a woman less likely to be self-employed. This finding stands in direct contrast to current trends in self-employment. One explanation for this difference relates to the pattern of immigration, which began to change dramatically in the years after 1901: increasingly, immigrants came from southern Europe rather than from Britain and northern Europe. Sharper discrimination may have funnelled more of these individuals into self-employment than was the case with the relatively familiar immigrants in the years before 1901.

The occupation ratios largely support the data presented in table 7.8. Women in sales and service were the most apt to be self-employed, followed by manufacturers and professionals; for men, sales and the professional/managerial sectors headed the list, followed by service and, much less likely, manufacturing. It bears noting that the regressions confirm that women in manufacturing were more likely than men in that sector to be self-employed artisans. Did this status confer on women more financial and decision-making independence? Decision-making capabilities are hard to test at a macro-level. The financial implications of self-employment in the manufacturing sphere for both men and women can, however, be explored. On average, self-employed men and women made more than their employee counterparts in the manufacturing sphere. The similarity ends there: self-employed women averaged 17 per cent more per year, while self-employed men averaged 74 per cent more.[94] Annual income for women remained marginal, whether the woman worked for wages or on her own account in the manufacturing sector. It is hard to see a class division in existence between women wage earners and women who worked on their own account or as employers in that sector. For men, the difference was substantial, probably at a level where it makes sense to speak of a meaningful class difference between manufacturing wage earners and their self-employed and employer counterparts.

Individual ownership of property was strongly associated with being self-employed. This was especially the case with women. However, familial property ownership – living in a family another member of which owned property – as we suggested earlier, did not affect the odds of being self-employed for women or men. Family cycle was in some ways a surprisingly weak predictor of being self-employed. The R statistic is somewhat higher for women, suggesting a stronger relationship between family cycle and self-employment. Very likely this difference relates to the strong likelihood of unmarried female heads living with some family members being self-employed: fully 68 per cent of women in the workforce in that family cycle were self-employed. It would seem reasonable to suppose that self-employment facilitated more freedom to attend to household duties than wage work would, although most of the families in that life-cycle category did not have children under the age of fourteen living with them. It is also worth noting that men in single-person households were more apt to be self-employed than were women in that category. Overall, however, for both sexes, the result is perhaps surprisingly flat. It would seem that family cycle was a more

significant predictor of workforce participation than it was for predict-
ing who would be self-employed within that workforce.

Marital status, another familial attribute, did not significantly affect
the odds of men being self-employed, but in the case of women it was a
powerful indicator. Married women were ten times more likely than
widows to be self-employed.[95] The reason for the large difference is, of
course, obvious: married women dominated the realm of boarding-
house keepers. This finding seems to stand in opposition to that
reported by Burley, who, on the basis of cross-tabulated data, suggests
that in Winnipeg "married women seldom were in business."[96] In fact,
his data suggest that single women dominated the ranks of the self-
employed.[97] If our unit of analysis is self-employed women excluding
boarding-house keepers missed by the census, then we find, as Burley
did, that single and widowed women outnumbered married in the
ranks of the self-employed.[98] We also find, on the basis of cross-tabula-
tions, that widowed women in the workforce were more likely than
their married counterparts to be self-employed.[99] Yet if the regression is
run with all self-employed women minus the boarding-house keepers
missed by the census, not only does marital status remain quite signifi-
cant, but married women were 1.5 times more likely than widows to be
self-employed.[100] In the context of variables such as age – on average,
widows were older – and family life cycle – single, unmarried female
heads were the most likely to be self-employed, and by definition, mar-
ried women were not in that category – the relationship between
marriage and self-employment remains strong, a relationship that sim-
ple cross-tabulations misrepresent.

The final two logistic regressions reported in table 7.10, men and
women with and without boarding-house keepers, confirm most of
what we have already discussed. Their significance lies in what they tell
us about the importance of one's sex in the odds of being self-
employed: women in the 1901 workforce were 5.3 times more likely to
be self-employed than were men. Some might argue, or quietly think,
that such a finding could be arrived at only by a "cooking of the books,"
in this case by the inclusion of a large number of women boarding-
house keepers. If one is of that frame of mind, then, the question
becomes just how greatly does such an addition "cook" the results? To
find out, the regression was run without boarding-house keepers
missed by the census. Even without those individuals in the model,
women in the workforce in 1901 remained, by a factor of 1.1, more
likely to be self-employed than men.

This is quite a significant result. In the first part of this chapter, we provided various measurements of the extent of self-employment on the part of women in the workforce. Various comparative contexts were used to assess the significance of those measurements. Self-employed women were seen to be at least as and in some ways more active in the workforce than were similar women at the end of the twentieth century. In 1901 married women bulked large amongst the female self-employed. As well, on average, women at the beginning of the twentieth century may have enjoyed greater material benefit from self-employment than was the case at the century's end, although far less than the benefits enjoyed by men. Regression analysis provides a further comparative frame within which to appreciate the extent of women's self-employment. Even without the inclusion of women boarding-house keepers missed by the census, the odds remained greater that a woman rather than a man in the workforce would be self-employed in 1901.

Society in the late nineteenth century and many scholars since have pictured married women as wedded to household duties of a non-earning nature. It is true that the separate spheres paradigm is no longer dominant in scholarly discourse. It is also true that recent studies of general labour-force participation by women have pointed to an upwards trend commencing well before the mid-twentieth century. Yet even in the context of this revisionist literature – literature that points to increasing independence and more varied economic endeavour for women – the fact that married women in the workforce were the most numerous amongst the female self-employed (see table 7.2) and that many of those women were demonstrably middle-class, the group presumed to be the most constrained by the separate spheres ideology, remains significant. It is an excellent example of the unearthing of what Bernard Bailyn has called the "latent tendencies" in society, trends that people at the time paid no attention to, enacting policy and prescribing social roles often in contradiction to what was taking place on their own doorsteps.[101]

Certainly, some women entered the entrepreneurial arena out of economic necessity; their choices were constrained by familial obligations – as single mothers, for example – and by the lack of opportunities within the domain of wage work. Many were, as one historian has suggested, "marginal in the occupational structure [and thus] turn[ed] to small business proprietorship, as an alternative to deprivation in the labour market."[102] Yet as this chapter has made clear, many others actively sought out an entrepreneurial career, a career that the MWPLS sanctioned in law. It is the case, too, that women tended to work in segmented areas of the economy. Yet this fact did not make them any less entrepreneurial. "The ingenuity of women is being strikingly evidenced these days," Lady Gay observed in one of a series of articles on "New Occupations for Women" published in *Saturday Night* at the end of the nineteenth and beginning of the twentieth century. They were discovering, she continued, "glaring long-felt wants which no one has heretofore seriously considered, and their promptness in devising ways and means of supplying themselves to fill the need of their neighbors" was, for Lady Gay, wonderful to observe.

The businesses that she identified as demonstrating ingenuity were firmly within the segmented sector of woman's endeavour. Yet the nature of those businesses emphasize that their owners possessed a fine sense of commercial possibilities, the ability to define and exploit economic opportunities. One such business was run by an educated young woman Lady Gay called the "Amuser." The woman hired herself out to homes with elderly people in the household, people who required attention that restricted the freedom to socialize on the part of the rest of the family. The Amuser became a companion and helpmate to the older people. Lady Gay gave the following examples of the "peripatetic Amuser" at work: "Does grandma knit? She is shown a fascinating new stitch. Is she fond of music? The Amuser plays old or new tunes for her or sings ballads of yesterday, or coon songs of to-day. Does grandpa like the news? The Amuser arms herself with the dailies and gives him Bobs until he drops asleep. She plays dominoes or checkers or chess with him, and laughs at his stories; makes his punch and fills his pipe, and grandma and grandpa hope the family will accept engagements en masse with perfectly free minds, so that the Amuser may brighten their happy solitude."

The second enterprise was an operation that provided in-home secretarial services, a business "intended for," according to its founder, "the accommodation of persons who have more money than energy." Obviously, there was an entrepreneurial instinct at work. Concerning another woman "with a large contract on her hands [and] a business that grows tremendously ... I have heard [her] say," Lady Gay reported, "she would not return to her dull monotony of small beer, ordering dinner, dressing for a tea, lying on the sofa with a novel and a box of sweets, yawning over life, if she could."[103]

Whatever these women's motivations, the prevalence of such activity among women underlines the contested nature of gendered discourses in this era. Those discourses both reflected and denied the ways women engaged in economic activities and in so doing, provided, for those women who cared, an ideological buttressing or scaffolding that allowed them to justify and make sense of their economic behaviour, their pursuit of economic agency and self-sufficiency both within and outside the home. The incidence of self-employment by women, arguably the most visible economic endeavour engaged in by them in this time period, sits nicely with the findings reported in this book concerning the presence of women in other significant financial and economic sectors.[104] Although not all contemporaries and later historians perceived or cared to admit it, women were active and in many ways indistinguishable from men as economic and financial players in the emerging liberal society of late nineteenth- and early twentieth-century Canada.

8

"A Retail Dry Goods Merchant on My Own Separate Account": Gender and Family Enterprise in Urban Canada at the Turn of the Twentieth Century

In Ontario in the nineteenth and twentieth centuries, sole proprietorship and partnership firms were required to register their businesses with the land registrar of the county in which the business office was located. Jane Kerr, a fifty-year-old married woman in Hamilton, registered A.R. Kerr and Company in January 1900. When asked by the registrar what her relationship to the business was, she declared in no uncertain terms: "a retail dry goods merchant on my own separate account. I am the only member of the firm."[1] On 12 April 1901 H.G. McMahon, the census enumerator for ward 2 in Hamilton, recorded a different relation to the means of production for Kerr. Now a widow, she was given no occupation and, befitting a widow, was recorded as living on her own means. But Kerr continued to rent a store, and her twenty-six-year-old son, Henry, an employee, was a dry goods clerk who earned $800 for twelve months' work.[2]

This example provides a fitting introduction to the sources and subject matter that this chapter confronts. The example is far from exceptional: as we have seen, different historical sources often recorded varying information about the economic and social characteristics of nineteenth-century individuals. Which source should one believe? Or, in this case, are both correct? Did Jane Kerr sell the business after her husband's apparent death, and did her son continue to work there as an employee? The latter scenario is unlikely because proprietor and partnership dissolutions were also often registered at the land office. There is no record there of any change to the ownership of A.R. Kerr and Company. Moreover, Kerr continued to rent a store: why would she do so if she had sold or dissolved the business? In this case we are, I think, safe in assuming that the census enumerator simply did not accord Jane Kerr the respect of being a sole proprietor of a family business, a proprietor for whom her son worked. Such disrespect did, as we have seen in chapter 7, accord well with the still prominent mores of the time: women looked after the home, and men worked for money.

As we also noted in the previous chapter, business history has tended to perpetuate the bias inherent in the 1901 census. While work is increasingly emerging on gender and business, family businesses and the role of women within them have received less attention from business historians.[3] Andrea Colli, in a recent succinct historical survey of family business notes, "The role of women ... even if frequently obscure and hidden, is a key resource for [family] entrepreneurs, who are often able to start up their firms only thanks to the aid of their wives, sisters or mothers, who provide active financial, administrative and technical support."[4] Such an interpretation, while valuable and certainly, as we noted in our analysis of chattel mortgaging in chapter 6, correct, accords to women only the position of helpmate. In fact, as this chapter seeks to demonstrate, female capitalism was alive and well in the haven of the home.

There has been little systematic exploration of the nature of Canadian family enterprise during a time of increasing urbanization and industrialization at the beginning of the twentieth century. Valuable work by Henry Klassen on a number of western Canadian entrepreneurial families has shed light on inheritance practices and management styles, as has an earlier study of a central Canadian enterprise by Ian Radforth. The most sophisticated study is that of David Monod on shopkeepers, a study which, among other points, stresses the resilience of petty shopkeepers in the face of emerging retail giants.[5] There exists, however, nothing comparable to the studies of family enterprise in 1880 Detroit published by Melanie Archer. In a series of articles, Archer has situated family enterprise in the context of occupational structure, middle-class formation, and family strategies. She points out that at a time when, according to general business historiography, family businesses were in a state of decline, such enterprise in late nineteenth-century Detroit was alive and well. Family entrepreneurs tended to be better off than their waged employee counterparts. The economic strategies adopted by these families further differentiated them from households headed by employees. They represented, she concludes, a more homogeneous group in terms of occupation, social characteristics, and economic strategies than their working-class counterparts.[6]

In chapter 7 we looked at the familial context of some businesses run by women. This chapter seeks to broaden that analysis and provide a more systematic examination of women in family businesses. In order to identify entrepreneurs, those who were self-employed, and employers, Archer had to link census and city directory information.[7] By contrast, as in chapter 7, we draw on a 5 per cent sample of the 1901 census to examine the relation between family entrepreneurship and women in business in urban Canada. The focus includes all of urban Canada and extends beyond the head of the household. The argument will be made that in several important ways, family business was quintessentially a women's endeavour. To put the proposition somewhat more provocatively: family business, it will be suggested, was firmly and often profitably situated within women's domain.

There is no standard definition of an entrepreneurial family.[8] Most scholars would accept Archer's seemingly unambiguous definition: "a family proprietor is ... any business proprietor who involved at least one family member in shared ownership, management, or labor," as Jane Kerr did.[9] Yet Archer, along with many other writers on this topic, routinely restricts her analysis to the social characteristics of the household head, and most often only to those household heads who were male. Intuitively and practically, there are good reasons to do so. One can probably safely assume that the male household head would be the major player in any substantive family business. Moreover, focusing on the male head of household as one's central unit of analysis simplifies the presentation of often complex associations between social characteristics and entrepreneurship. Nevertheless, it seems fair to ask if anything is lost by the adoption of such a research strategy.[10]

Table 8.1, based on a 5 per cent sample of the 1901 census, provides a first look at this issue. Because of the biases in the census detailed in the previous chapter, census figures relating to women's participation in family businesses must be seen as lower-bound estimates. We use census data in this chapter, not as absolute and definitive measurements, but as an introduction to the pattern and extent of gendered entrepreneurship in family businesses in urban Canada in the early twentieth century. The census is the only source that would enable such an overview. Micro-studies of particular communities would allow the linkage of family entrepreneurship across households by the use of information in city directories, local newspapers, Dun and Bradstreet credit reports, and legal records as well as census data. At one level this chapter can be seen as an attempt to provide a broad template within which such studies can be situated.

The answer to the question as to whether anything is lost by simply focusing on the household head is clear: much is lost. In the first place, as the data presented in table 8.1 indicate, focusing simply on male heads of families overlooks 13.1 per cent of self-employed heads. Two-thirds of female family heads in the workforce and only one-quarter of male heads were self-employed. This is a strong indication that self-employment was far more important for female than for male family heads. To ignore women in this sector is to distort an important part of the economy in early industrializing Canada. Yet the full extent of women's participation in self-employment cannot be understood by a narrow focus on family heads. Including all self-employed in families only increases the number of male entrepreneurs by a factor of 1.2; female participation increases by a factor of 5, and women represent just under two-fifths of all self-employed in nuclear or extended families.[11] In early twentieth-century urban Canada, most self-employed women lived in nuclear or extended families and occupied household positions other than that of head. Clearly, to understand the nature of family entrepreneurship one cannot focus simply on family heads and one cannot ignore women.[12]

The 1901 sample yielded 14,620 nuclear or extended urban families with at least one family member in the workforce. For the sake of analysis, these families can be divided into three economic groups: working-class families, where at least one family member was an employee and no family member was self-employed (9,379); entrepreneurial families, where at least one family member was self-employed (4,618); and family businesses, where a self-employed individual either employed or was in partnership with another family member in the same business (623). Thirty-six per cent of nuclear families with at least one person in the work force (5,241) contained at least one member who was self-employed. Of those families with self-employment, 623, or 11.9 per cent, could be identified as engaging in family businesses.[13]

Table 8.2 provides an introductory look at some social attributes of the heads of the three economic family types examined in this chapter.[14] Tables 8.3 and 8.4 provide information on the familial and economic characteristics of these three family types. Taken together, the tables are fairly fulsome, and with particular attention to the differences between working-class and business families, our discussion will focus on one central question: in what ways can business families be seen to be a women's endeavour? The social characteristics of the head provide a first indication that women gravitated to and were economically more (visibly) involved in non-working-class family households. Consistent with our central hypothesis, women bulked as heads of entrepreneurial and business families; men were more concentrated as heads of working-class families. One of every seven business families was headed by a woman, compared to one of eleven working-class families. Relatedly, male heads were always most likely to be in the workforce; female heads of entrepreneurial and business families were much more likely to be in the workforce than were female working-class family heads, further suggesting the relative importance of entrepreneurial/family business to women as compared to men.

A closer comparison of the social characteristics of female- and male-headed households across economic families points to the distinctiveness of women-led business families. Across all three economic family types, male heads were overwhelmingly married; female heads were not and were less likely to be married if they headed a business family than if they headed a working-class household.[15] As men aged, they tended to be more likely to head an entrepreneurial or business family; for men, there is evidence of a progression from working-class to entrepreneurial/business endeavour over time. The age of women heads varied little across the three economic family types. For women, heading an economic family generally occurred relatively late in their life course. Women who headed entrepreneurial and business families were more likely to be Canadian-born than women who headed working-class families, a finding, it will be recalled, also highlighted by the regressions in the last chapter. The reverse was true for men. The regressions in chapter 7 confirmed at a more general level that entrepreneurial women were more apt to engage in blue-collar work. Distinguishing amongst economic families allows us to refine that result. Women who headed *business* families were much more likely to be in the blue-collar sector than women who headed working-class or entrepreneurial families and more likely to head blue-collar businesses than men. The high white-collar representation for women in entrepreneurial families reflects the large number of women boarding-house keepers in the service sector. Simply looking at some characteristics of family heads, then, suggests that family businesses offered more scope for economic activity for women and that business families headed by women differed in some important ways from those headed by men.

But a focus on family heads tells only part of the story. If one broadens one's focus to include all members of entrepreneurial and business families who were self-employed or employers, then fully 41 per cent of entrepreneurs in entrepreneurial families were women, and a smaller but still impressive (especially given the bias of the source) 30 per cent of entrepreneurs were women in business families.[16] The broader familial characteristics of the three economic family types (table 8.3) further supports the proposition that business (and entrepreneurial) families were the location of high participation by women in the market economy.[17] If one were to look only at family businesses undifferentiated by the sex of the family head, then one could state that family businesses in general had larger families, a higher ratio of workers to family size and to those of working age, and fewer dependents than their working-class counterparts. By distinguishing between male- and female-headed business families and by the sex of workers in the families, however, one can see that many of these differences are attributable to women. What is perhaps most interesting is that much of the increase in workforce participation in business compared to working-class families is accounted for by the increased ratio of working-age women working. On average, family businesses had 1.5 times more women of work age than working-class families and 1.6 times more men of work age than working-class families.

The key difference is that women of work age in business families were 2.1 times more likely to be working than in working-class families. By comparison, there was negligible difference in participation rates by working-age men across families. It is true that business families headed by both men and women put more of their family members to work than did working-class families, but for both family types that increase was almost totally attributable to the increase in the participation of women in the workforce (from 13 to 24 per cent in male-headed families and 40 to 76 per cent in female-headed families). Moreover, women-headed business families were noticeably more successful in using their potential workers than were male-headed business families: 79 per cent of potential workers (92 per cent of men and 76 per cent of women) worked in female-headed business families, and only 60 per cent worked in male-headed business families (89 per cent of men and 24 per cent of women).

One further point is suggested by the familial data in table 8.3. Family businesses provided a means for women to look after themselves. Women in family businesses were far more apt to work with other women than to work with men.[18] Given the segregated market activity of woman in business, as noted in chapter 7, this employment pattern should come as no surprise. It is nevertheless significant. Three of every four individuals of working age in women-headed business families were women, compared to less than half of those in male-headed business families. Seventy per cent of female-headed business families included only women, and 75 per cent of male-headed business families included only men. Family business was a gendered affair.

The gender-divided nature of family businesses in 1901 seems to stand in contrast to the gendered makeup of family businesses in the 1990s. Commentators at the end of the twentieth century pointed to the high incidence of self-employed married couples working in the same business and suggested that for self-employed women, "family enterprise [was] near the norm."[19] Two qualifications should be noted here. In 1901, as we have seen in chapter 7, over 80 per cent of self-employed married women were boarding-house keepers, and their husbands, whether self-employed or not, worked in an unrelated business. More specifically with regard to family businesses in 1901, we must keep in mind that the 1901 census certainly obscured the degree to which women were active partners in the business affairs of their husbands. Such shared enterprise is common today in the areas of accommodation, food services, and retail businesses,[20] and most probably was also common in the earlier years of the twentieth century, but the census enumerators missed much of that activity.

Did it make economic sense for women to engage in family business? The simple answer is yes, but seemingly not to the degree that such enterprise benefitted men. Two of the four economic indices presented in table 8.4 – families with servants and with property owners – point to a slight positive benefit for women in business families and much greater benefits for male-headed business families. This result corresponds to the findings in chapter 7 concerning property ownership amongst self-employed women compared to women employees. But examining, as we do in this chapter, changes in family income across economic families provides a more complete picture. The two indices related to income suggest changes of a fairly dramatic sort.[21] On average, family income increased very little for women-headed entrepreneurial families compared to their working-class counterparts but increased a significant amount for women-headed business families compared to both their working-class counterparts (an increase of 40 per cent) and their entrepreneurial counterparts (an increase of 37 per cent). This difference is much smaller than the nearly 100 per cent increase for male-headed business families compared to their working-class family counterparts but is significant nonetheless. A more nuanced measurement of income is even more suggestive. In general, families headed by women were smaller than those headed by men. This was especially the case for business families. As a result, the average income per family member varied hardly at all between male- and female-headed families. In fact, measured in this way, the gains experienced by family members in business as compared to working-class families did not vary significantly by the head's sex. It made economic sense for women to engage together in family business.

As table 8.5 indicates, there was a slightly higher tendency for families with entrepreneurs to be located in the West and a higher tendency for family businesses to be found outside the West. The relatively lower incidence of family entrepreneurship in the West reflects the newness of settlement and the preponderance of "young," as opposed to "mature," families in that region. Comparing regional variation by sex of the head indicates that women-headed families throughout Canada were more apt than male-headed families to be involved in entrepreneurially related endeavours. This pattern is also true for city size. No matter the size of the city, women-headed families tended toward entrepreneurial/family business activities to a greater extent than their male counterparts. From a geographical perspective, the relative importance of entrepreneurial and business families for women spanned Canada.

In an effort to compare the factors that affect the probability of men and women in the workforce engaging in family business, table 8.6 reports the results of several logistic regression analyses on members of the workforce with business/working-class family as the dependent variable. The results are reported as odds ratios (the exponential [B] statistic) in relation to the reference group within each variable.

Our discussion of table 8.6 will focus primarily on what the data reveal about the gendered nature of business families. The first regression run in the table – female- and male-headed families – provides strong support for the notion that family business was in important ways a female endeavour. Women-headed families were twice as likely as male-headed families to run family businesses. A logistic regression was also run with two variables designed to determine whether the gender composition of the workforce differed across families. Various measures, including a simple count of women and men of work age, could have been employed, but the one used in table 8.6 captures the number of women and men workers as a percentage of women and men of work age in the family. The results were then separated into two categories: fewer than 50 per cent of women or men of work age who worked and 50 per cent or more. For male- and female-headed families, the regression discarded the sex of the head and the male worker ratio variables as not significant. Families with 50 per cent or more of their women of work age who worked were, however, 1.8 times more likely to be in business families than working-class families.[22] This finding supports what the data in table 8.3 suggested with regard to the gendered composition of the workforce. Business families put more of their women to work than did working-class families and in that sense can be seen to be supportive contexts for entrepreneurial women. Interestingly, when the worker ratios were run with only male-headed families, results for the male worker ratio variable were insignificant. For the female worker ratio variable, on the other hand, the odds remained at 1.8 per cent more likely for families with 50 per cent or more of their female workers in the workforce to be in family businesses.[23] Opportunities for women who wished to work were not limited simply to women-headed business families and thus were not simply a result of the segmented nature of women's participation in the workforce. Women who wished to work in the market economy found greater opportunities in male- as well as in female-headed business families than they did in working-class families.

Marital status did not differentiate significantly between male- and female-headed family businesses. For both, the log odds were higher that the head of a business family would be single and, for women, widowed than would the head of a working-class family. Almost all other variables in the regression runs, however, do point to differences between male- and female-headed business families.

The results for occupation support what the data in table 8.2 suggested: women-headed business families were more likely than their working-class counterparts to be in manufacturing/blue-collar enterprise (6.6 times as likely); by comparison, male-headed business families were only 1.8 times as likely as their working-class counterparts to be in manufacturing. Fully 59 per cent of women-headed business families were in that sector, compared to 42 per cent of those headed by men. Not surprisingly, women manufacturers clustered in the millinery, dressmaking, and seamstress sectors. As we noted in chapter 7, it is often assumed that nineteenth-century self-employed women – and, indeed, working women in general – found employment in segmented areas of the economy, most generally in pursuits that women might have carried out and continued to carry out as part of their household activities. We would expect this pattern to hold strongly for family business ventures and especially for those that are identified in the census which would not include cross-household interactions. Nevertheless, albeit on the basis of limited data, it is clear that not all female-headed family businesses identified in the census operated only in the home. Fifty per cent of those for whom we know the place of employment operated at least some of the time outside the home, compared to 65 per cent of male-headed family enterprises.[24] One of every eight of female-headed family businesses owned or rented a store. From a different perspective, it will be recalled, Wendy Gamber has also questioned the home-based interpretation for the millinery sector: milliners and dressmakers often learned their trades outside the home in a workshop.[25]

Female-headed family businesses, then, should not simply be seen as some sort of cloistered enterprise bound by the walls of the family home. Relatedly, the notion that such enterprise was prized by women because it allowed a mother to look after her children as well as participate in the market economy should be qualified. As we have seen in our comments on table 8.3, these businesses tended to have relatively few dependents in the family and were headed by relatively few married women. Our findings in table 8.6 strongly suggest that female-headed entrepreneurial families, rather than business families, better fit the notion of women combining home-care responsibilities and market-oriented enterprise. These distinctions in entrepreneurial practice are, however, not widely applied in the literature.

The results for age support what table 8.2 suggested: age differences were far more important for male-headed than for female-headed families. In fact, the regression for female-headed families discarded the age variable as being of no significance, while for male heads the odds of heading a family business increased for those over fifty-five compared to other age categories. The fact that the regression on women heads discarded age should not be interpreted as meaning that women heads of family businesses were likely to be of any age. Rather, it suggests that the age of a woman head did not change significantly across the economic type of the family. As the data in table 8.2 indicated, women heads were as likely to be older in working-class families as they were in business families.

The birthplace and religion variables are fascinating for what they indicate about family business. It is perhaps surprising that birthplace is discarded in all three regressions as insignificant. Literature on entrepreneurship notes that entrepreneurs are often immigrants, the general explanation being that they have difficulties in obtaining employment from members of the host society.[26] Indeed, if only birthplace and not religion is included in the regressions, then for male-headed families that variable is significant and suggests that the European-born were most likely to head a business, rather than a working-class family. When religion is added, however, the regression discards birthplace, and Catholics and Jews are the most likely to head businesses, rather than working-class families. Relatively speaking, there were few Jewish-headed families in our sample, but those that were included were most often born in Europe. One might argue that both religious groups were challenged by some degree of discrimination in parts if not all of Canada and found it better to work as a family unit than for people outside their religious sphere.

Another indication that certain minority groups found a safe economic haven in family business relates to colour. The 1901 census contains a question on colour: whether one was white, black, red, or yellow. People who were yellow represented .4 per cent of all respondents in the sample and 1.5 per cent of all self-employed/employers in family businesses. They were not overrepresented at all in entrepreneurial families. Colour was not included in the regression runs because of too few cases in most values.

Neither religion nor birthplace was a meaningful indicator of whether a woman was in a working-class or a business family. Regressions with both variables and with each alone always discarded them as not significant. It may be true, as the information in table 8.2 indicated, that female heads of family businesses were more apt to be born in Canada than their male counterparts, but they were not more likely to be native-born than their female working-class counterparts.

The final set of variables relate to the relative wealth of female- and male-headed business and working-class families. Male-headed business families had a greater tendency to own property than did working-class families headed by men. The same was not true for women. In fact, the odds of someone in the family owning property did not vary across economic families for women.[27] The odds of employing a domestic increased for both male- and female-headed business families compared to their working-class counterparts, and the variance was stronger for male-headed than for female-headed families. Of all the variables relating to wealth, the most tantalizing is family income. Income run without age for male-headed families resulted in generally positive log odds of an increase in family wealth for business over working-class families. Yet, as the data in table 8.6 indicate, when age is added to the mix, the picture changes. While our income data is far from complete, there is a suggestion that business families headed by men had higher odds than their working-class counterparts of being in the lowest wealth category (business families were relatively more apt to be in the lowest than in the second through fourth levels). We saw indications of this income dispersal in chapter 7 and in the high standard deviation numbers for family income in male-headed entrepreneurial and business families reported in table 8.4. In other words, measured by income, business families headed by men were far from homogenous, and indeed, as men aged, many might have, from the perspective of income, been better off in working-class than in family business endeavours.

The same could not be said for women. Age was not an important differentiating characteristic of women-headed business and working-class families. Thus even with age in the regression, the income variable results in generally strong positive odds of increasing income for women-headed business compared to working-class families. The regression confirms that, at least in terms of income, it made economic sense for women to participate in family business ventures.

From one perspective, that of the large-scale business corporation, family businesses populated by women were small-scale affairs. Yet for those involved, those businesses were crucial to their material and social existence. Where else, for example, could Violet McKee earn $1,300 in one year? She headed, as will be recalled, a family dressmaking business along with four of her daughters. Granted, McKee earned more than the average $296 for the self-employed/employer women who operated family businesses for whom we have financial information.[28] Yet that average was close to two-thirds higher than the average $182 made by all women employees in Canada in 1901 and higher than the average $246 for one common female occupation, that of teacher.[29] The average income even compared favourably with that of men who were "operatives" in mills and factories.[30] From some perspectives, family businesses run by women can be seen as "penny capitalism."[31] Such business activity has also been typed as evidence of domesticity continuing to restrict and circumscribe women's economic agency. A broader perspective suggests that, given available options, female family enterprise represented the possibility for significant economic income, to say nothing of the independence that such income could facilitate.[32] Or put another way, Violet McKee and the women in her family business stand as an example of women's ability to capitalize on "the opportunities offered by a segmented economy."[33] Female-headed family businesses were one further niche within which women exerted financial and economic agency and in so doing, managed their own wealth and contributed to the economic development of the regions in which they lived.[34]

By paying attention to gender, we have established a more nuanced portrait of family business than that provided by Melanie Archer. Family businesses were in an important way far from the homogeneous enterprises depicted in the Archer studies. Rather, they were very much a gendered affair. As we have seen in our discussion of tables 8.2 through 8.4, the nature of family enterprise varied in many significant ways according to the gender of the owner-operators. As well, business families headed by women differed from their working-class counterparts in ways different from the way business families headed by men contrasted with male-headed working-class families. Not only were women an important presence in family enterprise; they were also a distinctive presence, one that cannot be explained by simple reference to the social profiles and economic activity of their male counterparts.

By focusing on the role played by women in family-run businesses, this chapter underlines the permeability of the boundaries between home and working on one's own account, between family and the marketplace. Carole Shammas, as we noted in our introduction, pointed to the decline of family capitalism as a contributing factor underlying the passage of the MWPLs.[35] Yet in business historiography the degree to which family capitalism did indeed decline is hotly contested.[36] What this chapter has, it is hoped, made clear is that for women, family capitalism was certainly alive and well. Home and family were havens for women in more than the normal meaning conveyed by that descriptor. Home provided many women entrepreneurs the opportunity to engage in and manage their own enterprise free from direct male control. The activity of these women stands the notion of home as an island or sanctuary from the "hurly-burly of contention" of the outside economic world on its head.[37] From the perspective of women-headed family businesses, home was indeed a haven, but a haven in a totally opposite sense to that understood by separate spheres ideologists and, as well, in a sense opposite to that understood by many historical commentaries on the emergence of a middle-class liberal society in this period. Put simply, female-run family businesses extended the world of contracts and competition into the home, and in so doing, they undercut several widely accepted premises inherent in the emerging notion of a liberal society. To a considerable degree, women in late nineteenth- and early twentieth-century Canada developed in their economic behaviours that market orientation associated with the constitution of the liberal individual self. Wherever men cared to look, women were engaged in matters of contract, investment, and general entrepreneurial activity. One can perhaps be pardoned from thinking how potentially subversive such collective activity was.

Conclusion

This work has explored how close to four thousand women in Victoria, British Columbia, and nearly six thousand women in Hamilton, Ontario, managed aspects of their wealth in an era when women were not normally thought to be in a position to manage much wealth.[1] Where feasible, attempts have been made to situate these women in their immediate gendered and familial environments and within broader legal, financial, spatial, temporal, and historiographical contexts. Focusing on these women (and a larger number of men) in two urban communities, often over a period of some sixty years, and wherever possible, putting these comparative analyses in a national and international frame allows us to conclude, unequivocally, that women with wealth were far from marginal players in the world of capital in late nineteenth- and early twentieth-century urban Canada. It is no exaggeration to label the late nineteenth and early twentieth centuries as an era characterized by the largest redistribution of wealth since the takeover of Native lands by Europeans. In all of the financial and economic sectors examined in this book, women increased their proportion of owned assets even as, especially in the cases of landholdings and financial stock, men's proportions declined.

Consider the following trends:[2] women increased their percentage of probates from 15 in the early 1870s to 32 by 1900 and to 43 by 1930, a sure indication that more women had money to manage and bequeath over time; they increased their percentage of probated wealth from under 5 in the early 1870s to 23 in 1900 and 28 in the late 1920s;[3] they increased their share of the landed wealth owned by men and women from 5 per cent in 1871 to 23 per cent at the end of the nineteenth century; and Ontario women increased their proportion of bank shares from 26 per cent in 1860 to 61 per cent in 1911 and from 15 per cent of share value in 1860 to 38 per cent of share value in 1911. Similar trends occurred in the land and chattel mortgage sectors. It is true that, on average in most capital sectors – overall probated wealth, land, financial stocks, mortgage borrowing and lending, and entrepreneurial affairs – women owned and managed less than men did. They were closing but never completely closed the gap. Yet averages, while important, conceal much. Men usually dominated because of the wealth-holding and behaviour of a relatively small number of the very rich. This was true of probated wealth-holdings, the value of financial stock, the worth of land, and the size of businesses, to name a few sectors covered in this book. If one were to take away the very rich and obviously powerful, then women's activities and profiles in those areas were often virtually indistinguishable from those of most of their male counterparts.

That women controlled wealth to an extent similar to most men and invested and managed that wealth in ways increasingly similar to and in some cases even more aggressively than men are significant findings of an empirical and behavioural sort. Indeed, it is striking how active and visible they were in all the capital sectors examined in this book. In that sense, women as owners and managers of wealth were far from ghettoized. How might one best explain this unprecedented transferral of wealth from male to female hands? What were the major social and economic consequences of this movement of capital? In this book we have approached these questions from three different but overlapping perspectives. The first line of inquiry concerns the impact of legal change, most especially a series of MWPLs and laws relating to dower, on women's activity in economic and financial affairs. Women's behaviour has also been set within a second broad context, the robust debate in the late nineteenth century centred on appropriate definitions of gender roles. Thirdly, an attempt has been made to explore the interrelationships of law, ideology, and behaviour in different spatially defined contexts. Indeed, it is important to emphasize that each of these perspectives has been grounded in two explicit and, as much as possible, systematic comparative contexts: gender and location. In this way, significances are better appreciated. The general can be separated from the local. Explanations are richer and more nuanced. A few summative words on each of those perspectives are appropriate here.

The MWPLs were passed in an era of increasing general debate about the proper role for women in society. Feminists toured Canadian and

American cities arguing for voting and economic rights. As we have
seen in this study, a vigorous debate concerning women's rights took
place in newspapers, journals, and even novels. At some level this pub-
lic discourse undoubtedly emerged from and interacted with changes
in religious teachings and attitudes, but it would also have gained
strength from the customary practices of, for example, married women
who engaged in buying and selling in their own names before the pas-
sage of enabling laws.[4] Clearly, more work of a systematic sort is neces-
sary to ascertain the foundational sources that underlay what this book
has uncovered: a significant transferral of wealth from men to women
and a heightened, if bounded, sense of agency and possibilities on
the part of middle-class and some working-class women, all of which
occurred in a relatively few short years encompassing the end of the
nineteenth and the beginning of the twentieth century.

Whatever the constellation of reasons for the passage of the MWPLs in
the late nineteenth century (and current literature suggests that such
causes were often only tangentially concerned with increasing women's
economic rights), those acts were wonderfully enabling for married
women in capital affairs. Following the 1870s legislation, married
women could participate in their own name in business affairs and
could own but not sell real property free from their husbands' control.
By the end of the 1880s in both the jurisdictions covered in this book,
married women could own and dispose of all types of property free
from their husbands' legal control. Yet the importance of the MWPLs
goes beyond their direct impact on the potential role for married
women in economic affairs. In the nineteenth century, women were
known by, and very often enabled and restricted by, their marital status,
hence the term "married" in the MWPLs. Historians, in fact, often
define and situate nineteenth-century women in their social settings
with primary reference to their civil status. It is suggested here that
more clarity would be served were one to refer to the MWPLs as simply
the women's property laws. The positive impacts for women occasioned
by the (M)WPLs, despite the name, transcended marital status. Most
importantly, those laws precipitated a fundamental change in the way
men bequeathed wealth. The (M)WPLs initiated a complex system for
the transmission of wealth from male to female hands. The ensuing
redirection of wealth – from, generally, men to men to men to women
as well as to men – underlay the growing visibility of women in financial
and economic areas, sectors up to that point commonly considered the
province of men.

How did the passage of the (M)WPLs facilitate such changes? By doing away with the notion of *femme couvert*, these laws made it palatable for fathers increasingly to bequeath money and assets to daughters, secure in the belief that present or future husbands could not summarily assume control of that wealth on marriage. Similarly, husbands began to leave assets in the hands of their widows free of many traditional controls in the belief that, should their widows remarry, their new husbands could not simply take control of that wealth and, in the process, prevent future transmission to children of the first marriage. Married women, too, increasingly wrote wills and bequeathed to daughters as well as sons. Prompted by the (M)WPLs, these changing inheritance practices gave to daughters and widows more direct control over bequests from fathers and husbands. More women were acquiring in their own names the means for the exercise of some financial agency.

It seems reasonable to think that as more women gained greater control of wealth through the process of inheritance, they would become more assertive and visible in capital matters. The language women used in their own wills captures some of that assertiveness. The feminization of capital markets, such as financial stock investment in Ontario, provides another indication of collective assertiveness. What is perhaps most surprising is just how quickly this activity developed. By the end of the nineteenth century the heightened visibility of women in urban land and mortgage markets is quite significant. Indeed, in the context of the two mortgage markets – land and chattel – it is useful to recall that the participation of married women as lenders and buyers increased markedly in the years following the passage of the (M)WPLs, a pattern which suggests that the acts facilitated married women's access to more capital and that these women were increasingly active in their employment of that capital. Our studies of probated wealth and will bequests point to how members of an older generation of women benefited from the (M)WPLs. Our analysis of landholding, mortgaging, and perhaps especially investment in financial stocks demonstrates how a younger, often single segment of the population also benefited from a system of wealth transmission precipitated by the (M)WPLs.

The (M)WPLs directly facilitated the entrance of married women into the world of entrepreneurship. Some, indeed, were already there, a fact that, in part, prompted laws such as the (M)WPLs to protect the rights of creditors and customers. The interaction between behaviour and law was never simply one-way. Unfortunately, we lack good data on the extent to which women were self-employed/employers before the

passage of the enabling (M)WPLs. An indirect indication of increasing
participation is suggested in the chapter on chattel mortgaging. In the
early years, women, generally housewives, raised money or loaned
funds on the basis of household goods. Over the course of the late nine-
teenth century, women in business increasingly turned to the chattel
market to raise cash on the security of their business chattels, rather
than household goods, for their entrepreneurial endeavours. More
directly, we do know, even from very biased sources such as the census,
that by the end of the nineteenth century, women, including married
women, bulked large in the world of entrepreneurship, in some ways as
large if not larger than similar businesswomen one hundred years later.
Much of this enterprise was bounded or segmented by gender ideals,
but even when that was the case, women could and did act in an entre-
preneurial manner by creating new enterprises and in a more limited
sense by owning and operating more traditional endeavours. More-
over, as we detailed in chapter 8, many women nicely turned the notion
of home as a haven for male comfort into home as a haven for women-
headed business enterprise.

If the (M)WPLs made possible a redirection of inheritance practice
and freed up space for married women in financial and business affairs,
the interaction between law and behaviour also cut across and was
affected by a related and contested debate on appropriate notions of
gender behaviour. The activity of women in economic affairs as
detailed in this book cannot be understood simply within the ideology
of separate spheres. In fact, the notion of separate spheres is of limited
analytic utility in understanding the position/role of women in relation
to wealth in the late nineteenth and early twentieth century in urban
Canada. For example, to label men producers and women consumers
simply perpetuates a false dichotomy between production and con-
sumption. Such a perspective places women in a separate sphere of
household consumption when in fact, as we argued in chapter 6, pro-
duction and consumption existed along a continuum and women and
their goods stood at the convergence of both. Women's activities, espe-
cially the behaviour of many middle-class women, were far from con-
tained within the sphere of a home and far from adequately described
by the use of such words as a "helpmate" or a "resource" that husbands
and other males had recourse to in times of financial, administrative, or
technical need. Women with wealth may indeed have fulfilled such
roles, but many were also active in their own right, promoting and man-
aging wealth in their own interests and doing so with little regard to

notions of the home as a sanctuary from the "hurly-burley" of finan-
cial, investment, economic, and business marketplaces. Moreover, in
the aggregate, women's activity in land, investment, and mortgage
markets amounted to a significant sum; their capital directly under-
wrote significant urban infrastructural development and the prolif-
eration of local businesses and indirectly, through investments in a
variety of financial enterprises, supported development in wider busi-
ness and economic spheres.

As our discussions of gender discourses in the late nineteenth cen-
tury have indicated, however, the ideology of separate spheres was alive
and persistent. One has only to remember the comments of C.A. Hol-
land, manager of the British Columbia Loan and Investment Company
in Victoria; "please," he wrote to his Vancouver agent, "get the hus-
bands to join in the mortgages in the case of married women where
possible." That mode of thinking was nicely congruent with, and even a
subset of, what Ian McKay has called "a liberal order framework." The
liberal order, Carole Pateman has asserted, was dominated by men. Yet
we have noted in this work that even some "liberally" minded men were
rethinking the proper sphere for women. Remember the correspon-
dent who wrote to the Toronto *Globe* on 11 May 1889 and argued that
dower was best understood as an "inalienable" right rather than a pater-
nalistic bequest. Dower was "another name for compensation," a con-
tractual right. It is worth repeating here the words of Senator
Alexander Campbell concerning the changing role of married women
in economic affairs. Campbell was a man with extensive business inter-
ests, was an accomplished lawyer, and had a long career in politics: he
held many different cabinet positions in Sir John A. Macdonald's vari-
ous governments in the late nineteenth century and ended his public
career as lieutenant-governor of Ontario. An imperious man, a man his
biographer has characterized as "aloof ... contemptuous of the masses
and somewhat scornful of popular politics," he was surely a patriarchal
figure, one who, in Pateman's words, would be quick to promote "patri-
archal right[s] ... throughout civil society."[5] Instead, Campbell recog-
nized the winds of change and supported the idea of a married woman
controlling her own affairs. Such, he believed, was "a course which rec-
ommends itself to most men of liberal minds – that the wife should be
considered in every way, quite as capable of taking care of her own
property and as having a full right to deal with it – to mortgage or sell or
to do what she likes with it – as if she were not married ... It seems to me
that is a more liberal way to treat a woman."[6]

Yet it would be foolish to assume that all women who achieved increased agency in financial affairs in this era did so with the primary goal of individual gain and, in that sense, in the pursuit of a small "l" liberal agenda. Indeed, McKay notes in his article that "first-wave feminists placed great strains on liberal definitions ... of the 'individual' in favour of general family matters." As Nancy Folbre and Julie Nelson have noted, a wide range of motivations may have prompted women (and men) to participate in the "world of money and profit." In the light of fragmentary sources that reveal "motivation," that is the position adopted in this study.[7]

Clearly, the separate spheres ideology was one of several competing definitions of appropriate gender behaviour. Women could choose between and/or be influenced by one or other of these discourses. From a separate spheres perspective, women's activity in capital affairs may indeed have been, in the historian Barnard Bailyn's sense of the word, "latent." The fact that some nineteenth-century commentators, such as Senator Campbell, could extol and support women's behaviour in these areas suggests that for them, such activity was quite visible. Still, and tellingly, even Campbell's views were constrained by a separate spheres mentality. Recall his answer to one senator's jibe "that always, or at least for a long time, the average wife will be very considerably under the influence of her husband." Campbell agreed and was firm in his "hope [that] the average wife will continue to be considerably under the influence of her husband." Recall, too, the plight of Mary Kough Brown of Hamilton, who had loaned her husband money and found it more comfortable to inquire about the loan arrangements via her brother rather than directly asking Adam, her husband. As her brother advised, "money dealings between husband and wife are not always conducive to marital peace and love." Yet even in the face of these attitudinal restraints, many women persisted and expanded their presence in financial affairs. The activity of married women such as Mary McKee, who borrowed eleven separate times from the British Columbia Land and Investment Company and steadfastly refused to accept Holland's wish that her husband co-sign the loans, exemplify married women engaging in entrepreneurial affairs in the face of attitudes conditioned by separate spheres precepts. Women with wealth continued to be constrained by notions of proper spheres even as they were enabled by and, like Mary McKee, took advantage of permissive legislation and alternative discourses.

It is impossible (or at least unwise) to be categorical concerning the influence of ideology on behaviour and behaviour on ideology. It may be that even as "young" businesswomen became active as investors in the early twentieth century, they were blinded by generational and attitudinal perspectives that prevented them from properly appreciating the degree to which their mothers and grandmothers had engaged in similar activity. Certainly, as many chapters in this work make clear, a similar myopia was apparent in the late twentieth century when commentators on women's roles in business and other capital affairs routinely assumed new frontiers and pointed out how, for presumably the first time, women were breaking free from the constraints of home and domesticity. The persistence of a form of separate spheres ideology and the related persistence of the notion of a liberal state run by men has made it difficult to "see" behaviour on the ground and especially to appreciate the extent of such behaviour in the past. At some level the absence of such knowledge continues to weaken and undermine women's public roles in the present.

The impact of sets of "structuring dispositions" and legal entitlements on actual practice cannot be understood without also taking into account their interaction with socio-economic constraints operative in different spatially defined contexts. It mattered where women lived. Demographic, spatial, legal, and local infrastructural developments filtered ideology and legislation and combined to create a context that shaped economic activity by women differently in each of the two cities primarily examined in this book. Perhaps the three most defining processes operative at the local level related to contrasting demographic structures, different applications of the law of dower, and contrasting economic infrastructures. In Victoria, men of marriageable age significantly outnumbered women of similar age; in Hamilton women of marriageable age outnumbered their male counterparts. In ways detailed most explicitly in chapter 4, Victoria women benefited from this favourable marriage market and enjoyed more agency in economic matters than did women in Hamilton. This was especially the case for married women, although, as we show, benefits extended to widows as well.

Often overlooked by historians, the different laws relating to dower, discussed primarily in chapter 5, also affected women's agency in financial affairs, an impact that is best seen in conjunction with the enabling provisions of the (M)WPLS. The relatively protective dower regulations in Ontario may have made the need for married women to control property less acute there than in Victoria, where dower protection was virtually absent. Denied easy access to a third of their husbands' landed assets on the husband's death, Victoria's married women looked to and took advantage of the (m)WPLs to a greater extent than did Hamilton's married women. Yet ultimately Victoria's unbalanced sex ratio provided the necessary condition for realizing that end, a condition absent in Hamilton.

Sensitivity to local economic structures and the comparative frame adopted in this book allows one to shed light on the differences in the upward trend of probated wealth held by Hamilton women compared to Victoria women after 1911. Hamilton women continued to close the gap between themselves and their male counterparts; Victoria women lost much of what they had gained in the past. While both cities experienced a significant land boom, in Hamilton that speculation occurred within the context of increasing industrialization and of different local regulations relating to land taxes. In Victoria the speculative boom took place in *anticipation* of industrialization. The failure of industrial capital to arrive, coupled with a single tax on land and several other local municipal proceedings, led to a much more dramatic collapse in Victoria than in Hamilton, a collapse that Victoria's women were just beginning to recover from on the eve of the Depression. Our comparative frame allows us to qualify the provocative comment of Livio Di Matteo concerning a possible "national setback in women's wealth." A setback did indeed occur, but it was more one of regional than national extent. Local structures shaped the ways that (m)WPLs and gender discourses impacted women's behaviour.

It may be that the most significant changes that accompanied wealth transferrals did not occur at the public level. Beverly Lemire has shown that women in England were most active in the day-to-day matters of household maintenance and survival. Such "everyday practice and plebeian affairs," while of central importance to family welfare, were conducted at the margins and in the shadow of more public and institutional frames. Relatedly, Gerard Bouchard argued, in his study of married women in the peasant society of the Saguenay, that women's agency must be analyzed at both the macro-social level of church, state, and capital and the micro-social area of the family and the married couple. Bouchard found patriarchy reigning at the macro-social level and diversity to be characteristic of relations between men and women at the micro-social level. He noted that there are constant lines of interaction between the two levels, although he did not dwell on those in his study.[8] The analysis offered in this book suggests that those lines of interaction were of fundamental importance in understanding relations between men and women who lived in urban Canada. Legal change at the macro-social level directly affected wealth transferrals within the micro-sphere of the family. Over time these private transferrals led to a heightened presence of female capital in the public spheres of finance, investment, land, mortgages, and business. At the same time, as a reading of wills and sundry other qualitative sources suggests, women exercised increasing agency in the control and devolution of capital within the micro-social sphere of everyday life. Equality in either area remained elusive, but at the very least, women's activities became more diverse and more resistant to reification in the time period and areas under review in this book.

"It has been said," William O. Stoddard, observed in his essay "Women in Their Business Affairs," "that in transacting business affairs a woman should forget that she is a woman and proceed altogether as if she were a man." "This," in Stoddard's opinion, "is an exceedingly pernicious, stupid and false teaching."[9] After all, he noted, one cannot "set aside an immutable fact." At one level, Stoddard was quite correct: traditional views of just what constituted that "immutable fact" remained strong in late nineteenth- and early twentieth-century urban Canada. Such views had not been set aside. Yet in spite of and often in the face of those views, women with wealth carved out new public territory for themselves. They were exceptional women if only in the sense that they had some wealth to manage. But so too were men with wealth to manage. Collectively, these women aspired to the liberal bourgeois dream: ownership and management of capital affairs as equal individuals in that part – surely a very central part – of the public sphere that encompassed appropriate behaviour in matters to do with business and money. In this work we have identified thousands of women from only two cities who in various ways pushed the traditional boundaries of acceptable feminine practice. They, for the most part, did not espouse fundamental social reforms of a class-based sort. More prosaically, they wanted a piece of the liberal economic pie; whether for familial or for purely personal reasons is largely unknowable. To that extent these women can be seen as reformers, since, through their practice, their actual behaviour, they stretched the notion of a liberal state and in the process laid, however unconsciously, the groundwork or underpinning for similar and emerging reform of the political sphere.

The evidence of the pervasiveness of women's economic endeavours presented in this book allows us to reconsider a central lacuna in many studies of the nature of social classes, and especially of the middle class in the late nineteenth century. For both nineteenth-century contemporaries and for many historians, occupational identities stand at the centre of class definitions. Too often women have remained invisible in these areas. As Andrew Holman laments, "how can we study the class experience of women [since] most married women in the middling ranks ... had no classifiable paid occupation, and evidence of their unwaged work is fragmentary." For Holman, as for many others, the solution is to concentrate on women's social and cultural roles, such as child-rearing, education, and the cultivation of refinement. Via such pursuits women accorded themselves an important role in middle-class development.

Such a perspective, while at some levels understandable, really only perpetuates the separate spheres binary. It is certainly true, as Jurgen Kocka has noted and as Ian McKay has forcefully outlined in a different milieu, that men stood at the centre of the development of middle-classness. That "project," however, was, as Kocka notes, "hardly opposed by middle class women who in the long run would try to claim the principles of civil society for their own emancipation." Those principles encompassed more than the exercise by women of cultural and political rights, matters on which traditional historiography has mainly focused. Women acquired and exercised many economic rights as well. By so doing, they put pressure on men to reconceptualize the notion of the middle class and women's proper place therein.[10]

Despite their real gains, these women fell short, often far short, of equality with men in capital matters. As Constance Backhouse has written: "property allocation would continue to be gender imbalanced."[11] But such a summation is too absolutist and unrealistic in expectation. A better perspective is to underline what these women, most often operating as individuals, did achieve. Their gains over a short period were quite substantial. Their activities belied rigid gender stereotyping. In fact, their accomplishments in capital matters raise the question of whether one might term this a "revolutionary process." The answer might be yes in terms of the amount of wealth involved and the speed of the transfer of that wealth from men to women, no matter that the process was for the most part an intra-class happening. The answer must be more qualified when one views this process from the perspective of public power. The flow of power lagged behind the flow of capital. Few, if any, women sat on the boards of those corporations that were emerging as economic and financial leaders. But as we have argued throughout this book, women's visibility and power in the public sectors of finance and business only come into sharp relief when we narrow the lens and focus below the top level of economic activity. Thousands of individual women demonstrated that they could function quite well in the public (masculine) spheres of finance and business. Even as women gained confidence, some men began to rethink what a woman could do. In the aggregate their many public acts of competency in the fields of finance and business set the stage for reform in the public arena of politics.

Yet it seems clear that later generations of women have continued to lag behind men in matters of wealth and the potential power that accompanies money. It is possible that such power was more often realized at the micro-social level, a level very difficult for historians to systematically penetrate but of which this book has provided many glimpses through readings of women's wills and scattered correspondence with husbands, financiers, and the courts. Such assertiveness was slower to materialize at the macro-social level, the sphere of politics, the press, and conspicuous consumption.[12] It is by separating the micro-social life from macro-social activities that we might best understand how Annie Meyer and Julia Howe, two American feminists, could note in 1891 that via property law reforms, "the emancipation of married women has been gradually, *silently*, successfully accomplished."[13] In this sense we might conclude that the process we have uncovered and explored in this book was at best a silent revolution which in the public sphere engendered equally muted consequences. The fertile ground left by early twentieth-century women resulted in growth of a stunted sort. It is a question for a future work to determine why women's initiatives in the public sectors of finance, business, and general economic endeavour at the beginning of the twentieth century were not acknowledged, built upon, and extended effectively during the rest of that century.

APPENDICES

The Gendered Nature of Sources
for the Calculation of Property
Ownership Trends

Since the discussion of property ownership is based on assessment rolls and, for 1901, the census of that year, a brief indication of the gendered nature of these data is useful. Victoria's assessment rolls do not provide any information on the marital or occupational status of the property owner. In all cases that information has been found by linking the assessment data to the requisite census. For Hamilton, the situation is different. In 1881 whether a woman was single or "Mrs" was recorded, as was occupational status, some familial characteristics, in some cases indications as to whether one was a Protestant or Catholic, and some information about personal, as opposed to real, wealth. In 1886 the assessment rolls in Hamilton began to record whether a woman was married, a widow, or single.

Until 1901, we are entirely reliant on assessment data for information on ownership of real property. We have no real means for testing the gender bias of this source until 1901, when the census of that year recorded a great deal of information about the property holdings for men and women across Canada. I have closely compared and linked data from the 1899 Hamilton assessment roll (the last year to be microfilmed by the Mormons and thus easily available for analysis) to a complete machine-readable file of the 1901 census for Hamilton. I have done the same for Victoria's 1901 assessment roll and the 1901 census for Victoria. The results are both intriguing and frustrating. For Victoria, the number of male owners recorded in the census compares very closely to the number of male owners recorded on the assessment roll as living in Victoria (1,519 and 1,348 respectively). Since the census records property owned anywhere and the assessment records only property owned locally, the difference in number of property owners makes sense. As I do not have a complete count of male property owners for the 1899 Hamilton assessment roll, a similar comparison is not possible.

For Victoria, the number of women recorded as property owners on the assessment does not compare at all closely to the number of women recorded as property owners in the census (756 and 270 respectively). The prime reason for the census undercount is clear: Only 45 of 330 married women on the assessment roll who could be linked to the census were recorded as owning property in the census (13.6 per cent). Clearly, in the case of Victoria, the 1901 census was dramatically gender-biased in the sphere of property ownership.

The Hamilton sources, however, point to a somewhat different story. Unlike in Victoria, the number of women property owners on the Hamilton assessment roll compares more closely to the number of women property owners in the census (1,173 and 1,030 respectively). Moreover, the assessment lists only 12.7 per cent of women as married, whereas the census lists 22.4 per cent of women property owners as married.[1] The Victoria census, by comparison, recorded 29.3 per cent as married. However, when the assessment data is linked to the census data for each city, the proportion of married women property owners increases only slightly to 24 per cent for Hamilton but rises dramatically to 63 per cent of women property owners for Victoria. In the latter city the census is biased against women property owners and against married women property owners especially. In Hamilton the number of women property owners is comparable across the census and assessment roll, and the census captures proportionately more married women owners than does the assessment roll.

Clearly, the same type of source in one district can yield a different gendered picture of ownership patterns. What are the implications of these differences for this study, a study that at several levels attempts to be comparative? There are several possibilities. If one considers that the whole world is like Victoria, then both the assessment rolls and the census for Hamilton might severally undercount women property owners, especially married ones. Such a conclusion seems unjustified. The data regarding marital status of women who left probated wills in Hamilton and in Victoria indicate a significant difference in married women's participation in Victoria compared to Hamilton, similar to the differences in marital status of women property owners as revealed by the Victoria assessment rolls (see table 1.3).

The following are my operational conclusions. I take it that the assessment rolls for Hamilton provide a reasonably accurate and at least consistent picture of the extent of women's property holding; thus a trend line for that city based on assessment data is reasonable. Those assessment rolls may underestimate the extent of married women's property holding, but when put in the context of other indices of wealth-holding used in this study, I think that the bias would not alter the conclusions drawn in chapter 4 concerning the relative participation of married women as property holders in Victoria and Hamilton in this time period. Nevertheless, I have for 1901 offered a "blended" figure for women's participation, consisting of, for each city, women in the census plus women from the assessment roll who could be linked to the census. The result, I think, is a conservative count of women property owners in Victoria and a somewhat less conservative count of women property owners in Hamilton. It should be noted that even if just assessment roll data were used for each city and expressed as a percentage of women over nineteen in the census, then the direction of the trend lines within each city would not be altered and the comparisons of women's participation across each city would not change.

The Construction of
Tables 4.7 to 4.10

The following procedure was used to construct tables 4.7 through 4.10. The central assumption is that the cases which I have been unable to link to the census and for which, as a result, I lack personal data exhibit similar enough social characteristics to permit their being added to each cell in a proportion similar to that of the linked. For example, in Victoria in 1881, there are 741 men on the assessment roll. I have linked 388 of them to the census, and 353 are not linked. Eleven of the linked men were between twenty and twenty-nine and single. In the whole of Victoria, as per the census, there were 477 single men of that age range. If I just use 11 in that cell, then as a proportion of all men in Victoria of that age range and marital status they constitute 2.3 per cent. To get a possibly more realistic percentage I have calculated that 11 is 2.8 per cent of all 388 linked cases. I am assuming that 2.8 per cent of all unlinked cases (10 of 353) are also single and between the ages of twenty and twenty-nine. So table 4.8 includes linked and unlinked data, and 21 as a percentage of all 477 single men between twenty and twenty-nine in Victoria is 4.4.

Such a procedure runs the risk of ignoring the possibility that the unlinked are different in some systematic way from the linked. I estimate in general terms that the contrast would likely lie in a tendency to be able to link older, married individuals, rather than younger, unmarried, at least in part because the former tend to more stable in a residential sense. It is hard to test for this hypothesis, but one related measure would be the assumption that older, married/widowed individuals would, on average, own more property than younger individuals whether married or not. So if our linked group is missing younger individuals, one would expect to find a significant difference in average landed wealth between the two groups. For Victoria men in 1881–82, the average landed wealth for the linked population was $2,854, and for the unlinked, $2,473. The standard deviation is similar: $4,966 and $5,155 respectively. This finding suggests that there may be some bias in the direction noted above but not an unreasonably strong difference. In 1891 the difference in average wealth was greater: $9,354 for linked men and $5,340 for unlinked men. The procedure employed for the construction of the tables, then, likely underestimates the number of younger, probably single men on the assessment roll in 1891. For Victoria women in 1881, the average wealth for those linked is $1,651 and for those missed, $1,308, and for 1891, it is $4,966 for linked women and $5,328 for unlinked. In all cases, the standard deviations are similar. For women, then, a small bias may exist against linking older women in 1891. In fact, however, much of this bias is accounted for by a small number of relatively large unlinked estates. For Hamilton women in 1881, linked women had an average landed wealth of $2,159 and unlinked, $3,081, suggesting that somewhat more of the older women on the assessment roll might have been missed in the linkage. However, an examination of the wealth distribution of the linked and unlinked determined that the estates of five wealthy unlinked Hamilton women accounted for almost all the difference. Indeed, the proportion of wealth held by the lowest 60 per cent of the population was almost identical. Overall, the differences in average assessed worth point to a possible underestimation of younger men in the tables and a possible – but more for Hamilton than for Victoria – small underestimation of older women. On balance, I think the procedure adopted for the construction of tables 4.7 through 4.10 is reasonable.

Property Ownership by Relation to Means of Production: Women in Urban Canada, 1901

Because of the bias in the census toward the attribution of property owner-ship – generally only to the household head, and most heads were male – it is useful to explore the relation between being in business and owning land at a more micro-level, specifically in Victoria and Hamilton, where, as we did in chapter 4, we can combine assessment roll data and census informa-tion. As table A3.1 in this appendix indicates, property holding for employ-ers and the self-employed combined in Victoria was greater than the percentage reported for all cities simply on the basis of census data.[1] The percentages were roughly the same for Hamilton. That the difference is greater for Victoria women is consistent with our findings in chapter 4 to the effect that a higher percentage of women owned property in that city than in Hamilton and perhaps in many other Canadian cities. In both cities the odds of owning land increased if one were an employer or self-employed, compared to employees and women with no reported relation to the means of production. But in both cities and in urban Canada as a whole, women on their own means were by far the most likely to own prop-erty. This finding also is consistent with our discussion of general wealth-holding in chapter 1.

Table A3.1
Property ownership by relation to means of production: women in Victoria, Hamilton, and all urban Canada, 1901

Relation to means of production	Percentage/number women owning property		
	Victoria	Hamilton	Urban Canada
Employer	10.0/1	13.3/8	15.5/20
Self-employed	18.8/26	13.6/89	13.9/96
Total employer/ self-employed	18.2/27	13.5/97	14.1/116
Employee	4.8/35	4.4/163	2.2/104
Own means	31.8/116	42.7/262	41.3/454
No relation given	11.5/424	6.2/755	2.9/695

NOTE: The age is greater than or equal to twenty, and boarding-house keepers missed by the census are not included.

Women and the Business of Philanthropy: The Case of Victoria

Well before the late nineteenth century, middle- and upper-class women were quite visibly involved in managing charitable institutions. In one sense, charitable endeavours differed from the activities focused on in chapter 7 since they were not run for individual or familial gain. Nor was the money "owned" by the women who managed it. Yet managing these non-profit organizations often entailed the careful collection and dispersal of significant sums of money. It also often required the management of paid personnel and the exercise of no little degree of power over the men and women in need of the organization's services. Moreover, this management of wealth and people took place in a public, not private, venue. The strategies adopted by women to organize, finance, and manage philanthropy provide insights into the general business acumen that many women possessed in this era.

It might be assumed that women were especially appropriate custodians of philanthropic activities. After all, the separate spheres paradigm extolled charity and selflessness and saw these attributes as part of a woman's essential character. It is all the more interesting, then, that the major local charitable institution in Victoria, the British Columbia Benevolent Society, founded in 1872, had been initiated by and was managed by men. During the first twenty years of its existence, the society actively met the needs of the worthy poor no matter their "creed, colour or nationality."[1] Its records testify to a liberal charitable agenda: food and money were dispensed to single as well as married men, to women, and to old and young. Management and management philosophies changed abruptly in the depressed era of the 1890s. In that decade the dispensation of aid in Victoria became increasingly feminized. Some Victoria women in fact accused the British Columbia Benevolent Society of ignoring the plight of poor women and pandering to healthy, single men. Records indicate, however, that the society provided more aid to women than to men.[2] But that did not matter. Local Victoria women established a parallel charitable agency, the Friendly Help Society, in 1895 and competed with the Benevolent Society for local funds.

From the beginning, the female-managed Friendly Help Society's policies differed substantially from those of the male-run Benevolent Society. While the Benevolent Society gave cash or vouchers to needy poor for the purchase of clothes and other essential goods, the Friendly Help Society advertised for old clothes that memebrs could repair and then, since "our object was to make people independent + help them to keep their self respect, + not make paupers of them'" could sell "at a very low price rather than giving them away." In contrast to the Benevolent Society, the Friendly Help Society did not set up an employment registry and decided to deny any aid to "single" men, "as the Association had as much as they could do in helping families." It devised and applied measures to ascertain the worthiness of all applicants for aid. The women divided the city into twenty-nine zones and appointed "visitors" to check up on charity recipients in each zone by a system of home visiting. A black list was kept for people deemed unworthy. The names of "imposters" were published in the press.[3]

Discussions between the two societies failed to lead to amalgamation, but the women pressed for the exchange of monthly lists to "prevent a repetition of alms be[ing] given to any one individual."[4] Clearly, the policies espoused by the women redefined charitable initiatives in Victoria. The rigour, clear organization, and hard-edged – what one might term "business" – policies implemented by the women appealed to the local community: ultimately the Friendly agency trumped the Benevolent Society where it counted most, in the raising of funds from the local community and municipality. Donations to the Benevolent Society declined, even as subscriptions to the Friendly Help Society increased. The Benevolent Society limped into the twentieth century; the Friendly expanded its operations, networking and affiliating with such organizations as the National Council of Women of Canada, the King's Daughters, the Children's Aid Society, the Mission Hall Committee, and the Saint Mary's Friendly Aid in nearby Oak Bay, and by 1914 it even appeared on the directory of the Organized Charity Society of New York.

The approach to philanthropy put in place by these women reflected a larger and, by the late nineteenth century, well-established international agenda concerned with providing relief outside the boundaries of the state and reflective of values within the liberal bourgeois polity as a whole. In part, the wellspring for this desire to reform emerged from an evangelical religious tradition, and it is true that meetings of the Friendly Help Society always commenced with a prayer and its annual reports invoked the assistance and support of God. Moreover, the suitability of women for home visiting squared nicely with separate spheres notions. Some historians have suggested that a religious discourse allowed women to appear in public, and to that extent they continued to participate in the public discourse less as women and more in the role of saintly religious benefactresses. Yet in Victoria the Benevolent Society, too, in its reports paid homage to God. At some level, Christian ideals underlay the charitable endeavours of men and women in late nineteenth-century Victoria. What is most interesting in the context of this study is the role played by the city's women, rather than its men, in the introduction and management of a systematic philanthropic agenda. They, rather than men, were more successful in speaking to the public and appropriating the language and approaches that were best suited to elicit needed support and backing for their charitable endeavours. In this sense, Victoria's women were more centrally a part of the public sphere than were its men. They were more assertive, rational, systematic, "businesslike," and "scientific" in their managerial philosophy and practice. By comparison, charitable initiatives espoused by Victoria's men did not measure up to scientific precepts and consequently failed to meet the test of the "subscriber democracies" on which they depended for donations.[5] In a public sphere defined by liberal society as masculine, the city's women bested its men. In the context of this book, women's assertiveness in the public sphere of charity parallels the more private assertive actions of women financiers, investors, and will-writers, as well as paralleling the more public activity of women in the world of business.

TABLES

Table 1.1

Probated decedents who were women and percentage of total net wealth they owned: selected studies, 1868–1984

Place	Time	Number of probated decedents	Percentage women	Women's percentage of wealth
UNITED STATES				
Massachusetts	1879–81	11,142	36.9	16.5
Massachusetts	1889–91	14,608	42.8	26.7
Essex Co., NJ	1875	60	21.6	na
Essex Co., NJ	1900	60	40.0	28.2
Bucks Co., Pa	1790–1801	701	16.5	7.0
Bucks Co., Pa	1891–93	761	37.8	34.6
Bucks Co., Pa	1979	570	47.4	52.8
Sacramento Co., Calif.	1890–1910	307	34.5	na
Sacramento Co., Calif.	1968–84	342	51.2	na
CANADA[1]				
Hamilton	1869–71	74	23.0	5.0
Hamilton	1880–81	75	37.3	23.7
Hamilton	1890	93	48.4	33.8
Hamilton	1900	101	42.6	25.5
Hamilton	1911	208	45.2	39.2
Hamilton	1922	312	41.0	29.2
Hamilton	1930	311	54.0	40.8
Victoria	1868–72	56	5.4	na
Victoria	1880–86	140	22.1	17.4
Victoria	1894–1900[2]	287	28.2	20.6
Victoria	1910–13	461	29.7	26.6
Victoria	1918–21	661	36.1	15.6
Victoria	1928–31[3]	797	38.1	22.4

NOTE: US cases come from Shammas, "A New Look at Long-Term Trends," table 2, 423.

1 Note that there was no requirement in either Ontario or British Columbia in the first two time periods to report real property.

2 Includes all probates not, as in table 1.4, simply those with asset breakdowns.

3 One male case with a gross worth of $2,860,125 or, in other words, almost equal to the gross worth of all women has been omitted from the analysis. The next closest value was $725,043.

Table 1.2

Probated estates with wills: women in Hamilton and Victoria, 1880–1931

Date	Hamilton: percentage number	Victoria: percentage number
1868/69–71/72	52.9/9	0/0
1880–84	51.6/33	55.0/11
1888–92	54.6/95	61.9/26
1898–1900	73.2/90	75.7/28
1910–13	na	68.0/85
1918–21 (H=1922)	66.4/85	66.5/159
1928–31 (H=1930)	76.8/129	71.4/217

Table 1.3
Married women as a percentage of women's probates, wills, and probated wealth: Hamilton and Victoria, 1880–1931

Date	Hamilton: percentage number	Victoria: percentage number
PROBATES		
1868/69–1871/72	11.8/2	33.0/1
1880–84	27.4/17	31.6/6
1888–92	37.1/52	44.7/17
1898–1900	31.7/38	54.3/19
1910–13 (H= 1911)	22.3/21	58.5/55
1918–21 (H=1922)	33.6/43	60.9/98
1928–31 (H=1930)	35.7/55	46.4/117
WILLS		
1869–71	11.1/1	0.0/0
1880–84	21.2/7	27.3/3
1888–92	30.0/27	30.4/7
1898–1900	30.0/27	57.7/15
1910–13	na	50.9/29
1918–21(H=1922)	28.2/24	59.3/51
1928–31(H=1930)	29.9/35	44.0/77
PROBATED WEALTH		
1868/69–71/72	3.1/$770	0.0/0
1880–84	17.2/$25,357	41.7/$34,065
1888–92	30.4/$145,850	41.4/$74,780
1898–1900	25.5/$105,984	64.7/$107,921
1910–13 (H= 1911)	15.3/$110,165	75.7/$1,269,184
1918–21 (H=1922)	22.2/$275,806	51.6/$379,576
1928–31 (H=1930)	15.1/$260,907	48.1/$1,134,102

Table 1.4
Investment patterns of men and women in Victoria, 1894–1931, from probate data

	Percentage of total (gross) wealth/percentage of investors							
	Victoria: men, 1894–1900; women, 1894–1901		Victoria: Men and women: 1910–13		Victoria: Men and women: 1918–21		Victoria: Men and women: 1928–31	
Investment category[1]	Men	Women	Men	Women	Men	Women	Men[2]	Women
CONSERVATIVE/	84.1/97.6	84.8/94.3	65.4/92.0	84.8/91.2	48.4/95.3	70.1/94.6	39.2/94.1	40.3/91.4
TRADITIONAL RISK								
Land	62.9/61.0	55.7/71.4	55.0/68.5	77.4/59.9	35.6/70.4	51.5/64.0	23.5/67.1	24.7/59.9
Household goods	2.9/65.0	13.8/77.1	1.1/38.3	1.3/36.5	1.4/31.8	2.5/32.6	1.4/35.9	2.7/39.1
Cash in hand	0.1/4.1	0.0/0.0	0.8/12.8	0.3/15.3	0.4/26.3	0.3/19.2	0.1/26.9	0.1/19.9
Cash in bank	8.2/23.6	14.7/18.6	6.2/59.3	5.6/54.7	6.2/58.3	14.6/60.7	9.6/66.3	11.6/63.5
Life insurance	10.0/16.3	0.6/16.3	2.3/17.6	0.3/5.8	4.9/25.1	1.2/7.5	4.6/29.2	1.3/11.7
MODERATE RISK	4.2/12.9	9.9/12.9	19.2/48.8	10.1/40.1	30.0/54.7	20.0/41.4	29.6/53.3	34.4/49.7
Mortgages	2.5/5.7	8.8/8.6	15.1/27.2	8.7/32.8	14.2/21.6	12.5/20.5	8.7/19.6	8.1/16.6
Financial investments: bonds, debentures, notes, book debts	1.7/9.8	1.1/5.7	4.1/31.5	1.4/11.7	15.8/46.2	7.6/29.7	20.9/46.9	26.3/42.0
HIGHER RISK	11.3/15.3	3.5/4.3	13.4/32.1	3.3/20.4	20.3/25.6	6.2/15.9	28.0/43.6	21.2/28.3
Bank stock	0.0/0.0	3.4/2.9	0.7/6.5	0.3/5.1	0.4/2.6	1.4/5.0	3.0/1.6	0.9/2.3
Other stock	8.9/11.4	0.0/0.0	12.0/21.9	3.1/16.1	17.1/19.0	4.2/10.0	24.0/39.3	20.3/27.0
Stock in trade	2.3/5.7	0.1/1.4	0.5/5.2	0.0/0.0	2.5/5.0	0.5/1.3	0.9/4.3	0.1/0.7
Farm (including animals)	0.1/2.4	0.0/0.0	0.2/7.1	0.0/0.0	0.3/4.3	0.1/1.7	0.1/3.4	0.0/0.0
OTHER PROPERTY AND LEGACIES	0.5/0.8	1.9/2.9	1.9/25.9	1.9/27.0	1.3/31.8	3.6/30.5	3.2/50.3	4.0/37.8
Number of investors	123	70	324	137	422	239	493	304
Gross investment	1,382,301	368,443	6,903,251	2,275,964	8,829,300	1,591,929	10,093,165	2,895,299

Figure 1.4 continued

	Percentage of total (gross) wealth/percentage of investors							
	Victoria: men, 1894–1900; women, 1894–1901		Victoria: Men and women: 1910–13		Victoria: Men and women: 1918–21		Victoria: Men and women: 1928–31	
Investment category[1]	Men	Women	Men	Women	Men	Women	Men[2]	Women
Debts	310,886		1,104,346	98,139	1,387,100	22,1570	1,081,919	291,656
Net investment	1,071,415	368,443	5,798,905	2,177,825	7,442,200	1,370,359	9,011,246	2,603,643

1 The use of terms such as conservative, moderate, and higher risk does not mean to imply that speculation could not occur in any of these categories. Indeed, over-investment in a heated land market proved to be extremely hurtful to, especially, Victoria women. Rather, the terms are used to reflect the generally held attitude toward investment in the time period covered.

2 One male case with a gross worth of $2,860,125 or, in other words, almost equal to the gross worth of all women has been omitted from the analysis. The next closest value was $725,043.

Table 1.5
Investment patterns of men and women in Hamilton, 1898–1930, from probate data

	Percentage of total (gross) wealth/percentage of investors							
	Hamilton: men, 1900; women, 1898–1900		Hamilton, 1911		Hamilton, 1922		Hamilton, 1930	
Investment category[1]	Men	Women	Men	Women	Men	Women	Men	Women
CONSERVATIVE/ TRADITIONAL RISK	45.4/98.3	64.3/91.7	43.7/97.4	68.0/96.8	40.3/96.7	46.5/95.3	50.1/93.7	37.5/89.9
Land	25.2/67.2	42.0/57.9	25.8/64.9	45.7/63.8	28.0/58.2	31.6/52.7	27.2/53.9	25.2/57.7
Household goods	3.1/65.5	4.0/51.2	1.2/44.7	1.8/51.1	1.1/40.8	1.3/41.9	1.1/35.1	1.2/35.8
Cash in hand	0.3/20.7	1.3/11.6	0.2/14.9	0.2/21.3	0.2/17.4	1.2/22.5	0.1/13.1	0.2/11.9
Cash in bank	6.2/44.8	14.7/50.4	7.7/57.0	19.0/66.0	5.5/62.0	11.9/63.6	6.1/58.2	9.6/56.4
Life insurance	10.6/24.1	2.3/7.4	8.7/33.3	1.2/4.3	5.5/34.8	0.4/10.9	15.6/44.0	1.3/17.4

Figure 1.5 continued

	Percentage of total (gross) wealth/percentage of investors							
	Hamilton: men, 1900; women, 1898–1900		Hamilton, 1911		Hamilton, 1922		Hamilton, 1930	
Investment category[1]	Men	Women	Men	Women	Men	Women	Men	Women
MODERATE RISK	32.6/34.5	24.1/33.1	15.8/31.6	12.0/31.9	31.8/52.2	31.2/52.7	27.2/46.2	29.7/45.2
Mortgages	23.1/17.2	20.3/24.8	9.4/14.9	7.9/20.2	13.7/24.5	16.8/26.4	14.4/20.3	19.0/28.6
Financial investments: bonds, debentures, notes, book debts	9.5/25.9	3.8/13.2	6.3/21.1	4.1/17.0	18.1/41.3	14.4/37.2	12.9/39.2	10.7/29.1
HIGHER RISK	21.7/37.9	10.5/15.7	39.9/23.7	17.4/23.4	25.3/26.6	17.2/18.6	19.8/32.9	30.7/29.6
Bank stock	14.5/17.2	10.4/14.1	3.0/4.4	8.9/9.6	3.0/4.9	9.2/7.0	4.5/1.4	14.2/8.9
Other stock	1.3/3.4	0.0/0.0	36.0/12.3	7.9/13.8	21.0/22.8	8.0/15.5	12.5/25.9	16.5/23.8
Stock in trade	5.8/22.4	0.0/0.0	0.6/7.9	0.6/1.1	1.3/3.3	0.1/0.8	2.6/7.9	0.0/0.0
Farm (including animals)	0.1/10.3	0.1/1.7	0.2/3.5	0.1/4.3	0.1/1.6	0.0/0.0	0.1/0.1	0.1/0.1
OTHER PROPERTY AND LEGACIES	0.3/13.8	1.2/13.2	0.6/12.2	1.0/21.3	2.7/32.1	5.1/24.8	2.9/25.9	2.2/29.6
Number of investors	58	121	114	94	184	128	143	168
Gross investment	619,709	415,075	1,118,151	721,850	2,962,807	1,202,635	2,615,207[2]	1,883,211[3]
Debts			1,500	1,600	14,320	2,341	105,860	8,432
Net investment	619,709	415,075	1,116,651	720,250	2,948,487	1,200,294	2,721,067	1,874,779

1 See note 1 to table 1.5 regarding the use of terms such as conservative, moderate, and higher risk.
2 In 1930 Hamilton probates included money transferred before death. This sum of $60,259 was not included in gross total.
3 In 1930 Hamilton probates included money transferred before death. This sum of $4,189 was not included in gross total.

Table 1.6
Logistic regressions with risky investor or not as dependent variable: Victoria and Hamilton,
late nineteenth century

Variable	Victoria/Hamilton *Odds of risky investment*	Victoria *Odds of risky investment*	Hamilton *Odds of risky investment*
CITY Reference category: Victoria	3.49*	–	–
GENDER Reference category: women	3.14*	4.51**	2.88**
WEALTH Bottom 20 per cent Top 20 per cent Reference category: middle 60 per cent	.09** 3.07*	.34 7.25*	.00 2.29
MARITAL STATUS Single Widow Reference category: married	ns#	ns#	ns#
AGE <=40 50–69 Reference category: over 69	Unavailable	16.61** 3.74	unavailable
AGE SQUARED		ns***	

*   Significance is < .02.
** Significance is between .02 and .05.
***Variable was excluded as insignificant during the regression by the backward stepwise procedure.

Table 1.7
Logistic regressions with risky investor or not as dependent variable: Victoria, 1918–21, and Hamilton, 1922

Variable	Victoria/Hamilton Odds of risky investment	Victoria Odds of risky investment	Hamilton Odds of risky investment
CITY Reference category: Victoria	1.52	–	–
GENDER Reference category: women	1.68**	1.98**	1.86
WEALTH Bottom 20 per cent Top 20 per cent Reference category: middle 60 per cent	.36 * 5.93*	.43 5.33*	.29 6.55*
MARITAL STATUS Single Widow Reference category: Married	.54 .48**	.36** .34**	ns***

* Significance is < .02.
** Significance is between .02 and .05.
*** Variable was excluded as insignificant during the regression by the backward stepwise procedure.

Table 1.8
Logistic regressions with risky investor or not as dependent variable: Victoria, 1928–31, and Hamilton, 1930

Variable	Victoria/Hamilton Odds of risky investment	Victoria Odds of risky investment	Hamilton Odds of risky investment
CITY Reference category: Victoria	.76	–	–
GENDER Reference category: women	ns#	1.4	ns***
WEALTH Bottom 20 per cent Top 20 per cent Reference category: middle 60 per cent	.32 * 7.62*	.24 7.2*	.62 9.2*
MARITAL STATUS Single Widow Reference category: Married	.78** .40	.63 .35*	1.8 .77

* Significance is < .02.
** Significance is between .02 and .05.
*** Variable was excluded as insignificant during the regression by the backward stepwise procedure.

Table 1.9
Probated net wealth distribution: men and women in late nineteenth-century
Hamilton and Victoria

| | Bottom 20% | | Middle 60% | | Top 20% | |
Category	Hamilton	Victoria	Hamilton	Victoria	Hamilton	Victoria
% of men	20.7	24.8	46.5	51.9	32.8	23.3
% of women	17.4	13.4	69.5	73.2	13.2	13.4
No. men	12	51	27	107	19	48
No. women	21	13	84	71	16	13
Male wealth as a % total male wealth	0.5	–2.8	10.0	16.4	89.5	86.4
Female wealth as a % total female wealth	1.5	0.5	41.9	37.5	56.7	62.0
Average wealth men (standard deviation)	249 (123)	–834 (4,627)	2,304 (1,678)	2352 (16,56)	29,185 (30,444)	27,620 (31,925)
Average wealth women (standard deviation)	287 (117)	176 (111)	2,068 (1,688)	2,358 (1,720)	14,708 (10,356)	21,285 (7,539)
Average wealth men and women (standard deviation)	273 (119)	–629 (4,142)	2,125 (1,681)	2,354 (1,677)	22,567 (24,322)	26,270 (28,576)

NOTE: Victoria data include all probates between 1894 and 1900 for men and 1894 and 1901 for women. Hamilton probates are the same as in table 1.1.

Table 1.10
Probated net wealth distribution: men and women in Hamilton, 1922, and Victoria, 1918–21

| | Bottom 20% | | Middle 60% | | Top 20% | |
Category	Hamilton	Victoria	Hamilton	Victoria	Hamilton	Victoria
% of men	21.7	17.1	54.9	60.9	23.4	22.0
% of women	15.0	25.1	70.3	58.6	14.8	16.3
No. men	40	72	101	257	43	93
No. women	19	60	90	140	19	39
Male wealth as a % total male wealth	0.6	–0.1	16.5	11.8	82.9	88.2
Female wealth as a % total female wealth	0.8	0.6	30.5	39.4	68.7	60.0
Average wealth men (standard deviation)	449 (285)	–40 (1,479)	4,949 (3,498)	3,355 (2,652)	58,405 (83,931)	69,245 (121,917)
Average wealth women (standard deviation)	555 (226)	134 (692)	4,239 (3175)	3,708 (2,652)	45,258 (46,055)	20,287 (12,611)
Average wealth men and women (standard deviation)	483 (270)	39 (1,187)	4,615 (3,360)	3,479 (2,503)	54,377 (38,756)	54,780 (104,821)

Table 1.11
Probated net wealth distribution: men and women in Hamilton, 1930, and Victoria, 1928–31

	Bottom 20%		Middle 60%		Top 20%	
Category	Hamilton	Victoria	Hamilton	Victoria	Hamilton	Victoria
% of men	19.6	19.7	53.8	57.0	26.6	23.3
% of women	20.2	20.7	65.5	65.1	14.3	14.1
No. men	28	97	77	281	38	115
No. women	34	63	110	198	24	43
Male wealth as a % total male wealth	0.7	–2.6	15.7	16.2	83.6	86.4
Female wealth as a % total female wealth	1.3	0.3	27.4	35.0	71.3	64.7
Average wealth men (standard deviation)	684 (391)	–2,445 (17,612)	5,552 (3,622)	5,196 (3,526)	59,852 (60,811)	67,724 (101,613)
Average wealth women (standard deviation)	699 (363)	–114 (2,571)	4,671 (3,007)	4,607 (3,279)	55,713 (79,651)	39,176 (31,613)
Average wealth men and women (standard deviation)	692 (373)	–1,438 (13,777)	5,034 (3,294)	4,952 (3,435)	58,250 (68,112)	59,952 (89,034)

Table 2.1
Indicators of women's status in male wills: Victoria, 1880–1930

Category	1880–84 percent/ number	1887–91 percent/ number	1895–1900 percent/ number	1910–13 percent/ number	1918–21 percent/ number	1928–30 percent/ number
Sole women as prime beneficiaries	71.0/44	67.9/76	72.5/74	90.3/84	75.4/193	73.1/196
Women as other inheritors	40.9/9	48.3/14	37.5/12	42.9/12	48.5/48	51.0/52
Women as prime beneficiary under will controls	38.6/17	28.9/22	28.4/53	19.1/16	16.1/31	22.5/44
Women as executors	34.5/20	37.8/42	47.3/44	68.9/84	51.4/149	45.1/142
Women as prime beneficiary with protective language	25.0/11	18.4/14	14.9/11	0.0/0	1.6/3	0.5/1

NOTE: Total numbers of cases for men are: 1880–84, 62; 1887–91, 112; 1895–1900, 102; 1910–13, 93; 1918–21, 256; and 1928–30, 268. Prime beneficiary denotes the person who received the most wealth. Controls most often took the form of access to wealth only until death or remarriage. Protective language was used to ensure that the bequeathment could not be assumed by other than the individual to whom the goods were granted. It was most often used to protect a daughter's inheritance from an existing or future husband.

Table 2.2
Indicators of women's status in male wills: Hamilton, 1880–1930

Category	1880–81 percent/number	1890 percent/ number	1900 percent/ number	1922 percent/ number	1930 percent/ number
Sole women as prime beneficiaries	74.1/20	60.6/20	79.5/31	80.3/98	74.6/97
Women as other inheritors	55.5/5	40.02/2	54.2/13	50.0/42	53.1/43
Women as prime beneficiary under will controls	40.0/8	45.0/9	25.8/8	26.5/26	25.8/25
Women as executors	44.4/12	37.0/10	56.7/17	45.5/71	46.3/69
Women as prime beneficiary with protective language	11.1/2	15.0/3	12.9/4	na	na

NOTE: Total numbers of cases for men are: 1880–81, 27; 1890, 33; 1900, 39; 1922, 121; and 1930, 130. Dates are for year of probate.

Table 2.3
Indicators of wives' status in wills of married men: Victoria, 1880–1930

Category	1880–84 percent/ number	1887–91 percent/ number	1895–1900 percent/ number	1910–13 percent/ number	1918–21 percent/ number	1928–30 percent/ number
Wives as sole beneficiary	86.1/31	87.9/58	93.5/58	93.5/72	94.4/153	88.2/142
Sole wives under will controls	48.4/15	34.5/20	31.0/18	20.8/15	18.3/28	27.5/39
TYPE OF CONTROL						
Life rights to estate interest	40.6/6	75.0/15	72.2/13	46.7/7	57.1/16	76.9/30
Life rights to estate	0.0/0	0.0/0	0.0/0	26.7/4	25.0/7	5.1/2
Unmarried	26.7/4	15.0/3	16.7/3	6.7/1	10.7/3	0.0/0
Life/unmarried	33.3/5	10.0/2	11.1/2	6.7/1	0.0/0	15.4/6
Provide for another	0.0/0	0.0/0	0.0/0	6.7/1	3.6/1	0.0/0
Other	0.0/0	0.0/0	0.0/0	6.7/1	3.6/1	2.6/1
Sole wives who were executors	45.2/14	58.6/34	55.2/32	80.6/58	56.2/86	56.3/80
Sole wives with protective language	22.6/7	13.8/8	10.3/6	0.0/0	0.7/1	0.7/1

NOTE: Marital status known for: 1880–84, 82.3 per cent; 1887–91, 83.0 per cent; 1895–1900, 77.5 per cent; 1910–13, 83.0 per cent; 1918–22, 64.8 per cent; 1928–30, 61.7 per cent.

Table 2.4
Indicators of wives' status in wills of married men: Hamilton, 1880–1930

Category	1880–81 percent/ number	1890 percent/ number	1900 percent/ number	1922 percent/ number	1930 percent/ number
Wives as sole beneficiary	81.0/17	65.2/15	92.3/24	89.5/68	86.7/65
Sole wives under will controls	47.1/8	66.7/10	33.3/8	32.4/22	32.3/21
TYPE OF CONTROL					
Life rights to estate interest	37.5/3	50.0/5	87.5/7	72.7/16	61.9/13
Life rights to estate	0.0/0	0.0/0	0.0/0	9.1/2	9.5/2
Unmarried	12.5/1	00.0/0	12.5/1	0.0/0	0.0/0
Life/ unmarried	37.5/3	50.0/5	0.0/0	9.1/2	19.1/4
Provide for another	14.3/1	0.0/0	0.0/0	4.5/1	0.0/0
Other	0.0/0	0.0/0	0.0/0	4.5/1	9.5/2
Sole wives who were executors	41.2/7	26.7/4	50.0/12	77.9/53	64.6/42
Sole wives with protective language	17.6/3	20.0/3	12.5/3	na	na

NOTE: Marital status known for: 1880–81, 85.2 per cent; 1890, 69.7 per cent; 1900, 66.7 per cent; 1922, 67.2 per cent.

Table 2.5
Indicators of women's status in women's wills: Victoria, 1880–1930

Category	1880–84 percent/ number	1887–91 percent/ number	1895–1900 percent/ number	1910–13 percent/ number	1918–22 percent/ number	1928–30 percent/ number
Sole women as prime beneficiaries	29.4/6	36.4/12	39.0/23	28.6/14	37.0/64	36.7/67
Women as other inheritors	60.0/3	44.4/8	48.0/12	50.0/14	50.5/54	56.5/70
Women as prime beneficiary under will controls	0.0/0	16.7/2	21.7/5	21.4/3	17.2/10	17.9/12
Women as executors	25.0/3	21.4/3	28.1/9	22.6/14	24.2/55	29.8/76
Women as prime beneficiary with protective language	33.3/2	33.3/3	30.4/7	7.1/1	1.6/1	00.0/0
Male inheritors as prime beneficiary under will controls	30.0/3	23.5/4	17.9/5	19.2/5	7.2/5	17.7/14
Husbands as prime beneficiary under will controls	50.0/3	25.0/2	25.0/4	7.7/1	11.1/4	26.6/8

NOTE: Total number of cases for women are: 1880–84, 19; 1887–91, 33; 1895–1900, 59; 1910–13, 49; 1918–22, 173; 1928–30, 183.

Table 2.6
Indicators of women's status in women's wills: Hamilton, 1880–1930

Category	1880–84 percent/ number	1888–91 percent/ number	1898–1900 percent/ number	1922 percent/ number	1930 percent/ number
Sole women as prime beneficiaries	61.8/21	41.1/30	44.2/38	49.4/43	60.3/94
Women as other inheritors	38.5/5	50.0/17	44.0/22	48.2/27	52.4/65
Women as prime beneficiary under will controls	4.8/1	11.1/3	18.4/7	11.6/5	19.1/18
Women as executors	29.3/12	13.0/6	31.9/23	32.7/37	28.4/56
Women as prime beneficiary with protective language	23.8/5	10.0/3	15.8/6	na	na
Male inheritors as prime beneficiary under will controls	22.2/2	21.7/5	44.8/13	19.4/6	17.8/10
Husbands as prime beneficiary under will controls	33.3/1	42.9/3	45.5/5	25.0/4	28.6/8

NOTE: Total number of cases for women are: 1880–84, 34; 1888–91, 73; 1898–1900, 86; 1922, 87; and 1930, 156.

Table 2.7
Treatment of spouses in wills: Victoria and Hamilton, 1880–1930

Date	Women who ignored spouse in wills: percent/number		Men who ignored spouse in wills: percent/number	
	Victoria	Hamilton	Victoria	Hamilton
1880–84	25.0/2	57.1/4	15.0/3	19.0/4
1887–91	33.3/4	65.0/13	12.2/5	36.4/8
1898–1900	48.4/15	59.3/16	2.6/1	7.7/2
1910–13	35.0/7	na	6.4/5	na
1918–22 (H=1922)	32.7/18	28.6/6	3.7/6	3.9/3
1928–30 (H=1930)	38.9/21	31.9/15	9.9/16	0.0/0

NOTE: Hamilton men are from 1880–81, 1890, 1900, and 1922.

Table 2.8
Bequeathments to daughters and sons in mothers' wills: Victoria and Hamilton, 1887–1931

	Victoria			Hamilton		
Years	Percent of sons sole/co prime beneficiary	Percent of daughters sole/co prime beneficiary	Number of wills	Percent of sons sole/co prime beneficiary	Percent of daughters sole/co prime beneficiary	Number of wills
1887–1901	43.7	62.7	32	51.9	61.1	54
1910ff	60.8	68.4	132	42.5	63.8	80

NOTE: These are wills where there is evidence that daughters and sons were alive. The dates for Hamilton are 1890, 1900, 1922, and 1930. The dates for Victoria are 1887–1901, 1910–13, 1918–21, and 1928–31.

Table 2.9
Bequeathments to daughters and sons in fathers' wills: Victoria and Hamilton, 1887–1931

	Victoria			Hamilton		
Years	Percent of sons sole/co prime beneficiary	Percent of daughters sole/co prime beneficiary	Number of wills	Percent of sons sole/co prime beneficiary	Percent of daughters sole/co prime beneficiary	Number of wills
1887–1901	37.5	30.0	40	23.3	23.3	30
1910ff	38.4	40.8	125	31.5	42.5	73

NOTE: These are wills where there is evidence that daughters and sons were alive. The dates for Hamilton are 1890, 1900, 1922, and 1930. The dates for Victoria are 1887–1901, 1910–13, 1918–21, and 1928–31.

Table 2.10
Husbands who received inheritances from spouses free of control: Victoria and Hamilton, 1880–1930

	Of all possible husband inheritors percent/number	
Date	Victoria	Hamilton
1880–84	37.5/3	28.6/2
1887–91	50.0/6	20.0/4
1898–1900	38.7/12	22.2/6
1910–13	60.0/12	na
1918–22 (H=1922)	65.5/36	47.6/10
1928–30 (H=1930)	57.4/31	61.7/29

Table 3.1
Bank shares held by women: Ontario, 1860–1911

	Year			
	1860	1880	1900	1911
Per cent share value	14.8	NA	31.4	38.4
Per cent shares	NA	15.8	31.0	37.5

NOTE: Sources are the same as for figure 3.3.

Table 3.2
Women bank investors as a percentage of Hamilton women (all and by marital status),
1880–1900

	Year	
Category	1880	1900
All women investors as % of all women >=20	.4	.6
Single women investors as % of all single women >=20	.2	.6
Married women investors as % of all married women >=20	.2	.3
Widowed women investors as % of all widowed women >=20	.8	1.0

Table 3.3
The gender of bank shareholders by individual company: Ontario, 1880–1911

	Bank of Hamilton hareholders number/percent		Commercial Bank shareholders number/percent	
Date	Women	Men	Women	Men
1880	55/21.9	196/78.1	221/29.1	538/70.9
1900	143/47.8	156/52.2	476/49.9	477/50.1
1911	342/58.3	245/41.7	539/62.3	326/37.7

Table 3.4
The gender of insurance company shareholders by individual company: Ontario,
1880–1900

	1880 number/percent		1900 number/percent	
Company	Women	Men	Women	Men
British America Assurance	30/27.8	78/72.2	71/38.6	113/61.4
Western Assurance	44/28.0	113/72.0	182/46.8	207/53.2
Canada Life Assurance	22/31.0	49/69.0	18/26.9	49/73.1
Confederation Life Association	2/5.6	34/94.4	19/42.2	26/57.8
Total	98/26.3	274/73.7	290/42.3	395/57.7

Table 4.1
Real property owned by women over the age of nineteen years in urban Canada according to the 1901 census

Property type	Percent owned by women	Total number	Women as a percent of owners	Total number of owners
Acres	7.9	241,430	15.2	795
Lots	18.1	10,756	17.7	3848
Houses	18.5	8,418	17.0	4709
Stores	18.9	857	18.9	502
All, including barns, silos, and manufacturing establishments	NA	NA	17.4	5037

NOTE: The data are from the Canadian Families Project's 5 per cent sample of the 1901 Canadian census. "Urban" is all cities with 5,000 and more inhabitants. See appendix 1 for a discussion of the gendered bias of the census and other sources for an understanding of women's property ownership.

Table 4.2
Distribution of assessed wealth: Victoria and Hamilton, 1863–1901

	Percent of assessed wealth							
	Victoria				Hamilton			
Category	1863	1882	1891	1901	1871	1881	1891	1899
Lowest fifth	1.1	1.9	1.9	1.3	1.9	3.6	3.3	3.3
Second fifth	3.0	4.7	4.2	3.5	5.3	7.2	6.8	5.9
Third fifth	5.0	7.9	7.1	6.4	7.4	11.7	10.4	10.4
Fourth fifth	11.3	16.9	13.0	12.4	14.4	20.3	17.4	15.3
Top fifth	79.7	68.7	73.9	76.4	71.1	57.2	62.1	65.2
Top 10%	66.4	50.5	59.4	63.8	57.1	40.1	49.6	52.7
GINI COEFFICIENT:								
All	.752	.645	.687	.724	.670	.524	.579	.595
Women	.374	.526	.600	.629	.446	.490	.569	.541
Men	.723	.644	.670	.694	.678	.513	.569	.531
Companies	.784	.304	.582	.697	.480	.529	.595	.687
Other	–	.673	.694	.757	.526	–	–	.402

NOTE: For sources, see the discussion of assessment rolls in appendix 1.

Table 4.3
Ownership shares: Victoria and Hamilton assessment rolls, 1863–1901

| | % total wealth | % total wealth | | % total wealth | | % total wealth | | % total wealth | |
| | 1863 | 1871 | | 1881 | 1882 | 1891 | | 1899 | 1901 |
Owners	Victoria	Hamilton	Victoria	Hamilton	Victoria	Hamilton	Victoria	Hamilton	Victoria
Women	1.1	4.6	3.4	7.7	5.6	10.8	11.6	14.8	21.0
Men	72.1	83.3	88.5	81.0	81.9	80.3	68.1	65.2	51.5
Corps	24.3	10.0	8.1	9.5	3.3	7.8	8.9	16.1	10.6
Estates	2.4	2.1		1.0	7.1	1.0	7.4	3.4	10.2
Other				0.8	2.1	0.1	3.9	0.5	6.6
Total %	99.9	100	100	100	100	100	99.9	100	99.9
Total $	2,986,658	792,160	1,654,078	12,987,580	2,621,591	19,147,005	15,824,463	22,410,120	15,685,904

NOTE: For Hamilton in 1871, the figures are from a one-in-thirteen page sample of the 1871 assessment roll. All women were entered into a computer file from the Hamilton assessment rolls of 1881, 1891, and 1899. The worth of corporations, estates, and others was then tabulated for each assessment roll. The totals for women and the rest were added together, and the result was subtracted from the total assessment value to arrive at the value for men. The Victoria data is for the whole of the 1863, 1871, 1882, 1891 and 1901 assessment rolls. The figures reported in this table include all who whose gender could be determined from the assessment roll regardless of where the owner lived.

Table 4.4
Characteristics of property holding by women and men: Victoria, 1863–1901

Property	1863		1871		1881		1891		1901	
	Women	Men	Women	Men	Women	Men	Women	Men	Women	Men
Average value (dollars)	2,016	6,189	1,145	2,270	1,432	2,671	5,347	8,307	3,339	5,072
% of individual property owners	4.7	95.3	7.1	92.9	11.3	88.7	16.5	83.5	33.1	66.9
Women and men as % of individual wealth-holders in top fifth of all landed wealth holders[1]	0.0	100.0	na	na	5.8	94.3	13.5	86.5	30.8	69.2
Women and men as % of individual wealth-holders in bottom two-fifths of all landed wealth holders[2]	4.9	95.1			13.2	86.8	24.7	75.3	32.3	70.0
% lots with buildings	35.5	27.5	46.8	na	76.2	80.6	45.8	47.5	48.8	56.4
% assessed value in buildings	15.4	12.1	37.5	na	49.7	40.3	24.1	27.2	46.0	40.4
% of all property owners owning more than one building	5.9	17.3 (27.2)	na	na	26.0	28.3	12.8	23.3	20.1	23.3
% of all property owners owning more than one property	29.4	48.9	36.7	na	40.6	52.2	35.2	48.1	45.0	49.0
Number of property owners	17	347	49	645	102	804	343	1265	675	1363

1 All wealth-holders include corporations, estates, and others, as well as men and women.
2 All wealth-holders include corporations, estates, and others, as well as men and women.

Table 4.5
Landholding patterns: Victoria men and women, 1901

Category	Male %	Female %
Owns home and does not rent any property	48.5	46.0
Owns home and rents other property	11.9	11.8
Does not own home but rents other property	13.3	16.9
Owns only lot(s)	18.2	19.5
Unknown	8.1	5.6

NOTE: Calculated from the 1901 Victoria assessment roll and includes only women living in Victoria.

Table 4.6
Landholding patterns (percentage): Hamilton women, 1881–99

Category	1881	1891	1899
Owns home and does not rent any property	35.4	35.6	36.4
Owns home and rents other property	13.3	21.5	17.6
Does not own home but rents other property	43.5	38.1	41.2
Owns only lot(s)	7.7	4.8	4.7

NOTE: Calculations are from complete counts of women living in Hamilton who appear on the assessment rolls for 1881, 1891, and 1899.

Table 4.7
Share (percentage of population) of Victoria women owning real property, 1881–1901

Age	Married	Single	Widowed	All
1881/82[1]				
20–29	0.3	2.9	0.0	1.4
30–39	3.4	6.3	25.0	5.2
40–49	9.2	0.0	21.4	10.6
50–59	9.7	7.7	26.3	13.9
60+	9.1	11.1	27.0	17.8
All	4.8	4.2	23.7	6.5
1891[2]				
20–29	3.8	2.6	0.0	3.2
30–39	6.7	8.7	29.6	8.3
40–49	9.4	13.8	29.6	11.8
50–59	25.0	0.0	31.5	24.9
60+	9.6	22.2	23.1	17.0
All	8.3	4.3	26.3	9.0
1901[3]				
20–29	4.8	2.3	4.5	3.5
30–39	10.9	5.5	24.2	10.6
40–49	16.0	15.1	30.9	17.8
50–59	20.5	5.3	33.6	23.0
60+	22.4	16.7	32.0	26.8
All	12.2	4.2	30.1	12.3

NOTE: See appendix 2 for a discussion of the procedure used to construct this table.

1 There are 100 women on the 1882 assessment roll. After 8 per cent are deducted for non-resident owners, the number of resident owners is 92. Marital status and age are known for 66 of 92 cases (71.7 per cent). For this table, the assumption is that the missing cases closely replicate the age and marital status of the known cases; so all 92 cases were used in the calculation of percentages.

2 There are 343 women on the 1891 assessment roll. After 8 per cent are deducted for non-resident owners, the number of resident owners is 316. Marital status and age are known for 260 of 316 women (82.3 per cent). For this table, the assumption is that the missing cases closely replicate the age and marital status of the known cases; so all 316 cases were used in the calculation of percentages.

3 I have used the blended figure of 602 women property owners for the calculations for 1901. As noted in appendix 2, this is a conservative count of women property owners in 1901 Victoria.

Table 4.8
Share (percentage of population) of Victoria men owning real property, 1881–1901

Age	Married	Single	Widowed	All
1881/82[1]				
20–29	26.6	4.4	0.0	9.9
30–39	23.3	7.8	60.0	16.3
40–49	51.5	18.2	52.0	40.4
50–59	71.4	19.0	45.5	53.2
60–	71.8	28.8	74.4	59.7
All	46.0	10.4	58.3	29.6
1891[2]				
20–29	14.7	3.7	0.0	5.5
30–39	31.3	2.8	5.9	14.5
40–49	31.8	5.3	29.6	19.4
50–59	52.7	12.4	45.0	38.9
60–	62.8	18.6	35.2	43.5
All	35.2	4.7	31.5	16.2
1901[3]				
20–29	10.3	1.2	0.0	3.2
30–39	25.7	4.0	26.9	16.9
40–49	34.4	4.3	33.3	26.6
50–59	36.5	7.9	34.5	31.1
60+	56.1	20.0	39.4	45.3
All	30.3	3.2	34.8	17.9

1 There are 816 men on the 1882 assessment roll. After 8 per cent are deducted for non-resident owners, the number of resident owners is 741. Marital status and age are known for 388 of the 741 cases (52.4 per cent). For this table, the assumption is that the missing cases closely replicate the age and marital status of the known cases; so all 741 cases were used in the calculation of percentages.

2 There are 1,265 men on the 1891 assessment roll. After 8 per cent are deducted for non-resident owners, the number of resident owners is 1,164. Marital status and age are known for 824 of 1,164 cases (70.8 per cent). For this table, the assumption is that the missing cases closely replicate the age and marital status of the known cases; so all 1,164 cases were used in the calculation of percentages.

3 In order to use the same type of source – in this case, the census – I have compared Hamilton and Victoria owners who appear on the 1901 census. Had I used simply assessment roll data for 1901 Victoria, the number of owners would have been 1,348. Had I used a blended (assessment and census) figure, the number of owners would have been 1,595. I used the census; the number of owners was 1,519.

Tables

Table 4.9
Share (percentage of population) of Hamilton women owning real property, 1881–1901

Age	Married	Single	Widowed	All
1881/82[1]				
20–29	0.9	0.8	8.9	0.9
30–39	1.8	3.3	15.1	3.0
40–49	3.5	2.8	25.4	6.7
50–59	2.1	17.1	29.9	11.5
60–	2.4	17.1	19.8	13.2
All	2.0	1.9	27.0	4.7
1901[2]				
20–29	0.8	0.7	3.5	0.8
30–39	1.9	5.4	19.2	3.6
40–49	3.7	7.7	30.3	7.3
50–59	4.4	10.1	35.2	12.2
60–	6.8	10.9	33.7	20.7
All	2.9	2.9	31.3	6.5

1 On the 1881 assessment roll there are 475 women who lived in Hamilton. Marital status and age are known for 226 of 475 women (47.6 per cent). For this table, the assumption is that the missing cases closely replicated the age and marital status of the known cases; so all 475 cases were used in this tabulation.

2 See appendix 2 for the calculation of women property owners. I have used the blended figure of 1,089 women property owners for the calculations in this table. Had I just used women on the assessment roll, the number would be 1,173.

Table 4.10
Share (percentage of population) of Hamilton men owning real property, 1901

Age	Married	Single	Widowed	All
20–29	7.7	1.2	7.4	3.1
30–39	24.9	5.2	12.5	19.7
40–49	37.7	13.4	22.0	34.4
50–59	49.0	16.1	34.7	45.8
60–	50.7	15.5	32.3	44.3
All	33.6	3.6	28.3	23.8

Table 4.11
Marital status of women property holders (percentages): Guelph, Hamilton, and Victoria, 1871–1901

Marital Status	1871			1881–82			1891		1899–1901	
	Guelph	Hamilton	Victoria	Guelph	Hamilton	Victoria	Hamilton	Victoria	Hamilton	Victoria
Single	28.6	13.1	14.9	30.4	14.5	12.3	15.6	8.8		
Married	3.6	24.6	50.0	16.0	(13.2)	58.2	24.0	63.0		
Widow	67.9	62.3	35.2	53.6	72.2	29.6	60.1	28.2		
Number	28	191	74	194	717	318	1091	602		
Missing data	na	282	26	na	52	25	0	0		

NOTE: The data for Guelph are drawn from Inwood and Van Sligtenhorst, "The Social Consequences," 174–5. The data for 1881 Hamilton are those cases on the assessment roll that could be linked to the census. The data for 1891 Hamilton are from the assessment roll only, and as appendix 1 discusses, the assessment roll data for Hamilton undercount married women property owners; that is why the 13.2 figure for 1891 married women is in brackets. The data for 1899/1901 Hamilton combine census information and linked cases from the assessment roll. The data from 1882 and 1891 Victoria are those cases on the assessment that could be linked to the census. The data for 1899–1901 are the same as those for 1899–1901 in table 4.3. Had assessment data only been used for Hamilton in 1899, the marital distribution would have been: s, 17.9; M, 12.7; w, 66.9. If census data only for Hamilton in 1901 been used, the marital status would have been: s, 15.1; M, 23.0; w, 61.6. If linked assessment data only had been used, for Victoria, the marital status would have been: s, 9.2; M, 64.9; w, 25.9. If census data alone had been used for Victoria in 1901, the marital status would have been: s, 10.4; M, 28.8; w: 60.8.

Table 4.12
People per acre: Victoria and Hamilton, 1881–1901

Date	Victoria	Hamilton
1881	3.1	15.1
1891	9.1	12.8
1901	11.0	13.2

SOURCES: Census of Canada, 1881, vol. 4, table E; 1891, vol. 1, table 1; 1901, vol. 1, table 7.

Table 4.13
Women and vacant lots: Hamilton and Victoria, 1881–1901

Propertied women	1881/82		1891		1899/1901	
	Hamilton	Victoria	Hamilton	Victoria	Hamilton	Victoria
Vacant lots as % of all lots owned by women	15.5	47.0	8.5	54.2	14.4	50.9
% of women owners owning vacant lots	10.1	45.5	7.0	49.4	10.0	48.2
% of women owners who owned improved lots	92.3	75.2	95.2	71.8	95.4	80.4

NOTE: The data are my calculations from assessment rolls for the relevant years.

Table 4.14
Sex ratios for Victoria and Hamilton, 1881–1931: number of men per 100 women

Date	Hamilton	Victoria all men	Victoria excluding Chinese
1881	90	175	139
1891	87	221	174
1901	82	178	144
1921	96	115	na
1931	98	111	na

NOTE: Calculated from data in *Census of Canada*, 1881, vol. 1, table 1, and vol. 2, table 8; 1891, vol. 1, table 3, and vol. 2, table 1; 1901, vol. 1, table 7, and vol. 4, table 1; 1921, vol. 2, table 31; 1931, vol. 3, table 15. For Victoria in 1881 and 1891 a computer file of the nominal-level census compiled by the Public History Group, University of Victoria, was used. Only adults twenty and over were included. There were relatively few Native people counted by census enumerators as living in the city of Victoria in these years.

Table 4.15
Married women and widowed property owners as a percentage of all married women and widows age twenty and over: Hamilton and Victoria, 1881–1901

Year	Hamilton	Victoria
1881/82	5.3	7.4
1901	8.9	14.9

NOTE: The percentages are calculated from information in tables 4.7 and 4.9.

Table 5.1
Logistic regression with mortgagee/mortgagor as dependent variable: Victoria, 1881, 1891, and 1901, and Hamilton, 1881 and 1901

	Victoria		Hamilton	
Variables	Odds of being a mortgagee	Odds of being a mortgagor	Odds of being a mortgagee	Odds of being a mortgagor
MARITAL STATUS	*	*	ns**	ns**
Single	2.0*	.49*		
Widow	1.9*	.53*		
Reference category: married				
OCCUPATION	*	*	*	*
Professional/managerial	3.1*	.32*	3.4*	.29*
White collar/clerical	2.2*	.47*	1.2	.78
Sales	2.6*	.39*	2.4*	.41*
Service	1.2	.87	.78	1.3
Primary	1.4	.73	2.8	.36
Transportation	1.8	.57	2.4	.40
Labourer	.51	1.9	.16	6.2
Retired/no occupation listed		3.0*		2.3
Reference category: manufacturing				

Table 5.1 continued

Variables	Victoria		Hamilton	
	Odds of being a mortgagee	Odds of being a mortgagor	Odds of being a mortgagee	Odds of being a mortgagor
AGE	*	*	*	*
30–39	1.7*	.60*	1.7	.56
40–49	3.1*	.32*	2.8*	.36*
50–59	4.4*	.23*	2.3	.43
60+	7.7*	.13*	5.9*	.17*
Reference category: 20–29				
Gender	ns**	ns**	ns**	ns**
Birthplace	ns**	ns**	ns**	ns**
Religion	ns**	ns**	ns**	ns**
Year	ns**	ns**	ns**	ns**

* Significance is < .02.
** Variable was discarded as insignificant during the regression by the backward stepwise procedure.

Table 5.2
Mortgagee share of mortgage market by lenders, transactions, and value: Victoria, 1881–1921

Category	1881 %L	1881 %T	1881 %V	1891 %L	1891 %T	1891 %V	1901 %L	1901 %T	1901 %V	1911 %L	1911 %T	1911 %V	1921 %L	1921 %T	1921 %V
Men	79.1	82.4	71.7	67.4	61.7	61.9	58.3	54.7	56.5	60.2	55.4	66.8	61.0	60.6	52.6
Women	9.0	8.1	5.5	17.1	14.5	12.0	27.4	22.8	19.7	25.6	20.5	11.5	20.3	19.7	22.8
Male-male	3.7	4.2	14.2	5.9	4.3	4.3	5.4	6.1	8.0	5.8	5.5	4.5	4.9	6.3	5.0
Female-female	–	–	–	–	–	–	–	–	–	–	–	–	–	–	–
Male-female	–	–	–	0.4	0.2	0.1	1.2	1.5	1.0	2.3	2.8	1.8	3.3	2.8	3.4
Company	0.7	0.5	0.6	4.6	16.2	19.8	4.6	13.0	12.7	5.8	15.1	15.0	8.1	8.5	14.3
Trustee	6.7	4.1	8.0	3.7	1.9	1.6	0.5	0.2	0.9	–	–	–	–	–	–
Other	0.7	0.7	0.1	0.8	1.1	0.3	1.9	1.8	1.2	0.6	0.6	0.3	2.4	2.1	1.9
Total number	134	218	359,496	457	930	2,751,746	259	405	531,055	172	224	781,426	123	145	234,392

Table 5.3
Mortgagee share of mortgage market by lenders, transactions, and value: Hamilton, 1881–1901

Category	1881 %L	1881 %T	1881 %V	1891 %L	1891 %T	1891 %V	1901 %L	1901 %T	1901 %V
Men	61.9	57.8	48.6	51.3	50.7	37.4	46.2	43.0	39.1
Women	19.0	18.1	11.1	33.8	34.0	23.7	33.3	32.0	23.2
Male-male	2.2	2.9	2.2	3.1	2.8	1.0	2.6	2.0	2.1
Female-female	0.9	0.6	0.6	0.0	0.0	0.0	1.3	1.0	0.4
Male-female	2.2	1.5	2.8	0.5	0.4	0.4	3.9	3.0	4.0
Company	7.4	13.8	23.0	4.6	6.4	32.6	9.0	15.0	28.7
Trustee	4.3	3.4	8.6	3.6	3.2	2.9	3.8	4.0	2.7
Other	2.2	2.0	3.2	3.0	2.5	1.8	0.0	0.0	0.0
Total number	231	356	457,822	195	283	471,358	78	100	113,829

Table 5.4
Tendency of women to lend to other women: Victoria and Hamilton, 1881–1921

	Victoria			Hamilton		
Year	Loans by women as % of all loans	Loans by women to women as % of all loans to women	LQ	Loans by women as % of all loans	Loans by women to women as % of all loans to women	LQ
1881	8	20	2.5	20	14	0.7
1891	15	14	0.9	33	42	1.3
1901	23	30	1.3	34	20	0.6
1911	21	15	0.7	–	–	–
1921	20	30	1.5	–	–	–
All to 1901	16	21	1.3	28	23	0.8
All to 1921	17	21	1.2	–	–	–

Table 5.5
Loan management by women and men: Victoria, 1881–1921

	Interest rate (av.)		Repayment time (av. months)		Foreclosure rate (%)	
Year	Women	Men	Women	Men	Women	Men
1881	10.7	10.0	20.3	23.2	0.0	2.7
1891	8.6	8.7	21.2	23.2	23.7	13.6
1901	6.7	7.2	–	–	1.1	2.2
1911	7.1	7.1	–	–	–	–
1921	7.6	7.5	–	–	–	–

Table 5.6
Selected characteristics of those who borrowed from women and men: Victoria, 1891

Characteristics	Borrowers from women	Borrowers from men
Interest (av.)	8.7	8.5
Number of loans (av.)	1.4	1.2
Size loan (av.)	2,459	3,424
Age (av.)	37.3	38
Under age 30 (%)	34.7	25.4
Household head (%)	61	66
Married (%)	69.3	74.2
Single (%)	28.0	21.7
Female (%)	13.8	13.3
OCCUPATION (%)		
Professional	9.7	13.1
White-collar	13.9	5.2
Sales	12.5	20.4
Manufacturing	36.1	32.3
BIRTHPLACE (%)		
Canada	27.4	34.0
England	38.4	34.9
Scotland	16.4	9.3
RELIGION (%)		
Protestant	28	26.3
Anglican	42.7	37.4
Roman Catholic	1.3	6.6

NOTE: Social data were collected by linking names from the mortgage information to a machine-readable file of the nominal-level census returns for Victoria in 1891. Some 50 per cent of men in the file were linked to the census, and 60 per cent of the women were so linked.

Table 5.7
Debtor share of mortgage market by borrowers, transactions, and value: Victoria, 1881–1921

Category	1881			1891			1901			1911			1921		
	% B	% T	% V	% B	% T	% V	% B	% T	% V	% B	% T	% V	% B	% T	% V
Men	89.7	91.3	88.3	77.9	80.3	77.2	67.5	67.7	68.7	65.0	64.7	69.1	71.0	70.3	71.3
Women	4.1	3.7	1.1	11.0	11.0	8.5	19.4	18.8	15.8	24.8	24.1	17.5	26.2	26.2	25.0
Male-male	3.6	3.2	8.9	6.5	4.7	4.4	3.4	3.7	4.6	6.3	7.7	10.3	2.1	2.1	2.2
Female-female	0.1	1.4	0.1	–	–	–	–	–	–	–	–	–	–	–	–
Male-female	2.1	–	0.8	3.2	2.7	1.5	9.2	9.4	8.5	2.4	2.6	1.5	0.7	0.7	0.5
Company	0.5	0.5	1.0	0.8	0.9	8.4	0.5	0.5	2.4	1.0	0.9	1.7	–	–	–
Other	–	–	–	0.3	0.3	0.1	–	–	–	–	–	–	–	0.7	1.1
Total number	195	218	359,496	780	930	2,751,746	382	405	531,055	207	224	781,426	141	145	234,392

Table 5.8
Debtor share of mortgage market by borrowers, transactions, and value: Hamilton, 1881–1901

Category	1881			1891			1901		
	% B	% T	% V	% B	% T	% V	% B	% T	% V
Men	21.2	21.3	16.9	22.6	20.5	15.7	28.6	29.0	24.4
Women	6.7	6.7	4.6	9.5	9.2	4.2	9.9	9.0	22.6[1]
Male-male	0.9	0.8	2.5	1.6	1.4	1.6	2.2	2.0	1.7
Female-female	0.9	0.8	0.2	0.4	0.4	0.3	1.1	1.0	0.7
Male-female	68.4	68.6	72.9	60.5	63.6	59.8	57.2	58.0	50.4
Company	0.3	0.3	0.7	0.8	0.7	7.6	0.0	0.0	0.0
Trustee	0.9	0.9	1.4	2.1	2.1	2.2	0.0	0.0	0.0
Other	0.6	0.6	0.7	2.4	2.1	8.5	1.1	1.0	0.3
Total number	326	356	457,822	243	283	471,358	91	100	113,829

1 One of the nine transactions was for a sum of $21,000.

Table 5.9
British Columbia Land and Investment Company and Yorkshire Guarantee and Security
Corporation: borrowers, loans, and value, 1889–1896

	BCLI			YGSC		
Category	% B	% L	% V	% B	% L	% V
Men	75.8	77.4	69.9	8	81.0	63.5
				0.2		
Women	13.4	11.5	5.5	11.9	11.5	9.5
Men-women	2.8	2.2	2.1	4.3	4.1	7.3
Company	8.0	8.9	22.5	3.6	3.3	19.6
Total number	314	505	1,742,022	645	749	1,537,005

SOURCES: BCA, BCLI papers, sundry accounts and correspondence, UCB, Special Collections, and YGSC, papers, various account books. I examined the BCLI papers when they were housed at the Victoria City Archives in a rudimentary organizational state. I examined the YGSC Papers in Huddersfield, England, when they were in a totally unorganized state in a home of a descendant of one of the founders.

Table 5.10
Loan activity: Confederation Life, 1871–1902

	1871–79	1888–94		1895–1902	
Borrower	Loans granted (number/ per cent)	Loan applications (number/ per cent)	Loans granted (number/ per cent)	Loan applications (number/ per cent)	Loans granted (number/ per cent)
Men	137/81.5	568/83.4	376/84.9	919/90.7	765/92.4
Women	10/5.9	104/15.3	58/13.1	87/8.6	56/6.7
Male-female	21/12.5	9/1.3	9/2.1	7/0.7	7/0.8
Total	168	681	443	1013	828

SOURCES: LAC, Confederation Life Insurance Company Papers, Loan registry book, 1871–79; Financial Committee; Schedule of mortgages, 1888–1902. All tabulations are my own.

Table 6.1
Victoria bills of sale registry: transactions by gender, 1880–1902

Gender	1861–73 N	1861–73 %	1874–80 N	1874–80 %	1881–87 N	1881–87 %	1888–92 N	1888–92 %	1893–97 N	1893–97 %	1898–1902 N	1898–1902 %
Men	na	na	na	na	na	na	513	93.9	473	88.6	377	91.9
Women	34	5.9	29	8.2	87	15.2	123	22.5	143	26.8	104	25.4
Company	na	na	na	na	na	na	68	12.5	129	24.2	86	21.0
Total	581		355		574		546		534		410	

NOTE: All computations are my own from data in BCA, GR 1900, vol. 4. The transactions do not add up to 100 per cent because a man, a woman, and a company could be involved in the same transaction. The transactions involved people who did not live in Victoria as well as Victoria residents. Addresses and occupations were given for almost all grantors, but the same information was not recorded for the grantees. Thus in the 1888–92 period, 93 transactions included grantors who did not live in Victoria, and a further 3 included grantors for whom no address could be found. The comparable figures for grantors in 1898–1902 are 62 and 9 respectively. For the first period, 12 transactions involved grantees who lived outside Victoria, and a further 133 included grantees for whom no address could be found. The comparable figures for the second period are 8 and 103 respectively. Addresses for grantees were found by name linkage (first and last name and, where possible initial) to computerized files of the 1891 and 1901 Victoria censuses and to Victoria street directories for those years. The computerized files could be alphabetized, thus making it possible to discard matches in the case of multiple same names in the census. Most but not all of those for whom addresses could not be found probably lived close to but outside Victoria's city boundaries.

Table 6.2
Realty and chattel mortgage markets compared: Victoria, 1891 and 1901

Transactions	1891 Chattels	1891 Realty	1901 Chattels	1901 Realty
Number	127	930	70	405
Total value	$595,957	$2,755,606	$448,761	$530,555
Average value	$4,693	$2,963	$6,410	$1,310
Median value	$650	$1,000	$602	$800
Standard deviation	$27,283	$11,356	$27,185	$1,751

Table 6.3
Mortgagee share of chattel market by lenders, transactions, and value: Victoria, 1860–1902

Category	1860–73			1874–87			1888–92			1893–97[1]		1898–02		
	% L	% T	% V	% L	% T	% V	% L	% T	% V	% T	% V	% L	% T	% V
Men							61.1	69.0	72.8	64.9	38.5	64.1	63.5	23.9
Women		1.9			4.6		10.0	8.4	11.7	15.6	13.5	13.7	12.0	5.2
Male-male							12.6	11.4	6.1	–	–	9.2	8.3	19.4
Female-female							–	–	–	0.4	0.1	0.3	0.2	0.2
Male-female							0.8	0.6	1.0	–	–	1.4	1.0	0.4
Company							8.9	10.6	8.4	19.1	47.9	11.3	15.0	51.0
Total number (women)	(9)	581		(43)	929		381	546	1,640,623	534	1,982,303 (66)	293	410	2,079,812

1 For 1893-97 we do not have the names of the male and company participants; so we cannot calculate the number of different individuals or companies involved. Also, for those dates the male-male transactions have been counted as part of the male transactions.

Table 6.4
Mortgagor share of chattel market by borrowers, transactions, and value (percentages): Victoria, 1860–1902

Category	1860–73			1874–87			1888–92			1893–97[1]		1898–02		
	B	T	V	B	T	V	B	T	V	T	V	B	T	V
Men		4.1			8.4		69.6	71.4	53.8	79.7	46.4	66.5	67.2	17.9
Women							12.4	13.0	5.1	9.5	3.2	10.1	10.0	4.2
Male-male							10.5	9.2	11.7	–	–	11.0	9.6	30.0
Female-female							0.3	0.2	0.1	0.2	0.2	–	–	–
Male-female							4.0	3.7	3.0	2.6	1.9	3.9	4.8	2.0
Company							3.5	2.7	26.4	8.0	48.1	8.3	7.8	44.3
Total number (women)	(21)	581		(75)	929		428	546	1,640,263 (41)	534	1,982,303	337	408	2,079,812

1 For 1893-97 we do not have the names of the male and company participants; so we cannot calculate the number of different individuals or companies involved. Also for those dates the male-male transactions have been counted as part of the male transactions.

Table 6.5
Social characteristics of female grantors and grantees: Victoria chattel market, 1888–1902

Row	Personal characteristics	Grantor (%)	Grantee (%)	Women 20+ in Victoria 1901[1]
1	Foreign-born	70 (57/81)	64 (59/92)	59
2	Protestant	83 (68/82)	85 (78/92)	84
3A	Age under 40	68 (57/84)	60 (60/100)	64
3B	Age over 50	11 (9/84)	21 (21/100)	17
4	Married	70 (71/102)	61 (65/107)	63
5	Head of household	16 (13/81)	23 (22/95)	11
6[2]	Self-employed/employer	79 (66/84)	55 (11/20)	17
7	Own property	22 (18/81)	47 (46/97)	14
8	Number known to be living in Victoria[3]	135	136	4,949

NOTE: Several women were both grantees and grantors in this period. They have been counted in both columns.
1 Calculated from a computerized file of the 1901 census for the whole of Victoria.
2 In the 1891 and more fully in the 1901 census, questions were asked about one's relation to the means of production. Self-employed/employers are expressed as a percentage of them plus employees.
3 To calculate the number of Victoria women for whom social information is missing in rows 1 through 7, subtract the denominator (in brackets) from the appropriate figure in row 8.

Table 6.6
Social characteristics of male grantors and grantees: Victoria chattel market, 1888–1892 and 1898–1902

Row	Personal characteristics	Grantor (%)	Grantee (%)	Men 20+ in Victoria 1901 (%)[1]
1	Foreign-born	62 (208/338)	66 (216/326)	73
2	Protestant	91 (296/326)	89 (274/318)	70
3	Age under 40	64 (216/340)	55 (181/332)	63
4	Married	73 (251/343)	71 (236/331)	50
5	Head of household	75 (250/334)	80 (253/318)	50

Table 6.6 continued

Row	Personal characteristics	Grantor (%)	Grantee (%)	Men 20+ in Victoria 1901 (%)[1]
6[2]	Self-employed/employer	61 (269/441)	73 (229/313)	21
7	Own property	34 (102/303)	56 (165/296)	20
8	Number known to be living in Victoria[3]	535	385	8623

1 Calculated from a computerized file of the 1901 census for the whole of Victoria.
2 Self-employed/employers are expressed as a percentage of them plus employees.
3 To calculate the number of Victoria men for whom social information is missing in rows 1 through 7, express the denominator as a percentage of the appropriate figure in row 8.

Table 6.7
Relation of women and men in the chattel market to means of production: Victoria, 1888–1901

Relation to means of production	Women %			Men %		
	Grantor	Grantee	Victoria 1901	Grantor	Grantee	Victoria 1901
Employer	5	16	1	27	41	5
Self-employed	73	19	11	33	31	14
Employee	21	28	59	39	26	77
Own means	1	38	29	1	3	4
Total number	85	32	1,246	443	321	8,235

NOTE: The total number differs from the total number in row 6 of tables 6.5 and 6.6 because women on own means are included in this table and not in tables 6.5 and 6.6. To compute the number of cases in the files without relation to means of production information, subtract the number in the last row of this table from the relevant number in row 8 of tables 6.5 and 6.6.

Table 6.8
Family cycle and credit for male and female grantors and grantees compared: Victoria, 1901

Stage	Percentage of families in each stage				
	Male grantors	Female grantors	Male grantees	Female grantees	All Victoria families
Wife <45, no children	25	30	21	9	12
All children <10	38	20	35	26	28
Some children 10–14, none 14+	12	16	13	5	15
Some children 14+	20	29	27	49	39
Wife >= 45 no children	5	6	5	12	6
Number of families	275	70	223	43	3,326

NOTE: The numbers for women in some cells are quite small.

Table 6.9
Logistic regression with grantee/not as dependent variable: Victoria chattel market,
1888–1901

Variables	Log odds of being a grantee in the chattel market
GENDER	*
Men	2.4*
Reference category: women	
OCCUPATION	*
Clerical	.58
Service	.25*
Sales	.52**
Transportation	.26*
Primary	.82
Manufacturing	.51**
In home with relation to production indicating in workforce	.27
Reference category: professional/managerial	
RELATION TO MEANS OF PRODUCTION	**
Self-employed	1.4
Employer	1.6**
On own means	10.9*
Reference category: employee	
OWN/RENT	*
Own	2.0*
Reference category: rent	
AGE	ns
15–24	
25–34	
35–44	
45–54	
Reference category: 55+	
BIRTHPLACE	ns
Canada	
United States	
Europe	
England	
Scotland	
All other	
Reference category: Ireland	
RELIGION	ns
Roman Catholic	
Presbyterian	
Methodist	
Baptist	
Jew	

Table 6.9 continued

Variables	Log odds of being a grantee in the chattel market
Other	
Reference category: Anglican	
FAMILY CYCLE	ns
Wife <45, no children	
All children <10	
Some children 10–14, none 14+	
Some children 14+	
Reference category: wife >= 45, no children	

*   Significance is < .02.

** Significance is between .02 and .05.

ns not significant, having been removed from the equation by the backward stepwise procedure.

Table 7.1

Relationship of workforce to the means of production: men and women in six cities, 1891 and 1901

	Men (%)		Women (%)	
Workforce status	1891	1901	1891	1901
Own-account employed	9.3	13.0	12.7	11.2
Employer	10.5	4.5	4.2	1.4
Employee	80.2	82.5	83.0	87.4
Own-account employee/employer	19.8	17.5	16.9	12.6
Total number	10,946	11,817	3,207	3,790

NOTE: From a 10 per cent sample of the population in Victoria, Vancouver, Winnipeg, Hamilton, Montreal, and Halifax. Age is 15 and over. No rural occupations are included in the table.

Table 7.2

Relationship of workforce to the means of production for men and women, 1901 and 1996

	1901		1996	
Workforce status	Men (%)	Women (%)	Men (%)	Women (%)
Own account	13.2	28.3	11.0	8.6
Employer	6.1	1.7	8.7	3.2
Employee	80.7	70.0	80.3	88.2
Total number	23,908	9,238	1,475,600	733,400
Own account/ employer	19.3	30.0	19.7	11.8

NOTE: The 1901 figures are based on the 5 per cent public use sample of the 1901 Canadian census. Only people who lived in towns or cities with a population of 1,000 or more are included. Agricultural and other primary workers are excluded. For both years, age is 15 and over. Both years exclude non-paid family workers. The 1996 data are from Statistics Canada, *Labour Force Update*, 1997, 45, table 14. These figures include agricultural workers and thus are not strictly comparable to the 1901 data. If agricultural and other primary workers are taken out of the 1996 data, then the rate of self-employment and employers for males is 17.8 per cent, and for females is 11.4 per cent (figures were calculated from data in *Labour Force Update*, tables 1, 14, and 16). On the basis of available information, a finer breakdown is not possible. The data for the survey were collected in a much more comprehensive manner than was the case for the census of 1901, a point that we return to later in chapter 7.

Table 7.3
Incidence of self-employment among men and women in the workforce by age, 1901 and 1996 (percentage)

Age	1901		1996	
	Men	Women	Men	Women
15–24	4.3	7.4	6.9	7.2
25–34	16.4	32.2	13.9	9.6
35–44	24.3	53.9	20.9	13.6
45–54	28.9	58.0	25.1	14.9
55+	37.3	60.1	38.3	23.4

NOTE: Data for 1996 are from Statistics Canada, *Labour Force Survey*, 13, table 3, and for 1901 are from the 5 per cent sample of the 1901 national census and include all women boarding-house keepers.

Table 7.4
Age distribution of self-employed women and men: urban Canada, 1901

Age group	Female	Male
15–29	53.1	36.3
30–39	16.4	21.7
40–49	13.5	18.4
50+	17.0	23.6
Average	33.1	37.8

Table 7.5
Relationship of workforce to means of production by marital status: urban men and women, 1901 and 1991

Workforce status	Married		Single		Widowed	
	Men	Women	Men	Women	Men	Women
Self-employed 1901	17.1	80.2	6.7	7.9	26.0	52.4
Employer 1901	8.4	1.4	2.8	1.3	5.9	4.4
Employee 1901	74.5	18.4	90.5	90.8	68.1	43.2
Total number 1901	13,642	2,017	9,507	6,226	728	957
Self-employed/ employer 1901	25.5	81.6	9.5	9.2	31.9	56.8
Self-employed/ employer 1991	13.3	6.6	4.8	2.1	16.4	7.8

NOTE: The figures for 1991 are from Gardiner, *Focus on Canada*, 13, table 2.2. They are derived from the 1991 census and exclude all agricultural workers. The statistics on self-employment reported by Gardiner, it should be noted, differ from those taken from Statistics Canada, *Labour Force Update*.

Table 7.6
Income by employment status: women and men in urban Canada, 1901 (dollars)

Employment status	Women			Men		
	Average (standard deviation)	Number known	% known	Average (standard deviation)	Number known	% known
Employee	198 (143)	5,435	84	452 (350)	17,548	91
Self-employed	288 (260)	441	51	803 (919)	1,124	36
Employer	392 (335)	79	50	1,107 (1,226)	608	42

NOTE: This table does not include women boarding-house keepers missed by the census. None of them, of course, had incomes recorded. Only those earning under $20,000 a year have been included. One woman and six men were excluded.

Table 7.7
Property ownership by relationship to means of production: men and women in urban Canada, 1901 (percentage)

Property holding	Self-employed	Employee	Employer	All
WOMEN				
Own	11.3	1.7	17.1	433
Rent	13.5	3.3	22.4	603
Neither owns nor rents	75.2	94.9	60.5	8,202
All	2,616	6,470	152	9,238
MEN				
Own	43.0	18.1	48.4	5,551
Rent	30.9	28.5	30.5	6,912
Neither owns nor rents	26.1	53.5	21.2	11,445
All	3,162	19,288	1,458	23,908

NOTE: This table includes women boarding-house keepers missed by the census, and the selection is as described for table 7.2.

Table 7.8
Self-employment by industry for men and women, 1901

Industry	Men		Women	
	Share (%)	Incidence (%)	Share (%)	Incidence (%)
GOODS-PRODUCING	36.9	13.6	17.3	17.1
Manufacturing	23.2	14.8	16.9	17.3
Construction	12.3	22.8	.2	46.2
General labourer	1.4	2.2	0.2	7.1
SERVICE-PRODUCING	63.2	23.4	82.6	35.7
Transport	5.8	10.6	0.1	0.1
Trade	29.1	55.9	2.8	35.2

Table 7.8 continued

Industry	Men		Women	
	Share (%)	Incidence (%)	Share (%)	Incidence (%)
SERVICE	28.3	20.3	79.7	23.9
Professional	15.0	38.1	4.4	14.3
Accommodation	4.0	31.5	67.5	89.7
Other services	9.3	10.7	7.8	6.7
Total number	4,620	23,908	2,768	9,237

NOTE: The data are from the 5 per cent national sample of the 1901 census of Canada. Age is 15 and over. Agriculture and other primary industry are excluded.

Table 7.9
Self-employment by industry for men and women, 1996

Industry	Men		Women	
	Share (%)	Incidence (%)	Share (%)	Incidence (%)
GOODS-PRODUCING	26.0	15.0	7.1	7.3
Manufacturing	6.6	5.5	4.4	5.1
Construction	19.4	36.4	2.7	25.8
SERVICE-PRODUCING	74.0	21.1	92.9	12.7
Transport	6.8	11.2	2.1	5.0
Trade	29.6	22.3	25.1	11.3
SERVICE	37.8	23.8	65.8	14.1
Professional	21.4	23.9	26.6	8.7
Accommodation	4.7	15.4	6.1	8.1
Other services	11.6	35.5	33.2	39.5
Total number	1,232,809	6,476,179	683,598	6,009,686

NOTE: The data are calculated from Statistics Canada, *Labour Force Survey*, table 1. Agriculture and primary industries are removed.

Table 7.10
Logistic regression with self-employed/not self-employed as the dependent variable: men and women in the urban workforce compared, 1901

Variables	Men Expo (B)	R	Women with boarding-house keepers Expo (B)	R	Men and women with boarding-house keepers Expo (B)	R	Men and women without boarding-house keepers Expo (B)	R
CITY	*	.04	*	.03	*	.04	*	.04
20,000–200,000	.88#	–.01	.82#	–.02	.88*	–.01	.89#	–.01
5,000–19,999	.97	.00	1.0	.00	.99	.00	.98	.00
1,000–4,999	1.2*	.02	1.2	.01	1.2*	.02	1.2*	.02
Reference category: +200,000								
MARITAL STATUS	ns		*	.32	*	.14	*	.03
Married			10.3*	.17	1.5*	.03	.74*	–.02
Single			.37*	–.07	.34*	–.08	.62*	–.03
Reference category: widow(er)								
OCCUPATION	*	.32	*	.10	*	.27	*	.28
Clerical	.04*	–.12	.12*	–.05	.05*	–.10	.05*	–.12
Service	.70*	–.03	1.5*	.02	1.1	.00	.49*	–.06
Sales	2.1*	.07	1.9*	.07	2.5*	.08	2.4*	.08
Transportation	.20*	–.12	.05*	–.02	.23*	–.09	.23*	–.10
Manufacturer	.32*	–.13	1.3	.01	.42*	–.09	.43*	–.10
Gen. labourer	.03*	–.16	.08*	–.06	.04*	–.13	.04*	–.14
Reference category: manager/ professional								
AGE	*	.15	*	.12	*	.13	*	.13
15–24	.14*	–.14	.22*	–.10	.17*	–.12	.16*	–.13
25–34	.38*	–.09	.59*	–.04	.48*	–.06	.44*	–.07
35–44	.51*	–.07	.75#	–.02	.62*	–.05	.60*	–.05
45–54	.62*	–.05	.77#	–.02	.69*	–.04	.67*	–.04
Reference category: 55+								
BIRTHPLACE	*	.04	*	.03	*	.04	*	.04
Canada	1.4*	.02	1.7*	.03	1.5*	.03	1.5*	.03
United States	1.5*	.01	1.3	.00	1.5*	.02	1.5*	.02
Europe	2.1*	.03	1.3	.00	1.9*	.03	2.1*	.03
England	1.1	.00	1.2	.00	1.2	.00	1.2	.00
Scotland	1.2	.00	.90	.00	1.2	.00	1.2	.00
All other	1.7*	.02	.89	.00	1.9*	.02	2.2*	.03
Reference category: Ireland								
PROPERTY	*	.11	*	.10	*	.07	*	.10
Own	2.7*	.10	5.3*	.09	1.4*	.03	2.5*	.09

Table 7.10 continued

Variables	Men Expo (B)	R	Women with boarding-house keepers Expo (B)	R	Men and women with boarding-house keepers Expo (B)	R	Men and women without boarding-house keepers Expo (B)	R
Rent	1.9*	.07	3.4*	.08	.76*	−.03	1.5*	.04
Reference category: neither own nor rent								
FAMILY CYCLE	*	.03	*	.08	*	.09	*	.05
Wife <45, no children	1.1	.00	1.2	.00	1.0	.00	1.0	.00
All children <10	1.1	.00	1.3#	.02	.96	.00	.93	.00
Some children 10–14, none >14	1.1	.00	.94	.00	.97	.00	.99	.00
Wife >44, no children	1.1	.00	.67#	−.02	.96	.00	1.1	.00
Single-person households	1.3*	.02	.45*	−.05	.84#	−.01	1.1	.00
Single unmarried female heads with some nuclear family	–	–	2.7*	.06	4.2*	.05	3.1*	.04
Unmarried male heads with some nuclear family	1.9*	.03	–	–	5.3*	.07	2.0*	.03
Reference category: some children >14								
SEX	–	–	–	–				
Women					5.3*	.11	1.1#	.03
Reference category: men								

Table 8.1
Self-employment within families: urban Canada, 1901

Gender	Heads of nuclear/extended families No. self-emp.	Self-emp. as % heads in the workforce (same sex)	% of all self-emp. heads	All nuclear/extended family members No. self-emp.	Self-emp. as % of family workforce (same sex)	% self-emp. in nuc./ext. families
Male	3,295	24.2 (25.6)	86.9	3,911	15.0 (19.6)	61.0
Female	496	3.6 (65.3)	13.1	2,499	9.4 (40.5)	39.0

NOTE: Nuclear/extended families includes all families with related individuals. This is the only viable unit of analysis that will enable one to identify family businesses. When used in the text, the term "family" refers to nuclear/extended families. All households with farmers were excluded, as were all self-employed who were retired. This table includes women boarding-house keepers, as explained in chapter 7.

Table 8.2
Social characteristics of family heads by gender and type of economic family: urban Canada, 1901

Characteristics	Working-class families		Entrepreneurial families		Business families	
	Male	Female	Male	Female	Male	Female
Gender	90.6	9.4	87.6	12.4	84.8	15.2
% married heads	95.3	14.5	95.8	12.8	89.0	5.3
% heads in workforce	97.2	30.4	96.6	56.7	98.7	61.1
Of heads in workforce, % white-collar	25.8	53.6	48.0	75.9	52.2	36.1
% of heads' age >=45	39.1	74.3	45.2	70.4	77.8	73.7
% of heads born in Canada	71.9	62.4	73.7	69.2	63.6	72.6
% of heads Protestant	55.7	61.1	61.0	63.1	54.7	55.7

Table 8.3
Familial characteristics of families by gender and type of economic family: urban Canada, 1901

Characteristics	Working-class families		Entrepreneurial families		Business families	
	Male	Female	Male	Female	Male	Female
% >=7 in family	21.1	11.7	18.0	6.8	42.6	9.5
Av. size family	4.8	4.0	4.6	3.7	6.2	4.0
% of working age who were women	50.0	65.5	51.9	70.6	44.9	78.8
% working age in workforce	52.0	58.2	59.5	63.4	59.7	79.4
% women of working age in workforce	12.8	40.2	32.1	55.4	24.0	76.2
% men of working age in workforce	91.2	92.2	89.1	82.6	88.7	91.7
% of self-employed/ employer	–	–	59.3	40.7	70.3	29.7

Table 8.4
Economic characteristics of families by gender and type of economic family: urban Canada, 1901

Characteristics	Working-class families		Entrepreneurial families		Business families	
	Male	Female	Male	Female	Male	Female
% with servant in house	5.6	3.8	16.2	11.7	18.0	4.2
% with property owner in family	35.4	36.6	49.0	44.3	63.8	42.1
Mean family income (standard deviation)	670 (539)	575 (449)	910 (1,872)	601 (502)	1285 (2,139)	825 (538)
Average income per family member (standard deviation)	160 (147)	152 (110)	218 (447)	164 (130)	222 (311)	217 (290)

Table 8.5
Location of families with self-employment by region and city size according to sex of head: urban Canada, 1901

Place	Self-employment families as % (no.) of all families of same gender with employment		Family businesses as % (no.) of all families of same gender with self-employment	
	Male head	Female head	Male head	Female head
REGION				
West (BC and Manitoba)	42.1 (379)	46.9 (30)	7.6 (29)	6.7 (2)
Central (Ontario and Quebec)	33.7 (3,577)	42.7 (568)	11.7 (419)	15.0 (85)
East (Nova Scotia, New Brunswick; and Prince Edward Island)	39.3 (562)	41.2 (63)	13.3 (75)	11.1 (7)
CITY SIZE				
+ 200,000	35.2 (1,266)	45.8 (213)	11.5 (146)	15.5 (33)
20,000–199,999	33.1 (989)	39.6 (135)	12.7 (126)	11.9 (16)
5,000–19,999	34.2 (943)	39.5 (131)	11.7 (110)	13.0 (17)
1,000–4,999	37.3 (1,364)	45.7 (188)	10.7 (146)	15.4 (29)

Table 8.6

Logistic regression with business family/working-class family as dependent variable: urban Canada, 1901

Variables	Female- and male-headed families Log odds of being in family business	Female-headed families Log odds of being in family business	Male-headed families Log odds of being in family business
CITY	ns	ns	ns
20,000–200,000			
5,000–19,999			
1,000–4,999			
Reference category:			
+200,000			
SEX OF HEAD	*		
Women	2.1*		
Reference category: men		–	–
MARITAL STATUS	*	*	*
Married	.52*	.04*	.61
Single	9.5*	5.1*	10.4*
Reference category:			
widow(er)			
OCCUPATION	*		*
Clerical	.05*	.00	.041*
Service	2.41*	2.31	2.8*
Sales	11.9*	14.3*	9.5*
Transportation	.95	.00	.79
Manufacturer	2.4*	6.6*	1.8*
General labourer	.03*	.00	.02*
Not given	.00	13.5	.00
Reference category:			
manager/professional			
AGE	*	ns	*
15–24	.59		.29*
25–34	.70		.15*
35–44	2.2*		.18*
45–54	3.3*		.66*
Reference category: 55+			
BIRTHPLACE	ns	ns	ns
Canada			
United States			
Europe			
England			
Scotland			
All other			
Reference category:			
Ireland			

Table 8.6 continued

Variables	Female- and male-headed families	Female-headed families	Male-headed families
	Log odds of being in family business	Log odds of being in family business	Log odds of being in family business
RELIGION	*	ns	*
Roman Catholic	1.6*		1.7*
Presbyterian	.68		.71
Methodist	1.14		1.2
Baptist	.97		.93
Jew	7.9*		5.6*
Other	2.0		2.1
Reference category: Anglican			
PROPERTY			
Own	1.7*	ns	1.8*
Reference category: not own			
FAMILY INCOME	*	*	*
Second fifth	.61**	2.5	.48*
Third fifth	.71	3.1**	.57*
Fourth fifth	.76	2.86**	.59*
Top fifth	1.6*	11.0*	1.3
Reference category: lowest fifth			
FAMILY DOMESTIC			
Domestic in family	2.9*	13.6**	2.8*
Reference category: no domestic			

* Significance is < .02.

** Significance is between .02 and .05.

No * Significance >.05

ns Not significant, having been removed from the equation by the backward stepwise likelihood ratio procedure.

Notes

ABBREVIATIONS USED IN THE NOTES

AO   Archives of Ontario
BCA   British Columbia Archives
BCLI   British Columbia Land and Investment Company
HPL   Hamilton Public Library
LAC   Library and Archives Canada

INTRODUCTION

1 For a critical discussion of that literature, see Kerber, "Separate Spheres." For middle-class attitudes to women in nineteenth-century Canada, see Holman, *A Sense of Their Duty.*

2 Toronto *Mail,* 12 May 1893, cited in Rutherford, *A Victorian Authority,* 177; *Canada Christian Monthly,* cited in Holman, *A Sense of Their Duty,* 153; AO, RG 22, vol. 384, Wentworth Court of High Justice, Morton vs. Gage, Statement of Defence, August 1892, 11; Victoria *Standard,* 15 January 1873; *Canadian Grocer,* 23 March 1900, 30.

3 Victoria *Standard,* 13 February 1873; *Canadian Grocer,* 10 July 1891, 6; 15 January 1894, 20; 21 July 1893, 30.

4 *Canadian Grocer,* 9 June 1893, 12.

5 Paulette Falcon, "'If the evil ever occurs,'" 47; Ingram and Inwood, "Property Ownership," 414.

6 Clarkson, "Property Law"; Gerard and Veinott, "Married Women's Property Law," 71, 75–7.

7 The comments about dower refer to British Columbia and Nova Scotia. As we will see in chapter 5, Ontario's dower provisions differed from British

Columbia's. For an examination of aspects of dower in Quebec, see Bradbury, "Wife to Widow."

8 For a good overview see Backhouse, "Married Women's Property Law." For a comprehensive discussion of Ontario, see Chambers, *Married Women and Property Law*. The best discussion of the judicial and legislative context for the passage of the MWPLs in British Columbia is Clarkson, "Remoralizing Families."

9 *Upper Canada Law Journal* 2 (1856): 217, cited in Falcon, "'If the evil ever occurs,'" 16.

10 Victoria *Standard*, 15 January 1873.

11 Ward, *Courtship, Law and Marriage*, 42–6; Bradbury, "Wife to Widow"; Gerard and Veinott, "Married Women's Property Law," 72–3.

12 For some of the best of the literature covering this process, see Basch, *In the Eyes of the Law*; Chused, "Late Nineteenth Century Married Women's Property Law"; Holcombe, *Wives and Property*; Khan, "Married Women's Property Laws"; and Shammas, "Re-assessing the Married Women Property Acts".

13 John Robson, BC Assembly *Debates*, 14 January 1873, cited in Victoria *Standard*, 15 January 1873; Victoria *Colonist*, 7 February 1874.

14 Chambers and Weaver, "'The Story of Her Wrongs,'" 109; Gerard and Veinott, "Married Women's Property Law," 82–3.

15 Victoria *Standard*, 15 January 1873.

16 Clarkson, "Remoralizing Families."

17 Ibid., 194.

18 Ibid., 174.

19 Shammas, "Re-assessing the Married Women Property Acts," 24–6.

20 Chambers, *Married Women*, passim.

21 Both Backhouse and Shammas make that argument. The work of Clarkson and Chambers on the judiciary's relationship to the MWPLs in British Columbia and Ontario takes a more balanced view.

22 Backhouse, "Married Women's Property Law," 242.

23 Davidoff and Hall, *Family Fortunes*, especially 272–315. See also Davidoff, "The Separation of Home and Work?"

24 See chapter 1 for a discussion of that literature.

25 Hill, "The Economic Value," 411.

26 A fine collection of essays edited by Beachy et al., *Women, Business and Finance*, attempts a holistic approach.

27 Similar sources in British Columbia were very uneven; so the discussion focuses on Ontario and Hamilton.

28 Comparable data is not available for Hamilton.

29 Beachy et al., *Women, Business and Finance*, 11.

30 The quotation is from Toronto *Mail,* 12 May 1893, cited in Rutherford, *A Victorian Authority,* 177.

31 BCA, Canadian Pacific Land and Mortgage Company Letterbook, vol. 9, Holland to London Secretary, 7 November 1893, 17 May 1894; BCLI Letterbook, vol. 4, Holland to London Secretary, 5 May 1896 (first quotation); ibid., vol. 5, 7 January, 1897, (second quotation).

32 Baskerville, *Beyond the Island;* Lutz, "Losing Steam."

33 Weaver, "The Location of Manufacturing Enterprises"; Middleton and Walker, "Manufacturerers and Industrial Development Policy"; McCann, "Staples and the New Industrialism," table 3, 62.

34 Calculated from data in *Census of Canada,* 1901, vol. 1, table 7, and vol. 4, table 1. Adults twenty and over were included, and all of Victoria's Chinese males were removed since they rarely married "European" women.

35 A good introduction is Guttentag and Secord, *Too Many Women?*

36 Bailyn, "The Challenge of Modern Historiography".

CHAPTER ONE

1 AO, Hamilton wills, 1891, 3177 and 3147; 1930, 1273; BCA, Victoria wills, GR 1052, vol. 3, 458; vol. 16, 2362.

2 Morris, *Men, Women and Property,* 247.

3 BCA, Victoria wills, GR, 1052, 1915, 13818, and 1906, 2929. Women often bequeathed cars and often to other women; see, for example, Thomasina Stewart of Hamilton, who in her 1929 will ceded "my auto car to my daughter", AO, Hamilton wills, 1929, 1492.

4 For Canadian examples of this debate, see Backhouse, "Married Women's Property Law"; Chambers, *Married Women and Property Law.*

5 Shammas, "Re-assessing the Married Women Property Acts"; Khan, "Married Women's Property Laws"; Combs, "Wives and Household Wealth." Quotations are from Coombs, 159; Shammas, "Re-assessing the Married Women Property Acts," 23; and see Ingram and Inwood, "Property Ownership," 432, for a similar comment.

6 Ingram and Inwood, "Property Ownership," 406–9; and Inwood and Van Sligtenhorst, "The Social Consequences"; Di Matteo and George, "Patterns and Determinants"; Baskerville, "'She has already hinted,'" Women and Investment," and "Inheriting and Bequeathing."

7 Green and Owens, "Gentlewomanly Capitalism"; Owens, "'Making Some Provision"; Rutterford and Maltby, "'The Widow, the Clergyman"; Maltby and Rutterford, "'She Possessed Her Own Fortune'"; Yohn, "Crippled Capitalists."

8 For Canadian commentaries, see Di Matteo, "The Determinants of Wealth"; Di Matteo and George, "Canadian Wealth Inequality"; and "Patterns and Determinants"; Elliott, "Sources of Bias"; Gwyn and Siddiq, "Wealth Distribution"; Osborne, "Wills and Inventories"; Wagg, "The Bias of Probate"; Craig, "La transmission des patrimoines." For a recent survey and listing of international commentaries, see Shanahan, "Personal Wealth."

9 Ingram and Inwood are somewhat more skeptical in "Property Ownership," 414–6.

10 For Ontario see *Statutes of Canada*, 22 Vict., 1858, Surrogate Courts Act.

11 AO, Hamilton wills, 1887, 4689, and 1892, 3449; BCA, Victoria wills, GR 1052, vol. 42, 6159, vol. 21, 3014, and vol. 3, 473.

12 Owens, "Property, Gender," 301–2.

13 The relevant legislation for Ontario is *Statutes of Ontario*, 55 Vict., 1892 c. 6, Succession Duty Act, and for British Columbia, *Statutes of British Columbia*, 57 Vict., 1894, c. 47, Succession Duty Act.

14 *Statutes of Ontario*, 50 Vict., 1887; *Statutes of British Columbia*, 57 Vict., 1894, c. 47.

15 Footnotes to the tables make clear whether all Victoria probates or just Victoria probates with full information on asset distribution are being analyzed. After the passage of "An Act to Consolidate and Amend the 'Succession Duty Act'" in 1907 in British Columbia, (7 Ed., c. 39), reporting evened out in both jurisdictions.

16 Shammas, "A New Look," 422. Figure 1.1 is constructed from data in table 1.4.

17 Shammas, "A New Look," 422.

18 Shammas also suggests this; see "Re-assessing the Married Women Property Acts," 16–17.

19 The Ontario legislation is 47 Vic., c. 19, An Act respecting the Property of Married Women, clause 2. The British Columbia legislation is 50 Vic., c. 20, An Act respecting the Property of Married Women, clause 2. It is clear that many married women were writing wills before these acts with no apparent control being exercised by their husbands.

20 BCA, Victoria wills, GR 1052, vol. 16, 2289; Victoria probates, GR 1304, vol. 67, file 1290.

21 Shammas, "Re-assessing the Married Women Property Acts," 2; Schuele, "Community Property Law."

22 Victoria data include all probates for men and women between 1894 and 1900. Hamilton data include all probates for men and women for 1900.

23 Shanahan, "Personal Wealth," table 1, 58.

24 The Gini coefficient is a measure of inequality that takes on a value between 0 and 1, 0 being perfect equality and 1 perfect inequality. Gini coefficients for

the other eight jurisdictions ranged between .71 and .86. See Shanahan, "Personal Wealth," 58.

25 Bouchard, "Economic Inequalities," table 3, 680; Di Matteo and George, "Canadian Wealth Inequality," table 9, 481.

26 The dates are Hamilton men, 1900; Hamilton women, 1898–1900; Victoria men and women, 1894–1900.

27 For Victoria circa 1900 the figures are $1,324 for men and $2,020 for women; for Hamilton they are $1,672 for men and $1,712 for women. For Victoria circa 1921 the figures are 2,612 for men and 2,636 for women; for Hamilton in 1922 the figures are 3,673 for men and 3,597 for women.

28 In fact, circa 1900 the five Victoria women in the 80–90 percentile of wealth-holders owned, on average, only $16 less than the twenty-eight men in that category. The real gap emerged within the top 10 percentile: on average, men owned twice as much as women. There were no women in the top 1 per cent.

29 Toronto *Globe*, 27 January 1883.

30 First quotation in Griffen, "Class, Gender," 69; second quotation in Morris, *Men, Women and Property*," 390–1.

31 Collins, "A Conflict Theory of Stratification"; cited in Tickamyer, "Wealth and Power," 465.

32 Pierre Bourdieu, "Structure, Habitus, Practices," cited in Gottfried, "Beyond Patriarchy?" 456–7. Yohn, in "Crippled Capitalists," argues that women never have attained power commensurate with their wealth and that they are in that sense "crippled capitalists."

33 For the notion of crisis, see Rotundo, *American Manhood*; for evolution, see Bederman, *Manliness and Civilization.*

34 *About Women and Marketing*, 31 January 1999, 10. For a useful review of approaches to "gendered" investment decision-making in the late twentieth century, see Bajtelsmit and Bernasek, "Why Do Women Invest Differently than Men?"

35 Quotations from Galt *Reformer*, 3 March 1855, cited in Holman, *A Sense of Their Duty*, 155; Jarvis, *Geoffrey Hampsted*, 29; *Monetary Times*, 3 March, 1899, 1176; Lauder, *Pen and Pencil Sketches*, 52; Fairbairn, *Nothing Like Black on White*, 111.

36 Ryan, *Cradle of the Middle Class.*

37 Lizars, *Committed to His Charge*, 18; Victoria *Standard*, 15 January 1873; Clews, *Twenty-eight Years*, 437–46. Yohn, "You Can't Share."

38 Hilkey, *Character Is Capital*, 142–65.

39 As we have noted, some work is beginning to address this in the British context. See Green and Owens, "Gentlewomanly Capitalism"; Owens, "'Making Some Provision'"; and Rutterford and Maltby, "The Widow, the Clergyman."

40 Gottfreid, "Beyond Patriarchy?" 456–7.

41 This point is succinctly made in Dublin, "Gender."

42 National Council of Women of Canada, *Women of Canada*, 36; *Massey's Magazine* 1 (1896): 51.

43 Quotations from Mackendrick, "Robert Barr," 37; Barr, *The Woman Intervenes*, 27, 149. See also Barr, *The Woman Wins*.

44 Denison, *That Wife*, title page and c. 13.

45 Marshall, "Thomas Webster," 1079; Webster, *Woman Man's Equal*, 187.

46 Fairbairn, *Nothing Like Black on White*, 111.

47 Rutterford and Maltby, "'The Widow, the Clergyman," provide many examples of the existence of this literature in England.

48 Stoddard's book is listed in "Useful Arts: Livelyhood," in Iles and Leypodt, *List of Books*. See also Lewis, *Our Girls*, 85.

49 Articles on women financiers include *Monetary Times*, annual review, January 1913, 142, 144; *Maclean's*, November 1905, 44–9, March 1908, 89, April 1913, 148–50, July 1913, 101–3. For articles on investing advice for women, see *Maclean's*, April 1905, 64–5, and *Saturday Night*, 8 June 1912, 29.

50 Post Office Savings Bank, Canada, in Morgan, *The Canadian Parliamentary Companion*; *Monetary Times*, 4 May 1894, 1386; *Saturday Night*, 17 May 1913, 18.

51 *Saturday Night*, 8 June 1912, 29–30.

52 Rutterford and Maltby, "The Widow, the Clergyman," 11; and Green and Owens, "Gentlewomanly Capitalism," 515.

53 Unless otherwise noted, all calculations from the 1901 census are derived from the Canadian Family Project's 5 per cent public use sample of that census. A copy of the public use sample is available for downloading at the Data Liberation Network's website. See Sager, "The Canadian Families."

54 Baskerville, "Displaying."

55 There were sixty-two cities in Canada in 1901 with a population of 5,000 or more. Enumerators occasionally recorded more than one relationship to the means of production for an individual. If we exclude those men and women who, in addition to saying that they lived on their own means, also said they were employees, employers, or working on their own account, the percentage of men drops to 3.4 and that of women stays at 3.8.

56 In round numbers, 36 per cent of women living on their own means owned property, and only 3.1 per cent of other women owned property. If we include only those women who were employees, self-employed, or employers, those women living on their own means still were more likely to own property: 36 per cent to 3.7 per cent.

57 Eighteen per cent of male employees owned real property, and 21 per cent of all men not living on their own means owned property.

58 Women on their own means averaged 2.4 houses and 3.3 lots, compared to 1.7 and 2.7 for other women owners as a group and compared to 1.7 and 2.7 respectively for male property holders not living on their own means.

59 These figures were obtained by multiplying the 5 per cent sample by 20.

60 For Hamilton, see Weaver, *Hamilton*, and for Victoria, see Baskerville, *Beyond the Island*, chap. 3. The information on land comes from the 1891 and 1901 Victoria assessment rolls.

61 There seems to be little difference in the pattern of investment in banks, measured as a percentage of total wealth, between the residents of the two cities. But close to 50 per cent of Hamilton's investors had money in a savings bank, while less than 20 per cent of Victoria's investors did.

62 In Victoria 13 per cent of men and the same percentage of women invested in the moderately risky sector; in Hamilton 34 per cent of men and 33 per cent of women did.

63 *Maclean's*, April 1905, 64–5. On the restricted nature of education for Canadian women in the late nineteenth century, see Gaffield and Marks, "Student Populations," 14, 21; Ainley, *Despite the Odds*.

64 Anon., "Include More," 8; anon., "Women More Satisfied," 12; Wolf, "Genders Travel"; anon., "Women Could Be Compromising."

65 BCA, Victoria wills, 1920, 11123; *Saturday Night*, 8 June 1912, 17 May 1913. Broussard cited in Byrnes, "Money Mystique," 85; Sheridan cited in Kerr, "Change Comes Slowly."

66 The geographical location of many companies in which Victorians invested was not always apparent. Thus it is not possible to present precise figures on the transition. However, it is clear that in the post–World War One era, investments in companies and countries outside British Columbia and outside Canada were increasing.

67 In order of appearance in the paragraph: BCA, Victoria probates, GR 1304, 1917, 5135; 1919, 66; 1924, 323; 1930, 205; 1926, 78; 1926, 116.

68 We have only limited social data for Hamilton men in 1922 and 1930. But marital status remained fairly constant, as did the occupational profile.

69 For a more extended discussion of logistic regression, see Baskerville and Sager, *Unwilling Idlers*, 55–7.

70 The level of significance is the probability that, on the basis of the information in the sample, one could reject a hypothesis that is in fact true. With a level of significance of 5 per cent, one accepts the risk that one could be rejecting a true hypothesis 5 per cent of the time.

71 Similar data were not available for Hamilton.

72 Thirty-eight per cent of the Hamilton men who invested in that sector had over 50 per cent of their assets there. The comparable figure for Victoria men was 18 per cent.

73 Those who lived in Hamilton were 3.6 times more likely to invest in that sector at a significance level of .00. If one were in the top wealth category, one was 6.1 times more likely than those in the second wealth tier to invest in the moderately risky range of assets, with a significance level of .001.

74 The significance level for each was .001.

75 Logistic regressions run with only men and with only women and all else the same as in table 1.7 discarded residence as an insignificant variable.

76 Di Matteo, "Wealth and Inequality," 99–101, 104–5.

77 Quotation: National Archives, Washington, DC, Consular Post Files, Victoria Consul to Dept of State, 8 February 1910. Development figures from "Report of Inspector of Municipalities.

78 Victoria City Archives, Building Inspector, Reports, 1907–13; *Census of Canada*, 1911, vol. 3, p. xii.

79 Shortt, *Report*, 4.

80 For more discussion, see Baskerville, "Financial."

81 Weaver, *Hamilton*, 88–107; Doucet and Weaver, *Housing*, 90–6. Doucet and Weaver also write, "Impressive [as the Hamilton boom was it] paled in comparison to the exertions of platters in other Canadian cities, especially on the prairies" (90).

82 Feree, "Beyond Separate Spheres"; Folbre, "Hearts and Spades."

83 AO, Hamilton wills, 1920, 12469; BCA, Victoria wills, GR 1052, 10002, 10701, 21433, 10744, 10792, 13430, 18472.

84 AO, Hamilton wills, 1898, 4574; BCA, Victoria wills, GR 1052, 8652, vol. 18, 2661, vol. 21, 3023, 1915, 13818.

85 Morris, "Reading the Wills," 129. Some have argued that Morris mischaracterizes the situation in England; see Rutterford and Maltby, "The Widow, the Clergyman." 25.

86 On this point see Gordon and Nair, "The Economic Role," 792.

87 "Typically, being a loaner is a more conservative approach than being an owner" (Miller, "Investing," 14).

88 Quotation from Catherine White, president of Financial Architects, cited in Conklin, "Two Sides," 6; Jianakoplos and Bernasek, "Are Women More Risk Averse?"; anon., "Women Could Be Compromising."

89 I say "may" because some modern analyses argue that the "conservative" approach to stocks employed by women is more, not less, profitable, at least over the short term. See anon., "Are Women Better Investors?"; anon.,

"Women Stock Holders," 10; Barber and Odean, "Boys Will Be Boys." In the United States there are fewer wealthy women than wealthy men; see Tickamyer, "Wealth and Power," 468.

90 Green, "Why Women," 201; Clews, *Twenty-eight Years*, 441; Judy Phillips, VP, Harris Bank, quoted in anon., "Women Have a False Sense," 5; Gutner, "Girl's Night Out."

CHAPTER TWO

1 Stobart and Owens, *Urban Fortunes*, 14; Morris, *Men, Women and Property*, 77–8.
2 Gagan, *Hopeful Travellers*, 55; Cohen, *Women's Work*, 47–54; Elliott, *Irish Migrants*, 199. For exceptions to this pattern, see Baskerville, "Inheriting and Bequeathing," and Inwood and Van Sligtenhorst, "The Social Consequences."
3 Cohen, *Women's Work*, 161, argues that the position of wives deteriorated, but it is not clear whether she has controlled for wills of married men only; so the large number of wills that apparently ignore wives in 1890 in Wellington County may be a result of including widowed or single men in the file. See also Gagan, *Hopeful Travellers*, 52–7; Elliott, *Irish Migrants*, 198–9.
4 AO, Hamilton wills, 1880, 1603 and 1544; BCA, Victoria wills, GR 1052, vol. 49, 7654, and GR 1052, 1928, 18834.
5 Grigg, "Women and Family Property," 120–1; Smith, "Inheritance and the Social History," 64.
6 Grigg, "Women and Family Property," 121.
7 Shammas, "Re-assessing the Married Women Property Acts."
8 BCA, Victoria wills, GR 1052, 1926, 14086.
9 Ibid., 1929, 18787.
10 The percentage of women who appointed trust companies as executors was very similar to that for men at all times and for both cities.
11 BCA, Victoria wills, GR 1052, 1912, 10606; 1930, 20249..
12 BCA, Justice Crease, Bench books, GR 1727, vol. 572, 17 May 1895; AO, SCO, Wentworth County, RG 22, 45–50–7–1, Smith vs Ellis et al., Actions and Matters, 26 March 1881; box 373, Margaret Duncan vs Tom Partington, 10 April 1884; box 373 Matilda Hounsley vs Wm Mallory, May 1884.
13 BCA, Victoria wills, GR 1052 1882, 7708. Information on the Woollacott family is from a computerized file of the 1881 Canadian census, Victoria, nominal returns. See also AO, Hamilton wills, 1880, 1530.
14 Davis, "Patriarchy from the Grave"; Gagan, "The Indivisibility of Land," 134–5.
15 AO, Hamilton wills, 1890, 2864.
16 Goltz, "If a Man's Wife"; Backhouse, *Petticoats and Prejudice*.

17 For evidence that this was a realistic fear, see Elliott, *Irish Migrants*, 200–1.

18 Owens, "Property, Gender," 309–13.

19 AO, Hamilton wills, 1922, 12490, and 1924, 1548.

20 Owens, "Property, Gender," 317.

21 BCA, Victoria wills, GR 1052, vol. 48, April 1886, Richard Baker will; vol. 2, 363, Mary Baker will, September 1886. *Census of Canada*, Victoria, 1881, district 190, subdistrict B, family numbers 504 and 505.

22 Whitehern Museum Archives, McQuesten Family Collection, Mary Baker McQuesten to Calvin McQuesten, 5, 10 February 1902; Hilda to Calvin, 26 February 1902.

23 Quotation from BCA, Victoria wills, GR 1052, vol. 43, 7680; Hancock, vol. 21, 3031; Watson, 1913, 4388.

24 The total is for both cities from 1888 to 1930.

25 BCA, Victoria wills, GR 1052, 1913, 8652; AO, Hamilton wills, 1882, 1729 (my italics).

26 In order of mention in text: BCA, Victoria wills, GR 1052, 1334; 1233; 2, 404; 8702; 3, 469; and 13, 1920; AO, Hamilton wills, 1898, 4577 and 4554.

27 BCA, Victoria wills, GR 1052, McKay, 1926, 14673, and Victoria probates, GR 1304, 291, Edgington, probate, January 1927. William Edgington's lament was not uncommon. In 1885 Lavina Cates's husband wrote that the $456 in the Dominion Savings Bank "was at the time when it was deposited my property and was only deposited in my wife's name for our mutual convenience in depositing and withdrawing the same from time to time" (BCA, Victoria wills, GR 1304, vol. 4, 1885). See BCA, Victoria probates, GR 1304, 52, probate of Martha Campbell, October 1886, for a similar story.

28 BCA, Victoria wills, GR 1052, vol. 1, Aubin; and Willis, 1914, 8578; AO, Hamilton wills, 1881, 1694; personal information on the Charlton family from *Census of Canada*, Hamilton, division 3, district 149e, p. 45.

29 Gunderson, "Women and Inheritance," 110.

30 In order of reference in the paragraph: BCA, Victoria wills, GR 1052, 1906, 4035; 1919, 21551; 1905, 1337; 1896, 2662; and 1929, 18176.

31 This statement is based on those who did inherit; in many cases we do not know if sons or daughters were left out or if those who did not give to a son or daughter had none to give to.

32 Single women were excluded from the analysis.

33 It would be nice to further delimit this selection by the children's ages, but this is not possible with the data available.

34 Gunderson, "Women and Inheritance," 110.

35 Carole Shammas reports that over the course of the nineteenth century the favouring of sons over daughters fell sharply in parents' wills; see Shammas et al., *Inheritance Patterns*, 108–19.

36 Haslett, "Distributive Justice and Inheritance."

37 AO, Hamilton wills, 1892, 3380; BCA, Victoria wills, GR 1052, 1889, 1835; 1919, 13854.

38 BCA, Victoria wills, GR 1052, vol. 1; AO, Hamilton wills, 1930, 1504.

39 The percentage for Hamilton is from 1890 and 1900 data only.

40 Green and Owens, "Gentlewomanly Capitalism," 519.

41 AO, Hamilton wills, 1889, 2640; 1898, 4918; 1930, 1486; BCA, Victoria wills, GR 1052, 12381; vol. 9, 1232; 16176.

42 BCA, Victoria wills, GR 1052, 15, 2171.

43 Ibid., 1905, 3195.

CHAPTER THREE

1 Cromwell, *The American Business Woman*, 131; Stoddard, "Women in Their Business Affairs," 99–100.

2 Michie, "The Canadian Securities Market"; Whiteside, "The Toronto Stock Exchange;" Neufield, *The Financial System*, 476–7; Drummond, *Progress without Planning*, chapter 18; Toronto *Globe*, 7 May 1883, 20, 21 February 1882, 2 January 1901.

3 Dividend payouts are from the Toronto *Globe*, 3 May 1890, 4 April 1900, 2 January 1901, 23 October 1901; the quotation is from 21 February 1882. For returns on mortgages, see chapter 4 below.

4 Share volume calculated from Michie, "The Canadian Securities Market," table 2, 58; Canadian shareholder estimates from ibid., 48. My calculation of percentage of investors in the over-nineteen age population. British shareholder estimate from Michie, *The London Stock Exchange*, 71–2.

5 The figures are from table 1.5.

6 Individual shareholders who invested in more than one company are counted only once.

7 Mean value (V) and number (N) of shares held by men and women are as follows: 1860: V, $2,996 and $1246; 1880: N, 74 and 35; 1900: V, $7,104 and $2,397; N, 81 and 31; 1911: V, $4,239 and $1,542; N, 85 and 32.

8 Maltby and Rutterford, "'She Possessed,'" 229.

9 For a sampling of dividends, see Toronto *Globe*, 21 June 1883, 24 September 1884, 28 February, 24 June 1885, 3 July 1886, 19 December 1888, 26 February 1892, 2 January 17 February 1894, 8 March 1900, and 2 March 1901.

10 Toronto *Globe*, 4 April 1891, 18; 30 April 1892, 19; 26 April 1901, 12; and 1 May 1901, 12. For a cautionary note on investing in "new" life insurance companies, see *Globe*, 4 July 1901, 7.

11 The British data is taken from Maltby and Rutterford, "'She Possessed,'" 228–9, 239–40; and Acheson and Turner, "The Impact of Limited Liability," 334–5. For an earlier period, see Carlos et al., "Financial Acumen."

12 One possible difference in the women's activity in Ontario compared to England might lie in the average number of shares held. Over time, this number declined for women in England (Maltby and Rutterford, "'She Possessed,'" 240) and held amazingly constant for women in Ontario (see note 7 above).

13 LAC, RG 19 C1, v.1181, file 9, Lydia Payne to J. Browne, September 1866; *Saturday Night*, 8 June 1912, 29–30. Quotation from Strange, *Toronto's Girl Problem*, 3; this study focuses on "the rise of the single women as an economic and social actor" but includes nothing on investment, land or home ownership, or operating one's own business.

14 Shareholders' lists for these companies were not routinely published, unfortunately.

15 The standard deviations, as for Ontario as a whole, were always much higher for men than for women. In 1880 there were 38 female and 107 male investors in the Canadian Bank of Commerce and the Bank of Hamilton living in Hamilton. In 1900 the respective numbers were female 111 and male 87.

16 Fifty-five of the 107 male investors in 1880 were linked to the 1881 census, and 59 of the male investors in 1900 were linked to the 1901 census.

17 Men and women who invested in both banks and insurance companies are only counted once.

18 Unfortunately, the census data for testing this hypothesis is not machine-readable at this time and resources are not available to carry such a project.

19 The census indicates that she owned three stores. For dividend calculations, see below page 90.

20 Married women declined from 39 per cent of all women shareholders in 1880 to 32 per cent in 1900; and widows declined from 39 per cent in 1880 to 26 per cent in 1900. We know the marital status of 26 of 38 women shareholders in 1880 and 78 of 111 shareholders in 1901.

21 In 1900 the average age of single women investors was forty-two, of married women, forty-seven, and of widows, fifty-nine.

22 For a broader examination of demographic trends in Ontario in this era, see McInnis, "Women, Work" and "The Population of Canada." Maltby and Rutterford, in "She Possessed," 240, touch on a demographic explanation for the increased presence of women shareholders in England in the late nineteenth century.

23 Toronto *Globe*, 25 February 1887.

24 Quoted in Farni, "'Ruffled Mistress,'" 77–8.

25 McInnis emphasizes this in "Women, Work."

26 It is difficult to compare these figures with the behaviour of men since name changes are not a factor for men as they might be for women. At any rate, we know that 30 per cent of the men who had shares in 1900 continued to have shares in 1911. Ninety-four men increased their shareholdings, 40 reduced them, and 19 stayed the same. The activity of those who were in both registers varied only in the sense that women may have been somewhat more apt to stay put.

27 AO, Hamilton wills, 1922, 12679.

28 *Saturday Night*, 17 May 1913.

CHAPTER FOUR

1 *Homeowner* 10 (1994): 1. For the August 2004 report, see http:// www. royallepage.ca/CMSTemplates/Toolbox/News/NewsTemplate.aspx?id=968, and see a 2002 Harvard University report at http://www.cendant.com/media/ trends_information/trends_information. cgi/Real+Estate+Services/99.

2 Cromwell, *The American Business Woman*, 195–6, 198 (my italics); quotation in the chapter title, ibid., 195. The book was noted in the *Nation*, 28 June 1900, 505, and a second edition appeared in 1910.

3 Darroch and Soltow, *Property and Inequality*, 205.

4 Burley, "The Keepers"; Doucet and Weaver, "Town Fathers"; Doucet and Weaver, *Housing the North American City*; Darroch, "Occupational Structure"; Darroch, "Early Industrialization." See also Katz et al., *The Social Organization*.

5 BCA, Victoria wills, GR 1069, box 38, files 1–213; account of sales in land in section 18, February 1859–January 1862. The calculations are my own.

6 BCA, BCLI, Victoria to London, vol. 3, 17 May 1892; Baskerville, *Beyond the Island*.

7 See the sources in note 6; Soltow, *Men and Wealth*; and Haulman, "Change in Wealthholding."

8 Probated women in late nineteenth-century Victoria also owned one of every five dollars of probated land wealth. Hamilton probated women owned one of every three dollars in 1900. Corporate holdings are, of course, not included here.

9 On the basis of a one-in-thirteen page sample of the 1899 Hamilton assessment roll, the average for women was $2,581, and for men, $2,175. The figure for women closely approximates that for the complete count of women on that roll: $2,638.

10 AO, RG 22–451–1–31, Justice Ferguson, Bench books, 12 October 1891; Ford vs Landed Banking and Loan Company.

11 For information on lot development in Hamilton in this time period, see Doucet and Weaver, *Housing the North American City*, 20–112.

12 Inwood and Van Sligtenhorst, "The Social Consequences," quotation, 173; on the relationship between property ownership and age, see Darroch and Soltow, *Property and Inequality*, 71 and passim.

13 The exception is young married women in Hamilton.

14 This is a somewhat lower incidence than I reported in an earlier work. The difference is due to the fact that the earlier work relied on sample data. Both analyses, however, point to the same dramatic trends in women's property ownership in Victoria. See Baskerville, "Women and Investment."

15 When one controls for investment only in non-landed ventures, the proportion of women investors by marital status reflects for each city and every year the proportions for all wealth.

16 The "frontier spirit" is caught in Armitage and Jameson, *The Women's West*, and more systematically in Schlissel et al., *Western Women*.

17 BCA, Attorney Generals' Papers, GR 1323, reel B2133, file 5190–12–16, F.A. McDiarmid, solicitor, Union of British Columbia Municipalities, speech, 11 October 1916.

18 Khan, "'Not for Ornament,'" 175; Matsuda, "The West"; Clarkson, "Remoralizing Families," chap. 7, esp. 228–9.

19 *British Columbia Statutes*, An Act Respecting the Property of Married Women, 50 Vic, c. 20, section 17.

20 Clarkson, "Remoralizing Families," 229.

21 Ibid., first quotation, 211; second and third quotations, 205, 220, 225.

22 BCA, BCLI, Victoria to London, v. 5, C.A. Holland to Secretary, 31 May 1897. Concerning Davie's assets, Holland was correct: his probated estate recorded $42,000 in assets, all of which was in the form of insurance policies, and $65,000 in various debts. See BCA, Victoria probates, GR 1304, 2048, March 1898.

23 BCA, BCLI, Victoria to London, vol. 3, 30 June, 30 July 1892, 28 Sept. 1894; vol. 4, 14 March 1896; vol. 5, 31 December 1896.

24 Clarkson, "Remoralizing Families," 234.

25 AO, RG 22, 45–44–1–11, Supreme Court of Ontario records, Hortense Phelps vs W.P. and Hanna Mallory, 1891. The potential trouble with the deed may have related to the husband's right to courtesy in his wife's lands. If he had not waived that right, he might have been able to claim one-third life interest in the land after her death. See chapter 5 for a discussion of this right and the wife's right to dower and the impact of these laws on landholding by women.

26 Clarkson, "Remoralizing Families," 238.

27 The percentage was the same for Hamilton estates: only 26 of 581 estates, or 4.6 per cent, filed in Hamilton between 1880 and 1900 exceeded $25,000, and in Hamilton bequeathments to relatives under $100,000 were not taxed.

28 Noel, "New France." For a critique of this article and Noel's reply, see Dumont, "Les femmes." See also Landry, "Gender Imbalance." The most sustained critique of this model is Perry, "'Oh I'm just sick.'" For discussions of the sex ratio in the context of the history of Australian women, see Kingston, *The Oxford History of Australia*, 3: 114–21, and Anderson, "'Helpmeet for Man.'"

29 Jones, "The Economics of Women's Suffrage"; Geddes and Lueck, "The Gains," quotation, 1089.

30 Guttentag and Secord, *Too Many Women?* 130; South and Trent, "Sex Ratios."

31 Guttentag and Secord, *Too Many Women?* 30

32 Perry, "Oh I'm just sick"; Gee, "Marriage in Nineteenth Century Canada," 320.

33 These figures are derived from computerized files of the complete population in each city for 1901. The percentage of married women with land in Victoria and without husbands in 1882 was 5.9, and in 1891, 5.5.

34 The information on Victoria's marriages comes from a computer file created from data in the marriage registration records at BCA. Of the 3,344 marriages registered in Victoria between 1880 and 1900, 362 involved widows. I would like to thank Mark Trottier and Doug Thompson for help in organizing this file. The information on Hamilton marriages comes from a count of marriages in that city in 1881, 1891, and 1901, using AO, MS 932, reels 38, 73, and 106. The Hamilton figures are based on a 10 per cent sample of the nominal-level census returns in 1891 and from a file containing all of Hamilton in 1901. The Victoria figures are from complete files of the censuses for 1891 and 1901.

35 BCA, Marriage registration records; 145 married women with property were linked to this file.

36 Lepp, "Dis/Membering the Family"; Chambers and Weaver, "Alimony and Orders of Protection."

37 AO, RG 22, Supreme Court of Ontario, Wentworth County, box 374, Catherine Worrell vs David A Muir and John Colvin, 6 May 1886.

38 Ibid., box 366, 4 October 1887, and box 378, 5 March 1888.

39 BCA, E/C/M126, Mary Howard to Emma McCandlish, 18 June 1882.

40 Doucet and Weaver, "The North American Shelter Business," 235.

41 The count includes only men and women (not companies) and is compiled from the indexes of the following: HPL, Moore and Davis, Letter books, 1871–75, 1879–82, 1888–91, 1891–94, 1898–1901.

42 Ibid., 1879–82, Moore and Davis to Mrs E. Byrne, 5 May 1880, 13 May 1882.

43 Ibid., 1880–81, Moore and Davis to Mrs Eliza Thompson, 11 December 1880 and 2 April 1881. Assessed value is taken from the 1881 assessment role for Hamilton.

44 Ibid., 1882–85, Moore and Davis to Miss Kate A. Stamp, 26 July 1883; to Eliza Thompson, 18 June, 2 November 1883; see also 4 January, 1883.

45 Ibid., 1888–91, Moore and Davis to J.B. Eager, 18 April 1889.

46 Ibid., 1879–82, Moore and Davis to James Beaucroft, 21 January 1880; to Thomas Beasley, 24 January 1880; to J. Gillespie, 23 April 1880; to Thomas Woodruff, 30 April 1880; to Mrs E. Byrnne, 5 May 1880; to Eliza Thompson, 5, 8 May 1882; ibid., 1882–85, Moore and Davis to Thompson, 1 May 1883.

47 Ibid., 1879–82, Moore and Davis to E. Byrnne, 2 March 1880; to Eliza Thompson, 15 September 1881; ibid., 1882–85, Moore and Davis to Thompson, 15 June 1883.

48 See chapter 2 and also Lebsock, *The Free Women.*

49 See, for example, Vickers, "Competency and Competition," and the now-classic study Davidoff and Hall, *Family Fortunes.*

50 BCA, AIE/C86/C86T18, R.G. Tatlow to H.P. Crease, 11 June 1886. I am grateful to John Lutz for suggesting that I look at this correspondence.

51 BCA, Hayward Papers. I am grateful to Susan Johnston for bringing the collection to my attention.

52 BCA, BCLI papers, Vancouver to Victoria, 6 February 1892, and Victoria to Vancouver, 8 February 1892.

53 Chambers, *Married Women,* chap. 9; Shammas, "Re-assessing the Married Women Property Acts"; Clarkson, "Remoralizing Families."

54 *Canadian Grocer,* 9 June 1893, 12.

55 AO, RG 22, Supreme Court Records, Hamilton-Wentworth, vol. 403, Cammell vs. Cammell, 1904.

56 Bailyn, "The Challenge of Modern Historiography."

57 This is not meant to suggest that elements of this activity were not occurring before this period as well.

CHAPTER FIVE

1 Toronto *Globe,* 15 March 1870; Kiriazis, "Urban Mortgage Lending," 53, 69, 72, 119.

2 Doucet and Weaver, *Housing the North American City,* 259.

3 Warner, *Streetcar Suburbs,* 118–19.

4 Leavitt and Leavitt, *Wise or Otherwise,* 41.

5 Canada, House of Commons, Debates, 27 April 1889, 1620. For an analysis of his less public career, see Johnson, "John A. Macdonald."

6 Wood, *The Untempered Wind*, 49; Gardiner, The House of Cariboo, 105–6.

7 A creel is a frame for holding bobbins or spools in a spinning machine. See Barr, *A Knight of the Nets*, 173. Thompson, *Sketches from Life*, 221.

8 Cromwell, *The American Business Woman*, 99, 109, 188.

9 For pioneering work focusing mainly on men, see Bogue, *Money at Interest*; and for an early historiographical discussion, Bogue, "Land Credit." For studies focusing on Canada, see Gagan, *Hopeful Travellers*; Doucet and Weaver, *Housing the North American City*, esp., 243–304.

10 Heller and Houdek, "Women Lenders," 39, 49, 59, 66.

11 Inwood and Van Sligtenhorst, "The Social Consequences," 180.

12 Since I collected this information, the Victoria Land Registry Office has suffered significant turmoil. The actual status of the copybooks from which these data were taken is at present unclear.

13 AO, GS 1510–26. For this study, information was taken from the following reels: GS 1510, 1511, 1513, 1515, 1517, 1519, 1521, 1523, and 1525.

14 William Blackstone, cited in Salmon, *Women and the Law of Property*, 142. For an analysis of dower in the Roman Empire, see Geddes and Lueck, "The Rule of One-Third."

15 Gibbs, *Debates of the Legislative Assembly*, 15 February 1845.

16 Ibid., 1847, 6: 361–5, Baldwin and Boulton. On the pitiful provisions for the widow, see also the *Canada Law Journal*, November 1857, 209–10; Toronto *Globe*, 26 June 1847, and under the title of "To the Women of Canada! The Women Robbed of Their Matrimonial Rights," reprinted on 22 December 1847.

17 Toronto *Globe*, 25, 26, 27 November, 18 December 1868. In other ways the dower act was strengthened. See note 18 below.

18 Toronto *Globe*, 24 January 1880, 2 (my italics); Canada, House of Commons, *Debates*, 7 April 1884, 1400. For the laws governing dower and a married woman's signature with her husband as mortgagor, see Cameron, *A Treatise on the Law of Dower*; Ontario Revised Statutes, 1897, c. 164, An Act respecting Dower, and c. 165, An Act to facilitate the conveyance of Real Estate by Married Women; Hawkins, "Dower Abolition," 662n107; Chambers, *Married Women*, 19–21; Bradbury, "Debating Dower."

19 *English Statutes*, 3 and 4 Will., 1833, c. 105, Dower Act. This act appears in *Revised Statutes of British Columbia*, 1897, vol. 1, c. 63. A revised law in 1898 provided a widow of an intestate greater property rights than before but did nothing to hinder a husband from disposing of property during his lifetime or

of barring dower in his will; see *Statutes of British Columbia*, 61 Vic., 1898, c. 40. For the date of reception of English law, see Hogg, *Constitutional Law*, 32–3.

20 Clarkson, "Remoralizing Families," 57–65, 95–6.

21 *British Colonist*, 22 January 1873; *Daily Standard*, 9, 11, 19 April 1872; Clarkson, "Remoralizing Families," 117–23.

22 For a good summary and discussion of attempts to introduce dower law into British Columbia after 1910, see Clarkson, "Remoralizing Families," 327–38, 407–34.

23 *Prairie Farmer*, 17 June 1908, cited in Hawkins, "Lillian Beynon Thomas," 58–60. This letter kick-started a movement to institute dower in the West.

24 I became aware of this debate through the fine article by Hawkins, "Dower Abolition in Western Canada." In the first two decades of the twentieth century, discussion of dower, especially in Alberta, Saskatchewan, and Manitoba, was far more common. See McCallum, "Prairie Women"; Cavanaugh, "The Limitations"; and Hawkins, "Lillian Beynon Thomas."

25 Canada, Senate, *Debates*, 5 March 1885, 176–81 (David Macpherson). For the establishment of the Torrens system, see Stein, "Sir Robert Richard Torrens."

26 Canada, Senate, *Debates*, 18 March 1885, 361 (Kaulbach); 5 March 1885, 191 (Girard); 5 March 1885, 181 (Macpherson).

27 Ibid., 5 March 1885, 190–1 (Power); 5 March 1885, 195–6 (Howlan).

28 Ibid., 5 March 1885, 183; 15 March 1885, 361 (Plumb); 11 March 1985, 254; 5 March 1885, 186–7 (Trudel).

29 Sixty-two of 480 cases involving male-female partnerships as mortgagors listed the wife first.

30 Toronto *Globe*, 4 September 1863.

31 Rarely did a year go by without dower appearing in the indexes to these annual reports.

32 For the British Columbia law, see *Revised Statutes of British Columbia*, 1897, c. 111, An Act relating to the Transfer of Real Estate and to provide for the Registration of Titles to Land, section 56 and Second Schedule. For Ontario, see *Province of Canada Statutes*, 1858–59, c. 35, An Act to Amend the Law enabling Married Women to convey their Real Estate within Upper Canada. The examination may have been rendered optional in 1873 by *Statutes of Ontario*, 1873, c. 18, An Act to facilitate the conveyance of Real Estate by Married Women, section 12, 56; see Canada, Senate *Debates*, 5 March 1885, 183 (Scott). Canadian historians have all but ignored this procedure. It is mentioned briefly in Chambers, *Married Women and Property Law*, 19, 189n28, and in the context of Lower Canada in Bradbury, "Debating Dower." For the American context, see Salmon, *Women and the Law of Property*, 14–40, and Braukman and Ross, "Married Women's Property."

33 *Ontario Chancery Reports* 17 (1870): Romanes vs Fraser, 268.

34 Victoria Land Registry Office, Mortgage filing cabinet, DD5332. Married women who were mortgagees often underwent examination when the mortgage was discharged; see ibid., DD13388. This procedure was still being followed in 1911; ibid., see DD10661.

35 Braukman and Ross, "Married Women's Property," 62.

36 *Ontario Chancery Reports* 17 (1870): Romanes vs Fraser, 268–9.

37 Baker, "The Reconstitution of Upper Canadian Legal Thought."

38 Canada, Senate, *Debates*, 18 March 1885 (Campbell and Gowan).

39 Ibid., 5 March 1885, 193 (Kaulbach); 6 March 1885, 207 (Campbell).

40 AO, Hamilton wills and probates, 1900, 4986.

41 For Lower Canada, see Bradbury, "Debating Dower." For Upper Canada, see Chambers, *Married Women and Property Law*, 53–69.

42 HPL, Brown-Hendrie Collection, Mary Kough Brown, Journals, Adam Brown to Frazer, copied to journal, 12 June 1889.

43 Harris and Harris, *The Eldon House Diaries*, Amelia Ryerse Harris, 15, 21, 22 May, 15 June 1867, 277–9.

44 Ibid., Lucy Ronald Harris, 8 May 1873, 439.

45 Ibid., 4 June 1874, 440; 31 December 1878, 460–1.

46 Ibid., 16 November 1875, 446–7.

47 Ibid., 1 May 1869, 433; 30 July 1874, 441; 22 July 1875, 446; 15 February 1876, 448; 17 November 1876, 451; 20 February 1878, 458; 10 February 1881, 471; Canada, House of Commons, *Debates*, 1878, 2: 1522 (Plumb).

48 Buck, "'Blot on the Certificate."

49 Marital status rarely appears on the land records. These years have been linked to the 1881, 1891, and 1901 censuses.

50 Clarkson, "Remoralizing Families," 258–9, briefly speculates on this connection.

51 One possible qualification might be suggested by the fact that some married women may have had to have their husbands co-sign because of the rights of courtesy. As mentioned in the text, some wives had their names recorded before those of their husbands, and they might have fallen into this category. Even if this speculation is true, the different trends in each city remain evident.

52 Cited in Clarkson, "Remoralizing Families," 122–3.

53 Canada, Senate, *Debates*, 11 March 1885, 253 (Campbell)

54 McKay, "The Liberal Order Framework," 625–6; Kessler-Harris, "In Pursuit of Economic Citizenship," 160; Mary Deitz, cited McKay, 626n18.

55 Pateman, *The Sexual Contract*, 2.

56 Cited in Chambers, *Married Women and Property Law*, 189n28.

57 Toronto *Globe*, 11 May 1889.

58 'The Anxious and the Aimless," Toronto *Globe*, 9 March 1889; McInnis, "Women, Work."

59 Canada, Senate, *Debates*, 11 March 1985, 255 (Power and Campbell).

60 Kiriazis, in his Michigan study, found birthplace to be a significant factor, with the German-born particularly heavily involved in lending. He also suggests that women were more likely than men to be lenders in 1900. See Kiriazis, "Urban Mortgage Lending," 217–23.

61 A cross-tabulation of marital status and mortgage status generated a contingency coefficient of .002 and indicated that married women were overrepresented as borrowers and underrepresented as lenders. The regression run lost a significant number of single and especially widows; so the result should be qualified.

62 In Victoria single women were 5.1 times and widows 6.9 times more likely to be lenders than were married women. In the regression with men and women, the values for single women and widows were 2 and 1.9. In Victoria single women and widows were, compared to married women, very unlikely to be borrowers: in the regression for women only, the respective values were .19 and .14, compared to .49 and .53 in the regression with both men and women.

63 The sources for this paragraph are the nominal-level census returns for Victoria, 1881, 1891, and 1901; Victoria assessment rolls, 1882, 1891, and 1901; BCA, Victoria wills, GR 1052, Calder probate, 1903; BCA, Calder papers, MS 2615, Annie Calder, Account book, 1884–92. See page 127 for a statement concerning the investment of probated unmarried women in mortgages.

64 Hamilton nominal-level census return, 1881; HPL, Frances Gay Simpson, Diary, 1881.

65 The one-third representation is the same as Kiriazis found for Detroit and Wayne County, Michigan, in 1900; see Kiriazis, "Urban Mortgage Lending," 205.

66 If Hamilton in 1881 is taken as an example, the figures were arrived at in the following way. In that year Hamilton men accounted for 76.5 per cent of mortgagees and 47.4 per cent of the over-nineteens in the city. They were thus 1.6 times more likely to be a mortgagee than their population in the city would suggest. While men were overrepresented, women were underrepresented: they were .5 times less likely to be a mortgagee than their population in the city would suggest. Thus if we control for their population in the city, Hamilton men were 3.2 times more likely to be a mortgagee than Hamilton women.

67 The average number of loans for Victoria men and women for 1881, 1891, and 1901 were for men: 1.7, 1.9, and 1.5; for women: 1.4, 1.7, and 1.3. The

comparable figures for Hamilton were for men: 1.4, 1.4, and 1.2; for women: 1.4, 1.5, and 1.2.

68 In Hamilton the gap was only 6 per cent in 1891; in Victoria it was 18 per cent. The actual sums can be calculated from the data in tables 5.2 and 5.3.

69 BCA, MS 2615, Calder papers, Annie Calder, Account book, 1884–92.

70 This tendency was the least evident in 1881: 45 per cent of men were in the top 50 per cent, while 41 per cent of women were. In 1891 the comparable figures were 49 and 36, and in 1901, 54 and 45. For 1891, 25 per cent of men were involved in the top 25 per cent of loans by value, compared to 18 per cent of women. In 1901 the respective percentages were 25 and 16.

71 The figures for 1891 were women 57 and men 44, and for 1901 they were women 46 and men 44. The figures for the top 25 per cent were, in 1891, women 21 and men 25; in 1901 women 19 and men 22.

72 Heller and Houdek, "Women Lenders," 60.

73 The situation in 1901 is reflective of other years as well. In that year, on average, women mortgagors borrowed $1,133 and male mortgagors $1,434. On average, women mortgagees lent women $1,059 and men $1,153.

74 In Hamilton in 1881, for example, women mortgagors averaged $812 and men averaged $1,134, but as table 5.4 indicates, women were less, not more, likely to lend to other women.

75 In 1891 men charged women, on average, 8.6 per cent and men 8.7 percent. Women charged men and women 8.6 percent.

76 The figures on workers in the manufacturing sector are tabulated from machine-readable files from the 1891 and 1901 nominal-level census returns for Victoria.

77 Social data were collected by linking names from the mortgage information to a machine-readable file of the nominal-level census returns for Victoria in 1901. Some 54 per cent of men in the file were linked to the census, and 69 per cent of the women were linked.

78 In 1891, for example, household heads borrowed, on average, twice the amount of other household members from both men and women.

79 The data for the calculations are from tables 5.2 and 5.3.

80 Doucet and Weaver, *Housing the North American City*, 64.

81 For women as lenders in early modern England, see Sharpe, "Gender in the Economy," 302–3.

82 Seventy-one per cent of the women who applied for a loan to the BCLI received one, while only 61 per cent of male applicants were successful. Data that would allow for a similar tabulation for the YGSC do not exist.

83 BCA, BCLI, Vancouver to Victoria, 6 February 1892, and Victoria to Vancouver, 8 February 1892.

84 Ibid., Victoria to Vancouver, quotation, 10 February 1893, and see also 15 September, 8 July 1893.

85 Ibid., Victoria to London, 29 March 1893.

86 Dorsett, "Equality of Opportunity," 78–9.

87 William Beer was listed as a single male in the 1891 census. In December 1892 he and his new wife, Fannie, sought money for a home.

88 For an oft-cited statement for this position, see Becker, *A Treatise on the Family*. For a succinct critique, see Folbre, "Hearts and Spades."

89 BCA, BCLI, Victoria to London, 20 April 1893.

90 Ibid., Vancouver to Victoria, 19, 23, 29 December 1893; Victoria to Vancouver, 13 January 1896.

91 Six borrowed from the two local companies. One other borrowed from the YGSC and Confederation Life.

92 BCA, BCLI, Victoria to Vancouver, 15 September 1892.

93 Ibid., Victoria to Vancouver, 19 February 1892.

94 Ibid., Victoria to Vancouver, 15 September 1892.

95 "An Act for the relief of Charles Smith," 24–6.

96 HPL, Brown-Hendrie Collection, Mary Kough Brown, Journals, William Kough to Mary, 25 July 1885. Such cries for help must have occurred quite often. In 1875 in Virginia, Mary Ellet Cabel, a married woman, wrote to her uncle asking for advice concerning a similar "delicate" financial situation involving money advanced to her husband; see Censor, *The Reconstruction of White Southern Womenhood*, 98–100.

CHAPTER SIX

1 The drop-off after 1905 was probably due to the building boom in Victoria. As we noted in chapter 1, the real estate holdings of women in Victoria reached about 75 per cent of wealth in the pre–World War One years. For those who reported personal goods, the average worth declined from $976 in the years 1902–05 to about $600 for the rest of the period.

2 Lemire et al., *Women and Credit*; Lemire, "Consumerism in Preindustrial and Early Industrial England"; Finn, "Women, Consumption and Coverture"; Finn, "Working-Class Women"; Berg, "Women's Consumption"; Mancke, "At the Counter."

3 For women, see the work by Lemire, Finn, and Berg cited in note 2. The same assumption is explicit in Rotella and Alter, "Working Class Debt."

4 Finn, "Working-Class Women," 116–17.

5 In 1901, fewer than 30 per cent of industrial production workers in Victoria toiled in a factory setting. Three out of five worked in small artisanal shops

with fewer than five employees, and nearly one in ten worked in their homes. The number working at home increases considerably if we include those who worked in areas outside industrial production. See Baskerville and Sager, *Unwilling Idlers*, 89.

6 Mancke, "At the Counter," 169–71.

7 Trentmann, "Beyond Consumerism," 377, 387. See also Lemire, *The Business of Everyday Life*, 17.

8 Bogue et al., "Oxen to Organs," quotation, 421. Three Canadian studies that do consider chattels are Holman, "'Now this Indenture'"; Sylvester, *The Limits of Rural Capitalism*, 74–7; and Baskerville, "Chattel Mortgages." For broader discussions of credit, see Gagan, "The Security of Land," 140; Gagan, *Hopeful Travellers*; McCalla, *Planting the Province*, chap. 8; and Easterbrook, *Farm Credit in Canada*.

9 Chattel records for Hamilton have not been preserved. Nor have such records been preserved for any other comparable urban jurisdiction in Ontario; so this chapter focuses on Victoria only.

10 Canada, House of Commons, *Debates*, 28 March 1890, 2662.

11 Cromwell, *The American Business Woman*, 104–5, 117, 183–4.

12 In 1866 Vancouver Island united with mainland British Columbia. British Columbia entered the Canadian confederation in 1871.

13 For the legislative history of this act, see *British Columbia Statutes*, 25 Vict., 1861, c. 38; 30 Vict., 1866, c. 10; 33 Vict., 1870, c. 16; 36 Vict., 1873, c. 30; most conveniently for the period 1888–96, see Barron and O'Brien, *Chattel Mortgages*, 118–42. De Cosmos's comments are from the Victoria *Daily Colonist*, 11, 28 November 1863.

14 Entry on chattel mortgages in Bannock et al., *Penguin Dictionary of Economics*.

15 Barron and O'Brien, *Chattel Mortgages*, 8.

16 Ibid., 7.

17 Such activity on the part of widows has a long history. See Holderness, "Widows in Pre-industrial Society"; and Waciega, "A 'Man of Business.'"

18 The figures are calculated from machine-readable files of the nominal-level census returns for Victoria in each of those years.

19 The percentage of married women is from a file of women with known marital status: 28 of 61 were missing marital information for the 1881–87 period, 12 of 89 for the 1888–92 period, 39 of 107 for 1893–97, and 9 of 75 for the 1898–1902 period.

20 We know too few of the marital statuses of women lenders in 1881 to make a meaningful comparison here.

21 Lemire, *The Business of Everyday Life*, chap. 2.

22 In the period 1888–92, 21 per cent of women grantors dealt with women grantees, and 32 per cent of women grantees dealt with women grantors. Between 1898 and 1902 the respective figures were 10 and 8 percent.

23 Muldrew, *The Economy of Obligation.*

24 Where possible, values were computed from assessment roll data for 1901: the average value for 12 women grantor property owners was $4,048 and for 37 women grantees, $7,859. Ninety-two male grantors had an average property value of $9,173, and 147 male grantees had an average property value of $13,021. In all cases, large outliers were discarded, so that the standard deviations between women grantors and grantees and male grantors and grantees are similar.

25 These figures are percentages of all women and men in the file, not just of those for whom a relation to the means of production is known. The percentage would obviously be much higher if the latter relationship were used.

26 The names of the women who were so charged come from a file derived from arrest records held in the Victoria Police Archives and collected for her MA thesis, "Bodies Public, City Spaces," by Lisa Helps. I am very grateful to her for sharing this data. On the use of dressmaker as a synonym for prostitute, see Dunae, "Making the 1891 Census," 232–3.

27 For a discussion of another madam who owned property, see Backhouse, *Petticoats and Prejudice,* 244–59.

28 Lemire, *The Business of Everyday Life,* 17–47. There is no study of pawnbrokers in Canada. The classic study for England is Johnson, *Saving and Spending.* For a study of the culture and operations of prostitution in another city, see Hinther, "The Oldest Profession in Winnipeg."

29 A cross-tabulation of self-employed/employer or not grantor with the same for grantees indicated an expected count of 63 grantor employer/self-employed transacting business with their grantee counterparts. The actual number was twice that: 121. The contingency coefficient was .000.

30 Rotella and Alter, "Working Class Debt.".

31 The contingency coefficient was insignificant at .166.

32 I could not do a regression with just women since too many cases are lost as a result of insufficient information for all variables.

33 A three-way cross-tabulation between age (with five categories) and gender controlling for grantee/grantor generated insignificant results, thus reflecting the regression result.

34 Chambers, *Married Women and Property Law,* and Basch, *In the Eyes of the Law,* point to the narrow range of women affected by the MWPLs.

35 To some important degree, the absence of such evidence reflects the gender bias in the sources consulted rather than any wider reality.

36 Nineteen of the 38 transactions with family members used the absolute bill of sale, and 12 of 121 transactions by women with non-family used the absolute bill of sale.

37 Olson, "Feathering Her Nest," 5.

38 Male grantees also transacted 20 per cent of their dealings on the basis of household goods.

39 Appadurai, "Introduction: Commodities and the Politics of Value," in Appadurai, *The Social Life of Things*, 57–8.

40 Douglas and Isherwood, *The World of Goods*, xxiii.

CHAPTER SEVEN

1 *Financial Post*, 6 April 1907. Wendy Gamber has also noted the conflation of business woman and white-collar worker; see Gamber, "A Gendered Enterprise," 190.

2 *Census of Canada*, 1901, Hamilton, district 69, subdivision F, poll 6, p. 7; Symonds: Halifax, district 33, subdivision a, p. 4; Noble: Hamilton, district 69, subdivision c, poll 6, p. 3; Spencer: Vancouver, district 1, subdivision d, poll 10, p. 5; Humber: BCA, GG 1052, vol., 21n3066, November 1907.

3 On Arnold, see *Census of Canada*, 1901, Victoria, district 4, subdivision a, poll 15, p. 5; and Baskerville, "Giving Birth." See also AO, Hamilton wills and probates, Berney: 1891, 2864; Winslow: 1881, 1919; Kendall: 1900, 4943; Trumball: 1880, 1603.

4 Cochran, *Railroad Leaders* and "Cultural Factors"; Chandler, *The Visible Hand* and *Scale and Scope*.

5 A day-long session at the International Economic History Congress in Helsinki, Finland, on 23 August 2006 titled "Beyond Chandler: The Survival of the Family Firm in Europe, Asia and North America in the Nineteenth and Twentieth Centuries" sparked much heated debate.

6 Lamoureaux et al., "Beyond Markets" and "Against Whig History"; Scranton, *Endless Novelty*. Chandler, "Response to the Symposium," 134, 137.

7 *Business History Review* 72 (1998) published a theme issue on Gender and Business History, as did *Histoire sociale/Social History* on Women and Business in Eighteenth and Nineteenth Century Northwestern Europe in vol. 34 (2001), and *Enterprise and Society* in vol. 2 (2001). A useful collection of published essays on women and entrepreneurship covering a number of countries, with a wide time frame, and fitted with excellent introductions is Yeager, *Women in Business*.

8 Perhaps the most recent such lament, albeit a nicely balanced one, is Walsh, "Gendered Endeavours."

9 A sampling for the United States would include Gamber, *The Female Economy* and "A Gendered Enterprise." Kwolek-Folland has written a suggestive survey, *Incorporating Women*, that sparked a lively discussion on h-business@eh.net in October 1999. Other useful works include Lewis, "Female Entrepreneurs," "Beyond Horatio Alger," and Women in the Marketplace; Sparks, "Terms of Endearment," "Married Women and Economic Choice," and "Capital Instincts"; Murphy, "Business Ladies"; Dorsett, "Equality of Opportunity"; Myres, *Westering Women*, esp. chap. 9; Riley, *The Female Frontier*; Lebsock, *The Free Women*; and Bruchey, *Small Business*. For female self-employment in Britain and Europe, see Davidoff and Hall, *Family Fortunes*; Nenadic, "The Social Shaping"; and Beachy et al., *Women, Business and Finance*.

10 Murphy, "Business Ladies," 65; Riley, *The Female Frontier*, 4; Lebsock, *The Free Women*, chap. 5.

11 Scott, "Comment"; Sharpe, "Gender in the Economy," 306; Sparks, "Capital Instincts," xvii; and see her recently published book, *Capital Intentions*. See also Buddle, "The Business of Women"; and Beachy et al., *Women, Business and Finance*.

12 For literature on Canada, see Young, "Getting around Legal Incapacity"; Errington, *Wives and Mothers*; Guildford, "More than Idle Ladies"; Darroch and Soltow, *Property and Inequality*; Burley, "Frontier of Opportunity"; Baskerville, "'She has already hinted at board'"; Buddle, "The Business of Women."

13 Self-employment includes men and women fifteen years of age and over who worked on their own account with or without employees in the areas of production, trade, and service. Professionals are included, as they are in current estimates of self-employment by Statistics Canada. See Statistics Canada, *Labour Force Update*. Burley, in *A Particular Position* and "Frontier of Opportunity," and Archer, in "Self-employment and Occupational Structure," however, do not include professionals, or at least all professionals, in their estimates. Because much of the literature uses the term "self-employment" to refer to own-account and employers and because one of the themes of this chapter is the importance of differentiating between the two, whenever my use is not clear in a particular context, I use the somewhat awkward term "own-account employment" to refer to the self-employed with no employees.

14 What Angel Kwolek-Folland noted for the United States is equally true for Canada: "We have more information [on female entrepreneurs and women-owned businesses] for the years after 1970 than for any other period in the past." See Kwolek-Folland, *Incorporating Women*, 190–1, 212.

15 DeLollis, "Today's Female Passion," 42–5; Schwartz, "Entrepreneurship." For useful statistics on female self-employment currently in Canada and the

United States, see Devine, "Characteristics"; Statistics Canada, *Labour Force Update*; Manser and Picot, "Self-employment in Canada."

16 Burley, *A Particular Position*; but his more recent article, "Frontier of Opportunity," does employ nominal-level census data. See also Benson, *Entrepreneurism*; Monod, *Store Wars*; Katz, *The People of Hamilton*; and Katz et al., *The Social Organization*.

17 The Canadian Families Project is an interdisciplinary research project by eleven Canadian scholars at five universities. It is centred at the University of Victoria and was made possible by a Major Collaborative Research Initiative grant from the Social Sciences and Humanities Research Council of Canada. For further information, see Sager, "The Canadian Families Project".

18 A 10 per cent sample from six cities drawn from the 1891 and 1901 Canadian censuses by Eric Sager and myself for a book on unemployment is also used: Baskerville and Sager, *Unwilling Idlers*. For an introduction to the 1901 census and to general literature on nineteenth-century censuses, see Baskerville and Sager, "Finding the Work Force." For Hamilton and Victoria, a 100 per cent sample of 1901 is available.

19 For an exception, see Burley, "Frontier of Opportunity," 57.

20 For this book I surveyed the *Dun and Bradstreet Reference Book* for Hamilton for 1880–81, 1890–91, and 1901–2. information on Mary Fiset is from *ibid.*, July 1881, 183, and March 1892, 69. *Census of Canada*, 1891, Hamilton, district 72, subdistrict F, division 5, p. 7, l. 21; 1901, Hamilton, district 69, subdistrict F, p. 5, l. 44. She is not listed in the September 1892 *Dun and Bradstreet Reference Book*.

21 The number of men participating in such activity declined by 4.6 per cent, and women's participation declined by 11.8 per cent.

22 Burley, "Frontier of Opportunity," 57ff, has nicely documented in greater detail a similar trend for Winnipeg in this time period.

23 *Dun and Bradstreet Reference Book*, Hamilton, July 1881, 186; September 1891, 70; September 1901, 61. Information on employment status and number of employees is from *Census of Canada*, 1891, Hamilton, district 72, subdistrict E, division 1, p. 1, l. 17, and 1901, Hamilton district 69, subdistrict E, poll 1, p. 5, l. 32.

24 Despite a small decline in their rate of involvement in own-account enterprises, the number of women participating in such activity actually increased by 4 per cent. The figures for Hamilton and Victoria do not differ significantly from the averages in table 7.1.

25 Chaykowski and Powell, "Women and the Labour Market." They refer to the period between 1950 and 1970 as the "take-off period."

26 Frances et al., "Women and Wage Labour."

27 Denton and Ostry, *Historical Estimates*. Courchane and Redish, in "Women in the Labour Force," while recognizing the problem, use Denton and Ostry's figures as being the best available. Inwood and Reid, in "Gender and Occupational Identity," warn that under-enumeration may vary by type of occupation, location, marital status, number in the household, and age.

28 There is an expanding literature on this issue: Abel and Folbre, "A Methodology"; Conk, "Accuracy"; Goldin, "The Female Labour Force"; Herr, "The Census"; Bose, *Women in 1900*; Jones, "Occupational Statistics." Hatton and Bailey, in "Women's Work," 89–90, suggest that for England the censuses after 1901 might have over-counted women's work, but the British censuses are not directly comparable to Canadian censuses, especially in the official definitions of self-employment.

29 Inwood and Reid, "Gender and Occupational Identity."

30 *Instructions to Officers*, 15; *Enumeration Manual*, 45.

31 *Census of Canada*, 1901, Winnipeg, district 12, subdistrict E, poll 12, l. 4, p. 4–5. For a discussion of women shopkeepers in Canada at a later period, see Monod, *Store Wars*, and for a perceptive study of such activity in northern France, see Craig, "Petites Bourgeoises."

32 For advertisements, see Victoria *Standard*, 20 July 1870, 21 February 1874, and 29 January 1883. See also *Dun and Bradstreet Reference Book*, Victoria, July 1890, 668; *Census of Canada*, 1891, Victoria, district 4, subdistrict B, division 3, p. 56, l. 13–14; 1901, Victoria, district 4, subdistrict D, poll 8. In the 1881 census she *was* listed as a photographer: 1881, Victoria, district 190, subdistrict B. In addition to running the shoe store, Maynard's husband also acted as a photographer. But it seems clear that she remained active throughout his life and for the five years following his death in 1907. See Mattison, "Richard Maynard," 128.

33 AO, Hamilton wills, 1882, 1729 (my emphasis); *Dun and Bradstreet Reference Book*, Hamilton, January 1880, 173.

34 Vickery, "Golden Age."

35 Cohen, *Women's Work*, 130–2, comments on the probable undercount of boarding-house keepers and washerwomen. For a discussion of this issue in the United States (although not in the context of self-employment), see Bose, *Women in 1900*, chap. 2.

36 *Instructions to Commissioners and Enumerators*, 37. *Enumeration Manual*, 46.

37 Bradbury, "Pigs"; Gamber, "Tarnished Labor," esp. 189–90. For a recent study that does situate boarding within business history, see Kay, "A Little Enterprise."

38 On the notion of strangers, see Baskerville, "Familiar Strangers." Owners of boarding and lodging places often played on the notion of a home away from

home, as in this ad in the 19 January 1871 *Globe*: "First class accommodation. Vacancies for four gentlemen who would appreciate the comforts of home." And as this ad from the *Globe*, 3 September 1885, suggests, prospective board-ers looked for such "homes": "Two young gentlemen wish to hear of a family where they could have all comforts of home."

39 This figure does not include all women who had boarders but no listed occu-pation.

40 Elizabeth Kingsbury, *Work for Women* (London, 1884), cited in Kay, "A Little Enterprise," 42; Toronto *Globe*, 11 December 1877, 2; 4 October 1888, 5.

41 *Census of Canada*, 1901, Hamilton, district 69, subdistrict A, poll 5, p. 3, l. 12.

42 These were women who were either household heads or wives who had no other listed occupation and, in the case of the wives, whose husbands were employed as other than a boarding-house or hotel keeper.

43 The figures were 19 listed and 355 not recorded for Victoria and 72 listed and 1,116 not recorded for Hamilton.

44 *Census of Canada*, 1901, Hamilton, district 69, subdistrict B, poll 5, p. 8, l. 40–1.

45 Seventy-eight per cent of those not listed as boarding-house keepers had fewer than three boarders at the time of the census enumeration. Twenty-five per cent of those listed as boarding-house keepers had fewer than three boarders.

46 Forty-nine widows with three or more boarders were given the appropriate occupational title; eighty-seven were not. The returns for Victoria and Hamil-ton are very similar to the national figures.

47 For evidence of such fluctuations, see Medjuck, "The Importance of Board-ing," and especially Harris, "The End Justifies."

48 On risk see Kay, "A Little Enterprise," 51; Baskerville, "Familiar Strangers"; Gamber, "Tarnished Labor," 184. See also Bradbury's work on boarding, most conveniently summarized in *Working Families*.

49 The 20 per cent figure is derived from data in the 1901 public use sample. The figure for male own-account employment in Ontario is 15.7 per cent.

50 Calculated from data in *Census of Canada*, 1901, vol. 1, tables 5 and 22, and vol. 3, table 20.

51 Calculated from Statistics Canada, *Labour Force Update*, 45, table 14. Using a different data source, Kuhn and Schuetze report similar but more dramatic trend lines for the late twentieth century in "Self-employment Dynamics," table 6, 778.

52 Kuhn and Schuetze argue that men entering self-employment in the 1990s were doing so as a last resort in the context of declining opportunities as employees or employers; see "Self-employment dynamics."

53 Calculated from Statistics Canada, *Labour Force Update*, 45, table 14. This figure includes growth in own-account and employer status. The equivalent rate of growth for men was 19.5 per cent. See also, for similar statistics for the later twentieth century, Industry Canada, *Shattering the Glass Box?*

54 Lavoie, "A New Era"; Schwartz, "Entrepreneurship"; Brush and Hirsch, "Women Entrepreneurs."

55 Even if those women boarding-house keepers who were ignored by the census enumerators are left out, 14 per cent of women in the workforce were self-employed in 1901, compared to 12 per cent in 1996.

56 It should be noted that the figures for 1996 include agricultural and other primary workers and so in a relative sense "inflate" the numbers of self-employed.

57 Statistics Canada, *Labour Force Update*, 13. See also Mansur and Picot, "Self-employment," table 2, 40.

58 Burley, "Frontier of Opportunity," 55, found a similar trend for men.

59 These figures are derived from the 1891 and 1901 six-city file and exclude women boarding-house keepers missed by the census enumerators.

60 Eric Sager and I have argued that many of the aged were negatively affected by economic changes at the turn of the century. See Baskerville and Sager, *Unwilling Idlers*.

61 Without the addition of the boarding-house keepers, the percentages of self-employed women in each age cohort are 4.8, 14.2, 25.8, 31.8, and 39.8.

62 Goldin, *Understanding the Gender Gap*, 159–84; Sparks, "Married Women"; Buddle, "The Business of Women."

63 Quotation from Wolstenholme, "The Education of Girls", 43 (my emphasis). Murphy, "Business Ladies," ignores the possibility of absent husbands, and Myres, *Westering Women*, 268–9, gives the issue a brief comment. Sparks, in "Married Women and Economic Choice," while sensitive to the notion of divorce and desertion, does not examine the implications in any systematic way.

64 Most women boarding-house keepers missed by the census had a husband in the house, a fact that undoubtedly helps to account for their omission. Fifty-one per cent of married employees had no spouse in the house.

65 *Census of Canada*, 1891, Victoria, district 4, subdistrict B, division 4, p. 21, l. 25; district 4, subdistrict A, division 2, p. 1, l. 4; district 4, subdistrict A, division 1, p. 16, l. 11.

66 AO, Dundas wills and probates, 1884, 2036; BCA, Victoria wills, 1052-9-1345, January 1908; Victoria probates, GR 1304, 4, Eva Clarke to the Supreme Court, August 1888, in Mary Clarke's probate.

67 In Hamilton 60 per cent of married businesswomen were under the age of forty in 1891.

68 *Census of Canada*, 1891, Hamilton, district 72, subdistrict F, division 4, p. 9,
   l. 5; district 72, subdistrict D, division 2, p. 14, l. 20.

69 Sparks, "Married Women and Economic Choice," 288, is typical.

70 Statistics Canada, *Labour Force Update*, 25.

71 Ibid., 26. This gap is partially explained by the fact that women self-employed
   and employees worked, on average, fewer hours per week than their male
   counterparts. The 1901 census did record months employed but did so
   mainly for employees, and the under-reporting is greater than that for earn-
   ings in all employment categories. Nevertheless, the following table suggests
   that men and women in each employment status worked, on average, a simi-
   lar number of months per year (the table includes only men and women with
   earnings information, ie., only those men and women in table 7.6 who had
   months employed information recorded in the census) .

Employment status	Women		Men	
	Average no. of months worked	No. of cases	Average no. of months worked	No. of cases
Employee	11.1	4930	11.1	15910
Self-employed	11.1	289	11.2	670
Employer	11.5	59	11.6	408

72 The median earnings were, for the employees and self-employed respectively,
   $175 and $200, and the mode for both was $200.

73 The figure is arrived at by combining the data from both databases.

74 The figure is arrived at by the following calculation: 1,753 boarding-house
   keepers x 2 boarders x $170.

75 Toronto *Globe*, 4 October 1888, 5. Barrett, *Work and Community*, 97, argues
   that women could earn more running a lodging house than they could work-
   ing in the packing yards. Similarly, Bradbury, in *Working Families*, 175–81,
   states that Montreal women in the 1880s could earn as much taking in several
   boarders as they could working for wages. Shergood, *Working-Class Life*, 84–9,
   considers costs and concludes that for working-class families, boarding was
   not very remunerative.

76 *Census of Canada*, 1901, Hamilton, district 69, subdistrict F, poll 3, p. 9.

77 *Census of Canada*, 1891, Victoria, district 4, subdistrict A, division 1, p. 8;
   district 4, subdistrict C, division 3, p. 68. BCA, British Columbia Benevolent
   Society, 1890 report.

78 Baskerville, "Familiar Strangers," 329–31.

79 Researchers have found a positive relationship between having received an
   inheritance and the probability of being self-employed in the late twentieth
   century. See Blanchflower and Oswald, "What Makes an Entrepreneur?"

80 For women heads without spouses in the family, the results were different: 46 per cent of self-employed lived in a property-owning family, and only 29 per cent of women employees did.

81 In chapter 7 we examine family income by type of economic family in more detail.

82 Bird, *Enterprising Women*. First quotation from Myres, *Westering Women*, 270. second quotation from Murphy, "Business Ladies," 75. For a discussion of Murphy and her evidence, see Baskerville, "'She has already hinted at board.'"

83 Gamber, *The Female Economy*, 5, and "A Gendered Enterprise," 204–9.

84 Bertaux, "The Roots," 453. Courchane and Redish, in "Women in the Labour Force," table 9–3, 151, provide evidence of a similar freeze in segregated jobs in the early twentieth century for Canada.

85 If the boarding-house keepers missed by the enumerators are excluded, these contrasts become even more dramatic: only 52.3 per cent of self-employed women are in the service-producing sector in 1901.

86 I have yet to do a similar breakdown of the other industries, but I suspect the same patterns will hold true.

87 Denton and Ostry, *Historical Estimates*, 12n2 found that the labour force surveys of the late 1940s were far more comprehensive than censuses of that era in providing a detailed profile of the labour force.

88 Norusis/SPSS Inc., *SPSS/PC+*, chap. 2, b–42.

89 Belcourt, "Sociological Factors"; Saunders and Nee, "Immigrant Self-employment."

90 The small difference in the effect of city size on self-employment by gender is probably explained by the relatively large numbers of men living in cities and towns with populations under 5,000. The incidence of self-employment in those places was 26.5 per cent, much higher than their overall participation rate and just under a third of urban men in the workforce lived in those towns. For women, the incidence of self-employment was 33 per cent, much closer to their overall participation rate, and 24.5 per cent of women lived in those towns.

91 The finding is confirmed when age is entered as an interval variable.

92 Burley, "Frontier of Opportunity," 46, also found birthplace and religion to be poor predictors of self-employment for men.

93 Inwood and Reid, in "Gender and Occupational Identity," note that self-employed women in the manufacturing sector in Canada in 1871 were more apt than their male counterparts to be born in Canada.

94 Women wage earners realized, on average, $208 annually; their self-employed sisters earned, on average, $244. Male wage earners took home $426, on average, annually; their self-employed counterparts realized, on average, $743.

95 The regressions for women were run with relation to household head as an independent variable and wife-dominated within the category, followed by household head. This was the case with and without boarding-house keepers missed by the census, although the wife category's dominance was stronger with their inclusion.

96 Burley, "Frontier of Opportunity," 69.

97 Inwood and Reid, "Gender and Occupational Identity," note that in their sample of self-employed women in manufacturing sectors in Canada in 1871, women were most likely to be married, followed by single and then widowed. Lewis, "Business Women," found that single women were outnumbered by married and widowed women.

98 There were 537 single, 289 widowed, and 183 married self-employed women, excluding boarding-house keepers missed by the census. If we removed married women with no husband in the house, the number of married women would be 128. We do not do so here because it is not clear that either of the studies referred to in the previous note did so, nor is it clear that studies of the relation of women's marital status to their employment status in the late twentieth century did so.

99 Forty per cent of widows, 33 per cent of married, and 9 per cent of single women in the workforce were self-employed, excluding the boarding-house keepers missed by the census and including married women without a husband in the house. If we put married women without a husband in the house as a separate category, then the respective percentages are as follows: 40 per cent of widows, 9 per cent of single women, 41 per cent of married women, and 22 per cent of married women without a husband in the home were self-employed.

00 The result was significant at .01. It bears repeating here that the run with household relationship also resulted in a continued dominant position for the category of wife.

01 Bailyn, "The Challenge of Modern Historiography."

02 Kay, "Small Business, Self-employment," 193.

03 *Saturday Night*, 4 February 1899, 8, and 24 March 1900, 8.

04 See also appendix 4 for a discussion of women who managed charitable enterprises.

CHAPTER EIGHT

1 AO, Hamilton expired partnership and sole proprietorship registrations, pre-1975, box 57.

2 *Census of Canada*, 1901, Hamilton, ward 2, district 69, subdistrict B, Poll 6, p. 13.

3 Maltby and Rutterford, "'She Possessed,'" esp. 246.

4 Colli, *The History of Family Business*, 58.

5 Klassen, " Family Business"; Radforth, "Confronting Distance"; Monod, *Store Wars*.

6 Archer, "The Entrepreneurial Family Economy," "Self-employment," "Family Enterprise," and "Small Capitalism."

7 Archer found that 18.8 per cent of all employed male heads were self-employed; in urban Canada in 1901 the comparable figure was 26 per cent. The higher Canadian figure is at least partly a reflection of the different sources used: my sample would identify a greater number of male petty entrepreneurs than Archer's.

8 Colli, *The History of Family Business*, 9–22.

9 Archer, "The Entrepreneurial Family Economy," 263.

10 I have found only one article attentive to the gender of the owner of a family business, and that article focuses on a series of third-world countries in the 1990s. See Blumberg, "'We are family.'"

11 These figures exclude about 16 per cent of all self-employed in urban Canada in 1901: those who lived in non-kin families, single-person families, and who were lodgers.

12 The same points can be made without the inclusion of women boarding-house keepers, although the figures are less dramatic. Self-employed female heads represent one-half of all female heads in the workforce and 7.6 per cent of all self-employed heads. Including all nuclear family members increases female participation by a factor of 2.8, and women represent 17.0 per cent of all self-employed in nuclear families.

13 If married women boarding-house keepers are excluded, then business families as a percentage of all families with self-employed goes up to 15.4 per cent (624 of 4,043 families). This proportion remains lower than the 36.3 per cent Archer found for Detroit in 1880 (128 of 353); see Archer, "The Entrepreneurial Family Economy," 264. If the analysis here is restricted, as Archer did, to male household heads, then the figure is 14.3 per cent. The greater number of petty entrepreneurs in the Canadian sample probably adds more to entrepreneurial families, and thus business families expressed as a percentage of the whole would be lower. Archer also found (277–8) that the wealthiest family businesses spanned more than one household, a measurement not available here.

14 All families are economic in some sense of the word, but for simplicity sake I use the term "economic families" in this chapter to refer to the three types as outlined in table 8.2.

15 Blumberg, "'We are family,'" 275, found the same marital distinction in the countries she examined.

16 In entrepreneurial families there were 3,210 self-employed men and 2,203 self-employed women. In business families there were 701 men who were self-employed or employers and 296 women.

17 Women-headed entrepreneurial families generally occupied a position between working-class and business families headed by women in the economic/familial characteristics examined below.

18 Blumberg, "'We are family,'" 280, also found this to be true.

19 Gardiner, *Focus on Canada*, 14, and Statistics Canada, *Labour Force Update*, 16.

20 Gardiner, *Focus on Canada*, 15.

21 The income data is far from complete. Census enumerators were told to collect income only for wage earners, not for employers and self-employed. Information is available for 51 of 95 women heads of family businesses and for 219 of 528 male heads of family businesses. If one includes all self-employed/employers in family businesses, then income is available for 134 of 296 women and 290 of 701 men. The percentage missing does not vary significantly by province or by city size.

22 The significance was .000.

23 The run was attempted for female-headed families, but there were too few for meaningful analysis because the male ratio variable contained a large number of missing values. This outcome reflects the relatively few female-headed business families with male workers in the family.

24 The census provides spotty information on place of employment. For women-headed family businesses, we have information for 38 of 95, and for male heads, 153 of 528.

25 Gamber, *The Female Economy*, 5, and "A Gendered Enterprise," 204–9.

26 Belcourt, "Sociological Factors"; Saunders and Nee, "Immigrant Self-employment"; Fairlie and Meyer, "Ethnic and Racial Self-employment." Two Canadian studies have argued that factors such as religion, ethnicity, and colour have not been determinants of self-employment in this time period: Minns and Rizov, "The Spirit of Capitalism," and Burley, "Frontier of Opportunity."

27 Regressions were run with just ownership by the family head, and the same trends resulted.

28 We have data for 134 of the 296 women.

29 The data on employee income is tabulated in Census and Statistics (Canada), *Bulletin 1*, table 2, 82.

30 Ibid., table 2, Manufacturing Class, 11–75, esp. 35.

31 Benson, *Entrepreneurism in Canada.*
32 Blumberg, ("'We are family,'" 285), on the basis of "research on gender and development in over 30 countries in every continent except Antarctica," asserts, "In none have I ever found a case where women with income under their control proved more subjugated then women with no income."
33 Sharpe, "Gender in the Economy," 306. See also Beachy, "Business Was a Family Affair," and Scott, "Comment."
34 Some literature of female family enterprise underlines the social, "communal" values that might have fostered such activity. Our data do not permit a test for that. See Walsh, "Gendered Endeavours," 184.
35 Shammas, "Re-assessing the Married Women Property Acts," 24–5.
36 See page ooo above.
37 Toronto *Mail,* 12 May 1893, cited in Rutherford, *A Victorian Authority,* 177.

CONCLUSION

1 The figures are based on a consolidation of all the databases used in this study for women in each city. A similar consolidation of the databases for men in each city has not been undertaken.
2 The figures are the totals for both cities and do not take into account the different trajectories in each city, as explained in the relevant chapters of the book.
3 The increase was more dramatic in Hamilton: from 5 per cent to 26 to 41 per cent respectively.
4 A good study of such interaction in the context of one family is Van Die, *Religion, Family.* See also chapter 1 of this book for a brief discussion of Thomas Webster, a Methodist minister, and his views on women's place in Canadian society, and also appendix 4 on women and philanthropy. For customary economic practice by women, see chapter 6.
5 First quotation, Donald Swainson, "Campbell, Sir Alexander," *Dictionary of Canadian Biography,* 12: 151; second quotation, Pateman, *The Sexual Contract,* 4.
6 Canada, Senate, *Debates,* 11 March 1995, 253 (Campbell)
7 McKay, "The Liberal Order Framework," 635; Folbre and Nelson "For Love or Money," quotation, 123.
8 Lemire, *The Business of Everyday Life,* quotation, 1; Bouchard, "Through the Meshes of Patriarchy."
9 Stoddard, "Women in Their Business Affairs," 79.
10 Holman, *A Sense of Their Duty,* x; Kocka, "The Middle Classes," 786.
11 Backhouse, "Married Women's Property Law," 242.

12 For the use of the concepts of micro- and macro-social relations, see Bouchard, "Through the Meshes of Patriarchy."

13 Meyer and Howe, *Woman's Work in America*, 447. I am indebted to Evan Roberts for this reference.

APPENDIX ONE

1 A similar comparison to the Victoria assessment roll is not possible since marital status was not recorded on that city's assessment rolls.

APPENDIX THREE

1 The combined percentage for employers and self-employed in all cities was 11.6.

APPENDIX FOUR

1 BCA, British Columbia Benevolent Society, Cash book, 50–1.

2 Comments on the reality of giving are based on a computer file of all relief distributed between 1890 and 1895 by the society; see ibid., Minute book, 1. For comments about the gendered nature of giving, see Victoria City Archives, City Council Minutes, 19 March 1894, and Victoria *Colonist*, 4 February 1894.

3 Victoria City Archives, Friendly Help Society, Minute books, 2 March 1895–15 February 1896; 6 August 1895; 10 July 1906.

4 BCA, British Columbia Benevolent Society, Minute book, 2, 23; Victoria City Archives, Friendly Help Society, Minute books, 15 February 1896.

5 For a recent and comprehensive listing of work on women and philanthropy, see Varty, "'A Career,'" 254n2. The brief discussion here has benefited from the following: Varty, "'A Career'"; Kidd, "Civil Society"; Ginzburg, *Women and the Work of Benevolence*; Stage, "The Perils of [Post} Feminism."

Bibliography

ARCHIVAL SOURCES

ARCHIVES OF ONTARIO (AO)
Justice Ferguson, Bench books, 12 October 1891, RG 22–451–1–31, Ford vs
    Landed Banking and Loan Company,
Hamilton assessment records
Hamilton, expired partnership and sole proprietorship registrations,
    pre-1975, RG 55–17–62
Hamilton marriage records, MS 932, reels 38, 73, and 106
Hamilton mortgage records, GS 1510–GS1526
Hamilton wills and probates
Supreme Court Records, RG 22 [SCO], Wentworth County

BRITISH COLUMBIA ARCHIVES (BCA)
Attorney Generals' papers, GR 1323
British Columbia Benevolent Society records, N/D/B77
British Columbia Land and Investment Company papers
Calder papers, Annie Calder, Account book, 1884–92, MS 2615
Canadian Pacific Land and Mortgage Company papers
Justice Crease, Bench books, GR 1727, vol. 572
Hayward papers
Mary Howard to Emma McCandlish, 18 June 1882, E/C/M126
Marriage registration records
R.G Tatlow to H.P. Crease, 11 June 1886, AIE/C86/C86T18
Victoria probates, 1860–1930, GR1304
Victoria wills, 1860–1930, GR 1052

HAMILTON PUBLIC LIBRARY (HPL)
Brown-Hendrie Collection, Mary Kough Brown, Journals
Moore and Davis, Letterbooks, 1871–1901
Frances Gay Simpson, Diary, 1881

LIBRARY AND ARCHIVES CANADA (LAC)
Department of Finance, Bank of Upper Canada, RG 19 C1, v.1181, file 9
Confederation Life Insurance Company papers: loan registry book, 1871–79;
 Financial Committee; Schedule of mortgages, 1888–1902

UNIVERSITY OF BRITISH COLUMBIA, SPECIAL COLLECTIONS
Yorkshire Guarantee and Securities Corporation papers

VICTORIA CITY ARCHIVES
Building Inspector, report, 1907–13
City Council, Minutes
Friendly Help Society, Minute books
Assessment rolls

VICTORIA LAND REGISTRY OFFICE
Mortgage filing cabinet, DD5332, DD13388
Victoria mortgage records. 1880–1921

WHITEHERN MUSEUM ARCHIVES
McQuesten Family Collection, http://www.whitehern.ca

PUBLISHED SOURCES

"An Act for the Relief of Charles Smith." In Select Committee of the Senate of
 Canada, *Minutes of Evidence*, Appendix 4, 24–5. Ottawa, 1885
Abel, Marjorie, and Nancy Folbre. "A Methodology for Revising Estimates:
 Female Participation in Five Massachusetts Towns in 1880." *Historical
 Methods* 23 (1990): 167–76
Acheson, Graeme, and John Turner. "The Impact of Limited Liability on
 Ownership and Control: Irish Banking, 1877–1914." *Economic History Review*
 59 (2006): 320–46
Ainley, Marianne G., ed. *Despite the Odds: Essays on Canadian Women in Science.*
 Montreal: Véhicule Press 1990
Allen, Robert C., and G. Rosenbluth, eds. *False Promises: The Failure of
 Conservative Economics.* Vancouver: New Star Books 1992

Anderson, Margaret. "'Helpmeet for Man': Women in Mid-Nineteenth
   Century Western Australia." In Pat Crawford, ed., *Exploring Women's Past*,
   87–127. Sydney: Allen and Unwin 1983

Anon. *About Women and Marketing*, 31 January 1999, 10

– "Are Women Better Investors?" *American Woman: Road and Travel*, 1 August
   2001

– "Include More than Traditional Bank Savings in Financial Advice to
   Women." *About Women and Marketing* 10 (October 1997): 8

– "Mortgage before Marriage? Women to Increase Participation in the
   Housing Market: Royal LePage Report Finds More Women than Men
   Likely to Give Up Wedding." Available at http://www.royallepage.ca/
   CMSTemplates/Toolbox/News/NewsTemplate.aspx?id=968

– "Women Could Be Compromising Their Financial Future, according to a
   New Poll by TD Wealth Management and Environics Research." *Canada
   News Wire*, December 2001

– "Women Have a False Sense of Security, Say Bankers." *Women's Business
   Exclusive*, 30 April 1997, 5

– "Women More Satisfied Cautious Investors than Men." *Marketing to Women*
   9 (February 1996): 12

– "Women Stock Holders Earn More than Men." *About Women and Marketing*
   12 (1 January 1999): 10

Appadurai, Arjun, ed. *The Social Life of Things: Commodities in Cultural
   Perspective*. Cambridge: Cambridge University Press 1986

Archer, Melanie. "The Entrepreneurial Family Economy: Family Strategies
   and Self-employment in Detroit, 1880." *Journal of Family History* 15 (1990):
   261–83

– "Family Enterprise in an Industrial City: Strategies for the Family Organi-
   zation of Business in Detroit, 1880." *Social Science History* 15 (1991): 67–95

– "Self-employment and Occupational Structure in an Industrializing City:
   Detroit, 1880." *Social Forces* 69 (1991): 785–801

– "Small Capitalism and Middle-Class Formation in Industrializing Detroit,
   1880–1900." *Journal of Urban History* 21 (1995): 218–55

Armitage, Susan, and Elizabeth Jameson, eds. *The Women's West*. Norman:
   University of Oklahoma Press 1987

Axelrod, Paul, and John Reid, eds. *Youth, University and Canadian Society*.
   Montreal: McGill-Queen's University Press 1989

Backhouse, Constance. "Married Women's Property Law in Nineteenth
   Century Canada." *Law and History Review* 6 (1988): 211–57

– *Petticoats and Prejudice: Women and Law in Nineteenth Century Canada*.
   Toronto: Osgoode Society 1991

Bailyn, Bernard. "The Challenge of Modern Historiography." *American Historical Review* 87A (1982): 1–24

Bajtelsmit, Vickie L., and Alexandra Bernasek. "Why Do Women Invest Differently than Men?" *Financial Counseling and Planning: The Journal of the Association of Financial Counseling and Planning Education* 7 (1996): 1–10

Baker, Blaine. "The Reconstitution of Upper Canadian Legal Thought in the Late Victorian Empire." *Law and History Review* 3 (1985): 219–92

Bannock, Graham, R.E. Baxter, and Evan Davis, eds. *Penguin Dictionary of Economics*. New York: Penguin 1999

Barber, Brad M., and Terrance Odean. "Boys Will Be Boys: Gender, Overconfidence and Common Stock Investment." *Quarterly Journal of Economics* 116 (2001): 261–92

Barr, Amelia E. *A Knight of the Nets*. New York: Dodd Meads 1896

Barr, Robert. *A Woman Intervenes*. London: F.A. Stokes and Co. 1896. CIHM no. 03358

– *The Woman Wins*. New York: Stokes 1894. CIHM no. 03358

Barrett, James R. *Work and Community in the Jungle: Chicago's Packinghouse Workers, 1894–1922*. Chicago: University of Illinois Press 1987

Barron, John A., and A.H. O'Brien. *Chattel Mortgages and Bills of Sale*. Toronto: Canada Law Book Co. 1897

Basch, Norma. *In the Eyes of the Law: Women, Marriage, and Property in Nineteenth-Century New York*. Ithaca: Cornell University Press 1982

Baskerville, Peter. *Beyond the Island: Victoria, an Illustrated History*. Burlington, Ont.: Windsor Publications 1986

– "Chattel Mortgages and Community in Perth County, Ontario." *Canadian Historical Review* 87 (2006): 583–619

– "Displaying the Working Class: The 1901 Census of Canada." *Historical Methods: A Journal of Quantitative and Interdisciplinary History* 33, no. 4 (2001): 229–35

– "Familiar Strangers: Urban Families with Boarders, Canada, 1901." *Social Science History* 25, no. 3 (2001): 321–46

– "Financial Capital and the Municipal State: The Case of Victoria British Columbia, 1910–1936." *Studies in Political Economy* 21 (1986): 83–106

– "Giving Birth: Families and the Medical Marketplace in Victoria British Columbia, 1880–1901." In Eric Sager and Peter Baskerville, eds., *Household Counts: Canadian Families and Households in 1901*, 405–22. Toronto: University of Toronto Press 2006

– "Inheriting and Bequeathing: The Place of Urban Women in Late Nineteenth Century Canadian Wills." in Emiko Ochiai, ed. *The Logic of Female Succession: Rethinking Patriarchy and Patrilineality in Global and*

Historical Perspective, 129–46. Kyoto: International Research Center for Japanese Studies 2003

– "'She has already hinted at board': Enterprising Urban Women in British Columbia, 1863–1896." *Histoire sociale/Social History* 26 (1993): 205–29

– "Women and Investment in Late Nineteenth Century Urban Canada: Victoria and Hamilton, 1880–1901." *Canadian Historical Review* 80 (1999): 191–219

– ed. *Canadian Papers in Business History*. Vol. 1–2. Victoria: Public History Group 1989–91

Baskerville, Peter, and Eric Sager. "Finding the Work Force in the 1901 Census of Canada." *Histoire sociale/Social History* 28 (Nov. 1995): 521–39

– *Unwilling Idlers: The Urban Unemployed and Their Families in Late Victorian Canada*. Toronto: University of Toronto Press 1998

Beachy, Robert. "Business Was a Family Affair: Women of Commerce in Central Europe, 1650–1880." *Histoire sociale/Social History* 34 (2001): 307–30

Beachy, Robert, Beatrice Craig, and Alastair Owens. *Women, Business and Finance in Nineteenth Century Europe: Rethinking Separate Spheres*. New York: Berg 2006

Becker, Gary. *A Treatise on the Family*. Cambridge: Harvard University Press 1981

Bederman, Gail. *Manliness and Civilization: A Cultural History of Gender and Race in the United States, 1880–1917*. Chicago: University of Chicago Press 1995

Belcourt, Monica. "Sociological Factors Associated with Female Entrepreneurship." *Journal of Small Business and Entrepreneurship* 4 (1986–87): 22–31

Benson, John. *Entrepreneurism in Canada: A History of "Penny Capitalists."* Lewiston, NY: E. Mellon Press 1990

Berg, Maxine. "Women's Consumption and the Industrial Classes of Eighteenth Century England." *Journal of Social History* 30 (1996–97): 415–34

Bertaux, Nancy. "The Roots of Today's 'Women's Jobs' and 'Men's Jobs': Using the Index of Dissimilarity to Measure Occupational Segregation by Gender." *Explorations in Economic History* 28 (1991): 433–59

Bird, Caroline. *Enterprising Women*. New York: Norton 1976

Blanchflower, David G., and Andrew J. Oswald. "What Makes an Entrepreneur?" *Journal of Labor Economics* 16 (1998): 26–60

Blumberg, Rae Lesser. "'We are family': Gender, Microenterprise, Family Work, and Well-being in Ecuador and the Dominican Republic – with Comparative Data from Guatemala, Swaziland, and Guinea-Bissau." *History of the Family* 6 (2001): 271–99

Bogue, Allan. "Land Credit for Northern Farmers, 1789–1940." *Agricultural History* 50 (1975): 68–100

– *Money at Interest: The Farm Mortgage on the Middle Border.* Ithaca: Cornell University Press 1955

Bogue, Allan G., Brian Q. Cannon, and Kenneth J. Winkle. "Oxen to Organs: Chattel Credit in Springdale Town, 1849–1900." *Agricultural History* 72 (2003): 420–52

Bose, Christine E. *Women in 1900: Gateway to the Political Economy of the 20th Century.* Philadelphia: Temple University Press 2001

Bouchard, Gerard. "Economic Inequalities in the Saguenay Society, 1879–1949: A Descriptive Analysis." *Canadian Historical Review* 79 (1998): 660–90

– "Through the Meshes of Patriarchy: The Male/Female Relationship in the Saguenay Peasant Society (1860–1930)." *History of the Family* 4 (2000): 397–425

Bradbury, Bettina. "Debating Dower: Patriarchy, Capitalism and Widows' Rights in Lower Canada." In Tamara Myers et al., eds., *Power, Place and Identity: Historical Studies of Social and Legal Regulation in Quebec*, 55–78. Montreal: Montreal History Group 1998

– "Pigs, Cows and Boarders: Non-Wage Forms of Survival among Montreal Families, 1861–1891." *Labour/le travail* 14, (1984): 9–46

– "Wife to Widow: Class, Culture, Family and the Law in Nineteenth Century Quebec." Les Grandes Conferences Desjardins, McGill University, 1997, 1–36

– *Working Families: Age, Gender and Daily Survival in Industrializing Montreal.* Toronto: McClelland and Stewart 1993

Braukman, Stacey Lorraine, and Michael A. Ross. "Married Women's Property and Male Coercion: United States Courts and the Privy Examination, 1864–1887." *Journal of Women's History* 12 (2000): 57–80

British Columbia Statutes. 1861–1900

Bruchey, Stuart, ed. *Small Business in American Life.* New York: Columbia University Press 1982

Brush, C.G., and R.D. Hirsch. "Women Entrepreneurs: Strategic Origins, Impact on Growth." In Bruce Kirchoff, ed., *Frontiers of Entrepreneurship Research*, 612–25. Babson Park, Mass.: Babson College 1988

Buck, A.R. "'Blot on the Certificate': Dower and Women's Property Rights in Colonial New South Wales." *Australian Journal of Law and Society* 4 (1987): 87–102

Buddle, Melanie. "The Business of Women: Gender, Family and
Entrepreneurship in British Columbia, 1901–1971." PhD dissertation,
University of Victoria 2003

Burley, David G. "Frontier of Opportunity: The Social Organization of
Self-employment in Winnipeg, Manitoba, 1881–1901." *Histoire sociale/Social
History* 31 (1998): 35–70

– "The Keepers of the Gate: The Inequality of Property Ownership during
the Winnipeg Real Estate Boom of 1881–82." *Urban History Review* 17
(1988): 63–76

– *A Particular Position in Life: Self-employment and Social Mobility in Mid-Victorian
Brantford, Ontario.* Montreal: McGill-Queen's University Press 1994

Burman, S., ed. *Fit Work for Women.* London: Croom Helm 1979

Butler, J.E.G. *Woman's Work and Woman's Culture: A Series of Essays.* London:
Macmillan 1869

Byrnes, Tracey. "Money Mystique." *Black Enterprise* 30 (May 2000): 85

Cameron, Malcolm Graeme. *A Treatise on the Law of Dower.* Toronto: Carswell
and Co. 1882

Canada. House of Commons. *Debates.* 1870–1900

Canada. Senate. *Debates.* 1880–1900

Canada Law Journal. 1857

Canadian Grocer. 1890–1900

Carlos, Ann, Karen Maguire, and Larry Neale. "Financial Acumen, Women
Speculators and the Royal African Company during the South Sea Bubble."
Accounting, Finance and Business History 16 (2006): 219–43

Cavanaugh, Catherine. "The Limitations of the Pioneering Partnership: The
Alberta Campaign for Homestead Dower, 1909–1925." *Canadian Historical
Review* 74 (1993): 198–225

Censor, Jane Turner. *The Reconstruction of White Southern Womanhood,
1865–1895.* Baton Rouge: Louisiana State University Press 2003

Census and Statistics (Canada) *Bulletin 1, Wage Earners by Occupations.* Ottawa,
1907

Census of Canada. 1881–1911

Chambers, Lori. *Married Women and Property Law in Victorian Ontario.* Toronto:
University of Toronto Press 1997

Chambers, Lori, and John Weaver. "Alimony and Orders of Protection:
Escaping Abuse in Hamilton-Wentworth, 1837–1900." *Ontario History* 95
(2003): 113–35

– "'The Story of Her Wrongs': Abuse and Desertion in Hamilton,
1859–1892." *Ontario History* 93 (2001): 107–26

Chandler, Alfred D., Jr. "Response to the Symposium: Framing Business History." *Enterprise and Society* (2005): 134–7

– *Scale and Scope: The Dynamics of Industrial Capitalism.* Cambridge: Belknap Press 1990

– *The Visible Hand: The Managerial Revolution in American Business.* Cambridge: Belknap Press 1977

Chaykowski, Richard, and Lisa M. Powell. "Women and the Labour Market: Recent Trends and Policy Issues." *Canadian Public Policy* 25, supplement (1999): S1-S25

Chused, R.H. "Late Nineteenth Century Married Women's Property Law: Receptions of the Early Married Women's Property Acts by Courts and Legislatures." *American Journal of Legal History* 29 (1985): 3–35

Clarkson, Chris. "Property Law and Family Regulation in Pacific British North America, 1862–1873." *Histoire sociale/Social History.* 30 (1997): 392–98

– "Remoralizing Families: Family Regulation and State Formation in British Columbia, 1862–1940." PhD dissertation, University of Ottawa 2001

Clews, Henry. *Twenty-eight Years in Wall Street.* New York: Irving Publication Co. 1888

Cochran, Thomas C. *The Age of Enterprise: A Social History of Industrial America.* New York: Harper 1961

– "Cultural Factors in Economic Growth." *Journal of Economic History* 20 (1960): 515–30

– *Railroad Leaders, 1845–1890: The Business Mind in Action.* Cambridge: Harvard University Press 1953

Cohen, Marjorie Griffen. *Women's Work, Markets, and Economic Development in Nineteenth Century Ontario.* Toronto: University of Toronto Press 1988

Colli, Andrea. *The History of Family Business ,1850–2000.* New York: Cambridge University Press 2003

Collins, Randall. "A Conflict Theory of Stratification." *Social Problems* 19, no. 1 (1971): 3–21

Combs, Mary Beth. "Wives and Household Wealth: The Impact of the 1870 British Married Women's Property Act on Wealth Holding and Share of Household Resources." *Continuity and Change: A Journal of Social Structure, Law and Demography in Past Societies* 19 (2004): 141–63

Conk, Margot. "Accuracy, Efficiency and Bias: The Interpretation of Women's Work in the U.S. Statistics of Occupation, 1880–1960." *Historical Methods* 14 (1981): 65–72

Conklin, Tara. "Two Sides of the Coin." *Women's Times* 3 (31 October 1995): 6

Conrad, Margaret, ed. *Intimate Relations: Family and Community in Planter Nova Scotia, 1759–1800.* Fredericton: Acadiensis Press 1995

Courchane, Marsha, and Angela Redish. "Women in the Labour Force, 1911–1986: An Historical Perspective." In Robert C. Allen and G. Rosenbluth, eds., *False Promises: The Failure of Conservative Economics.* Vancouver: New Star Books 1992

Craig, Beatrice. "Petites Bourgeoises and Penny Capitalists: Women and Retail in the Lille Area during the Nineteenth Century." *Enterprise and Society* 2 (2001): 198–224

– "La transmission des patrimoines fonciers dans le Haut-Saint-Jean au XIXe siècle." *Revue d'histoire de l'Amérique française* 45, no. 2 (1991): 207–28

Cromwell, John Howard. *The American Business Woman: A Guide for the Investment, Preservation and Accumulation of Property: Containing Full Explanations and Illustrations of All Necessary Methods of Business.* New York: Putnam and Sons 1900

Darroch, Gordon. "Early Industrialization and Inequality in Toronto, 1861–1899." *Labour/Le Travail* 11 (1983): 31–61

– "Occupational Structure, Assessed Wealth and Home Owning during Toronto's Early Industrialization, 1861–1899." *Histoire sociale/Social History* 16 (1983): 381–410

Darroch, Gordon, and Lee Soltow. *Property and Inequality in Victorian Ontario: Structural Patterns and Cultural Communities in the 1871 Census.* Toronto: University of Toronto Press 1994

Davidoff, Leonore. "The Separation of Home and Work? Landladies and Lodgers in Nineteenth and Twentieth Century England." In Sandra Burman, ed., *Fit Work for Women*, 64–97. London: Croom Helm 1979

Davidoff, Leonore, and Catherine Hall, *Family Fortunes: Men and Women of the English Middle Class, 1780–1850.* Chicago: University of Chicago Press 1987

Davis, Nanciellen. "Patriarchy from the Grave: Family Relations in Nineteenth Century New Brunswick Wills." *Acadiensis* 13, no. 2 (1984): 91–100

DeLollis, Barbara. "Today's Female Passion for Entrepreneurship." *American Enterprise* 8 (1997): 42–5

Denison, Mary A. *That Wife of Mine.* Toronto: J.R. Robertson 1877. CIHM no. 33991

Denton, Frank, and Sylvia Ostry. *Historical Estimates of the Canadian Labour Force.* Ottawa: Dominion Bureau of Statistics 1967

Devine, T.J. "Characteristics of Self-employed Women in the United States." *Monthly Labor Review* 117, no. 3 (1994): 20–34

Dictionary of Canadian Biography. Vols 10–14. Toronto: University of Toronto Press 1972–98

Di Matteo, Livio. "The Determinants of Wealth and Asset Holding in
    Nineteenth Century Canada: Evidence from Microdata." *Journal of Economic
    History* 57, no. 4 (1997): 907–34
– "Wealth and Inequality on Ontario's Northwestern Frontier: Evidence from
    Probate." *Histoire sociale/Social History* 38 (2005): 79–104
Di Matteo, Livio, and Peter George. "Canadian Wealth Inequality in the Late
    Nineteenth Century: A Study of Wentworth County Ontario, 1872–1902."
    Canadian Historical Review 73, no. 4 (1992): 452–83
– "Patterns and Determinants of Wealth among Probated Decedents in
    Wentworth County, Ontario, 1872–1902." *Histoire sociale/Social History* 31
    (1998): 1–34
Dorsett, Lyle W. "Equality of Opportunity on the Urban Frontier: Access to
    Credit in Denver, Colorado Territory, 1858–1876." *Journal of the West* 18
    (Fall 1979): 75–81
Doucet, Michael, and John Weaver. *Housing the North American City*. Montreal:
    McGill-Queen's University Press 1991
– "The North American Shelter Business, 1860–1920: A Study of a Canadian
    Real Estate and Property Management Agency." *Business History Review* 58
    (1984): 234–62
– "Town Fathers and Urban Community: The Roots of Community Power
    and Physical Form in Hamilton, Upper Canada, in the 1830s." *Urban
    History Review* 13 (1984): 75–90
Douglas, Mary, and Baron Isherwood. *The World of Goods: Towards an
    Anthropology of Consumption*. New York: Basic Books (1979) 1996
Drummond, Ian M. *Progress without Planning: The Economic History of Ontario,
    from Confederation to the Second World War*. Toronto: University of Toronto
    Press 1987
Dublin, Thomas. "Gender, Class and Historical Analysis: A Commentary."
    Gender and History 13 (2001): 21–3
Dumont, M. "Les femmes de la Nouvelle-France étaient-elles favorisées?"
    Atlantis 8 (1982): 118–24
Dunae, Patrick A. "Making the 1891 Census in British Columbia." *Histoire
    sociale/Social History* 31 (1988): 223–39
Dun and Bradstreet Reference Book. For Hamilton and Victoria, 1870–1901
Easterbrook, W.T. *Farm Credit in Canada*. Toronto: University of Toronto Press
    1938
Elliott, Bruce. *Irish Migrants in the Canadas: A New Approach*. Montreal:
    McGill-Queen's University Press 1988
– "Sources of Bias in Nineteenth Century Ontario Wills." *Histoire sociale/Social
    History* 18 (May 1985): 125–32

English Statutes, 3 and 4 Will., 1833, Dower Act, c. 105.

Enumeration Manual. Ninth Census of Canada, 1951. Ottawa: Dominion Bureau of Statistics, 1951

Errington, Jane. *Wives and Mothers: Schoolmistresses and Scullery Maids: Working Women in Upper Canada, 1790–1840.* Montreal: McGill-Queen's University Press, 1995

Fahrni, Magda. "'Ruffled Mistresses and Discontented Maids': Respectability and the Case of Domestic Service, 1880–1914." *Labour/Le Travail* 39 (1997): 69–97

Fairbairn, E. *Nothing Like Black on White.* Ottawa: Maclean, Rogers 1878. CIHM no. 95852

Fairlie, R.W., and B.D. Meyer. "Ethnic and Racial Self-employment Differences and Possible Explanations." *Journal of Human Resources* 31 (1996): 757–93

Falcon, Paulette. "'If the evil ever occurs': The 1873 Married Women's Property Act, Law, Property and Gender Relations in Nineteenth Century British Columbia." MA thesis, University of British Columbia 1991

Feree, M.M. "Beyond Separate Spheres: Feminism and Family Research." *Journal of Marriage and the Family* 52 (1990): 866–84

Financial Post. 1907

Finn, Margo. "Women, Consumption and Coverture in England, c. 1760–1860." *Historical Journal* 39, no. 3 (1996): 703–22

– "Working-Class Women and the Contest for Consumer Control in Victorian County Courts." *Past and Present* 161 (1998): 116–54

Folbre, Nancy. "Hearts and Spades: Paradigms of Household Economics." *World Development* 14, no. 2 (1986): 245–55

Folbre, Nancy, and Julie Nelson. "For Love or Money – or Both." *Journal of Economic Perspectives* 14 (2000): 123–40

Frances, Raelene, Linda Kealey, and Joan Sangster. "Women and Wage Labour in Australia and Canada." *Labour/Le Travail* 38 (1996): 54–89

Gaffield, Chad, and Lynne Marks. "Student Populations and Graduate Careers: Queen's University, 1895–1900." In Paul Axelrod and John Reid, eds., *Youth, University and Canadian Society*, Montreal: McGill-Queen's University Press 1989

Gagan, David. *Hopeful Travellers: Families, Land, and Social Change in Mid-Victorian Peel County, Canada West.* Toronto: University of Toronto Press 1981

– "The Indivisibility of Land: A Microanalysis of the System of Inheritance in Nineteenth Century Ontario." *Journal of Economic History* 36 (1976): 126–41

– "The Security of Land: Mortgaging in Toronto Gore Township, 1835–1895." In F.H. Armstrong et al., eds., *Aspects of Nineteenth Century*

Ontario: Essays Presented to James J. Talman, 135–53. Toronto: University of Toronto Press 1974

Gamber, Wendy. *The Female Economy: The Millinery and Dressmaking Trades, 1860–1930.* Chicago: University of Illinois Press 1997

– "A Gendered Enterprise: Placing Nineteenth Businesswomen in History." *Business History Review* 72 (1998): 188–218

– "Tarnished Labor: The Home, the Market and the Boardinghouse in Antebellum America." *Journal of the Early Republic* 22 (2002): 177–204

Gardiner, Arthur. *Focus on Canada: The Self-Employed.* Toronto: Prentice Hall 1994

Gardiner, Paul A. *The House of Cariboo and Other Tales from Arcadia.* New York: A.P. Gardiner 1900

Geddes, Rick, and Dean Lueck, "The Gains from Self-ownership and the Expansion of Women's Rights." *American Economic Review* 92 (2002): 1079–92

– "The Rule of One-Third." *Journal of Legal Studies* 31 (2002): 119–37

Gee, Ellen. "Marriage in Nineteenth Century Canada." *Canadian Review of Anthropology and Sociology* 19 (1982): 311–25

Gender and Business History theme issue. *Business History Review* 72 (1998): 185–366

Gender and Business History theme issue. *Histoire sociale/Social History* 34 (November 2001): 275–375

Gerard, Philip, and Rebecca Veinott, "Married Women's Property Law in Nova Scotia, 1850–1910." In Janet Guildford and Suzanne Morton, eds., *Separate Spheres: Women's Worlds in the Nineteenth Century Maritimes.* Fredericton: Acadiensis Press 1994

Gibbs, Elizabeth, ed. *Debates of the Legislative Assembly of United Canada .* Montreal: Presses de l'École des Hautes études commerciales 1975

Ginzberg, Lori D., *Women and the Work of Benevolence: Morality, Politics and Class in the Nineteenth Century United States.* New Haven: Yale University Press 1990

Goldin, Claudia. "The Female Labor Force and American Economic Growth." In Stanley Engerman and Robert Gallman, eds., *Long-Term Factors in American Economic Growth* , 557–604. Chicago: University of Chicago Press 1986

– *Understanding the Gender Gap: An Economic History of American Women.* New York: Oxford University Press 1990

Goltz, Annalee. "'If a Man's Wife Does Not Obey Him, What Can He Do?' Marital Breakdown and Wife Abuse in Late Nineteenth and Early Twentieth Century Ontario." In L.A. Knafla and Susan W.S. Binnie, eds.,

Law, Society and the State: Essays in Modern Legal History, 323–50. Toronto: University of Toronto Press, 1995

Gordon, Eleanor, and Gwyneth Nair. "The Economic Role of Middle-Class Women in Victorian Glasgow." *Women's History Review* 9 (2000): 791–814

Gottfreid, Heidi. "Beyond Patriarchy? Theorising Gender and Class." *Sociology* 32, no. 3 (1998): 451–68

Green, David, and Alastair Owens, "Gentlewomanly Capitalism: Spinsters, Widows and Wealth Holding in England and Wales, 1800–1860." *Economic History Review* 56 (2003): 510–36

Green, Hetty. "Why Women Are Not Money Makers." *Harper's Bazaar,* 10 March 1900

Griffen, Ben. "Class, Gender and Liberalism in Parliament, 1868–1882: The Case of the Married Women's Property Acts." *Historical Journal* 46 (2003): 59–87

Grigg, Susan. "Women and Family Property: A Review of U.S. Inheritance Studies." *Historical Methods* 22 (1989): 116–22

Guildford, Janet. "More than Idle Ladies: Business Women in Nineteenth Century Halifax." Paper presented to Atlantic Studies/BC Studies Conference, May 1992, St John's, Nfld

Gunderson, Joan R. "Women and Inheritance in America: Virginia and New York as a Case Study, 1700–1860." In Robert K. Miller and Stephen J. McNamee, eds., *Inheritance and Wealth in America.* New York: Plenham Press 1998

Gutner, Todi. "Girl's Night Out with a Focus on Finance." *Business Week,* 17 April 2000

Guttentag, Marcia, and P. Secord. *Too Many Women? The Sex Ratio Question.* Beverley Hills: Sage Publications 1983

Gwyn, Julian, and Fazley Siddiq. "Wealth Distribution in Nova Scotia during the Confederation Era, 1851 and 1871." *Canadian Historical Review* 73, no. 4 (1992): 435–52

Haines, Michael R., and Richard H. Steckel, eds. *A Population History of North America.* New York: Cambridge University Press 2000

Harris, Richard. "The End Justifies the Means: Boarding and Rooming in a City of Homes, 1890–1951." *Journal of Social History* 26 (1992): 331–58

Harris, Robin S., and Terry G Harris, eds. *The Eldon House Diaries: Five Women's Views of the Nineteenth Century.* Toronto: Champlain Society 1994

Harvard University report, 2002. Available at http://www.cendant.com/media/trends_information/trends_information.cgi/Real+Estate+Services/99

Haslett, D. W. "Distributive Justice and Inheritance." In G. Erreygers and T. Vandervelde, eds., *Is Inheritance Legitimate? Ethical and Economic Aspects of Wealth Transfers*, 135–55. Heidelberg, 1997

Hatton, Timothy, and Roy E. Bailey. "Women's Work in Census and Survey, 1911–1931." *Economic History Review* 54 (2001): 87–107

Haulman, Clyde A. "Change in Wealthholding in Richmond Virginia, 1840–1870." *Journal of Urban History* 13 (1977): 54–71

Hawkins, Robert E. "Dower Abolition in Western Canada: How Law Reform Failed." *Manitoba Law Journal* 24 (1996–97): 635–64

– "Lillian Beynon Thomas, Woman's Suffrage and the Return of Dower to Manitoba." *Manitoba Law Journal* 27 (1999): 45–113

Heller, Charles F., Jr, and John T. Houdek. "Women Lenders as Sources of Land Credit in Nineteenth Century Michigan." *Journal of Interdisciplinary History* 35 (2001): 37–67

Helps, Lisa. "Bodies Public, City Spaces: Becoming Modern in Victoria British Columbia, 1871–1901." MA thesis, University of Victoria 2002

Herr, Elizabeth. "The Census, Estimation Biases and Female Labor Force Participation Rates in 1880 Colorado." *Historical Methods* 28 (1995): 167–81

Hilkey, Judy. *Character Is Capital: Success Manuals and Manhood in Gilded Age America*. Chapel Hill: University of North Carolina Press 1997

Hill, Caroline M. "The Economic Value of the Home." *Journal of Political Economy* 12 (1904): 408–19

Hinther, Rhonda L. "The Oldest Profession in Winnipeg: The Culture of Prostitution in the Point Douglas Segregated District, 1909–1912." *Manitoba History* 41 (2001): 2–13

Hoffman, Ronald, and Peter J. Albert, eds. *Women in the Age of the American Revolution*. Charlottesville: University Press of Virginia, 1989

Hogg, Peter W. *Constitutional Law of Canada*. Toronto: Carswell 1985

Holcombe, Lee. *Wives and Property: Reform of the Married Women's Property Law in Nineteenth-Century England*. Toronto: University of Toronto Press 1983

Holderness, B.A. "Widows in Pre-industrial Society: An Essay upon their Economic Functions." In R.M. Smith, ed., *Land, Kinship and Life Cycle*. New York: Cambridge University Press 1984

Holman, Andrew C. *A Sense of Their Duty: Middle-Class Formation in Victorian Ontario Towns*. Montreal: McGill-Queen's University Press 2000

Holman, H.T. "'Now this Indenture Witnesseth . . .': Some Comments on the Use of Chattel Mortgages in Material History Research." *Material History Bulletin* 19 (1984): 52–6

Iles, George, and Augusta Leypodt, eds. *List of Books for Girls and Women and Their Clubs: with Descriptive and Critical Notes and a List of Periodicals and Hints for Girls' and Women's Clubs*. Boston: American Library Association 1895

Industry Canada. *Shattering the Glass Box? Women Entrepreneurs and the Knowledge-Based Economy*. Micro-Economic Monitor, Special Report. Ottawa, December 1998

Ingram, Susan, and Kris Inwood. "Property Ownership by Married Women in Victorian Ontario." *Dalhousie Law Journal* 23 (2000): 406–49

Instructions to Commissioners and Enumerators, Seventh Census, Dominion Bureau of Statistics. Ottawa 1931

Instructions to Officers, Fourth Census of Canada, 1901. Ottawa 1901

Inwood, Kris, and Richard Reid. "Gender and Occupational Identity in a Canadian Census." *Historical Methods: A Journal of Quantitative and Interdisciplinary History* 34 (2001): 57–71

Inwood, Kris, and Sarah Van Sligtenhorst. "The Social Consequences of Legal Reform: Women and Property in a Canadian Community." *Continuity and Change: A Journal of Social Structure, Law and Demography in Past Societies* 19 (2004): 163–97

Jarrell, R.A., and A. E. Ross, eds. *Critical issues in the History of Canadian Science, Technology and Medicine*. Thornhill: HSCT Publications 1983

Jarvis, Stinson. *Geoffrey Hampsted: A Novel*. New York: D. Appleton 1890. CIMH no. 07240

Jianakoplo, Nancy A., and Alexandra Bernasek. "Are Women More Risk Averse?" *Economic Inquiry* 36 (1998): 620–30

Johnson, J.K. "John A. Macdonald, the Young Non-Politician." *Canadian Historical Association, Historical Papers*, 1971, 138–53

Johnson, Paul. *Saving and Spending: The Working-Class Economy in Britain, 1870–1939*. New York: Oxford University Press 1985

Jones, Ethel B. "The Economics of Women's Suffrage." *Journal of Legal Studies* 20 (1991): 423–37

Jones, F.L. "Occupational Statistics Revisited: The Female Labor Force in Early British and Australian Censuses." *Australian Economic History Review* 27 (1987): 56–76

Katz, Michael. *The People of Hamilton, Canada West: Family and Class in a Mid-Nineteenth Century City*. Cambridge: Harvard University Press 1975

Katz, Michael, M.J. Stern, and M.J. Doucett. *The Social Organization of Early Industrial Capitalism*. Cambridge: Harvard University Press 1982

Kay, Alison. "A Little Enterprise of Her Own: Lodging-House Keeping and the Accommodation Business in Nineteenth Century London." *London Journal* 28 (2003): 41–53

– "Small Business, Self-employment and Women's Work-Life Choices in Nineteenth Century London." In David Mitch, John Brown, and Marco H.D. Van Leeuven, eds., *Origins of the Modern Career*, 191–206. Burlington, Vt: Ashgate 2004

Kerber, Linda. "Separate Spheres, Female Worlds, Women's Place: The Rhetoric of Women's History." *Journal of American History* 75A (1988): 9–39

Kerr, Ann. "Change Comes Slowly to Female Investors." *Globeinvestor.com*, 30 October 2003

Kessler-Harris, Alice. "In Pursuit of Economic Citizenship." *Social Politics* 10 (2003): 157–75

Khan, Zorina. "Married Women's Property Laws and Female Commercial Activity: Evidence from the United States Patent Records, 1790–1895." *Journal of Economic History* 56, (1996): 356–88

– "'Not for Ornament': Patenting Activity by Nineteenth Century Women Inventors." *Journal of Interdisciplinary History* 31 (2000): 159–95

Kidd, Alan. "Civil Society or the State? Recent Approaches to the History of Voluntary Welfare." *Journal of Historical Sociology*. 15 (2002): 328–42

Kidd, Alan, and David Nicholls, eds. *The Making of the British Middle Class? Studies of Regional and Cultural Diversity since the Eighteenth Century*. Stroud, Gloucestershire: Sutton 1998

Kingsbury, Elizabeth. *Work for Women*. London: Bickers and Son 1884

Kingston, Beverly. *The Oxford History of Australia*. Vol. 3. Melbourne: Oxford University Press 1988

Kirchoff, Bruce, ed. *Frontiers of Entrepreneurship Research*. Babson Park, Mass.: Babson College 1988

Kiriazis, David. "Urban Mortgage Lending in the Late Nineteenth Century: Detroit and Wayne County Michigan, 1880–1900." PhD dissertation, Wayne State University 1997

Klassen, Henry C. "Family Business and Inheritance and Succession in Alberta and Montana in the Late Nineteenth and Early Twentieth Centuries." In Peter Baskerville, ed., *Canadian Papers in Business History*, 2: 45–70. Victoria: Public History Group 1991

Knafla, L.A., and Susan W.S. Binnie, eds. *Law, Society and the State: Essays in Modern Legal History*. Toronto: University of Toronto Press, 1995

Kocka, Jurgen. "The Middle Classes in Europe." *Journal of Modern History* 67 (1995): 783–806

Kuhn, Peter, and Herb Schuetze. "Self-employment Dynamics and Self-employment Trends: A Study of Canadian Men and Women, 1982–1998." *Canadian Journal of Economics* 34 (2001): 760–84

Kwolek-Folland, Angel. *Incorporating Women: A History of Women and Business in the United States*. New York: Twayne Publishers 1998

Lamoureaux, Naomi, Daniel M.G. Raff, and Peter Temin. "Against Whig History." *Enterprise and Society* 5 (2004): 376–87

– "Beyond Markets and Hierarchies: Toward a New Synthesis of American Business History." *American Historical Review* 108: 404–33

Landry, Yves. "Gender Imbalance: Les filles du roi and Choice of Spouse in New France." In Bettina Bradbury, ed., *Canadian Family History*, 14–32. Toronto: Copp Clark Pitman 1992

Lauder, Mrs Dick. *Pen and Pencil Sketches of Wentworth Landmarks: A Series of Articles Descriptive of Quaint Places and Interesting Localities in the Surrounding County*. Hamilton: Spectator Print Co 1897. CIHM no. 11833

Lavoie, Dina. "A New Era for Female Entrepreneurship in the 80's." *Journal of Small Business–Canada* 2 (1984–85) 34–43

Leavitt, Lydia, and Thad W.H. Leavitt. *Wise or Otherwise*. Toronto: Wells Pub. Co. 1898. CIHM 01309

Lebsock, Suzanne. *The Free Women of Petersburgh: Status and Culture in a Southern Town, 1784–1860*. New York: Norton 1984

Lemire, Beverly. *The Business of Everyday Life: Gender, Practice and Social Politics in England, c. 1600–1900*. Manchester: Manchester University Press 2005

– "Consumerism in Preindustrial and Early Industrial England: The Trade in Secondhand Clothes." *Journal of British Studies* 27, no. 1 (1988): 1–24

Lemire, Beverly, Ruth Pearson, and Gail Campbell, eds. *Women and Credit: Researching the Past, Refiguring the Future*. New York: Oxford University Press 2001

Lepp, Anna Lee. "Dis/Membering the Family: Marital Breakdown, Domestic Conflict, and Family Violence in Ontario, 1830–1920." PhD thesis, Queen's University 2001

Lewis, Dio. *Our Girls*. New York: Harper and Brothers 1871. CIHM no. 61483

Lewis, Susan Ingalls. "Beyond Horatio Alger: Breaking through Gendered Assumptions about Business 'Success' in Mid-Nineteenth Century America." *Business and Economic History* 24 (1995): 97–105

– "Business Women in the Land of Opportunity: First and Second Generation Immigrant Proprietresses in Albany, New York, 1880." *Hudson Valley Regional Review* 14 (1997): 56–70

– "Female Entrepreneurs in Albany, 1840–1885." *Business and Economic History* 21 (1992): 65–73

– "Women in the Marketplace: Female Entrepreneurship, Business Patterns and Working Families in Mid Nineteenth Century Albany, New York,

1830–1885." PhD dissertation, Binghamton University, State University of New York, 2002

Lizars, Robina. *Committed to His Charge: A Canadian Chronicle.* Toronto: G.N. Morang 1900. CIHM no. 09186

Lutz, John. "Losing Steam: The Boiler and Engine Industry as an Index of British Columbia's Deindustrialization, 1880–1915." *Canadian Historical Association, Historical Papers,* 1988, 168–208

MacKendrick, Louis K. "Barr, Robert." *Dictionary of Canadian Biography,* vol. 14

Maclean's. 1890–1914

Maltby, Josephine, and Janette Rutterford. "'She Possessed Her Own Fortune': Women Investors from the Late Nineteenth Century to the Early Twentieth Century." *Business History* 48 (2006): 220–53

Mancke, Elizabeth. "At the Counter of the General Store: Women and the Economy in Eighteenth-Century Horton, Nova Scotia." In Margaret Conrad, ed., *Intimate Relations: Family and Community in Planter Nova Scotia, 1759–1800,* 167–81. Fredericton: Acadiensis Press 1995

Manser, Marilyn E., and Garnett Picot. "Self-employment in Canada and the United States." *Perspectives,* Autumn 1999, 37–44

Marshall, David B. "Webster, Thomas." *Dictionary of Canadian Biography,* vol. 13

Massey's Magazine 1 (1896). CIHM no. 32948

Matsuda, Mari. "The West and the Legal Status of Women: Explanations of Frontier Feminism." *Journal of the West* 24 (1985): 47–56

Mattison, David. "Richard Maynard, Photographer of Victoria, B.C." *History of Photography* 9 (1985): 109–29

McCalla, Doug. *Planting the Province: The Economic History of Upper Canada, 1784–1870.* Toronto: University of Toronto Press 1993

McCallum, Margaret E. "Prairie Women and the Struggle for a Dower Law, 1905–1920." *Prairie Forum* 18–19 (1993–94): 19–34

McCann, Larry. "Staples and the New Industrialism in the Growth of Post Confederation Halifax." *Acadiensis* 8, no. 1 (1979): 47–79

McInnis, Marvin. "The Population of Canada in the Nineteenth Century." In Michael R. Haines and Richard H. Steckel, eds., *A Population History of North America,* 371–432. New York: Cambridge University Press 2000

– "Women, Work and Childbearing: Ontario in the Second Half of the Nineteenth Century." *Histoire sociale/Social History* 34 (1991): 237–62

McKay, Ian. "The Liberal Order Framework: A Prospectus for a Reconnaissance of Canadian History." *Canadian Historical Review* 81 (2000): 617–46

Medjuck, Sheva. "The Importance of Boarding for the Structure of the Household in the Nineteenth Century: Moncton, New Brunswick and Hamilton, Canada West." *Histoire sociale/Social History* 13 (1980): 207–13

Meyer, Annie Nathan, and Julia Ward Howe, eds. *Woman's Work in America.* New York: Henry Holt, 1891

Michie, Ranald. "The Canadian Securities Market, 1850–1914." *Business History Review* 62 (1988): 35–73

– *The London Stock Exchange: A History.* New York: Oxford University Press 1999

Middleton, D.J., and D.F. Walker. "Manufacturers and Industrial Development Policy in Hamilton, 1890–1910." *Urban History Review* 8, no. 1 (1980): 20–46

Miller, Kathleen. "Investing in Your Future." *Divorce Magazine,* 31 October 1997, 2, 14

Miller, Robert K., and Stephen J. McNamee, eds. *Inheritance and Wealth in America.* New York: Plenham Press 1998

Minns, Chris, and Marian Rizov. "The Spirit of Capitalism: Ethnicity, Religion and Self-employment in Early Twentieth Century Canada." *Explorations in Economic History* 42 (2005): 259–81

Mitch, David, John Brown, and Marco H.D. Van Leeuwen, eds. *Origins of the Modern Career.* Burlington, Vt: Ashgate 2004

Monetary Times. 1890–1914

Monod, David. *Store Wars: Shopkeepers and the Culture of Mass Marketing, 1890–1939.* Toronto: University of Toronto Press 1996

Morgan, Henry. *The Canadian Parliamentary Companion.* Montreal: s.n. 1874

Morris, R.J. *Men, Women and Property in England, 1780–1870: A Social and Economic History of Family Strategies amongst the Leeds Middle Classes.* New York: Cambridge University Press 2005

– "Reading the Wills: Cash Economy Capitalists and Urban Peasants in the 1830s." In Alan Kidd and David Nicholls, eds., *The Making of the British Middle Class? Studies of Regional and Cultural Diversity since the Eighteenth Century.* Stroud, Gloucestershire: Sutton 1998

Muldrew, Craig. *The Economy of Obligation: The Culture of Credit and Social Relations in Early Modern England.* New York: St. Martin's Press, 1998

Murphy, L.E. "Business Ladies: Midwestern Women and Enterprise, 1850–1880." *Journal of Women's History* 3, no. 1 (1991): 65–89

Myers, Tamara, et al., eds. *Power, Place and Identity: Historical Studies of Social and Legal Regulation in Quebec.* Montreal: Montreal History Group, 1998

Myres, Sandra L. *Westering Women and the Frontier Experience, 1800–1915.* Albuquerque: University of New Mexico Press 1982

Nation. 1900

National Council of Women of Canada. *Women of Canada: Their Life and Work.* Montreal 1900. CIHM no. 11965

Nenadic, Stana. "The Social Shaping of Business Behaviour in the Nineteenth Century Women's Garment Trades." *Journal of Social History* 31 (1998): 625–45

Neufeld, E.P. *The Financial System of Canada.* Toronto: Macmillan of Canada 1972

Noel, Jan. "New France: Les femmes favorisées." In Veronica Strong-Boag and Anita Clair Fellman, eds., *Rethinking Canada: The Promise of Women's History*, 33–56. Toronto: Oxford University Press 1997

Norusis, Marija J. / spss Inc. *SPSS/PC+ Advanced Statistics 4.0.* Chicago 1990

Olson, Sherry. "Feathering Her Nest in Nineteenth Century Montreal." *Histoire sociale/Social History* 33 (May 2000): 1–35

Ontario Chancery Reports. 1870–1900

Ontario Statutes. 1860–1900

Osborne, Brian. "Wills and Inventories: Records of Life and Death in a Developing Society." *Families* 19, no. 4 (1980): 235–47

Owens, Alastair. "'Making Some Provision for the Contingencies to which Their Sex Is Particularly Liable': Women and Investment in Early Nineteenth Century England." In Robert Beachy, Beatrice Craig, and Alastair Owens, eds., *Women, Business and Finance in Nineteenth Century Europe: Rethinking Separate Spheres,* 20–37. New York: Berg 2006

– "Property, Gender and the Life Course: Inheritance and Family Welfare Provision in Early Nineteenth Century England." *Social History* 26 (2001): 299–317

Pateman, Carole. *The Sexual Contract.* Stanford: Stanford University Press 1988

Perry, Adele. "'Oh I'm just sick of the faces of men': Gender-Imbalance, Race, Sexuality, and Sociability in Nineteenth Century British Columbia." *BC Studies* 105–6 (1995): 27–44

Radforth, Ian. "Confronting Distance: Managing Jacques and Hay's New Lowell Operations, 1853–73." In Peter Baskerville, ed., *Canadian Papers in Business History*, 1: 75–100. Victoria: Public History Group 1989

Riley, Glenda. *The Female Frontier: A Comparative View of Women on the Prairies and the Plains.* Laurence: University Press of Kansas 1988

"Report of Inspector of Municipalities." British Columbia. *Sessional Papers,* 1919, vol. 1: G1–22

Rotella, Elyce, and George Alter. "Working Class Debt in the Late Nineteenth Century United States." *Journal of Family History* 18 (1993): 111–34

Rotundo, E. Anthony. *American Manhood: Transformations in Masculinity from the Revolution to the Modern Era.* New York: Basic Books 1993

Royal LePage. *Homeowner* 10 (1994): 1

Rutherford, Paul. *A Victorian Authority: The Daily Press in Late Nineteenth-Century Canada.* Toronto: University of Toronto Press 1982

Rutterford, Janette, and Josephine Maltby. "'The Widow, the Clergyman and the Reckless': Women Investors in England, 1830–1913." *Feminist Economics* 12 (2006): 111–38

Ryan, Mary P. *Cradle of the Middle Class: The Family in Oneida County, New York, 1790–1865.* New York: Cambridge University Press 1981

Sager, Eric. "The Canadian Families Project." *History of the Family* 3 (1998): 117–23

Salmon, Marylynn. *Women and the Law of Property in Early America.* Chapel Hill: University of North Carolina Press 1986

Saturday Night. 1900–14

Saunders, Jimy M., and Victor Nee. "Immigrant Self-employment: The Family as Social Capital and the Value of Human Capital." *American Sociological Review* 61 (1996): 231–49

Schlissel, Lillian, V. Ruis, and J. Monk, eds. *Western Women: Their Land, Their Lives.* Albuquerque: University of New Mexico Press 1988

Schuele, Donna C. "Community Property Law and the Politics of Married Women's Rights in Nineteenth Century California." *Western Legal History* 7 (1994): 244–81

Schwartz, Eleanor. "Entrepreneurship: A New Female Frontier." *Journal of Contemporary Business* 5 (1976): 47–77

Scott, Joan W. "Comment: Conceptualising Gender in American Business History." *Business History Review* 72 (1998): 242–9

Scranton, Philip. *Endless Novelty: Specialty Production and American Industrialization, 1865–1925.* Princeton: Princeton University Press 1997

Shammas, Carole. "A New Look at Long Term Trends in Wealth Inequality in the United States." *American Historical Review* 98, no. 2 (1993): 412–31

– "Re-assessing the Married Women Property Acts." *Journal of Women's History* 5 (1994): 7–30

Shammas, Carole, Marylynn Salmon, and Michel Dahlin. *Inheritance Patterns in the United States, 1685–1980.* Ann Arbor: Inter University Consortium for Political and Social Research 1990

Shanahan, Martin P. "Personal Wealth in South Australia." *Journal of Interdisciplinary History* 32, no. 1 (2001): 55–80

Sharpe, Pamela. "Gender in the Economy: Female Merchants and Family Business in the British Isles, 1600–1850." *Histoire sociale/Social History* 34 (2001): 283–306

Shergood, Peter R. *Working-Class Life: The 'American Standard' in Comparative Perspective, 1899–1913*. Pittsburgh: University of Pittsburgh Press 1982

Shortt, Adam. *Report of Dr. Adam Shortt Investigating the Financial Condition of the City of Victoria, BC*. Victoria 1922

Smith, Daniel Scott. "Inheritance and the Social History of Early American Women." In Ronald Hoffman and Peter J. Albert, eds., *Women in the Age of the American Revolution*, 45–66. Charlottesville: University Press of Virginia 1989

Smith, R.M., ed. *Land, Kinship and Life Cycle*. New York: Cambridge University Press 1984

Soltow, Lee. *Men and Wealth in the United States, 1850–1870*. New Haven: Yale University Press 1975

South, Scott J., and C. Trent. "Sex Ratios and Women's Roles: A Cross National Analysis." *Journal of Sociology* 93 (1988): 1096–1115

Sparks, Edith. "Capital Instincts: The Economics of Female Proprietorship in San Francisco, 1850–1920." PhD dissertation, University of California, Los Angeles, 1999

– *Capital Intentions: Female Proprietors in San Francisco, 1850–1920*. Chapel Hill: University of North Carolina Press 2006

– "Married Women and Economic Choice: Explaining Why Women Started Business in San Francisco between 1890 and 1930." *Business and Economic History* 28 (1999): 287–300

– "Terms of Endearment: Informal Borrowing Networks among Northern California Businesswomen, 1870–1920." *Business and Economic History On-line* 2 (2004): 1–12

Stage, Sarah. "The Perils of [Post]Feminism: Gender, Class and Female Benevolence." *Reviews in American History* 19 (1991): 511–16

Statistics Canada. *Labour Force Update: The Self-employed*. Ottawa 1997

Stein, Robert. "Sir Robert Richard Torrens and the Introduction of the Torrens System." *Journal of the Royal Australian Historical Society* 67 (1981): 119–31

Stobart, Jon, and Alastair Owens, eds. *Urban Fortunes: Property and Inheritance in the Town, 1700–1900*. Aldershot: Ashgate 2000

Stoddard, William O. "Women in Their Business Affairs." In *The House and Home: A Practical Book*. New York: Scribner's 1896

Strange, Carolyn. *Toronto's Girl Problem: The Perils and Pleasures of the City, 1880–1930*. Toronto. University of Toronto Press 1995

Strong-Boag, Veronica, and Anita Clair Fellman, eds. *Rethinking Canada: The Promise of Women's History*. Toronto: Oxford University Press 1991

Sylvester, Ken. *The Limits of Rural Capitalism: Family, Culture and Markets in Montcalm, Manitoba, 1870–1940*. Toronto: University of Toronto Press 2001

Thompson, Mrs James C. *Sketches from Life: Being Tales on the Ten Commandments and Various Texts of the Scripture: including Remarks on the Service of the Episcopal Church, Intended for the Use of Sunday Schools.* Toronto: Hunter Rose 1876

Tickamyer, Ann R. "Wealth and Power: A Comparison of Men and Women in the Property Elite." *Social Forces* 60, no. 2 (1981): 463–81

Toronto *Globe*. 1847–1914

Trentmann, Frank. "Beyond Consumerism: New Historical Perspectives on Consumption." *Journal of Contemporary History* 39 (2004): 373–401

Van Die, Marguerite. *Religion, Family and Community in Victorian Canada: The Colbys of Carrollcroft.* Montreal: McGill-Queen's University Press 2005

Varty, Carmen Nielson, "'A Career in Christian Charity': Women's Benevolence and the Public Sphere in a Mid-Nineteenth Century Canadian City." *Women's History Review* 14 (2005): 243–64

Vickers, Daniel. "Competency and Competition: Economic Culture in Early America." *William and Mary Quarterly* 47 (1990): 3–29

Vickery, Amanda. "Golden Age to Separate Spheres? A Review of the Categories and Chronology of English Women's History." *Historical Journal* 36: 383–414

Victoria *Daily Colonist*. 1863–79

Victoria *Standard*. 1870–79

Waciega, Lisa Wilson. "A 'Man of Business': The Widow of Means in Southeastern Pennsylvania, 1750–1850." *William and Mary Quarterly* 44 (1987): 41–64

Wagg, Phyllis. "The Bias of Probate: Using Deeds to Transfer Estates in Nineteenth Century Nova Scotia." *Nova Scotia Historical Review* 10, no. 1 (1990): 74–87

Walsh, Margaret. "Gendered Endeavours: Women and the Reshaping of Business Culture." *Women's History Review* 14 (2005): 181–202

Ward, Peter. *Courtship, Law and Marriage in Nineteenth-Century English Canada.* Montreal: McGill-Queen's University Press 1990

Warner, Sam Bass. *Streetcar Suburbs: The Process of Growth in Boston, 1870–1900.* Cambridge: Harvard University Press 1962

Weaver, J.C. *Hamilton: An Illustrated History.* Toronto: J. Lorimer 1982

– "The Location of Manufacturing Enterprises: The Case of Hamilton's Attraction of Foundries, 1830–1890." In R.A. Jarrell and A.E. Ross, eds., *Critical Issues in the History of Canadian Science, Technology and Medicine.* Thornhill: HSCT Publications 1983

Webster, Thomas. *Woman Man's Equal.* New York: Nelson and Phillips 1873. CHIM no. 29459

Whiteside, John F. "The Toronto Stock Exchange and the Development of the Share Market to 1885." *Journal of Canadian Studies* 20 (1985): 64–81

Wolf, Carol. "Genders Travel Different Routes with Investments." *Crain's Cleveland Business,* 24 January 1994

Wolstenholme, Elizabeth. "The Education of Girls: Its Present and Its Future." In J.E.G. Butler, ed., *Woman's Work and Woman's Culture: A Series of Essays.* London: Macmillan, 1869

Wood, Joanna. *The Untempered Wind.* Ottawa: Tecumseh Press 1994

Yeager, Mary A., ed., *Women in Business.* 3 vols. Northhampton, Mass.: Elgar Pub. 1999

Yohn, Susan. "Crippled Capitalists: Gender Ideology, the Inscription of Economic Independence and Female Entrepreneurs in Nineteenth Century America." *Feminist Economics* 12 (2006): 85–109

– "You Can't Share Babies with Bonds: How Americans Think about Women Making Money." *Iris: A Journal about Women* 40 (30 April 2000): 20–7

Young, Brian. "Getting around Legal Incapacity: The Legal Status of Married Women in Trade in Mid–19th-Century Lower Canada." In Peter Baskerville, ed., *Canadian Papers in Business History,* 1: 1–16. Victoria: Public History Group, 1989

Index